# Access your Online Resource

CW01497324

*No Child is Missed, No Child Misses Out* is accompanied by
materials, designed to ensure this resource best supports your professional needs

Go to https://resourcecentre.routledge.com/speechmark and click on the cover of this
book

Answer the question prompt using your copy of the book to gain access to the online
content.

# NO CHILD IS MISSED, NO CHILD MISSES OUT

This book offers an evidence-based approach to empower early years, primary and secondary education professionals to identify individual pupil needs quickly and carefully, without the long wait or cost for a specialist diagnosis.

The resource guides the reader through aspects of core cognitive testing, showing how to identify specific areas of need from phonological and visual processing to executive functioning and mental health. It advocates for child-centred and school-based solutions for "what now?" and "what next?", based on screening data, and supports SEND teams to provide targeted strategies and advice for colleagues and families alike. At a strategic level, the book enables school leaders to use cohort data over time to anticipate trends and to develop and improve provision, policies, and practice, ensuring that no child misses out.

With suggestions for quick, free, easy and timely assessments, this comprehensive resource is an invaluable tool for all SEND professionals working in or alongside mainstream and alternative provision at early years, primary or secondary level.

**Hannah Moloney** is a SEND specialist with many years of experience in the education and care sectors. She is passionate about working to improve the SENCO role in practice, as well as build recognition for children with special educational needs and disabilities through strategic development of education, health and social care partnership working. Instigator of the Bath Spa University National SENCO Surveys, Hannah is devoted to improving SEND provision in schools nationally. A qualified, practising SENCO and specialist assessor, she currently leads strategically on SEND provision across a group of primary and secondary schools.

"*No Child is Missed, No Child Misses Out* is an excellent book which is so much more than it first appears. It delves not only into the '*what*' and '*how*' of screening, assessment and implications for support but (perhaps most importantly) also describes, from a research-based perspective, the '*why*'. Written by a SEND leader with deep knowledge and first-hand experience, this book is an essential read for any colleague wanting to better understand and support learners' needs and, ultimately, to play their part in bringing about a more inclusive society."

—**Natalie Packer**, SEND Consultant and Director, NPEC Ltd

"This book is so necessary as a practical guide to SEND assessment for teachers and leaders. The most significant impact on a child's pathway through education is early identification of need and this handbook details evidence-based strategies for just that. It supports the swift identification of individual pupil needs, equips readers with tools for core cognitive testing, with an emphasis on child-centric solutions and school-based interventions."

—**Margaret Mulholland**, ASCL SEND and
Inclusion Policy Specialist

"This book arrives at a crucial moment when inclusivity in schools is under scrutiny, and students are facing consequences for needs that are not recognised or addressed. It offers a structured method for effectively identifying these needs, detailing a comprehensive process that engages various stakeholders. With clear, actionable steps and practical tools for implementation, this resource will be invaluable for practitioners in the field."

—**Mrs Taneisha Pascoe-Matthews**, AHT-Inclusion/SENCO,
Board Advisor at UCL Inclusive Centre

"This is a must-have for any SENCO wondering how to continue supporting the needs of children and their families. Hannah gives practical and inspiring strategies and guidance about how to understand, identify and support SEN. Being a SENCO, in any setting, can be an overwhelming responsibility but Hannah unites us in our passion to work towards providing children with the start in life we know they deserve. I am itching to share this book with my early years team to deepen our understanding and improve our inclusive practice."

—**Kiri Turner**, Early Years SENCO and Manager
at Battenhall Nursery

"It is tragic that so many children's needs are just missed in schools and often it is too late. If you are striving to make a real difference to children's educational experiences in a positive way, read this book. Hannah explains the power of screening leaving no stone unturned. She identifies a multitude of areas to screen and provides links to practical materials that any teacher can use. This book is packed full of crucial information for everyone working in the world of SEN."

—**Amy Leeke**, SENCO, Bredon School

"Accurate identification and assessment of need is the foundation of high-quality SEND provision. Hannah draws on her extraordinary wealth of expertise and knowledge to produce a book that will help all schools deliver more informed provision. *No Child is Missed, No Child Misses Out* is an accessible framework for better understanding the children in our classrooms. Comprehensive, practical and well-informed, it will be invaluable reading for all SEND leaders. It is a book I wish I'd had as a SENCO."

—**David Bartram OBE**, SEND Advisor

"Working with children is both a wonderful and rewarding job, but it can also be a hugely challenging task trying to unearth what each child really needs to unlock their full potential. *No Child is Missed, No Child Misses Out* is a genuine must-read for anyone who wants to empower themselves to improve children's ability to engage and learn, and ultimately to give them a really positive foundation in life. It's both informative and entertaining and includes really comprehensive approaches to screening to use back in school. If you're a SENDCo and want a refreshing look at supporting children, look no further!"

—**Rebecca Sedgley**, Behaviour Consultant,
Perryfields Primary PRU

"The depth of research within this book highlights a number of key points and is a much-needed guide for educators within mainstream and special school settings to ensure that students with additional learning needs are no longer left behind. This is a book that will need to be read in more than one sitting. If you're serious about empowering young people, then this is a book you will repeatedly read and then actively apply. I wish I read something like this as a trainee teacher."

—**Bukky Yusuf FCCT FRSA**, Senior Leader and Leadership
Development Coach, Edith Kay Independent School

# NO CHILD IS MISSED, NO CHILD MISSES OUT

How to Identify and Support Special Educational Needs and Disabilities in Your Setting

Hannah Moloney

Routledge
Taylor & Francis Group

LONDON AND NEW YORK

Designed cover image: Getty Images

First published 2025
by Routledge
4 Park Square, Milton Park, Abingdon, Oxon OX14 4RN

and by Routledge
605 Third Avenue, New York, NY 10158

*Routledge is an imprint of the Taylor & Francis Group, an informa business*

© 2025 Hannah Moloney

*British Library Cataloguing-in-Publication Data*
A catalogue record for this book is available from the British Library

ISBN: 978-1-032-66383-8 (hbk)
ISBN: 978-1-032-66381-4 (pbk)
ISBN: 978-1-032-66396-8 (ebk)

DOI: 10.4324/9781032663968

Typeset in Sitka
by Apex CoVantage, LLC

Access the Support Material: https://resourcecentre.routledge.com/speechmark

For all children and young people everywhere.
May you get to live the happy and purposeful lives you deserve.
&
For Teresa, Richard, Simeon and Theodore.
I couldn't have done this without you.

# CONTENTS

# HOW TO READ THIS BOOK

This book is a mix of story, theory and practice. Ultimately, it's written to be read cover to cover, but you work in education – that's a luxury you might not get very often! So, I'm giving you a head's up, then you can use the time you do have to best effect.

Part One is about how we got here: the highs, the lows, and the barrel-scraping lowest of lows. It's a mandate for change, a call for action and the basics for why and how to do it. Giving us the grounding we need to understand the steps ahead, it sets us off on the screening journey.

Part Two introduces us to the world of screening. It is an overview of what to screen for: tools you can use and ways to support children and young people if you identify an area of need through your screening. The chapters cover research and theory, and are jam-packed with practical tools and strategies. Each chapter can be read in isolation if you need/want to, but they build upon each other – concepts introduced in detail early on are referenced only in passing later. I've included a working glossary so you can still get the gist if you're dipping in.

Part Three brings us home. We cover what we can do about it: practical, experience-won steps for how to bring it all together, at scale, and with impact. We cover the practical steps to help you use the data so that no child is missed and no child misses out. The final chapter brings us to a seminal point in history – now – and gives us all a chance to leave an extraordinary legacy for humankind.

www.nochildismissed.org

# PREFACE

Working in education really is, or at least should be, about changing people's lives for the better; enabling every child and young person to achieve their goals and live a meaningful and purposeful life. Sadly, this is not yet everyone's future, which is why every English educational institution now has, and really desperately needs, a **SENCO** - and their team. This SEND team must be empowered to influence their setting and they must be funded with sufficient time and resources to be able to do so.[1]

> **SENCO:** Special Educational Needs Co-Ordinator. A leadership role in schools, co-ordinating provision for children and young people with special educational needs and disabilities (SEND).

For me, having been a SENCO for well over a decade, one of the absolute joys of the role is the permission, in fact the expectation, to continue to research, learn and share important findings about learning and wellbeing with colleagues across the school. But, in a relentless day with an ever-growing crisis-level to-do list, this can also feel overwhelming at times. A lack of knowledge and skillset in identifying and assessing for SENDs, in a deeply complex, often underrated role, is not just a limitation for the individual professional but it has significant and long-lasting impact upon the pupils within the school. Research from 2021 by the Education Policy Institute[2] showed that the school a child attends makes a far greater difference to their chances of being identified with SEND than other factors, such as children's individual learning needs or experiences. The responsibility of identifying children's needs lies squarely then with *us*. And at the moment, we're not very consistent at it.

As much as I enjoyed my **National Award for SEN Co-ordination**, and as much as it fast-tracked my understanding of the depth and breadth of the role, it wasn't until I did my postgraduate qualification in Specific Learning Difficulties, to be able to assess for dyslexia, that I really felt empowered to enact it fully; to begin to identify the needs of children and young people, and to make a meaningful difference in their lives at school.

**National Award for SEND Co-Ordination:** This was a qualification that SENCOs had to achieve within three years of taking on the role. From September 2024, this qualification changed to become the National Professional Qualification for SEND Co-Ordination.

What this training gave me was the knowledge and confidence to begin to use screening tests with my pupils and to form my own evidence-based opinions about their needs. This then meant I felt much more confident in both advising colleagues and organising interventions for support. Over a decade on, and literally thousands of assessments later, I can honestly say that it is my team's ability to screen and assess children - now with a much more nuanced and refined battery of tests covering a greater spectrum of indicators, which we'll cover in this book - that has had the greatest effect on provision in my schools. It has been nothing short of transformational.

The ability and confidence to screen children remains a large skillset gap in our educational workforce however. A skillset gap which not only has epic implications on the current wellbeing and economic futures of millions of children and young people and their families, but also on the field of special educational needs and disabilities itself. This gap is amplified by a lack of SENCO time, protection and positioning;[3] a ruthless underfunding for schools to be able to provide support that could make a difference;[4] and a lack of external specialists, such as educational psychologists (EP) and community paediatricians available to support schools to bridge this gap.[5] As a result, millions of children are being missed; and millions of children are missing out.

Having worked with children and young people from all different socioeconomic backgrounds, and across the 2–18 age range, I have spent a lot of time asking how we identify and support children's needs better, using only the people and the tools that we have to hand. I've obsessed about understanding not just how an individual functions and what support they might need to succeed, but also how a child's environment impacts upon their development and potential. And the more I read and developed our SEND screening practice as a result, the more I could see its impact rippling across the schools I oversee: in lessons, exam halls, parents' evenings, professional dialogue and pupil outcomes.

So, this book is for you if you want inclusion to look different and better in your setting. This book is for you if you've been waiting months to get the EP to see a child but they can't fit them in til next August. This book is for you if you've got colleagues, parents, social workers, or health providers seeking advice about a child and you need answers but have no budget. This book is for you if you need help in evidencing why a child needs more funding and support than they currently have.

Above all, this book is about agency. It's about navigating the stuckness you might feel. And I hope that, when we journey through this approach to screening together, it'll be about dismantling the barriers and discrimination that have dominated our field for so long: child by child, SENCO by SENCO and school by school. No one is too small to make a difference.

I can't wait for us to get started.

# PART 1
# Education: A Powerful Weapon to Change the World

# 1 Rupture and Repair

If you've ever been to the English city of Bath, you'll know it's incredibly beautiful. Filled with sumptuous Georgian buildings rising up from its basin in the Cotswold hills, these architectural gems reference its significant global economic past. Embarking upon my teacher training there in secondary History, it felt like an apt and inspiring place to be, which definitely helped – because like everyone one else, I found my PGCE crushingly difficult.

This overwhelm began to shift slightly in my second year when coping with the mechanics of teaching started to ease, and I began to really enjoy my lessons. I even felt an inkling to rekindle my studies. For a start, I was baffled by some new whimsical ideologies that were filtering into my classroom: the allure of **"VAK"** and Howard Gardner's eight **"Multiple Intelligences"**.[1]

My initial euphoria of thinking that teaching was suddenly going to get a whole lot easier, now that I simply had to work out which type my pupils were and teach to that, quickly dwindled into a confusion of whether it was three learning styles or eight intelligences? Which then became nine, when a new one suddenly got discovered. And so it was in my second year of teaching that I found myself scurrying along on a wet Thursday evening to a brutalist seminar room at the University of Bath, on a mission to find out.

**VAK:** This theory suggested that everyone had a preferred style of learning – visual, auditory or kinaesthetic. It has now been debunked.

**Multiple Intelligences:** This theory proposes that there are at least eight modalities of intelligence: Musical, Bodily-Kinaesthetic, Interpersonal, Verbal-Linguistic, Logical-Mathematical, Naturalistic, Intrapersonal and Visuo-spatial.

It would be fair to say I was a little unsure. Firstly, although I was intrigued to resolve my pressing dilemma, the welcome email from the professor running the course was signed "Love Jack" and, whilst I felt it was probably nothing more than a benign sign-off

DOI: 10.4324/9781032663968-2

he sent to everyone, I had never met a professor who shared their validation so liberally – especially with a student he had not yet met. I thought it decidedly odd. Secondly, I still felt I was a newbie in this teaching world and I wondered if I was getting a bit ahead of myself signing up for a Masters in a discipline where I sometimes still struggled to take my registers.

Perching on the hard, plastic chair, hair still damp after the dash from the car, I found myself in the company of a few like-minded strangers, also grappling with their own questions about education. Sitting at the table, with deep wrinkles around his eyes from a lifetime of smiles and a shirt unbuttoned at the collar, Jack turned out to be as welcoming and generous as his email suggested. Over the course of the coming weeks and months, he graciously allowed me the space and time to realise that I was asking the wrong question. I couldn't know if it was "three" or "eight" if I didn't actually know what "intelligence" was in the first place. And so I began a new, revised quest to answer just that. It led me to uncover a story so harrowing, I nearly left education for good.

*

## Rupture

Crises, it seems, are actually fertile ground. For Sir Francis Galton (half-cousin of the Victorian explorer and biologist, Charles Darwin) also had one when he began to consider the magnitude of the Origin of the Species.[2]

Evolution may have caused him to question the very existence of God, but within the existential chaos that ensued, it also afforded him a new insight that he might be able to define a genetic order across humanity, just as his cousin had with animals.

The context of this fascination is also important because, if you're familiar with your Victorian history you'll know, the 1800s were a significant century establishing Britain as the dominant global power. At its peak, the British Empire covered about a quarter of the Earth's land surface and its population was about 450 million people. This was a time where Britain's language, culture, economy, engineering and ideology were firmly seeded across the world, supplanting unique cultures and heritages under the regime of Rule Britannia. It is perhaps not unsurprising then that Sir Francis Galton's fascination with innate human ability was deeply infused with outrageous racist beliefs.[3]

If you've ever found yourself decrying the heinous work of the Nazi regime, let me tell you that its origins in fact lay firmly with the eugenics movement developing at University College London (UCL), under the tutelage of Sir Francis Galton himself.

In the desire to develop a perfected human race, Sir Francis Galton conducted many studies on willing volunteers. In 1884, at the International Health Exhibition, an event not dissimilar to our Ideal Home exhibition demonstrating the very best of British Imperial health, wellbeing and interior design, Sir Francis Galton set up a laboratory which visitors paid a small sum to enter. Over the course of their fourteen-minute visit, he and his team gathered data across seventeen different categories, ranging from their height, facial features, fingerprint patterns, eye-sight and mental characteristics. In total, he saw 9,937 participants and banked the largest human dataset then ever conceived, beginning a whole new field of research, known as differential psychology.

By the late 1880s he had inspired and influenced many, but arguably none more important than a small boy named Cyril Burt and a mathematician, Karl Pearson. Cyril was a precocious learner, so much so that his medical doctor father would take him on his rounds to keep him occupied. It was on one of these appointments where he met Darwin Galton, the brother of Francis. Throughout these visits, Cyril also became fascinated with the study of human ability and, after a somewhat circuitous educational route, ended up as a school psychologist in London in the early 1900s.

Karl, on the other hand, took on a position at UCL in the field of mathematics and ultimately became Galton's protégé, continuing on his work long after Galton's death in 1911. He worked relentlessly to quantify and statistically correlate humanity within the field of biometrics. And if you recognise the surname, it's because it's stamped annually on countless GCSE and A-Level examination papers today – his legacy and fascination for quantifying humanity lives on. Back in 1900, however, his name may have been less ubiquitous but his beliefs and values were just as clear. On a cold and dry Monday in mid-November, Pearson spoke at a conference in Newcastle. "You cannot change the leopard's spots" he exhorted, "You cannot change bad stock to good; you may dilute it, possibly spread it over a wide area, spoiling good stock, but until it ceases to multiply it will not cease to be."[4]

Perhaps caught up by the recent hysteria that 8,000 of the 11,000 recruits who had just tried to sign up to fight in the Boer War were not deemed fit enough, the concept that there were some people who were simply "better stock" didn't seem particularly offensive or even radical to some. To me however, reading those words a hundred years later and knowing what was to come, they seemed pretty grotesque.

### Better stock

In 1909, Cyril Burt (by then a school psychologist-turned-researcher) published a study which evidenced that upper class children in private education did better than those children being educated by the state, and that the cause of these outcomes was down to the innate differences between the two groups. So influential were his findings about "feeble-minded" children that they shaped the content and language used in the Mental Deficiency Act of 1913.

Galton's work also caught on beyond the Empire. In the early 1900s, the French government asked Alfred Binet to design a test to establish which children needed help in school, and by 1916 this had been developed into the first IQ test, the Stanford-Binet Test enabling people to be categorised by "mental age". In 1917, Robert Yerkes developed the Alpha and Beta tests to evaluate the intellectual calibre of recruits to the US Army. Coming straight off the boats in New York, nearly two million of the soldiers taking the tests were immigrants. The results were used to determine who would help command, and who could be considered "cannon-fodder".

Just like Burt's research, the results of these tests were as shocking as they were influential. Divided into categories of cognitive ability ranging from "very superior" to "very inferior", it appeared that at the top end of recruits was the white American. Although their scores were still rather disappointing – at about a mental age of 13, the European immigrants were worse. The Italians had an average mental age of 11.34, the Polish came in at 10.74. Notably, the darker skinned people from southern Europe and the Slavs of Eastern Europe were less intelligent than the fair people of western and northern Europe. Unfortunately for "the Negro", they came bottom (with an average mental age of 10.41).[5]

This data was used to legitimise propaganda not just for atrocities like the Final Solution in Nazi Germany and acts of white supremacy in America and South Africa, but to further engender racial fear and division. Moreover, it limited immigration across the world at a time when escaping over a boundary line had a life-or-death reality associated with it.

The widely publicised results of Yerkes Alpha and Beta tests validated the concept of intelligence testing to the masses, bringing it outside of the research lab and into everyday life. Suddenly, organisations and families alike started to request to use them too. We are, after all, innately interested in learning a bit more about who we really are – especially if we think we're going to do rather well out of it. But, there was a bind. And it's the kind of eye-watering, sickening, lose-your-tummy-in-a-lift kind of bind. When they looked into it, it turned out that Yerkes' Alpha and Beta tests weren't measuring intellectual calibre at all. They were measuring mileage from New York.

Of course, being illiterate and in search of a better life in this brave new world, the likelihood you'd succeed in a test which relied on cultural knowledge and previous educational experience was much reduced, particularly, too, if you'd just stepped off a boat. The further away your origin, the less likely you were to have been influenced by American middle-class, male, professional cultural insights and language to be able to answer the questions correctly. At the time these considerations didn't seem to have been heeded by the Army, and hideous decisions were made from publishing hideous headlines categorising people by race. Years later, and with far less column space than the original findings, the truth quietly came out. Too late, unfortunately, for the six million Jews, Roma, Sinti, black and disabled people who were tortured and murdered in order to purify the Aryan race.

When news began to seep out from the concentration camps of Europe that doctors were carrying out barbaric research on humans in the name of science, most rational people were deeply shocked. Starvation, vivisection, drug testing and mutilation were all validated through the ambitions of "racial hygiene". Through the Nuremberg Trials and Code that followed the toppled Nazi Regime, even though wounds inflicted between countries were still open and weeping, a global agreement emerged. Medical and psychological research must hold ethics and morals above the power dynamic of the researcher-patient relationship, especially in the venture to understand the human mind and body. Its legacy still influences us today.

### Ethics of research

Back in early 1940s England with the war still raging however, Cyril Burt was still focused on education. Soon to be knighted for his contributions to psychology through his Professorship at University College London, he was now President of the British Psychological Society. In readiness for upskilling post-war Britain and not yet fully aware of the vulnerabilities to bias in intelligence testing, the government at the time were keen to develop an education system which fitted the profile of the people. Anxious to capitalise on and engage with the aspirations of the growing middle- and professional-classes, it was important to allow the brightest and best to receive a world-class education, not dissimilar to the best private schools across the country.

The type of school you went to would ensure that your needs could be adequately met. And so, with the Butler Education Act of 1944, the 11+ was birthed into existence, based firmly upon Burt's twins study research which categorically and undeniably proved that intelligence was not only innate but fixed.[6] "Those that could" went to a grammar school. And those that "couldn't" went to a secondary modern to follow a different kind of curriculum. The Butler Act also gave us new medicalised vocabulary with which to describe another category of children who "definitely couldn't", including the "uneducable", the "maladjusted" and the "educationally subnormal". Many of the children grouped into these categories would never attend school, given the perceptions of their limited intellectual ability.

As the Yerkes debacle taught us, the problem with intelligence testing (as with any scientific research I might add) is that it is really important to ask the right questions and to critically consider the potential limitations of your data. Ensuring that your methodology actually serves the work is vital, as is being aware of potential blind spots, otherwise you might get an answer you *think* is the answer, but actually isn't. The same is true for the importance of reliability of that data; findings must be replicable for them to be considered secure. In the case of Sir Cyril Burt, it took decades for the truth to come out, but eventually in 1971, some plucky researchers reviewed his notes posthumously, to discover that he had *falsified* some of his results.[7] Imagine that? Our whole education system from 1944 to the mid-1970s – leading to millions of people following differentiated academic routes and changing their life chances irrevocably – was predicated on research findings that were completely unreliable.

At this point, I was beginning to lose my faith in the purpose of school. What exactly were we trying to achieve in categorising and grouping children? My fellow Masters students listened respectfully on as I discussed my latest findings, as equally galled by them as I was. I don't really remember if anything special was said to make me feel any better, but over time Jack helped me to see that regardless of what had gone before, I was the custodian of my classroom now. It was my own research insights that mattered to today's children,[8] and that I could make a difference where I was. I clung on and found a new inner reserve.

*

## Repair

Probably as a result of this ongoing professional crisis and after my school realised it had a slight shortage of French teachers that year ("don't worry Hannah, it'll be fine, we'll give you one of our bottom set Year Sevens so it doesn't affect our GCSE data"),

I came to realise that, broken system or not, it wasn't the subject I loved teaching but the children. Especially those in the bottom sets. The joy I felt when I watched a pupil flawlessly recite the verb *être* still makes me smile. Word soon got out, and after a few months of reflecting on this new revelation, when the Headteacher asked me to be the school's **Special Educational Needs Co-Ordinator**, I felt somewhat drawn to the idea. Of course, I initially said no – I mean, what on earth did a **SENCO** do?! Weren't they just the raving loony women who gave the children biscuits in the stationery cupboard to keep them quiet?

> **Special Educational Needs Co-Ordinator/SENCO:** A leadership role in schools, co-ordinating provision for children and young people with special educational needs and disabilities (SEND).

Recognising that I didn't have to conform to this stereotype and sensing that it was a step I needed to take regardless, I found myself turning up the following September as the school SENCO. Naïve. Desperately lacking the knowledge to do the job. But willing to give the whole thing a try. It felt like a small way I could take back some power from Sir Cyril Burt and his mendacious impact upon generations of children and young people; my first real step to exploring and unravelling the endemic bias steeped within my school walls.

Although I won't spend too much longer detailing the history of IQ, partly because we've got a lot to get through over these next few chapters together and we need to get going, I did want to start by sharing with you some of the stories that have profoundly shaped the structure of our education system today. Legacies of the beliefs and values from more than a century ago, which still influence how we perceive children in classrooms across the world. Legacies that need re-evaluating in light of newer, more valid and more reliable research into our genes and their expression. Legacies which need exposing in view of a growing commitment to decolonising the curriculum. Roots which burrow far, far deeper than we might ever have imagined.

In terms of the IQ debate, by 1983, the conversation had begun to widen when Howard Gardner publicly questioned the linear nature of intelligence, suggesting that it was more complex than a single number.[9] In 1991, evolutionary biologist Stephen J.Gould described IQ as a "pseudo science" to justify discrimination.[10] In 1996, Daniel Goleman wrote that "Emotional Intelligence" mattered more than IQ.[11] And in 2008, Malcolm Gladwell published, *Outliers*,[12] which carefully deconstructed everything we might assume about the roots of genius and success, suggesting that factors unrelated to IQ, like date of birth and hours of practice, can have an extraordinarily powerful effect. On top of these challenges, by 2009, after more than a decade of publications, "the Flynn Effect"[13] was finally widely accepted. Research by James Flynn had convincingly shown that IQ increases generationally as access to education improves. Far from being fixed and limited, as Burt had "proved", it turns out that access to education *does* make a difference to cognitive ability.

For me, it's not that IQ tests don't give us useful information about someone, I think they actually do, as we'll cover in Chapter Two, but it's that humans are so much more complex and valuable than a single number could possibly capture, that to base our whole education system around it embeds structural discrimination into its very heart. And that's what we need to remember and better understand, because it *really* matters to the children, young people and families that we work with. Not just in relation to their time experiencing school but for the years and years that follow; for the way they might feel for the rest of their lives.

### Discrimination: from IQ to SEND via parenting and postcodes

As I was reminding myself of the atrocities of the IQ story in preparation for this chapter, I became acutely aware that listed on the time-lines I had scribbled, detailing the histories of education, psychology and global events within the twentieth century, were exclusively white, upper- and professional-class males. It really brought home to me one of the greatest criticisms often aimed at early intelligence testing, that the people who seemed to do best were the ones most similar in profile to the men who wrote them. And when I reflected a little deeper, and started to add in the names associated with advocating for children with "special educational needs", it was clear that the voice calling for the rights of children and young people became decidedly more female towards the end of the century. Whether newly empowered in the post 1960s world of bra-burning and professionalism or from pushing back against the shame of being considered a "refrigerator mother",[14] the story of education is also as much about class and gender, as is it about race.

> **Special Educational Needs (& Disabilities) (SEN/SEND):** A ground-breaking term coined in the 1970s by Professor Ronald Gulliford, popularised by Mary Warnock in 1978 in her seminal report and legalised in the Education Act of 1981. This term moved descriptive language away from the term "handicapped" to be more cognisant of the context in which difficulties were observed, not just the characteristics of the individual themselves. "Disabilities" was added to the acronym in 2014–5 to make it "SEND". In practice SEN and SEND tend to be used interchangeably.

### Parenting – the mother load

Word blindness, or **dyslexia**, as we now more commonly refer to it, was first talked about at the end of the nineteenth century. In 1896, a fourteen-year-old named Percy came to the attention of Dr Pringle Morgan who described him as "bright" but with "an inability to read". Over the next century, the diagnosis pathway for dyslexia developed upon a discrepancy model which compared IQ with literacy ability; a disparity between the two would indicate dyslexia. In spite of a mushrooming of associations in support of this apparent learning difficulty, politics remained sceptical and avoided acknowledging it as a special educational need until the late twentieth century. It was just the complaints of a bunch of overly dramatic mums, they said; a middle-class "myth". But thanks to the amazing work of Helen Arkell, Bevé Hornsby, Marion Welshman and Susan Hampshire, all of whom were pivotal in setting up or leading dyslexia organisations, dyslexia was firmly placed on the SEND map through later legislation and then protected through the Equality Act (2010).

Likewise, the turn of the twentieth century also saw the beginnings of what is now considered **autism**. Paul Eugen Bleuler coined the term, later to be more comprehensively developed by Hans Asperger and Leo Kanner in the 1940s. It was Kanner who also suggested that autism in children resulted from having been reared in emotional refrigerators. And, here we begin to see a slightly different misogynistic approach with the growth of a mother-blaming culture which is still alive and flourishing today. In 1964, Bernard Rimland[15] a psychologist researcher and a father of a non-verbal son, challenged this theory, suggesting that autism was actually the result of neurological factors, not a lack of mother care. But his research was rebuked in 1967 by fellow psychologist Bruno Bettelheim:[16] the critique cemented the concept of "mother failure" as a regular and pivotal cause of autism. As this framing of mothers became a common part of the diagnostic narrative, it also settled in more comfortably across other learning difficulties and behaviours, too.

> **Dyslexia:** A learning difficulty which primarily affects the development of accurate reading and spelling. It can occur across the intellectual spectrum.
>
> **Autism (ASD):** A condition associated with a triad of impairments, including difficulties with social interaction, communication and sensory processing, resulting in restrictive or repetitive behaviours.

Contemporary clinical psychologist Dr Naomi Fisher considers one of the most damaging parts of Western motherhood culture is the emphasis of children as the outcome of their mother's mothering.[17] There is, of course, plenty of research that has demonstrated the importance of affection and attachment with at least one primary caregiver, as well as the importance of a stimulating home environment, some of which we'll cover in later chapters. But I raise this because I want to draw your attention to a powerful paradox that exists: there is a really interesting and stark disparity when we line up the mid-twentieth century research into IQ and autism spectrum disorder (ASD), placing them next to each other. The former, a **construct** measured against the strengths and virtues of the male presentation; the virility of nature. The latter, a construct borne from the failure of a female to fulfil her evolutionary purpose as a nurturer. Weakness seen in both the mother's and the child's observable characteristics against constructed ideals. And here's the catch. Whilst IQ was the gift of heredity – good genes passed on from generation to generation – the opposite was true for autism where lack of nurture was pivotal to a child's outcomes. Could both be true? Perhaps more importantly, who gets to decide?

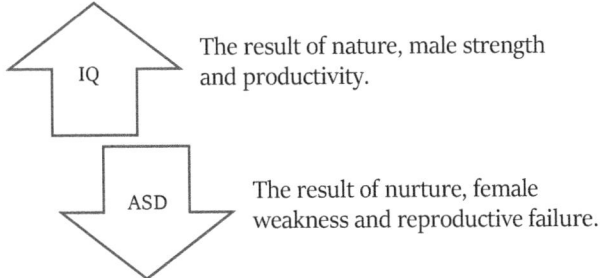

The result of nature, male strength and productivity.

The result of nurture, female weakness and reproductive failure.

*Figure 1.1* The paradox of IQ and autism

**Construct:** A concept theorised by humans in order to make sense of the world. Social construct theory argues that humans make meaning by structuring what they see, by picking out patterns and dividing their knowledge and experience into categories.

**Attention Deficit Hyperactivity Disorder (ADHD):** A condition which causes inattention and overly reactive responses.

**Hippocrates:** Believed to be the first person to promote the idea that diseases were caused naturally, not through superstition. He used clinical observation to take a considered approach to diagnosis and cure.

**Diagnostic and Statistical Manual of Mental Disorders (DSM):** Listing the criteria used by diagnosticians for mental health disorders, such as autism and ADHD. This was first published in 1952 and has had several revised editions since. The third was published in 1980 with a revised edition in 1987. The current edition is the DSM-5, published in 2013.

Parent blaming has infiltrated mainstream ADHD assessment pathways too. **Hippocrates** (460–375 BC) no less, is sometimes considered the first to record observations of **ADHD** behaviours. He noted there were patients who could not keep their focus on any one thing, who had "quickened responses to sensory experience" but who were "also less tenaciousness because the soul moves on quickly to the next impression"."[18] Broadly it is George F. Still in 1902 who is credited with bringing together the constellation of symptoms now considered "ADHD", although he termed it rather less favourably, the "Abnormal Defect of Moral Control". It took another eighty years for it to be fully recognised as a diagnosable mental health disorder in the **DSM**-3 but, depending on your local area assessment funding criteria, many health teams will require parents to have done a parenting course before even joining the waiting list to see a specialist.

In the world of SEND, mothers have been both blamed as the cause of their children's behaviours and gaslit for pointing out their child's difficulties. From parents who don't care enough to parents who care too much. More recently, we've also become more aware of how rooted diagnostic descriptors are in the male presentation, especially in ADHD and autism, meaning that young girls have often missed out from receiving specialist assessment and support because "they don't fit the criteria" for either referral or diagnosis. This disparity continues to the present day, with a recent report from the National Audit Office[19] stating that "significantly more boys than girls are identified as having SEND – 20.2% of boys aged 5 to 17 in state-funded schools . . ., compared with 10.7% of girls". I find it interesting, too, that 91% of SENCOs are women.[20]

Whether we've consciously noticed it or not, gender norms and behaviours are critically enmeshed in much of this current world of SEND. Gender norms and behaviours that are increasingly under scrutiny in both education and the wider world.

### Postcodes

Finally, when we look at the current SEND crisis whereby hundreds of thousands of children remain languishing on waiting lists, we see discrimination through the postcode lottery of resourcing. Dyslexia is still more regularly diagnosed in children of wealthier socio-economic classes, driven partly by the cost of a private assessment and also access to dyslexia specialists.[21] (Interestingly, Dyslexia Action, the British Dyslexia Association and the Helen Arkell Centre are all centred on the Surrey/Berkshire border, two of the wealthiest counties in England.) The cost of a private autism assessment can be eye-watering, putting it in the gift of only a few. The same is true of private ADHD assessment, recently under the spotlight for operating in a somewhat unregulated pathology market.[22] And for what? Why do people travel down the route of diagnosis?

Most parents will give the following two reasons: to better understand their child's behaviours and needs (often as a result of the stressful experience of parenting), and to get their children the help and support they need to succeed (whether that *actually* happens as a result of a diagnosis is another matter). Many teachers will agree, quoting an under-funded education sector preventing children's needs being met within the ordinarily available budget. Others might perceive this differently: criticising parents' escalation of their children's needs as a "golden ticket"[23] to more expensive provision paid for by the state, and to better outcomes. The reality is that access to funding and support is a postcode lottery. If you can pay, you are able to purchase options that simply aren't available to others who cannot. This desperately needs to change.

### Where are we now and where are we going?

One thing is for sure: navigating the realms of IQ, education and SEND is complex and fraught with hidden twists and turns. Some say that it is a Jungle.[24] Back at the turn of the twentieth century, Sir Francis Galton apparently pondered in his dotage whether there was a connection between his obsessiveness in quantifying humanity and his own possible **"insanity"**.[25] When I read this, I raised my eyebrows, chuckled and nodded my head in solidarity: if nothing else, his work on calculating genius and its subsequent history has indeed caused *me* considerable insanity. I may not identify with being the loony old woman in the cupboard (* there goes the gender discrimination klaxon again!) but at times this job has certainly brought me close.

> **Insanity:** This term is often used pejoratively, as a criticism of self or others, in description of their poor mental ill-health. As such, it is no longer used within the field of psychology, as it is considered offensive. It is however still used in the legal system. One can plead insanity. I reference the term here, because it is the one Sir Francis Galton used of himself and, for poetic licence, I continue the use of language to expose the discrimination which continues within the field of SEND.

And so we find ourselves here, at the start of a book about the complex needs of children and young people with an aim to help you to identify and support them in your setting. Needs, which were succinctly summarised in the legal definition from 1981 as "a learning difficulty or disability which calls for special educational provision to be made for him", (*!) but which are rather clouded by the fact the practice of assessing for them is so limited in resource and practice, that getting enough data to define them reliably continues to be extraordinarily difficult. I hope this book helps us to move forward together on this: to better identify, understand and support the diversity of need in our settings. I hope it's also the beginning of a re-evaluation about what it means to be a human with purpose and value, and particularly what it means to be a child, in light of our growing awareness of the need for some kind of change in education.

Encouragingly, this same energy for review has been building in the field of evolutionary biology for a while. Given the relationship between Darwin and Galton, this field is perhaps unsurprisingly closely related to education. We might even call it our "half-cousin"? Younger generations of scientists and researchers exploring the animal kingdom are becoming more vocal in articulating the importance of diversity and transparency in research practices, as a way to remove the mask of Victorian beliefs and values that have infiltrated so much of our current knowledge. As the Oxford graduate zoologist and science journalist Lucy Cooke explains: "The fight for biological truth is crucial if we are to forge a more inclusive society that can work together to protect the future of our planet and all that live on it."[26] I believe we need to take a similar approach to our field of education if we want to do the same.

Not only do I believe in you to be able to develop the knowledge and skills to screen children through the tools and advice in this book – even if you feel as naïve and inexperienced as I once did – but I believe that, combined, *we* as leaders in education can use this practice to help bring about a more inclusive society. One which better understands and values the importance of diversity.

"Never doubt that a small group of thoughtful, committed, citizens can change the world. Indeed, it is the only thing that ever has."[27]

You can do this.
*We* can do this.

Love Hannah

# 2 IQ and the Power of Screening

For Sir Francis Galton, the marker of intelligence was speed and accuracy of sensorimotor response to a stimulus. This is why we say things like "she's as sharp as a knife" or "there's no flies on him" – because they've "got it" quickly and have already moved on. In a world that had recently standardised time so that the new steam trains could run efficiently, and with industrialisation growing busy factories with start times and finish times, there was no doubt for Galton: time was money. Doing things efficiently was good for business. And if it was good for business, it was good for Britain.

He wasn't the first to consider speed of response a marker of intellectual prowess. As you'll remember, even Hippocrates had noted the "quickened responses to sensory experience".[1] The difference was that Galton wanted to measure it. And for that, a general description and a shared awareness wasn't enough. It had to be tied down and tightly defined to be quantified. The standardised measurements would then indicate someone's efficiency, someone's worth.

Time is central to education, too. We carve up curriculums into age-related expectations across a school year. We divide weeks into timetables. We slice days into lessons. We plan those lessons with a meticulous awareness of the number of minutes we are going to allow for each task to be completed. And when the bell finally tolls, and pupils are sitting in the battlefield of the exam hall, the only weapon they've got is the number of words per minute they can get down on that booklet, before the invigilator tells them that time is up. Speed and accuracy of sensorimotor response matters a lot in school.

It makes sense: the school curriculum is intended to develop our children and young people into the citizens of the future that we need. Those who can interpret information quickly and accurately are therefore more likely to make better judgements about how to grow our businesses, to sustain our position on the global stage and to develop new products and services which will make our lives easier, giving us more . . . time.

Of course, the stage of global politics tells us over and over again that our perceptions about what, or *whom*, this looks like in practice is inherently affected by much more complex psychological evaluative processes. This suggests that what we *actually* value in humans is far more nuanced than simply someone's speed and accuracy of response. But politics, perceptions and economics aside for the time being, when we look at what is going on in the brains and bodies of those who score highly on intelligence tests, we see

DOI: 10.4324/9781032663968-3

humans who are able make fine sensory discriminations within their body. Intelligence then is really an indication of the workings of our central nervous system.

## IOS – our Internal Operating System

Now it's been a very long time since I studied biology at school, so if it's as hazy for you as it was for me, allow me to (re-)introduce you to a few "bio-basics" as we go through this chapter. Let's start with the fact that there are twelve pairs of cranial nerves[1] which conduct energy through our bodies. Leading into and out from our skull, they travel to different parts of the body. Some are sensing nerves – the ones we use to gather information about our surroundings, resourcing our eyes and our ears, for example. Some are motor (movement) nerves – the ones we use to do something in response to this information, to resource our muscles. And some do both, like the ones which empower our hands and our mouth. Nerves are absolutely core to our survival.

Day and night, our central nervous system spends its entire time looking for changes to communicate to the brain: temperature, sound, visual stimuli, smells, tastes, terrain (balance and space), hunger, bladder and bowel, pain – to name but a few. Nerves are our information highways. Some of them lead us to understand our external environment, known as **exteroceptions**, and some help us to understand what's going on internally, known as **interoceptions**. Together they give us our awareness of the world. These sensations and perceptions, or what we more commonly refer to as "senses" are very literally keeping us safe, alive and well.

> **Exteroception:** Perception of stimuli outside the body, like hearing a fire alarm and knowing we need to leave the building.
>
> **Interoception:** The awareness of internal sensations in the body, including heart rate, respiration, hunger, fullness, temperature, pain as well as emotions.
>
> **Transduce:** To convert something (e.g. energy) into another form.

Perhaps, because we tend to over-simplify looking for rules of thumb to live by, we typically think there are only five senses: hearing, sight, touch, taste and smell. But given what I've just listed, it won't surprise you to know that there are at least nine senses and even up to twenty and beyond, depending on who you ask.[2] Moreover, just as different nerves are dedicated to different sensory and motor roles, so too are

---

1  They are paired to resource each side of the body.
2  The idea of five senses can be traced back to at least Aristotle's De Anima, where he devotes a different chapter to the five senses we quote today. Neurologists would consider there are more but putting a number on it can be tricky because it depends on the definition chosen and how the experience is grouped, even including whether there is in fact a "sixth" – known as "X" – sense.

different parts of the brain and the brainstem. The energy **transduced** from what we see and what we hear for example, goes along different nerves to different places in the brain to be interpreted. Hercule Poirot solved cases with the help of his "little grey cells", more commonly known as grey matter. It is this, in our brain and spinal cord, which houses our neurons (nerve cells) allowing messages to travel. You may also have heard of white matter. This is found deep inside the brain, enabling messages to pass from brain region to brain region. So, as the late, great Sir Ken Robinson once posed, "if we underestimate something as straightforward as our senses, what about more complex capacities like intelligence?"[2]

## Linking nerves to the classroom

You might think that sensing and perceiving messages within our central nervous system is pretty immediate, but actually the time it takes for information to travel from one part of the body to be interpreted by the brain can be measured. For example, you'll perceive a blow to the shoulder more quickly than the shin. The reason for this is that the energy from the signal literally has to travel through the body in a kind of domino effect with information shared from one neuron to the next. The further away from the brain, the longer it'll take for the message to get there.

When we think about the demands of the classroom – the energy produced and used within all those bodies in such a comparatively small space; the constant and varied signals being processed simultaneously by multiple central nervous systems each with twelve sets of nerves; all in pursuit of survival as well as attempting the task at hand within the time allotted – what we expect of children and young people, and of ourselves as teachers, is pretty intense. No wonder we're all shattered at the end of the day.

Amongst those we might consider find this more difficult, children who appear more distracted – the ones who Hippocrates observed had a good speed of response but were "less tenacious"[3] – what we're noticing is the sensory load in their information highways. It's just more obvious in some than others. Nerve efficiency can be affected by all kinds of developments, at all stages of life, both through genetics and experience. Often, what we're observing in pupils who stand out is a hyper- or hyposensitive response from the brain: too quick or too slow, too loud or too quiet, too much or not enough.

Even when children and young people are broadly able to balance the demands of these sensory stimulations and cope with the classroom expectations for their age – the ones in the middle, who we don't tend to notice as much – there is still great diversity in the speed at which they're all sensing and perceiving information through their neural networks. It is this which leads to the difference we see in attainment in our mark books.

Intelligence then, in a broader sense, is the result of our body's constant monitoring and learning from the environment. And, as an aside, this is actually what sets us apart from all other mammals and why humans have come to dominate. Whilst we are born the most helpless of all animals because we're so underdeveloped when we emerge from the womb, unable to move or feed ourselves independently until several years of nurturing have taken place, it is ultimately to our advantage. We do not arrive in the world with a fixed and pre-determined set of skills and behaviours. We arrive into the world with a plasticity which allows us to learn and to adapt to our environment, meaning that – come what may – we are more likely to master or develop the necessary responses for survival. Evolution is coded into our very DNA.

## Measuring intelligence

The history of measuring intelligence, as I have written about in Chapter One, is littered with controversy and is still a highly divisive topic – particularly when it is used to justify acts of soft and hard **eugenics**. Your Educational Psychologist (EP) might also have different views to me with regards its place in evaluating the needs of children and young people, which I discuss in this note.[4] But, for me, Sherlock Holmes would be nothing without Watson and Moriarty. Likewise, I've come to see intelligence as an important protagonist within the education system now that its testing is more reliable; but one who should only get to tell a part of our story. Before we learn about those other characters in the coming chapters, let's take a closer look at how we measure this thing we call "intelligence".

> **Eugenics:** Aims to perfect the human race by reducing undesirable characteristics from the genes within the population. This can be through mating people with desirable qualities to produce lots of children. It can also be through practices which enable an early death of those deemed to have undesirable characteristics. "Soft" eugenics refers to subtle nudges and indirect action, whereas "hard" eugenics refers to specific programmes to reduce undesirable characteristics as its aim.
>
> **g:** Charles Spearman was an English psychologist who noticed that children's performance in school across subjects seemed to correlate. He suggested that "general ability" could therefore be conceptualised as a single number – their g-factor, or simply "g".

From early research into general ability which led to establishing a number known as "**g**", we have now largely settled on an approach called "deviation IQ" which provides us with a number that falls on a bell curve of normal distribution. It's called a bell curve because it looks a bit like a bell. If you look at Figure 2.1, you will see what I mean. People are divided up along a scale, the centre of which is the number 100.[3] The majority of people fall in the two central sections, which is known as the average range.

---

3   In education we standardise people, but the same concept is used to measure and norm-reference in medicine too, just with a different scale called percentiles. You might have come across this, already.

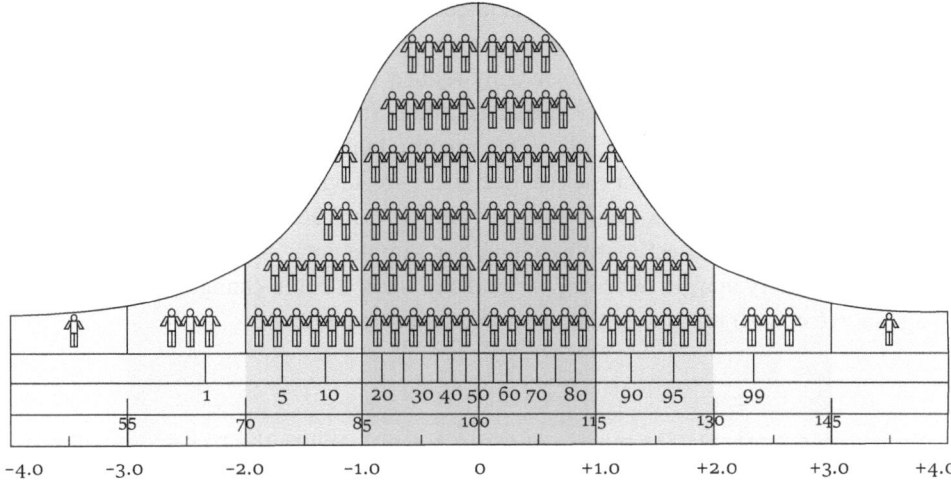

*Figure 2.1* The Gaussian bell curve of normal distribution

It means that if your IQ is 100, you are bang on average for your age. However, if you score anywhere between 85 and 114, it means it falls *within* the average range. Clearly there's quite a big difference between a score of 87 and a score of 112 however, which makes "average" seem rather a vague term. As such, it's helpful to use 100 as your guide to look at which half of the bell the score falls in, too. If you score particularly highly – 115 or above, you've scored in the above average range; and likewise, anything 84 or below is considered below average. It's a sliding scale: there is only a sliver between 84 and 85 but that one point takes you into a different category.

The Gaussian bell curve, as it's known in the trade, gives us a tool to compare results by age in years and months with a population norm. Let's say you score 16/20 on a maths test. As a teacher, we'd congratulate you for scoring 80% and be able to say how that compared to your fellow classmates. Our appreciation for your score however could change depending on your age in relation to the challenge of the test. If you're nine and it's a degree level test, we'd be calling you the next Einstein. If you're degree level and it's a test for a nine-year-old, you might not get such a charming accolade. So, the bell curve helps us to understand not just how you did in a test, but how you did in relation to other people of *exactly* the same age as you in years *and months*. And it's a very useful measure – of whatever quality it is you are measuring – because it communicates a lot of complex information very efficiently.

It can help us to understand someone's profile and to make perceptive and evidence-based decisions about next steps with and for them. And in organisational terms, when data is grouped together, it can also help leaders to understand the demographic of their patients/pupils/clients, preparing for future need, allocating resources to desired groups and implementing thresholds to manage systems and demand. (If you've worked in the field of SEND for a while, you will know how significant a standardised score can be in terms of accessing resources.)

It has its risks, too, of course, and a modicum of caution always needs to be factored in when making any judgments based on the numbers. There is a margin of error in recognition of the fact that we can never truly reduce someone's ability in a specific area to a single number given the many variables of life. So, any result will also come with a range of accuracy.[4] For example, the single result might be 92, but the 90% **confidence interval** might be 87–96. What the test designers are saying here is "we are 90% confident that the true score lies somewhere between 87 and 96 and we're going to put our money on 92 as the best estimate based on our sample data". You might still think this leaves quite a hefty margin of error (particularly when it could change someone's access to a resource or not) but that is the price we pay for expedience.

> **Confidence interval:** The margin of error; the probability the true score will fall within the range given.

Other than that, the *big* risk is the quality of the data the bell curve has been standardised on in the first place. And this is rapidly growing in importance. For example, if data from certain demographic groups have *not* been captured or included – intentionally or not – this can mean decisions are made for and with someone based on their scores alone, but they might not necessarily be in their best interests. This is because they haven't been represented in the data at the test design stage. Those most at risk of this are the usual suspects: women – and, particularly pregnant or breast-feeding women; people of low socioeconomic status; certain racial, ethnic or religious identities; people with disabilities. Societal and cultural biases can arise simply from the insufficiency of the dataset in the first place, gaps which aren't generally intended to be malicious, or even deliberate.[5] This has always been a huge issue but with the rise of AI, its significance is magnified exponentially. We'll come back to this later on in the book.

Currently we're pretty good at testing for cognitive ability in most secondary schools and because of this our datasets are robust for the majority of the teenage population, albeit with the caveats briefly described above. However, harvesting IQ data is not a consistent practice across all schools and it's much less common in primary schools, which means that there is more of a practitioner knowledge gap about children's cognitive ability in early years and primary. Being me, I dug around to try and find out why this is. It seems to be a legacy of the selection process brought into fruition with the 1944 Education Act, whereby pupils' cognitive ability was tested on the 11+ as a way to discern if they should attend a secondary modern or a grammar school. Given this is practice stemming from another era, there doesn't seem to be any rational argument to not test

---

4   Whether it's shared with the test user directly or not.

earlier, it's just legacy that we typically don't. We've grown up and inherited normative practice without much question or reason to do any different.

The lack of consistent testing of cognitive ability in schools, particularly in primary schools when it could *really* make a difference, means we don't always have enough data to identify underachievement with enough *sensitivity* and *specificity*. Our standard classroom data from classwork or observation isn't always sensitive enough to pick up on whether a child is struggling, particularly in the blurry middle. And it's definitely not specific enough to be able to tell us why. Testing for cognitive ability can therefore be a really helpful first step towards getting better data.

## What intelligence tests measure

If you've ever sat and watched a child sit an intelligence test, be it with an educational assessor or on a computer, you will have noticed that it's a sedate and calm affair with minimal speaking and movement. It doesn't loudly allude to testing nerve energies and speeds. Children don't pelt across a hall in a beep test frantically finding answers. But it is the cognitive equivalent. We are measuring intellectual reaction times formed from senses and perceptions. Research conducted by John Carroll in 1993, reviewing test scores from nearly 500 studies of IQ, found a pattern of correlations between several abilities and it is largely these skills that are being put through their paces when someone is going through an IQ test. They are:

- *General comprehension, knowledge and reasoning* – previously learned experiences or procedures (*Gc*)
- *Fluid reasoning* – the ability to solve problems with unfamiliar or novel information (*Gf*)
- *Quantitative knowledge* – understanding numerical concepts and relationships, and manipulating numerical symbols (*Gq*)
- *Reading and writing ability* (*Gr*)
- *Short-term/working memory* – the ability to hold and use immediate information within a few seconds and then discard what is irrelevant (*Gsm*)
- *Long term storage and retrieval* – the ability to store information and fluently retrieve it later in the process of thinking (*Glr*)
- *Visual processing* – to perceive, analyse, synthesise and think in visual patterns, including visual memory (*Gv*)
- *Auditory processing* – the ability to perceive, analyse, synthesise and discriminate auditory stimuli, including pitch, rhythm, timbre, distance, location (*Ga*)
- *Processing speed* – actioning tasks particularly requiring continued focus and attention under time pressure (*Gs*)

Not all IQ tests will cover all of these facets but, overall, this is what Carroll constitutes as the main qualities of intellect. If you've come across cognitive testing in schools, you'll probably know that they cherry-pick about three or four to measure: most commonly vocabulary/verbal ability *(Gr)*; maths/quantitative ability *(Gq)* and non-verbal ability

*(Gf).* Sometimes they might select aspects of others as a fourth, commonly aspects of visual patterns or 3D shapes *(Gv).* The reason for this abbreviated version is time and cost – of course. The more qualities you test, the longer it takes to administer and analyse, the more it costs. In a busy curriculum it's efficacious to streamline the data capturing. However, we're then left with a dot-to-dot picture with quite a few key numbers still missing. Does this really matter?

Well, remember these scores correlate so in some respects, no, it doesn't. IQ testing is *big* business – it's now as reliable and valid as any psychological testing ever can be. What we learn from these school cognitive tests will tell us reasonably accurately what we should expect of a pupil's progress whilst in school, based on the millions of other children's data that has been fed back into the algorithm over time, in a massive IQ-outcomes feedback loop. But remember, too, that Galton, Pearson and Burt were driven by different values and ultimately wrong when "proving" that nature was the only influencer of IQ. Some aspects of a person's IQ *can* change with educational experience, so it's not such a foregone conclusion. That's why we talk about "value added" – schools can and do make a difference to outcomes. Some make a greater difference than others and *this* is where those data gaps can really matter.

The qualities that can change are known as **crystallised** dimensions. Like crystals, they will grow over time in the right conditions – verbal ability and knowledge of maths facts are a good example of this. Great teaching and an inclusive school environment can make a real difference. Those which seem to be less susceptible to the same influences – the ones which are fixed and heritable[6] – are known as **fluid** intelligences. Non-verbal skills like logic, pattern and error spotting are examples of natural aptitudes which don't seem to change very much over the course of someone's life. When we're looking to understand a child's profile in order to capitalise on the adaptations we might make, we need as full a picture as possible. Without a detailed data picture, we don't know which areas we might have some additional influence over – and, as a result, how we might affect each child's life for the better. There is real power in this nuanced approach: analysis of PISA [Programme for International Student Assessment] test results in 2015 showed that "adaptive instruction" was the second most powerful predictor of academic success – second only to socioeconomic status.[7]

> **Crystallised intelligence:** This is dynamic and can change with educational experience, for example, knowledge of vocabulary and maths facts.
> **Dimension:** An attribute or construct that we value and seek to measure.
> **Fluid intelligence:** This is considered fixed and heritable, for example, logic, pattern and error spotting.
> **Composite:** To combine two or more pieces of information (in this case, data) into one overall single outcome.

We make it even harder for ourselves too when we **composite** the three or four scores we do get from the tests into one overall cognitive ability score and turn a pupil into a single number. We leave ourselves less room for manoeuvre because now the data is just too blended to really get to grips with. Sure, it's mathematically likely to be well-founded, but for teachers in the business of making a difference, a single average score makes it virtually impossible to get a foothold in the rockface. "Everything should be made as simple as possible", noted Einstein, "but not simpler".[8] Even averaging good data makes things just too blurry. Let's take a look at some imaginary pupils and their cognitive ability scores to see what I'm talking about.

## What we learn from school cognitive data (and what we don't)

All of these scores below are written as standardised scores, so, remember that 100 is bang-on average. Anything above 115 is above average. Anything 84 or under is below average.

Let's start simple. The following scores are the composite of the three main test results from a school cognitive ability test.

*Table 2.1* Example composite scores from four pupils in a school cognitive ability test

| | Overall cognitive ability |
|---|---|
| Pupil A | 78 |
| Pupil B | 111 |
| Pupil C | 118 |
| Pupil D | 105 |

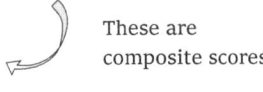 These are composite scores

In terms of outcomes, Pupil C is likely to be our best performer, followed by Pupil B, then Pupil D and finally Pupil A. Our school systems are generally set up to focus on the top and the bottom – the outliers – because they are the exception to the norm. Pupil A, it seems, needs a lot of help. At the other end of the spectrum, Pupil C could go on to do something impressive, so we might be tempted to invest some extra help into them too. But what? We've not really learned any more than what we'd see in the classroom or on report cards. I've also barely noticed the ones in the middle – they're doing fine. Or are they?

Let's take it up a notch. Same pupils. More data. This table now includes the sub-test scores as well as their composite.

*Table 2.2* Example verbal, quantitative, non-verbal and composite scores from four pupils in a school cognitive ability test

| | Verbal | Quantitative | Non-verbal | Overall cognitive ability |
|---|---|---|---|---|
| Pupil A | 75 | 80 | 80 | 78 |
| Pupil B | 100 | 102 | 131 | 111 |
| Pupil C | 125 | 122 | 106 | 118 |
| Pupil D | 104 | 106 | 105 | 105 |

Pupil A continues to be a pupil whom teachers are aware of towards the bottom of the class. Their literacy and numeracy abilities are both within the below average range, so these crystallised intelligence scores (verbal and quantitative) indicate that their learning has been slower to develop than peers'. However, when we look at their fluid intelligence score (non-verbal), we notice that their educational progress is in line with their underlying problem-solving/pattern-spotting ability and therefore this pupil will certainly need support to access the curriculum in the classroom, but actually their progress is pretty in line with what we might expect. They are doing just as well as Pupil D, in this regard, who is also performing as expected, albeit within the middle of the cohort, some twenty points higher.

Let's take a look at Pupil C. We were impressed before, but actually they have a profile that cognitive assessors would call "spiky". Pupil C is doing *really* well in school. Better than expected. Something about the environment and the teaching is really working here. They are "over-achieving" by some margin and, especially sitting next to Pupil D, will seem quite different in terms of their literacy and numeracy skills. And yet, look, their non-verbal abilities are virtually the same. Why is Pupil C doing quite so spectacularly well?

What about Pupil B? We had considered them average and barely noticed them on the list. It now appears, however, that they also have a "spiky profile" but for them the opposite is true. Their problem-solving skills are exceptional, so why is there such a difference between this and their verbal and quantitative scores? These are indicators of crystallised abilities – ones that we can statistically influence so something must be amiss. If you speak to their class teacher(s), everyone will have their hypothesis and, just like **Occam's Razor**, perhaps the simplest, most obvious, answer is indeed the right one. I've taught a Pupil B and they were just a bit silly, a bit lazy and often didn't listen in lessons. I've also taught a Pupil C and they were motivated, hard-working and a delight to teach. Maybe it's just as simple as that?

But maybe it's not.

> **Occam's Razor:** A philosophical model also known as "the law of parsimony". Its theory states that the simplest explanation is most likely the right one.

## Sliding doors

If you've ever watched the famous Gwyneth Paltrow movie *Sliding Doors* where two completely different life stories emerge from a single moment in time – the one where she does catch the train and the one where she doesn't – you'll see where I'm going with this example. Let's imagine two different parents-carers' evenings for Pupil B who is currently in Year Five:[5] the one where the class teacher doesn't know their cognitive ability scores (1) and the one where they do (2).

---

5   Year Five is the penultimate year of the British primary curriculum, covering the ages 9–10.

*Table 2.3* Verbal, quantitative, non-verbal and composite scores from Pupil B's performance in a school cognitive ability test

|  | Verbal | Quantitative | Non-verbal | Overall cognitive ability |
| --- | --- | --- | --- | --- |
| Pupil B | 100 | 102 | 131 | 111 |

- *Scenario 1: The one where the teacher has no knowledge of Pupil B's cognitive ability scores (not even the single score)*

  "Hello Parent-Carer B, lovely to see you. B is doing just fine. They're meeting their age expectations: reading, spelling, handwriting are all fine; maths is, too. They are performing at age-expectations in their classwork. Sometimes they can be a little silly in lessons, they can lack a bit of motivation at times and they do tend to have a few spats on the playground. This is probably because they can take things too far sometimes. Overall though, I'm pleased with their progress and they're doing fine."

After this conversation Pupil B continues through the year making average progress but over time appears increasingly frustrated, disengaged and more and more isolated through ongoing friendship issues.

- *Scenario 2: The one where they do know the range of cognitive ability scores*

  "Hello Parent-Carer B, lovely to see you. On the surface of things, B is doing just fine. They're meeting their age expectations: reading, spelling, handwriting are all fine; maths is, too. However, I think they're much more able than the work they produce in class and I've observed that sometimes they can be a little silly in lessons. I'm wondering if they find concentrating difficult because I'm often having to bring them back on task? Sometimes I even have to get a bit snappy with them. I notice that I often have to help them sort out friendship difficulties from spats on the playground and this makes me wonder if they're finding it difficult to make secure friendships too? Have you noticed any of these things at home or does this match with experiences from your perspective? Do you think anything else could be going on . . .?"

Now this second conversation might seem a little trickier and perhaps a teacher wouldn't want to have this conversation without their SENCO or a senior leader on hand. This "difficult" conversation might cause people to shy away from the topic and brush it under the carpet, reassuring themselves that the pupil is performing as expected so all is ok. Except what if I were to tell you that three years later, Pupil B goes on to be permanently excluded from their secondary school because of their persistent low-level disruption? An opportunity has been missed. Inattention and aspects of hyperactivity, which have caused their own poor progress and disruptive behaviour in the classroom and on the playground, have begun to seriously affect the outcomes and wellbeing of others, too. That the extent of their inattention hasn't been picked up earlier also means that there is now a (very long) wait for assessment, causing even further barriers to their future learning.

The reality is that, despite every good intention and senior leaders working exceptionally hard to minimise the risks, secondary schools are much less predictable and far more complex environments than primary schools, due to the increased number of variables. There are now lots more and different pupils, a much larger campus, different teachers, different subjects, different classrooms, different expectations, different equipment required which needs to be carried around, and different homeworks due on different days which need to be remembered. This adds greater complexity of sensory information to process and manage on top of coping with the ever-increasing expectations of the curriculum as it rises in challenge. Hormones are also starting to change with puberty – which affect brain function and nerve efficiency, too.

As such, Pupil B is now engulfed by this new environment and the diverse demands on their central nervous system and simply hasn't got the strategies or support to adapt successfully. Remember, this is a pupil who'd been able to cope with the challenge of Year Six work performing at age-expectations and with peers whom they knew and who knew them, despite underperforming considerably in relation to other areas of cognitive ability, because they're able. But through transition and over time, little by little, the balance of risk tips and coasting is no longer possible. Without the cognitive tools and support to cope, they are now very definitely no longer "fine".

## Beyond Occam's Razor

*You* know, too, that your classroom is a microcosm, greatly affected by the environment. Too hot or too noisy and it's much harder to concentrate. Just before lunch and there are some who are too hangry to work nicely in pairs on a fresh task. A bee buzzes into the classroom on a warm summer's day and you might as well have rung the fire alarm or called "home time". It's not just a single quotient that will influence how well we perform on a task. It's really how well our brains are able to manage the internal and external "noise" being transduced by the many different sensing and perceiving highways of our body simultaneously. How quickly it can decide on the importance of an incoming message and how swiftly it can action a decision to re-balance. The context of where and when those messages are being received is critical, too.

This ability to sense, perceive and act in response to the internal and external noise, is arguably pretty stable over a longer period of time,[9] which might commonly lead us to find an overall figure of IQ, but if we haven't fully understood the nuance of a child's sensing and perceiving abilities and the impact that their normative environment has on them then we aren't fully armed with knowledge to support and empower change. When we measure ability solely through the dimension of cognitive ability in a singular number along one line, we compress a human into a 2D entity. When actually, we need to be a bit more Pixar.

## To infinity and beyond!

I don't think I can ever recall being so close to the edge of my seat as the moment where Woody, Buzz and the *Toy Story* gang are heading helplessly towards the incinerator in the third film. Watching it, even now when I know the outcome, my throat still squeezes tightly and my eyes brim with tears. The music; the pathos; the wordless, tender and affectionate moment when they embrace each other and in a shared look acknowledge their impending fate . . . oof! It captures me in heart-wrenching suspense every time. They draw me in with carefully crafted imaginative details, applied layer by layer throughout the movie, leading me to this moment of catharsis.

When Woody and Buzz Lightyear first entered our lives, they brought joy, laughter, panic and thrill; and they also brought us into a new age of cinema. With *Toy Story* came the realisation that the *details really do matter*. Stories matter. Engaging with a world in high-definition matters. We are far more than the sum of our parts and engaging with them takes us forward, beyond anywhere we could ever have imagined before.

The same is absolutely true of school achievement: we can do a lot better than a 2D sketch of a pupil's cognitive profile. We can even do better than considering the three main data captures in standard cognitive ability tests, like we did with Pupil B. Through a greater treasure trove of data, we can engage more intelligently (with greater speed and accuracy, I might add) with the levers for change. Levers that we might be able to nudge to improve the outcomes of the children in our schools. For this, we need to explore many more quantitative dimensions, but this doesn't necessarily make it any more complex than trying to navigate with only half the instructions. In fact, I think it makes it a lot *easier*. As Hyman G. Rickover famously said, "The devil is in the details, but so is salvation."

Let me introduce you to Pupil E.

### Pupil E

Pupil E is in Year Seven[6] and they've just sat their cognitive ability tests. Let's take a look at their three main scores. Crikey! I hear you say. That verbal score is *really* low. When compared to their non-verbal score, there's 47 points difference! Wow. Something has to be going on there. . . . They're not just slightly underachieving in their verbal abilities. To quote Buzz Lightyear, they're "falling in style".

Table 2.4 Example verbal, quantitative, non-verbal scores from Pupil E's performance in a school cognitive ability test

| Verbal | Quantitative | Non-verbal |
|--------|--------------|------------|
| 72 | 109 | 119 |

If we stopped at this point, the obvious conclusion would be some kind of literacy difficulty and most people would probably jump straight to dyslexia. But now we're going

---

6  Year Seven is the first year of the British secondary curriculum, covering the ages 11–12.

to see the power of high-definition data. Let's do a few more screening tests, to add in some more data and see if we're right.

Table 2.5 Example reading efficiency, reading comprehension, spelling and free writing scores from Pupil E's performance in a school screening

| Reading efficiency | Reading comprehension | Spelling | Free writing |
|---|---|---|---|
| 81 | 110 | 112 | 100 |

Their reading efficiency (speed and accuracy) is low. However, it doesn't seem to be impacting too much on their comprehension. That score is much, much higher. They must be working exceptionally hard when they're reading, to understand the text in spite of the many barriers associated with low speed and poor accuracy. Apart from anything, this pupil is likely to be absolutely exhausted at the end of the day from all that additional energy that's being used up trying to interpret meaning from in between all those inaccurate sensations and perceptions. Reading for Pupil E is a tightrope experience.

Their handwriting is of average speed and their spelling is surprisingly good however. Perhaps unexpectedly so. It's not dyslexia. . . .

Just as an aside here, there are actually several definitions for dyslexia – and they keep being tweaked. This means that, as well as the significant influence of personal opinion, practitioners might have different views on whether this could be dyslexia or not, depending on the definition that they choose to use. But with such a high spelling score, in *my* view the evidence for dyslexia is wobbly whatever the definition you use.

Furthermore, this data still doesn't give us a range of levers we can pull to intervene, other than some reading fluency intervention. This will probably help, but we could have learnt this just from listening to them read and with such a low score and such laboured reading, they have probably already been picked up and had a lot of reading support at primary. It doesn't seem to have made that much difference. We need to explore further to see if we can glean any other information, and find additional options.

What else could we consider? Common practice in dyslexia assessing would expect us to consider the following tests and, given it's a literacy difficulty, following this path a little further could help. Let's run a few more tests.

Table 2.6 Example short-term memory, working memory, visual processing and self-concept scores from Pupil E's performance in a school screening

| Short-term memory | Working memory | Visual processing speed | Self-concept |
|---|---|---|---|
| 105 | 125 | 80 | 103 |

Ok, what can we learn now?

We learn that when they are asked to recite a string of information, word for word (their short-term memory), they're pretty average at it. However, when they have to *do* something with that information – mix it up somehow and remember it in a differ-ent order (their working memory) – they are approaching *exceptional*. This suggests that their academic success is likely being protected by their short-term and work-ing memory – but imagine what their progress might look like if their reading abil-ity matched their memory? Because of their memory, the classroom is likely to be an engaging space where they're able to keep focus and manage the multi-step demands of learning that have been set. They are able to process many of the different signals and decide which ones they need to zone in on and remember to complete the task. It's not this dimension that's affecting the low verbal score.

It also tells us that their self-concept is secure – they believe in themselves and their competence to approach learning in school. Their reading difficulty doesn't appear to be holding them back too much, emotionally. This pupil has many protective factors for success in the classroom. Things are looking pretty good.

But look, the data also exposes to us the most likely root cause of the poor verbal cognitive ability score: their eyes. Or more precisely – and to return to our initial discussion – something about their ocular nerve conduction – how energy is trans-duced by the eyes and transported to the brain. That's a connection that we are unlikely to have made if we hadn't have explored more quantitative dimensions because at sec-ondary level we are far less likely to hear them read one-to-one. Certainly, if we'd only had their overall cognitive ability (which, by the way, is bang-on 100[7]) we'd have had very little clue. They would barely have stood out. And yet, when it comes to exams and time pressure, details matter. This pupil is ripe for underachievement, affecting their life opportunities considerably and also their school results. It's in everyone's interest to try to reduce that risk.

So, what would I recommend we do about it?

Some levers we might have for improving outcomes for Pupil E are:

- reading fluency intervention
- seeing an optometrist, exploring vision and possibly getting glasses
- computer reader technology

What else might *you* do or try?

This is the kind of work my team and I do when looking at pupil data. It has been transformational for us and for the thousands of children, young people, parents-carers we've worked with over the years, and for the many hundreds of teachers who have come into the profession to make a difference.

Cases can be a lot more complex than this example, of course, because there are many more dimensions we could add into the mix and much more nuanced stories to extract. Literacy difficulties aren't the only challenge pupils face in school. We haven't yet looked

---

7  And probably shouldn't even be calculated as a composite as the differences between the three cognitive ability scores are too vast to make it meaningful, as you can see here.

at their gender, their birth date, their other senses, their medical history, their lived experiences or their schooling so far, and what else we might be able to discern from these data. There is, therefore, even more we could learn and suggest to try, but we'll cover that as we travel through the next few chapters together, exploring the screening process in more detail. I sense we've probably covered enough for now.

### Final thoughts: the DNA "mixing desk" of dimensions

Before we bring this chapter to a close however, I just want to spend a moment or two helping you to pin this new information to a visual analogy that really helps me to understand it better conceptually.

Imagine a mixing desk. You know, like the ones you see at any kind of performance which requires sound amplification and lighting. The tech team at the back, dressed in black, hovering over a board with lots of twiddly knobs and sliders. As I collect data about pupil skills and abilities, instead of thinking about pupils by their diagnosis or their ability, I imagine each child's DNA as a mixing desk of dimensions, where the presentation of each of their (many) dimensions can be positioned along a spectrum from low to high.

Take a look at the following diagram to see what I mean.

Given that we know that not all ability is fixed, and neither then is potential, the position of each slider evidences the extent of the dimension in its presentation: how high, how middling or how low it is. Its positioning is the result of a child's genes, their environment and their lived experiences over time. Knobs and sliders which, with some careful thinking and strategic work like we've just done, could be targeted to see if we can improve a child's educational experience.

"Experience" states Gabor Maté, the renowned Canadian physician, "determines how our genetic potential expresses itself in the end".[10] Neuroscientist Candace Lewis agrees. "One of the biggest takehome messages from my work is how malleable we are as an organism, how responsive [we are] to environmental cues throughout the lifespan",[11] she says.

The world that Darwin and Galton inhabited is different to the one we live in now. Science is changing. It increasingly shows that humans are dynamic and adaptive in real

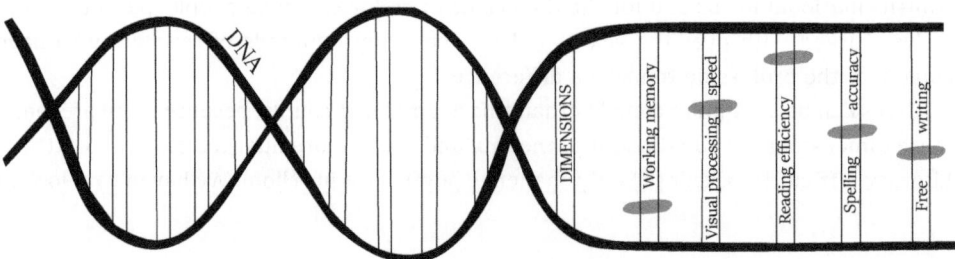

*Figure 2.2* A DNA mixing desk of psychological dimensions – Hannah's visual analogy to help you picture the screening scores and influences

time, not a leopard unable to change its spots. We're dependent both on our body and everything it is surrounded by. Being born helpless and underdeveloped means we are cued to adapt to our environment with a plasticity that seems to be unrivalled within the animal kingdom. We can grow. We can change.

Rather than eugenics then, the new science is **epigenetics**: understanding how our genes express themselves in response to our lived experiences. So it's time to leave Galton et al. behind and meet some other researchers and practitioners who have since added to the complex story of education. We'll cover new theories that you need to know, other tests you can try and, importantly, what you can do to help. It's time to learn how you, too, can screen.

**Epigenetics:** An emerging scientific field of research which explores how environmental influences can affect how genes are expressed; how genes can be modified in terms of their activity without changing the DNA sequence itself.

## No Child is Missed – Action Point 2.1: Assess Cognitive Ability

In terms of assessing cognitive ability, here are some tests which you might want to consider.

*UK:*

- *CAT-4 (age 6+)*
- *Cambridge Primary Insight (5-11)*
- *InCAS AfE (5-11, Scotland)*
- *MidYIS (11-14)*
- *Yellis (14-16)*

*USA:*

- *CogAT (K-12)*

*Australia:*

- *PAT Assessments (Foundation–10)*

Although I wouldn't recommend them for testing IQ at scale, there are different tests which specialist assessors might use to measure IQ in a one-to-one environment. You will often come across these referenced in diagnostic reports written by specialist teachers and educational psychologists. Common ones include: the *Wechsler Intelligence Scale for Children (WISC)*, the *Wide Range Intelligence Test (WRIT – although this is being phased out)* or the *Reynolds Intellectual Assessment Scales (RIAS)*.

# 3 First, Do No Harm

If early twentieth century **differential psychology** was the shiny and sleek hare, mid-late twentieth **humanistic psychology** was definitely the less sexy but arguably more careful tortoise. As the world grappled with the legacy of world war, psychologists such as Abraham Maslow and Carl Rogers sat at the helm of a new perspective: one which identified people's "needs" and encouraged people to give each other "unconditional positive regard"; one which sought to understand people in their wholeness and within their context, rather than stripping them down to a single, quivering figure. Our first step to developing a screening process in our settings begins with this more empathic approach.

Valid and useful though the differential model of assessing speed and accuracy may be, it's still a pretty narrow view of humanity and one which has questionable roots. Screening children and young people takes more nuance than that if you want to get a sense of the depth and breadth of their profile and how we might make a difference to their outcomes. My ongoing experience of **access arrangements** testing whole year groups at a time – and *still* not getting a clear enough picture – was testament to that, too. So I was reassured to read the opening page of a recently published seminal, weighty tome – all 734 full-sized pages of it, thrice revised in quick succession, which stated: "To all students of psychology; may you find the answers you are looking for."[1] I chuckled at the irony. It *must* be hard if even the seasoned experts are advocating caution about neatly boxing people up into theories, and rapidly re-writing their work at the same time.

> **Differential psychology:** The study of the ways that humans are different, including the biostatistical measurement of intellect (IQ).
> **Humanistic psychology:** The movement in psychology that we met at the beginning of the chapter which emerged after World War Two, focussing on happiness, wellbeing and purpose. Abraham Maslow and Carl Rogers are important figureheads of this movement.
> **Access arrangements:** Adaptations for access to learning. In England, they are considered important as a normal way of working in lessons but are especially important in assessments involving timed conditions, such as internal and

DOI: 10.4324/9781032663968-4

external examinations. Common examples of access arrangements are extra time, technology to support reading, typing, being in a smaller room rather than the examination hall etc.

Far from being disheartening however, it gave me confidence in my opinion that we, as educators and SEND professionals, have a valuable and experienced viewpoint to add. One which isn't well-embedded into the wider psychological debates about the needs of children and young people – yet.

## Diagnosis, diversity and difficult decisions

Although our screening process is not intent on labelling or diagnosing, it's helpful first of all to begin with concepts we know. In SEND, we tend to focus heavily on diagnosis, often as a way to help us understand someone's profile and to access additional resources. Diagnosing is, however, rather a delicate art. This is because diagnoses of disability are given on a continuum scale rather than being binary and simplistic. At some point the balance tips and what is a difficulty becomes a disability. This forces diagnostic descriptors to be necessarily broad. Continuums might help with real-life validity but they are "the bane" of bureaucratic and legal decision-makers[1] because "abnormality" is on the exact same sliding scale as "normality": where is the cut-off point? When exactly does this difficulty become a disability? What role is the environment playing? Is it mitigated by other changing circumstances? And is it a constant, or a predisposition which is sometimes unexpressed unless triggered?[1] This is known as the Diathesis-Stress model which theorises that a person may be genetically or contextually predisposed to a mental disorder that remains unexpressed until it is triggered by stress.

These big, and sometimes overwhelmingly complex questions can make it challenging for assessors to decide how to frame children's needs and whether to apply a diagnostic label or not. No wonder it can trigger rather impassioned debate, especially between professionals sitting in different camps. Even with professional guidance from different governing bodies,[2] opinions are a critical part of the process. And opinions can be different. Not only that but the presentations of individuals seeking assessment in the first place can too. You might have come across Dr Stephen Shore's famous quotation:

---

1   For example, assessment for specific learning difficulties like dyslexia are guided in the UK by professional bodies such as PATOSS, the British Dyslexia Association, Dyslexia Action. Assessors for medical diagnoses can use guidance in the DSM, other overarching bodies focused on assessing for specific conditions, or within the NICE guidelines. These governing bodies are diverse from each other with differing views and opinions, too, which adds to the complexity. Overall however, the definition of disability in UK law uses time and severity as an indicator: the difficulty should be "substantial" (more than minor or trivial) and "long-term" (twelve months or more).

"If you've met one person with autism, you've met one person with autism". There is also another rather lovely phrase which captures the same sentiment: "autism is one word attempting to describe millions of different stories".[3] Indeed. I would even go so far as to say that there are millions of different stories within the SEND community as a whole. Framing them accurately is a challenge.

This means that if we want to attempt to capture the needs of our children and young people through screening, to begin to identify their needs sensitively and specifically enough, somehow our process needs to try and summarise something as complex as a million different stories into a swift yet compassionate operation. No small task at all. Where should we begin?

## Understanding the nuance and complexity of profiles

In 1977, fellow humanist George Engel published his theory of the **biopsychosocial model**.[4] Apart from being a bit of a mouthful, when I eventually managed to say it and grasp its concept, many of my experiences, observations and unanswered questions fell into place. The biopsychosocial model is a really useful and comprehensive framework which recognises that there are often multiple causes to someone's ill-health or disability and they can be broadly summed up through the three areas of biology, psychology and social environment which interact with one another within any given individual. Recent research confirms that it continues to be a valid concept: "a multitude of inter-related factors influence each child's developmental course and academic growth".[5] The theory felt very relevant to both my own lived experiences and also to the screening challenge I'd set myself.

The interesting, and perhaps daunting, consequence of the biopsychosocial model theory, however, is that if something has multiple causes, then it stands to reason that the solutions are likely to be equally multi-faceted. No singular cause of a diagnosis, no singular solution.

I sat and thought about this for a while. It didn't really change anything. We had our carousel of interventions and approaches between and across our different roles in school. And in all my meetings with parents-carers, we always looked at multiple actions we could take between home and school. If anything, it validated this more nuanced approach. It felt Hippocratic: using observation and logic to produce a plan of action.

The biopsychosocial model is not without its critics however; they argue that its broadness can mean it is difficult to confidently establish causality of an illness or disability and therefore clarity about what to do.[6] Some might say that the biopsychosocial model can lead people to get distracted by its nebulousness or to feel dispirited and confused that there is no instruction manual detailing a strategy or approach. Both can potentially result in inaction. It is, however, heralded by many as a really helpful way to understand a very complex individual human picture. To somehow encapsulate millions of different stories.

**Biopsychosocial model:** A psychological model by George Engel which theorises that there are often multiple and layered factors which combine to cause ill-health. These factors often fall within someone's biology, psychology and social worlds.

**Nebulous:** Cloudy, misty, difficult to pin down, ambiguous.

## The biopsychosocial model

Figure 3.1 shows us the broad overview of the biopsychosocial model and breaks it down into its constituent parts. It evidences the specific aspects within someone's life which might fall within one of the three zones highlighted by the model.

When I looked at this model in detail, I could see just how much of this information was relevant to us in school. To help with developing a screening protocol to suit it, I started to transpose the themes embedded within the model into questions that I could ask of myself and others. Figure 3.2 shows you what I mean as I looked at the theory through our educational lens.

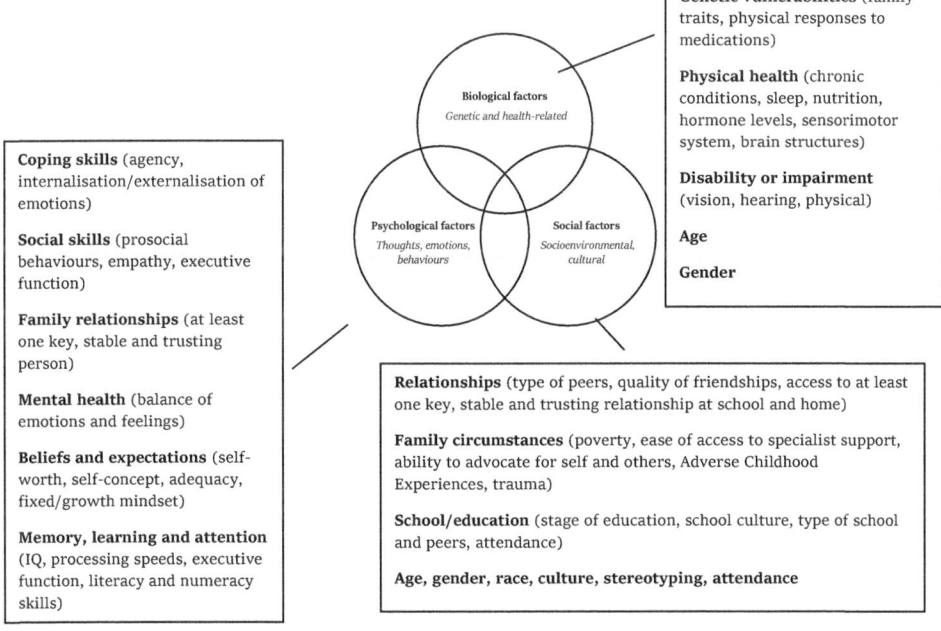

*Figure 3.1* An overview of the biopsychosocial model and examples of its constituent parts

**Information from a class teacher, a pastoral or a safeguarding lead:**

What is their behaviour like in lessons and during social time?* How many rewards and sanctions have they received, and what does the pattern suggest?

What do culture and relationships at home seem like? How might they help to explain the behaviours we are seeing in school?

**Information from whole year group academic assessments and questionnaires**

What is their IQ? (verbal, numerical, non-verbal)

How is their spelling?

Is their pencil grip or handwriting (comfort, clarity, speed) efficient?

Is their grasp of the four basic operations age-appropriate?

How does this child/young person perceive themselves as a learner?

What do their school reports say?

**Information from a short SEND 1:1 screening assessment:**

How efficient is this child/young person's reading accuracy, working memory and visual processing (speed and colour)?

What else might it be helpful to unpick? E.g. reasons for school avoidance, other factors affecting their learning or wellbeing.

* we can often see this in pupil observations too

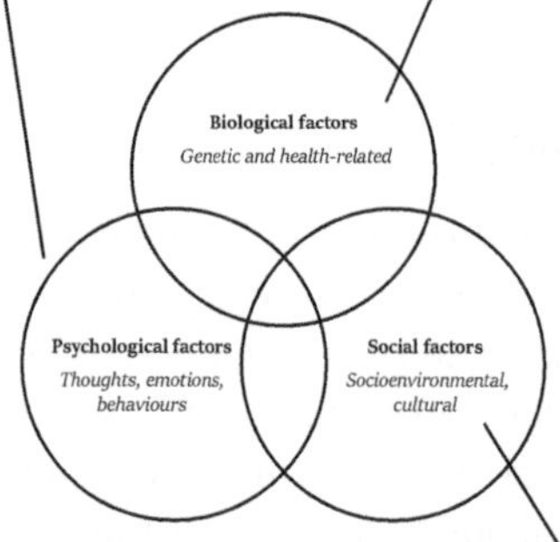

Biological factors
*Genetic and health-related*

Psychological factors
*Thoughts, emotions, behaviours*

Social factors
*Socioenvironmental, cultural*

**Information from a parent-carer or child/young person conversation:**

How are they sleeping and eating at the moment?

How do they seem to cope with different sensory experiences?*

Have they had their vision and hearing checked recently?

Is there anyone else in the family who is similar? If so, what helps them?

**Information from health service:**

School nurse and/or other health professionals involved with the family already.

**Information from a class teacher, a pastoral or a safeguarding lead:**

What is their friendship group like? How well do they create and sustain relationships?* How is their attendance?

To what extent could contextual circumstances such as poverty or cultural identity be affecting this child/young person?

How competent does their parent-carer appear to be in advocating for and providing for the child/young person's needs?

Has the child/young person been exposed to a number of adverse childhood effects, or trauma?

Is this child/young person's behaviour age appropriate?*

What is their behaviour like at home? How are family relationships between their child and other family members?

How might the school culture or type of school be impacting on the child/young person?

**Information from a pupil:**

What are their views about their life, their progress, their experiences?

*Figure 3.2* The biopsychosocial model through an educational lens

This next version of the diagram includes examples of our normal, in-school qualitative and quantitative data gathering practices, but also considers what else we could specifically add in to support a short 1:1 screening assessment. The extras we don't always consider are highlighted in grey.

What we quickly see when we transpose the model into tangible day-to-day roles and actions is that we already know - or can easily find out - a great deal about each child, really vital puzzle pieces in helping us to piece together many of their skills and barriers in education. And if we understand their skills and barriers in education, then we are already well-placed to identify a variety of strategies to support them.

However, there are also crucial aspects of the biopsychosocial data, particularly from the 1:1 screening which we (schools) are not yet routinely capturing – data which are in fact really big keys to unlocking academic success, removing discrimination and reducing stigma around SEND. We started to see the potential power of this process when we met Pupil E in Chapter Two.

## 1:1 screening to better understand our children and young people

There are several reasons that we don't tend to screen systematically: perhaps because administering screening tests is considered beyond our remit; or, perhaps we don't feel we know enough; or, they're so eye-wateringly expensive that we can't afford to invest in them; or, we don't have time; or, we think they're only for a few children; or, we were never trained. Likely any or all of these reasons combined. But I'm increasingly convinced that because we don't routinely screen as part of our normal practice, children and young people are missed and then miss out – with life-limiting consequences.

With such a high stakes introduction to screening as that, you'll be relieved to know that the screening process which we're going to cover over the next few chapters together is actually not that difficult.

It could be considered complex because humans are complex and we need to consider a wide range of biological, psychological and social indicators in a matter of minutes. But in practice it's pretty easy to manage once you've mapped it out and finely honed it into a strategic battery of questions and tests, which I have done and which I'm going to share with you throughout the following chapters. It can also be complex because it involves **"holding people in mind"** during the assessment process and then making sure that the information gleaned and advice offered as a result is shared with, and acknowledged by, stakeholders so that the child or young person feels supported. And it's complex because, when done at scale, it involves this process many, many times over, which increases the amount of data we're harvesting significantly, which in turn, increases the number of children and families we need to "hold" during this time. But before we get carried too far down stream and start to feel completely overwhelmed with that idea, let's just keep it simple:

The 1:1 screening process is not difficult.

> **Holding in mind:** A phrase often used in counselling and psychology to describe the state of being aware of what someone else might be thinking and feeling, particularly in a situation which might make them feel vulnerable, stressed or at risk.

Although, ultimately, I am proposing a new overall approach for educational settings by screening *everyone* every two to three years, which could be embedded systematically into the school year, first of all this is about doing what you can when you can. It is unlikely that you will be able to implement a whole new system of screening overnight for many reasons, but I encourage you to start with one child. And then another when you need to. And build up from there as you can. I guarantee you will be grateful that you have these tools and a new skillset to use to help the children and young people you work with. The adults around each child will value the outcomes from this process too and it will naturally evolve over time.

But before I introduce you to the dimensions we will look at in more detail together, we're going to look at one final and really important factor you need to think about first: *how you're going to get started.*

## First, do no harm

As Bananarama chanted on repeat, "it ain't what you do, it's the way that you do it". This is a critical thought in assessing, too. As educators, we are not routinely trained to consider how negatively we can impact on children's wellbeing with our own actions and behaviour. (Most of the focus is sat squarely with ensuring good behaviour in our pupils, isn't it?) For example, we don't have to take the equivalent of the teachers' **Hippocratic Oath** to work with children and young people. And yet, ask anyone of any age about their time in school and they will be able to name a teacher who caused them great fear or frustration. One of mine was a teacher who used to pick his nails with a long-bladed kitchen knife and when he got angry, he would stab it into the wooden teacher's desk where it would wobble for a few mesmerising seconds whilst we all breathed a sigh of grateful relief that it wasn't anywhere near us. (I know . . . it was the 1980s . . .) We can also equally name a few educators who we feel deeply grateful to, of course. We met one of mine in Chapter One. The rest sort of sit somewhere in the middle.

> **The Hippocratic Oath:** A promise taken by medical practitioners to act ethically when working with a patient. It covers key themes such as doing no harm, prioritising the patient over other influential factors, treating the whole person rather than just the symptom, obtaining prior informed consent, and calling on experts where needed. Religious texts also echo these sentiments. The Bible warns us of the Golden Rule – "do unto others, as you would have them do unto you" (Matthew 7:12) and psychotherapists, similarly: If you do something for a patient that you would not do to your friends or children, warns Bessel van der Kolk, consider first why and the potential negative impact it might cause. (*The Body Keeps Score: Mind, brain and body in the transformation of trauma*, 2014)

Teachers are, however, at odds with other frontline professionals such as doctors and social workers who practice from an agreed code of standards based heavily on ethics. Psychologists, too, are highly attuned to and mindful of the potential risks they have on children's wellbeing when conducting tests and feeding back results. The medical and social research professions have not just created codes and declarations by which to practice (for example, in Nuremberg in 1947 and in Helsinki in 1964, and by the Royal College of Paediatrics and Child Health in 2014) but these practices are constantly re-evaluated as research takes on new directions, faces new dilemmas, and ultimately reflects the diversity and the context of the people it meets. Whether we consider our individual classrooms as places of research or not, our actions have impact on children – sometimes forging memories which can be recalled very vividly at a moment's notice. We would be naïve and careless not to consider this seriously as professionals involved in helping children to grow and become the successful, happy and independent adults we want them to be.

In looking to act ethically and protect our pupils' wellbeing then, we need to consider our screening process through multiple lenses and stages. Although there actually are four overall phases of the process – screen, support, share and strategy – we're going to focus in on the first three in this chapter, breaking them down into smaller steps, as you can see in Figure 3.3.

*Figure 3.3* An overview of the initial steps to consider when carrying out a screening

**1. Designing the screening protocol**

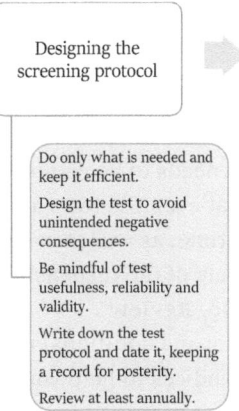

A screening protocol should always be evolving. Not necessarily huge changes, although they do happen from time to time. But little tweaks. A wording adaptation and new question, here and there. This is because we should always be looking to maximise each minute to be as perceptive and insightful as it can be. This means that when introducing something, just like a brand new lesson plan, the first time through at scale is always a bit of a dry run. With experience, ongoing deep reflection and debate about how we make the screening process ever better in its design, our protocol centres around the following:

- That we start from the place of wanting to ensure the classroom experience is positive for every child through better understanding of the specific barriers which might impede their progress. Because of this, every child experiences the same core tests. This protocol is always written down and dated to show what was protocol at any one time.
- That the core battery is cost-efficient – ideally no more than 15 minutes per child for the in-person process. Where it is possible to gather data in a group, this should be capitalised upon so parts of the process are streamlined by being included in normal class time, too.
- That, after this, we can personalise the screening process to the pupil in front of us either because of something they've said, something we've observed, or a trigger cause for referral (e.g. school avoidance) which causes us to want to explore something more fully and specifically.
- That the pupil experience is sensitive to potential unintended consequences from any questions we ask. We want to avoid any kind of distress or harm so questions are worded carefully and some topics are left out, potentially to explore at another time and in another way, if we feel they could trigger negative feelings or behaviours.
- That the tests we use give us data that we can act on.
- That we choose our tests wisely at the outset – particularly, when they are standardised. We consider how reliable and valid they are. (NB when purchasing tests from reputable companies, this will have already been done, but it's still good to be mindful of the data upon which any test was designed and ensure it is age- and culturally-appropriate for your pupils.)
- That we discuss protocol at least once, if not twice, a year and refine it so it captures our reflections and observations in writing so we can then refer back to it.

The screening protocol ultimately needs to be responsive and ever-evolving to the needs in front of you. I have no doubt that even the tests and choices I explore in this book will continue to gradually evolve over time, as we learn more and meet new challenges. It's a deeply satisfying and important part of the responsibility of screening, and an extension of the concept of "**Assess, Plan, Do, Review**".

We will explore the core protocol and additional tests in Chapter Ten and you will also find further resources in the Appendices to help you.

**Assess, Plan, Do, Review:** is a process which is commonly used to evaluate progress and to help design next steps for a child. We will touch again on this in Chapter Four.

## 2. Informing, guiding and respecting stakeholders

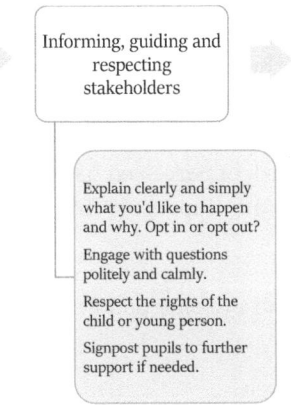

Once you've decided on what you're doing and when, you then need to think about communicating with stakeholders. How you choose to communicate about the screening will be based on your context, your culture and your senior leadership.

Best psychological and research practice would suggest that additional **informed consent** is ethically necessary. This means contacting the adult with parental responsibility, engaging with them about the process, checking that they're in agreement with it – and, crucially, respecting their decision if they're not.

Schools are not considered to be centres of psychological research, however, and we assess children all the time in all subject areas. In sending their child to your school, parents-carers have already given consent for them to be assessed at school. So whilst the above principle is important to heed, you may not need to seek additional explicit informed consent from parents-carers to carry out the screening. It would be wise to check your parental contract to see what wording has been used in your home-school agreement, and talk with your senior leadership team about it.

**Informed Consent:** Permission granted with knowledge of both the positive and possible negative consequences of the course of action. This is often in written form.

**Assent:** Agreement given, either explicitly or implicitly, to something taking place. This is often verbal or non-verbal.

Alongside this, during a screening assessment that has been consented to, it is vital to ensure the individual child is **assenting** to what's happening to them in that moment in time. A pupil must be content when being assessed. If they are not, the assessment must stop immediately and appropriate support be given.

As a minimum, I would encourage you to inform parents that the process is happening and offer an opportunity for them to ask questions. This is why:

- Parent-carers are then aware of what's happening in school and are open to and expecting feedback from the process when it comes.
- Parent-carers are given an opportunity to ask questions, to reflect on the process and to dis/agree to a screening process (enabling parents-carers to "protect" their child, thereby reducing the risk of perceived harm).
- Children and young people are supported from home in this unique and new experience.

It is however worth being mindful of some potentially unintended, and less desirable, consequences:

- It is additional workload writing to parents-carers which can trigger lots of follow-up communications answering questions and queries. This is manageable when it's just one child but if you're doing a whole year group, it can be time-consuming. It is worth thinking about how you are going to manage this efficiently. Even if you write some FAQs at the bottom of the letter and make sure a contact is given, this will help reduce the number of queries.
- It can cause parents-carers unnecessary alarm and anxiety ("My child has never had SEND before! What's wrong?") which can require sensitivity and considerable reassurance to placate.

### Opt-in or opt-out?

If you decide upon seeking consent specifically, you also need to consider if you'd prefer consent to be "opt-in" or "opt-out". Opt-in means you will wait for their written agreement before acting. Opt-out means you will wait until a certain date and if no disagreement is received, you will assume consent has been given.

*Opt-in*

- If you decide to seek additional opt-in consent, one communication isn't usually enough, so it can be time-consuming to manage.
- As you will know from parents' evenings attendance, it can be very difficult to engage certain groups of parents, which could lead to some of the most vulnerable children missing out (a situation you want to avoid at all costs).

*Opt-out*

- If you decide to choose to use opt-out consent, this may mean that one communication isn't enough either, as communication can easily be missed in the busyness of life.
- If this is the case, it can mean parents-carers are surprised when they receive a report detailing the process their child has gone through, which may cause alarm.

What I would say, however, is that once this process is embedded in your school, everyone gets used to it and you won't be fielding questions about it any longer. In fact, it becomes a much-valued experience which children and parents-carers tend to look forward to because it is so helpful in guiding everyone as to specific next steps for progress and success. Really, it's just about bedding it in.

In deciding how to communicate to parents-carers, in practice, I tend to operate on a case-by-case basis. If we are doing a big cohort screening, I will write to parents-carers and consider other ways to inform them, such as at a year group parents-carers event, allowing them to ask questions. We will also go into a year group assembly to inform the pupils about what's going to happen and demystify the process. I've even filmed a short film to show pupils the room and how it will look, to introduce the team and to explain exactly what's going to happen. This goes a long way to reducing any pupil worries about the process and to minimise any stigma of being seen by the SEND team, too.

If we are seeing someone from a referral or who has flagged through our internal monitoring systems, we will often give the parent-carer a quick call just to let them know. I have yet to have a parent out-right refuse. Usually, they just want to be reassured that their child is, and will be, ok and then they're happy for it to go ahead.

Genuinely, I can count the complaints that we've had about the screening process on one hand and I've overseen many, many hundreds of assessments over the last decade and more. Complaints have either been about too much or too little information. Sometimes, you can't win! Never have they been about a child or young person who has been upset by the process though, because we're really careful about designing a positive experience for our pupils throughout. It's something you'll need to consider carefully, too, so we're going to look into this in more detail now.

## 3.   Carrying out the screening

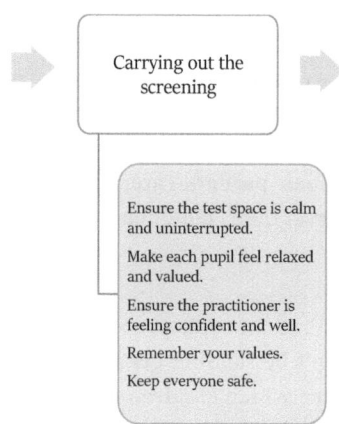

### *Considerations for the test environment*

Obvious though it may seem, test environments need to be calm, quiet and uninterrupted for the data to be reliable. I make a point of saying this at the get-go because schools are busy interchanges and small, calm, quiet and uninterrupted spaces are often at a premium. You will need to think carefully about how, when and where you carry out these assessments. When taking a large cohort approach, it is necessary to organise a composed and systematised approach, not dissimilar to year group vaccinations, in somewhere like a library or school hall. When testing on an individual basis, it is easy to screen in an office: turning the volume off on phones and sticking a note on the door to avoid interruption. As your practice increases and in heeding advice about safeguarding yourself and the children in your care, you will find what works for you.

### *Considerations for the adults carrying out the testing*

The tests are not complicated, as you will soon learn. Neither are they stressful to conduct when you are practiced at doing them. But there are some important factors to bear in mind when deciding who will carry out the testing.

Each educational professional should:

1.  Be educated and trained well enough to be able to manage the test process responsibly and reliably.
2.  Respect each child, ensuring they are well enough and happy to undergo the assessment.

3. Recognise that they are in a position of power and need to be very sensitive to not overstepping personal boundaries, in their questioning or their approach.
4. Be mentally and physically well enough to conduct the assessment.
5. Recognise that they need to take informed decisions in the moment – for example, stopping the process early if a pupil is upset, or doing an additional activity or questionnaire if the indications suggest it might be useful.
6. Be sensitive to discrimination in all forms, but especially with regards to the relevant protected characteristics, such as gender, race, religion and disability, found detailed in the Equality Act (2010).
7. Respect and be mindful of the need for confidentiality when sharing information, whilst also being aware of their duty to safeguard the pupil whilst in their care.
8. Be able to communicate effectively, clearly and kindly with each pupil they assess, as well as with colleagues.
9. Be aware of the school culture, systems and processes within which they are practicing.

A summary of the Health & Care Professions Council, Practitioner Psychologists Standards of Proficiency, valid from September 2023[7]

The above list of practice standards is really important to take on board and I hope, in time, the wider teaching profession will form its own ethical practice standards to which we will all adhere. Until then, these are a really useful guide to help us work carefully and respectfully with the children and young people in our care. If you want to read them in more detail, you can search for the document title above. It is freely available to all online.

### Considerations for a positive experience for the child or young person

So long as the assessor adheres to the above ethical practice, the pupil experience should be at least neutral and, in many cases, even positive. Certainly, most of the pupils I've worked with over time quite enjoy the one-on-one attention and an opportunity to "escape" their current lesson. The tests themselves aren't created to be stressful and some are designed to end at the point at which the child begins to struggle, so they never have a lasting and overwhelming sense of failure. If a child feels celebrated, nurtured, valued and safe throughout the screening, then they are unlikely to be or feel harmed, no matter how hard they find the tests. Their memory of how they felt in the experience is important to bear in mind and this is formed right from the very first moment. To help with this, make sure you have someone who can support a child if they're upset or need to reflect with. Even if someone isn't visibly upset by the process, you might be surprised at how the experience can be differently interpreted by children over the smallest of details, so at the end of the tests it helps to let them know who they can see to talk about the screening experience, if needed. It's why we've introduced pre- and post-assessment wellbeing checks to help us identify pupils who might need that extra reassurance.

Feeling psychologically safe before, during and after the screening is absolutely critical. In fact, psychological safety is vital for us all. Research by Amy C. Edmondson suggests that psychological safety is the number one factor for learning, innovation and growth. She states, "Given that our sense of danger is so natural and automatic, organisations have to do some pretty special things to overcome that natural trigger."[8] In part, how safe a pupil feels in your presence will be dictated by how safe you both feel in the school as a whole, but as practitioners we can do a lot to help the pupil to feel safe when they are with us. The "belonging cues" sent in the initial moments of interaction matter more than anything said.[9]

As such, I encourage you to consider your values and how you want people to feel when they've interacted with you and your team. What do you want them to observe and feel when they're with you? And what does this look like in practical actions and words? This is such a powerful and unifying process which enables you to enter this process more confidently. Thinking about what is important to you and as a team in your "initial moments of interaction" will help you to determine how you want the assessment process to be for the child or young person on the day itself. I highly recommend doing the following activity, personally and with your team if you have one, before you implement screening in your setting. As we learnt in Chapter One, values are critical to the process.

You might also want to reflect on the following too to help you design your process carefully:

- The United Nations Rights of the Child (1989)
- Millennium Development Goals (2000–2015)
- Sustainable Development Goals (2016)
- *Keeping Children Safe in Education* (the most recent edition)
- Gillick Competence

## No Child is Missed – Action Point 3.1: Reflect Upon your Shared Values

Brené Brown defines a value as "a way of being or believing that we hold most important". Trying to define what's important to you and distilling this into a set of core values can feel difficult. How do you choose one or two values that are more important than other really important values? I have, however, found it to be a really defining and confidence-boosting process. It has been worth the wrestle for that alone. But there is another reason I think acknowledging your values and listing them is so crucial in this screening process. And that is because, when your values are alive to you, it gives you (and your team) a guide for what to do in any eventuality. You will never be able to predict every single event or problem which may occur during a screening and write a policy about how to handle each one. For a start, screening is quick. No one will have time to turn to page 374 and carry out a seventeen-step process. Instead, having a set of values about how you want children, young people and parents-carers to experience the process, whatever happens, means that professionals will use this and their own professional judgement and expertise to navigate the challenge. It's infinitely smarter and means people use their own integrity, which is likely to be a much more successful and efficient way to run a safe and supportive process. This, of course, goes hand in hand with following robust safeguarding practice and a clear strategic overall protocol.

In terms of assessing your core values, an activity I highly rate is Brené Brown's *Living into Our Values* exercise which you can find on her website. It's also explained more fully in her book *Dare to Lead*. She says: "Living into our values means that we do more than profess our values, we practice them. We walk our talk – we are clear about what we believe and hold important, and we take care that our intentions, words, thoughts, and behaviors align with those beliefs."

> Brown, B. (2018). *Dare to Lead: Brave Work.*
> *Tough Conversations. Whole Hearts*
> (p. 186). Random House.

(And in case you're wondering..? Mine are 'trust' and 'growth.')

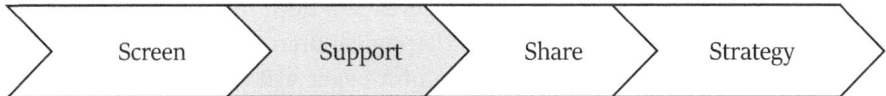

## 4. Crunching the data

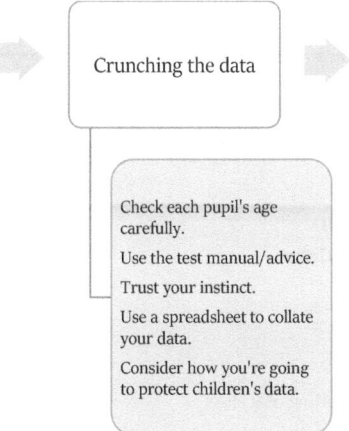

Crunching the data

- Check each pupil's age carefully.
- Use the test manual/advice.
- Trust your instinct.
- Use a spreadsheet to collate your data.
- Consider how you're going to protect children's data.

The word "data" can fill some people with dread. Within this chapter, it's difficult to talk specifically about data when there are many tests we can use, which have many different types of possible data outcomes. The best advice will be found in each test manual as to how you can interpret the data from a specific test. The best catch-all advice I can give you here is this:

- If you need to convert a raw score into a standardised score, make sure you have got the pupil's chronological age correctly worked out. Easy mistakes can be made by simply transposing the correct raw score into an incorrect standardised score by either miscalculating the child's age or by referring to the wrong column or page. (Don't forget, if you need a reminder about standardised scores, you can refer back to the diagram in Chapter Two.)

- Tests give strong indications but occasionally outcomes can be wrong or suggest something that you aren't convinced about. Don't cling to the data over your own gut reaction. You are the professional and you need to believe in the value you also bring to this process of evaluation. Gut reaction is incredibly powerful – our subconscious mind can pick up on subtle cues that our conscious mind might overlook.[10] The best outcome is really combining the strengths of human perception with the algorithm of the test.

- I find putting the data into excel helps in evaluating the scores (as I conditionally format them) and in speeding up reporting by mail merging the data. If you'd like to see an example of a conditionally formatted spreadsheet designed for the screening process, one is available to download on the website www.nochildismissed.org.

- Finally, respecting someone's rights also means being mindful of what data you are gathering and how it is stored and then shared. Your Data Protection Officer will need to be informed and appropriate measures will need to be in place to ensure compliance. As settings involved with gathering children's data are part of normal practice anyway, this is likely to be more of a paper exercise than a whole-scale change to working practice. Nevertheless, thinking about how you're actively going to protect children and young people through careful management of their screening data is a critical part of the process.

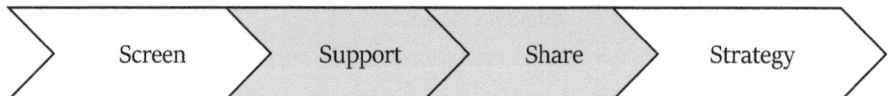

| Screen | Support | Share | Strategy |

5. **Supporting next steps, *and***
6. **Feeding back to stakeholders**

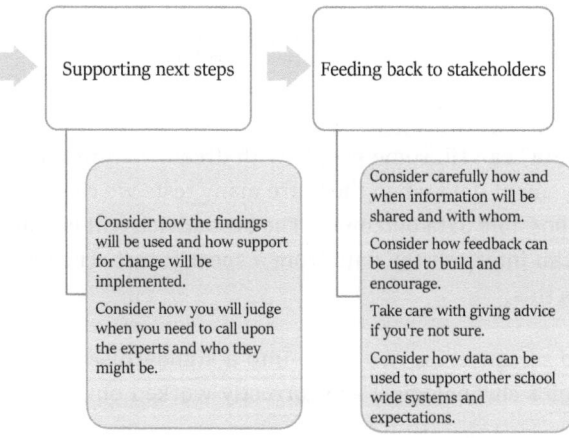

| Supporting next steps | Feeding back to stakeholders |
| Consider how the findings will be used and how support for change will be implemented. | Consider carefully how and when information will be shared and with whom. |
| Consider how you will judge when you need to call upon the experts and who they might be. | Consider how feedback can be used to build and encourage. |
| | Take care with giving advice if you're not sure. |
| | Consider how data can be used to support other school wide systems and expectations. |

## Supporting next steps and reporting back to stakeholders

### *Pupils and parents-carers*

How we feed back to people after screening can make a huge difference to how they perceive themselves. For me, growth is a critical value I hold and therefore, I will always provide concrete advice and steps to take to support any changes or adaptations that someone might want to make in response to any areas of weakness. Remember that even if a score is statistically likely to remain constant, there are still actions people can take to manage and improve how it affects them, or tools and technology which can help. This takes a solution-focussed approach, aligning itself more closely with the fields of **positive** and humanistic **psychology**, which aims to improve quality of life. It is even better when this list of next steps is sensitively created in discussion with the child or young person as well as their parents-carers recognising what's important to them, too. And I would recommend for more complex and higher needs cases, you try to do this if you can.

**Positive psychology:** A style of practice which emerged from the American Psychological Association in the late 1990s from the Humanistic field of psychology. It looks to find strategies and approaches which foster flourishing, subjective wellbeing and happiness.

**Deficit model:** An approach to testing which locates the difficulties identified within the child rather than seeing them as an interaction of biology and environment together. It also advocates a narrow range of tests which explore deficits within the microcosm of the classroom and the playground.

**CAMHS:** Child and Adolescent Mental Health Services.

Particularly when a child is struggling in school, I've learnt that parents-carers can often be keen to "try anything" and this can make them vulnerable to suggestion. As such, your actions and your conclusions require a diligent and compassionate approach, putting the child in the centre and being mindful to balance your level of experience with your level of influence. For example, I am always researching new supports and interventions and if I think something is worth suggesting I will mention it, but I also make sure parents-carers know that it is an unsubstantiated field of practice (e.g. see my recommendation for Binaural Beats in Chapter Seven, No Child Misses Out Response Point 7.1) so they are empowered to make a more rational decision about whether it's for them or not.

What this screening process does not yet do well enough – because cognitive screening tests aren't yet consistently designed with this end-goal in mind – is to identify and focus on a full range of someone's strengths, too. It focuses on skills for learning, relevant in the majority of subjects, and it focuses on them to identify "lack". We don't, for example, measure other personal strengths like someone's sense of humour, their creative ability, or their vast knowledge of a specialist area, like different train timetables and engine types. What we're looking to evaluate is rather different than what Instagram or TikTok followers might appreciate. I don't say this lightly. The way someone is defined, by another or by themselves, gives the one who defines considerable power. It's an important theme in our civil rights. Who are you? Who am I? And how does this change throughout the day, in different contexts and across a lifetime? Well, it really depends who gets the final say.

This idea of the power to define is an interesting thought in the process of dismantling injustice. Should we continue to use this "**deficit model**" to define weakness over strengths? And to locate them as barriers within the child, rather than stemming from the barriers they experience within their world? I think there is a lot more we could be doing globally in this regard, but we are where we are – for now, at least. We'll revisit this theme more definitively in the final chapter.

Nevertheless, by taking a positive approach to celebrating strengths that have emerged in an assessment and by trying to use those strengths – and others which might come out through later discussion, we will construct feedback which is more likely to help people to feel valued and encouraged. We will be endeavouring to give them our "unconditional positive regard". If you'd like to see an example of a report designed for the screening process, one which aims to foster growth and agency and one you can adapt to suit your context, you can visit the website www.nochildismissed.org.

### Colleagues

We'll cover the practical steps you can take in terms of reporting back to colleagues in a later chapter but to continue on this theme of positive psychology, I think there are a couple of areas to consider. Firstly, I think we need to be helping colleagues to see their classrooms as diverse, with children who arrive in school straight from other parts of their life; parts that may or may not be comfortable for many hundreds of reasons. The practical consequences that then arise from this level of empathy can jar and feel overwhelming at times when they can seem to be at odds with behavioural and curriculum expectations. We need to help colleagues manage any feelings of fear, frustration or inferiority which might come from the size of that expectation. It is the enormous challenge we all face in education: how to personalise a system which is ultimately designed to train the masses. Secondly, this screening needs to resolve itself in thinking about training needs of staff which might emerge from the data and to give them tools which are manageable and reasonable to embed. Staff need to feel they can and do make a difference – otherwise what's the point of school?

### Final thoughts: Do no harm . . .

There may be some education professionals who are aghast at the idea of mass screening. "Schools are doing enough already" they cry and that as a sector we cannot keep propping up insufficient services in other areas. In part, I agree. We cannot be expected to keep providing mental health and social care support without adequate staffing and funding. It's simply untenable: something has got to give. At the moment, the data suggests that it's children and young people who are. But unpicking how someone learns and what barriers they may be experiencing in the classroom is core Education business and I *do* think we should be doing that. We just need more training and support to do this effectively however – hence this book.

But why so many? Why not just those whose needs are flagging? In short, because every child and young person deserves the best chance of educational success and each of them deserve to have as many invisible barriers as possible acknowledged and removed/reduced. So many children get missed when we rely on appearances – they can be deceptive. Education needs to be far more equitable than it currently is.

There may also be some specialist assessors reading this book who are somewhat concerned at the overall SEND practice developments I'm suggesting: in essence, that further qualifications should not be required in order to carry out psychological testing. I tread cautiously here for I am well aware how complex individual cases can be and therefore I share a view that the practice in assessing vulnerable children and young people should be well-protected to avoid harm and to help enable good support. In that sense, I am keen that anyone engaging with screening should feel adequately trained to conduct the screening and, as Hippocrates necessitated all those years ago, that they feel confident about calling on the experts when needed. However, from where I'm standing, we have millions of children who aren't lucky enough to be able to see a professional assessor freely and in a timely manner. Children and young people are waiting, sometimes years, whilst symptoms worsen and attainment dwindles. This risks significant life-limiting impact.

In a six-month period in 2021, nearly half a million children and young people were referred to **CAMHS**.[11] In the Good Childhood Report 2022, 14.2% of children identified they were unhappy in school.[12] Their more recent report suggests this has deteriorated even further. In December 2022, NHS published data that there were 140,000 people awaiting an autism assessment[13] – a 40% increase from the previous year, with waiting times well in excess of NICE guidelines. In 2017, a workforce review of Community Paediatrics estimated there needed to be a 25% increase in doctors to cater for demand[14] – and that was *before* the data above. And, on top of this, training enough educational psychologists to keep pace with demand, isn't just a current issue[15] either but one which well predates our current SEND Crisis.[16]

It's not just a recruitment and training issue though; retention isn't looking good either. Twenty-four per cent of educational psychologists have left the profession since 2010. A DfE report published in June 2023 stated that "96% of Principle Educational Psychologists working in local authorities experienced difficulties in recruiting or retaining staff, or both" and "that these difficulties affected outcomes from children and young people requiring support".[17] All of this, at precisely the time when the number of children waiting for assessment has exploded off the chart.

In summary, I have come to the conclusion that we are *causing* more harm through ringfencing this kind of testing to postgraduate level qualified educational assessors, than preventing it. We need to carefully triage these needs at school level so that only the most significant needs reach those with the greatest level of qualification, and that children are seen by the right professional, at the right time. In Chapter Ten, we'll explore this further. But if this book motivates you to become one of these specialists yourself (hooray!), then below I also detail some organisations where you can find further information about how you can do just that.

*If you want to consider further training in a specialist area related to children and young people in education, you can learn more here*:

**Psychology**
UK: www.bps.org.uk; USA: www.apa.org;
Australia: www.psychology.org.au

**Specialist Teacher or Assessor**
UK: www.realtraining.co.uk; www.communicate-ed.org.uk; www.bdadyslexia.org.uk; www.dyslexiaaction.org.uk
USA: https://www.dyslexia.com/question/who-can-diagnose/
Australia: https://dyslexiaassociation.org.au/ada-training/

**Speech and Language Therapy**
UK: https://www.rcslt.org/speech-and-language-therapy/become-a-speech-and-language-therapist/;
USA: https://www.asha.org/Certification/Clinical-Specialty-Certification/; Australia: https://www.speechpathologyaustralia.org.au/

**Behavioural Optometry**
UK: https://babo.co.uk/TRAIN-WITH-US; USA: https://www.covd.org/; Australia: https://www.acbo.org.au/professionals/menu/education

**Irlen Screening and Assessing**
https://irlen.com/get-trained/

**Occupational Therapy**
UK: https://www.rcot.co.uk/rcot-education-hub/becoming-ot
USA: https://www.aota.org/career/become-an-ot-ota
Australia: https://otaus.com.au/

## Chapter Summary

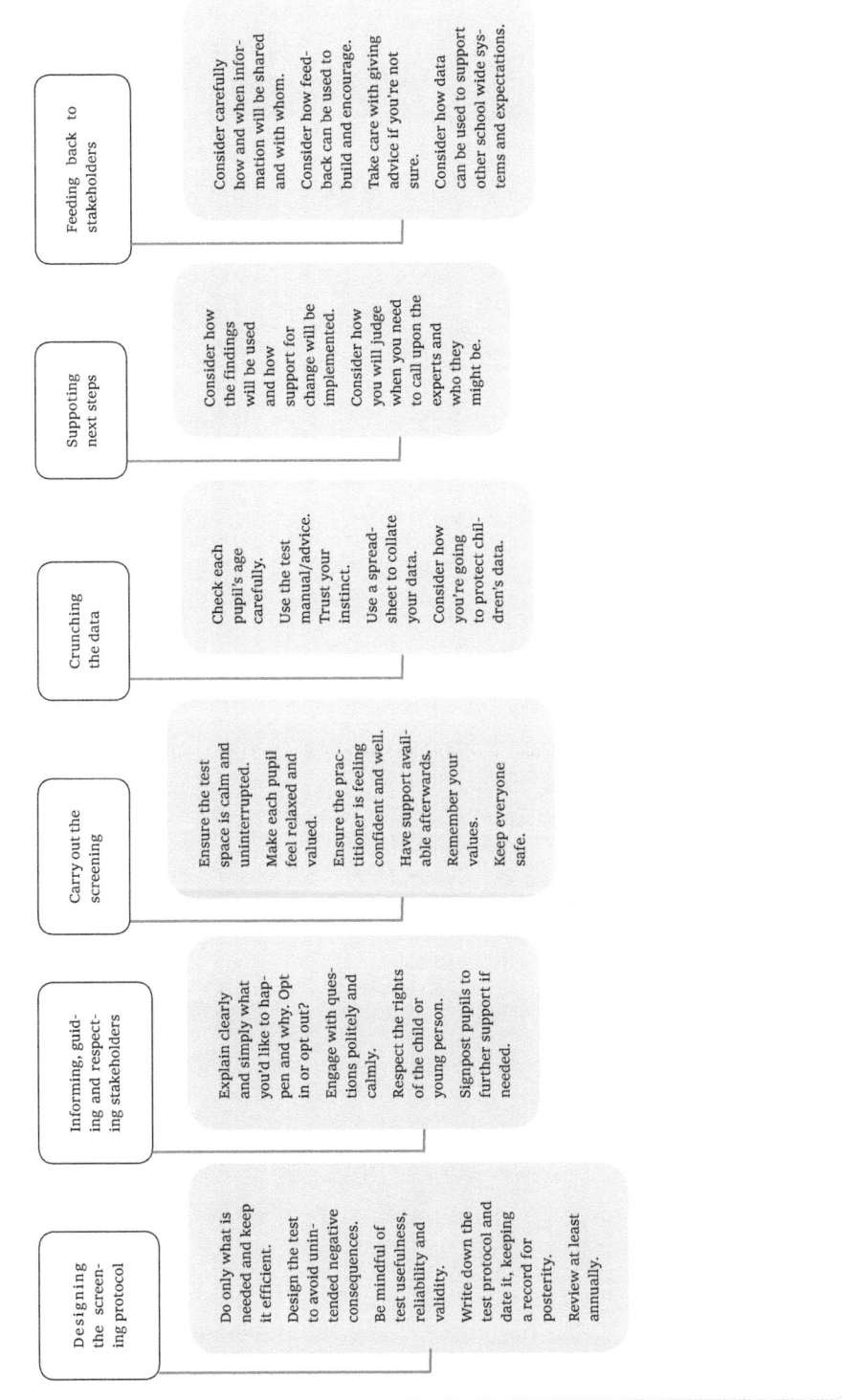

**Designing the screening protocol**

Do only what is needed and keep it efficient.

Design the test to avoid unintended negative consequences.

Be mindful of test usefulness, reliability and validity.

Write down the test protocol and date it, keeping a record for posterity.

Review at least annually.

**Informing, guiding and respecting stakeholders**

Explain clearly and simply what you'd like to happen and why. Opt in or opt out?

Engage with questions politely and calmly.

Respect the rights of the child or young person.

Signpost pupils to further support if needed.

**Carry out the screening**

Ensure the test space is calm and uninterrupted.

Make each pupil feel relaxed and valued.

Ensure the practitioner is feeling confident and well.

Have support available afterwards.

Remember your values.

Keep everyone safe.

**Crunching the data**

Check each pupil's age carefully.

Use the test manual/advice. Trust your instinct.

Use a spreadsheet to collate your data.

Consider how you're going to protect children's data.

**Supporting next steps**

Consider how the findings will be used and how support for change will be implemented.

Consider how you will judge when you need to call upon the experts and who they might be.

**Feeding back to stakeholders**

Consider carefully how and when information will be shared and with whom.

Consider how feedback can be used to build and encourage.

Take care with giving advice if you're not sure.

Consider how data can be used to support other school wide systems and expectations.

# PART 2
# An Overview of Screening

Each chapter in Part 2 follows the same format. It begins with longstanding and the latest research – the what and why of each dimension I'm guiding you towards, so you understand what it is you're testing and its importance. Following each explainer you'll find *No Child is Missed* advice about recommended tests. These are in grey boxes throughout the chapter. All tests recommended have been written by specialists in their field – many are freely available online, and I've also tried to share with you some that are costed, which you may want to consider purchasing in due course once you're further invested. Alongside these recommended tests, I've designed some resources which combine and streamline expertise into lightning quick check-ins, which you'll find in the *Appendices* and online. These have been put together to develop the quality and range of your information gathering in light of research and to support conversations with parent-carers that you might wish to have as a result of any findings.

In addition to the recommended tests and resources, you will also find advice about what I've learnt and noticed along the way. Firstly, I've put *Top Tips* in little break-out boxes as we go. These might help you to interpret observations or results to help inform the case, and even to encourage you in the power and value of your own observations. Secondly, I've added similar style boxes including **vocabulary** and their meanings, which might currently be unknown to you, as you will have already started to notice. In learning about screening and psychology, I have met and had to get to grips with many new terms and concepts so I hope that providing a working glossary is helpful for you as we go along. Finally, in the second half of each of the chapters, I have brought together expertise from professionals in research and practice in the relevant field to suggest actions you can take in response to any findings. I've put this advice into white boxes at the second half of the chapters entitled *No Child Misses Out*.

Closing each chapter, I briefly explore some *Final thoughts*. These are not designed to summarise the chapter, but to place it within a wider overall picture instead; encouraging us to see the chapter focus within its historical, social and/or political context – just like we did with IQ in Chapter 1.

DOI: 10.4324/9781032663968-5

# 4 Phonological Processing

It is no coincidence that I've begun the screening chapters with the processing of sound. Within hours of birth, babies will have their hearing checked; within weeks, they will begin to make their own babble; and within months they will be uttering their first magical words. Hearing is arguably one of our first and most important senses to develop. It is also one of the last to go when we slip into unconsciousness at the end of our lives; beginning and ending our relationship with the world. Critical to learning, sound helps us learn to speak, to read and to write. No less important, it also captures our attention, helps us to infer emotion and to help shift our behaviours in response, to play and to bond. The awareness of sound is very evident in early learning but perhaps becomes less overt the higher up the school you go. So, let's jump straight in and think about sound in your setting, wherever you are, and how you'll measure and support the development of **phonological processing**.

## Sensation: the hearing of sounds

In Chapter Two we learnt that learning is the result of **sensation** – nerve efficiency in conducting signals from within our bodies or from the environment (resulting from our DNA and early development) and **perception** – interpretation of the sensation (resulting from our lived experiences). Phonological processing describes sound being received by the ears and travelling along the auditory pathways from ear to brain and then, where relevant, from brain to action (be that speaking, writing, doing). In learning to speak, to read and to spell, we must first be able to hear.

> **Phonological processing:** The term used to describe how sound is interpreted by our brains through spoken and written language.
> **Sensation:** The ability to detect a stimulus through nerve efficiency, conducting signals from within our bodies or from the environment (resulting from our DNA and early development).
> **Perception:** Giving meaning to/interpreting the stimulus, which might lead to a response (resulting from our lived experiences).

DOI: 10.4324/9781032663968-6

**Visual orienting:** Moving the eyes to help identify and interpret the sound (important in supporting focus and attention). We are able to do this by rapidly calculating the difference in loudness between the sound as it enters our two ears, alongside awareness of our head position, the acoustics of the room and the range of wanted and unwanted sounds also being heard.

Pitch (frequency), amplitude (volume) and complexity (type/complexity) are all critical to efficient hearing, but it is pitch which is most critical. Pitch enables us to interpret the location and content of the sounds. As a result, we will move our head to locate sound using **visual orienting**. Pitch enables us to "hear" the different sounds within a word to learn and use it, too. The efficiency of this nerve conduction even affects our sense of time and timing. In fact, research has shown that the ability to clap in time to the beat strongly correlates with future literacy abilities.[1] So if you watch a class carefully in a music lesson, you may well notice that some of your known struggling readers are also the ones who seem to clap ever so slightly off the beat. Sound enables us to communicate with others and the world around us, sharing collective experiences and allowing us to create meaning together. Being able to communicate through sound is fundamental to our survival as a species. As such, perhaps it won't surprise you to learn that phonological processing, as indicated by delayed speech and language development, is one of *the* earliest and most important indicators of a potential learning difficulty.

## Perception: the understanding of sounds

How easy you find it to distinguish the individual phonemes, syllables or rhythms in a word is one thing. Giving these sounds meaning is quite another. For this, we need exposure within our environment, which is vital for building perception. The complexity of the soundscape will also affect our brain's ability to learn to identify and distinguish different sounds. This is particularly crucial in periods of high plasticity: notably our early years and adolescence. The more complex and repetitive the sounds we are exposed to, the more we will learn to distinguish the differences between them. So, even babies whose brains have enough phonological genes for efficient sensation of sound waves but who have had *limited* exposure to complex sounds, specifically including music and speech sounds, are likely to sense and perceive fewer sounds accurately and produce fewer and a smaller range of sounds compared to those in busy households with lots of adult chatter.[2] Our ability to perceive sound accurately directly leads to the building of our **receptive vocabulary**.

There's some pretty sobering research which evidences this. You might have come across the shocking finding that there is a "thirty-million word gap"[3] from birth to three years old (the difference in number of words spoken by parents to children in the home) across the socio-economic range, from "professional" to "welfare" families. Although this research has now been questioned both in terms of its design and the veracity of its stark conclusions,[4] the reality is that there *is* a difference in the number of words spoken across different households, and less singing and fewer words spoken do have a cumulative effect on child language development regardless of DNA. It stands to reason too that barriers of exposure to a diverse soundscape, full of varied language, rhythm, music, noises, volumes, are understandably often linked to familial financial resources: access to baby groups, early years childcare, going out into the community shopping and mixing with people, having a good level of previous education to enjoy reading books together or listening to different music genres. All of these types of experiences are often exclusive to certain demographics, perpetuating the cyclical grip of poverty.

**Top Tip:** In your setting, aim that the adults involved with a target child monitor and record the number of five minute conversations they have with them to build up conversational experience, vocabulary exposure, word finding skills, using their voice to communicate and empower. If not you, then who?

**Receptive vocabulary:** The words we are able to <u>understand</u> in text or speech.

**Phonics:** a method of teaching people to read and spell by linking sounds to their letter symbols. E.g. the sound "cuh" can be made by the following letter combinations: c, ck, and k.

**Onset:** The first sound in a word – e.g. "f" in "first"

**Rhyme:** The final sound(s) in a word – e.g. "ant" in "plant".

**Perceptual quality:** The sound energy within the word.

**Multi-sensory:** Simultaneous stimulation of at least two information gathering pathways (senses) within the body e.g. sound *and* light (vision) which provide complementary messaging, supporting greater overall confidence in accuracy and recall of comprehension (perception).

**Expressive vocabulary:** The words we are able to <u>use</u> in our speech to communicate our thoughts and ideas.

Experience of complex sounds enable us to distinguish beginnings and endings, gaps and patterns, particularly within continuous streams of sounds, which all help us to recognise and then develop our own vocabulary. Regular speech is often made up of lots of words rarely spaced, when spoken fluently, and often abbreviated or modified for ease. This makes them complex to understand. For example, if you listened to me say the first sentence of this paragraph out loud, as a fluent speaker of English I would produce these speech sounds at a rapid pace and, assuming that you are also a fluent speaker of English, you would be able to discern the patterns of the words and perceive gaps within them, even though they'd actually sound like one long sound:

"experienceofcomplexsoundsenableustodistinguishbeginningsandendings". A non-fluent speaker, or one whose vocabulary was quite limited, might hear some familiar words and perhaps guess at the overall meaning, but they would not be able to "hear" all of the words as separate entities. The sound would simply blur into a relentless battery, just like it does when we listen to foreign radio.

An experienced teacher of **phonics** will know that words are segmented into different parts: the initial sound is the **"onset"** also known as the "*attack*"; the final sound is the **"rhyme"** also known as the "*decay*". For example, we must be able to distinguish the difference between the "ch" and "sh" onset sounds to be able to perceive whether the speaker has said "chip" or "ship". Likewise, we need to be able to perceive the difference between rhyme sounds such as "ip" and "op" to know whether it's "chips" or "chops" that we're having for tea tonight. There are about 50 different onsets, and about 2,000 different rhymes,[5] which gives about 100,000 possible syllable sounds! In practice, we only use about 15,000 of these in English. Nevertheless, this is still a hefty figure, especially when compared to Japanese, for example, which is said to only have between 100–200 syllables.[6] English speaking children have a lot of sounds to be able to process and remember in order to develop their literacy skills.

## The development of speech and language

The more we experience words and develop our discernment of onsets and rhymes, the more we begin to apportion meaning to the different words we hear, especially when we hear them often and then start to recognise them in different sentences and contexts. This all takes time and lots of repetition. Research shows that children remember more words if they hear them through reading the same book over and over again,[7] even if it is a bit dull for the adults around them. But as we develop our phonological awareness, we become increasingly aware of the **perceptual qualities** of words, which then allows us to notice the difference between "hot", "heat" and "hoot", for example; and our vocabulary develops rapidly.

This perceptual quality comes from the speed of the sound energy required for the correct pronunciation of the word. Whilst natural nerve speed helps us to sense perceptual quality, comprehension is very much experience-dependent. And we perform even better, the more we *hear and see* words being spoken simultaneously, which is why it's much better for parents to push their babies in inward-facing pushchairs and prams rather than forward-facing pushchairs, and why parents scrolling into their phone with limited engagement with their babies can impede vocabulary development in little ones. It's the same reason why we want to see people when they're speaking, or why we might close our eyes to concentrate and "hear" better if our visual experience is distracting from what we are trying to listen to and understand.

The more we are stimulated with the same message, through different nerve pathways, the greater the chance of this message reaching the brain clearly. Synchronous **multi-sensory** experiences produce an enhanced response that represents the combined activity of the senses.[8] It's a fundamental reason for developing dual-coding within teaching – if you've come across this term: that when teaching we should introduce new concepts and language with multi-sensory cues to support stronger encoding of new memories. The integration of the senses ignites a much more powerful encoding of meaning for recall.

In terms of developing and extending word knowledge, vocabulary is divided into three tiers, as detailed in the following diagram. Being aware of tiers of vocabulary can help teachers to think about the types of vocabulary they are using in lessons and predict the typical language barriers and supports needed for pupils to access the topic and to build on their learning. We tend to focus on Tier 3 words because we recognise that these are naturally less common and therefore less well known, but the battleground for understanding is often Tier 2 vocabulary because we might make assumptions about pupils' knowledge and awareness of these typically more common words – and yet, assuming knowledge of Tier 2 words may lead to pupils missing out.

**Expressive vocabulary** skills predict later reading competency[9] and a pupil's range of vocabulary relates to their reading comprehension and also their understanding of the curriculum. Students whose vocabulary knowledge is low are also unlikely to develop their vocabulary through typical classroom instruction approaches.[10] This means that developing pupils' expressive vocabulary should positively impact on their reading comprehension, their understanding of the curriculum and prevent continued exclusion from learning higher up the school; but it also needs careful and specific attention in order to develop. There are lots of resources online with word lists to support teachers in their planning – have a look at Academic Word Lists as a starting point.

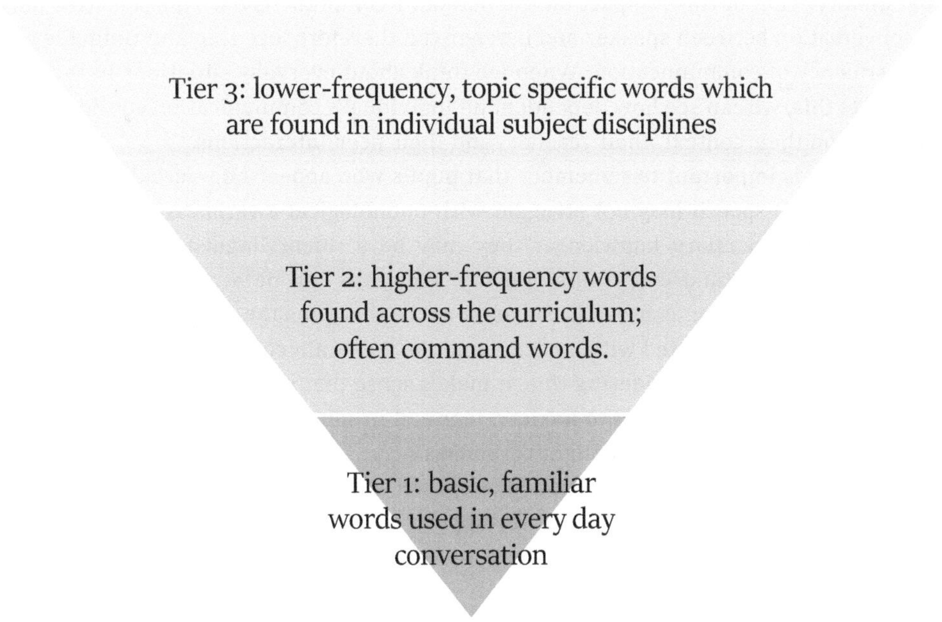

Tier 3: lower-frequency, topic specific words which are found in individual subject disciplines

Tier 2: higher-frequency words found across the curriculum; often command words.

Tier 1: basic, familiar words used in every day conversation

*Figure 4.1* The three tiers of vocabulary

## Speech

Being able to speak words is a separate ability in itself, working alongside and intricately linked with phonological processing. The mechanics of speech itself is beyond the remit and scope of this book. However, there are a few points worth making.

Firstly, speech is also the product of our cranial nerves: the hypoglossal nerve which is responsible for tongue movement and is vital for speech and swallowing; and the vagus nerve which is responsible for the muscles involved in swallowing, voice and resonance. Accurate speech also relies on sound conduction from our voice box through the bones in our head and our ears to reach our brain for perception. Like with other nerves, the speed it takes for information to travel from the brain to produce speech also varies within people. Speech also takes *practice and refinement* and that's much easier if someone is speaking to us and stimulating us to speak in a reciprocal exchange with them. As we progress in our skill and sound awareness, it also takes our *planning*. We need to think quickly and get our mouth and tongue ready for the correct series of positions needed to speak the words we want to say. It's complex. Giving pupils enough time for thinking through a response and then planning the speech production is critical, even though we might feel pressure to move on with the lesson.

Secondly, speech clarity can be affected by conditions such as cerebral palsy which can cause muscle weakness and/or nerve damage affecting a child's ability to use their tongue and facial muscles to enunciate words. Likewise, the palate is fundamental to making speech sounds as it lifts and closes, preventing air from leaking through the nose. A cleft palate or overly soft palate may mean that closing the palate is difficult causing the voice to sound nasal, affecting speech clarity. Lack of speech clarity (perceptual quality) can, in turn, impact on the listener's comprehension. This sensitive dance of conversation between speaker and listener can therefore lose step and timing leading to dysfluency of communication. When we think about everyday situations in the classroom like this, we can see how dependent an individual's communication confidence and skill is upon their context, their teacher- and their peer-interactions.

Finally, it is important to remember that pupils who appear non-verbal, or who have slow or limited speech may not struggle with phonological awareness, speech production or poor vocabulary knowledge: they may be a fluent linguist underneath their silence and understand everything you say. Emotions can be a powerful inhibitor of speech fluency. The vagus nerve is the main nerve that runs the length of our spine and it is increasingly associated with emotion and the gut-brain connection, as well as swallowing and the voice. Considering this, it makes sense that some speech conditions such as selective mutism are linked to anxiety, fear and in some cases, post-traumatic stress: manifestations of the freeze or flight responses.

In all cases of speech difficulties, if a speech and language service is not already involved, a swift referral for specialist support is vital to prevent long-term and life-limiting impact. In the UK currently, there are too few speech and language therapists to meet need which is why being very proactive with in-house screening early on is important for evidencing need and getting children accepted onto waiting lists quickly. In the UK, The Bercow Report: Ten Years On[11] highlighted continuing difficulties accessing specialists, showing that only 12% of pupils with speech and language needs were picked up by a professional. Research from adult prisons has found that up to 79% of adults have speech, language or communication need.[12] It just goes to show how significant the processing of sound is for overall life success and happiness.

**Top Tips:**

- Seek out vocabulary lists by searching for "Academic Word Lists". Consider dual-coding of new language providing glossaries with images and/or examples in context. Build short vocabulary lists which parents-carers and form teachers can work on in short bursts each week.
- Encourage teachers to allow more thinking and speech planning time when asking a pupil a question.
- Speech confidence and clarity can also be affected by eating highly processed foods that don't require much chewing. Jaw and tongue strength, as well as other aspects of facial development, require us to chew. If a child is struggling with speech, it might be worth speaking to parents-carers about their diet.
- With waiting lists as long as they are, some parents may want to see a private therapist. Build relationships with and put together a contact list of local private speech and language therapists who can be approached for advice, support and assessment, especially if your access to local authority services is very limited.

## No Child is Missed – Action Point 4.1: Screen Speech, Language and Communication

In terms of assessing how well each child has developed with their speech, language and communication, there are key areas to look at and think about. How well does this young person perform in these areas?

- Attention and listening
- Understanding (receptive language)
- Talking (expressive language)
- Social communication and use of language
- Speech sounds
- Play

If you would like to look further into this, there are some brilliant resources by *Bedfordshire and Luton Speech and Language Therapy Service* who have an *Early*

*Years Language and Communication Toolkit. Herefordshire and Worcestershire Speech and Language Therapy Service* are also nationally renowned for their expertise and resources. I particularly like their *Every Child a Talker Speech, Language and Communication Development Chart* and their *Identification of Need* tools. They also give some useful advice about pupils who are multi-lingual learners. If you are aware that a child is multi-lingual and their first language is not English, I would also recommend the *Bell Foundation* resources (also free) to help you assess their level of fluency and competency in English language.

If you would like to purchase a test, one that is highly recommended by many speech and language therapists is the *Wellcomm* screener. We use it across our nursery provision – it's brilliant: particularly useful for picking up difficulties and plotting a clear action plan. There is also a primary edition. You may be familiar with the *British Picture Vocabulary Scale* (BPVS) which helps practitioners to assess receptive vocabulary - useful when assessing multi-lingual children or non-readers because it doesn't require the child to speak or to read. *Speech* Link is also a respected screening resource at secondary. The *Renfrew Language Scales Expressive Vocabulary Test* measures a pupil's spoken language skills.

## Reading for meaning

Being able to read is another product of **phonological awareness**. Synthetic phonics is a way of teaching reading and writing through sounds. Pupils will learn about the correspondence between the written letter patterns (known as *graphemes*) and their speech sounds (known as *phonemes*). Pupils learn these as isolated grapheme–phoneme units and then they gradually learn to *blend* and to *segment* these sounds in order to build words and break words down: both vital skills in reading and spelling accurately. So, first you might learn the grapheme–phoneme correspondence for "d" and then "u" and then "ck". When you see them grouped together, you will begin to blend all of those sounds closely together and, with a favourable wind, you will hopefully say "duck'. Likewise, when you come to spell it, you might hear the three different phonemes within the word which need writing down. It might take you a while to master the correct "ck" grapheme–phoneme correspondence but three sounds will get you most of the way to accuracy at least, even if you choose to write "duk". In total, English has 44 phonemes represented by 26 letters, individually and in combination.

You might have noticed that I have deliberately used the conditional tense when describing someone learning grapheme–phoneme correspondence skills because, for some, "hearing" those sounds – that's to say, learning the **phonology** to reproduce them correctly – (being able to blend sounds to form words and break words down into their constituent sound parts) – is actually really quite difficult. Whilst there may be no hearing difficulties in terms of recognising volume or type of sound, challenges distinguishing and recognising the individual units of sound - their pitch – and reproducing them accurately through reading and spelling does not come as naturally for some as others. It's one of the reasons why, when children are first learning, speech may be slower to develop.

Uta Frith, a hugely influential professor in the world of SEND, suggests that there are three stages in learning to read which are more like gradual transitions rather than abrupt, demarcated changes.[13]

> **Phonological awareness:** the ability to hear and distinguish between the sounds within words, allowing people to segment words into their individual sounds and to blend a series of sounds into whole words.
> **Phonology:** The sound structure of words – e.g. the fact that the word "bring" has three separable sounds in it ("br", "i" and "ng")
> **Analytic reading:** reading/knowing words by sight rather than using phonological skills to (learn to) read.

Her a reading model encompasses both phonological skills and also **analytic** (sight word) skills. Both processes are important in learning to read as there are some words in English which are incredibly difficult to decode accurately through sound alone (e.g. though/thought/enough) and just need to be learnt by their whole word visual pattern. We will look at this in more depth in the next chapter, when we explore the impact of vision on reading fluency.

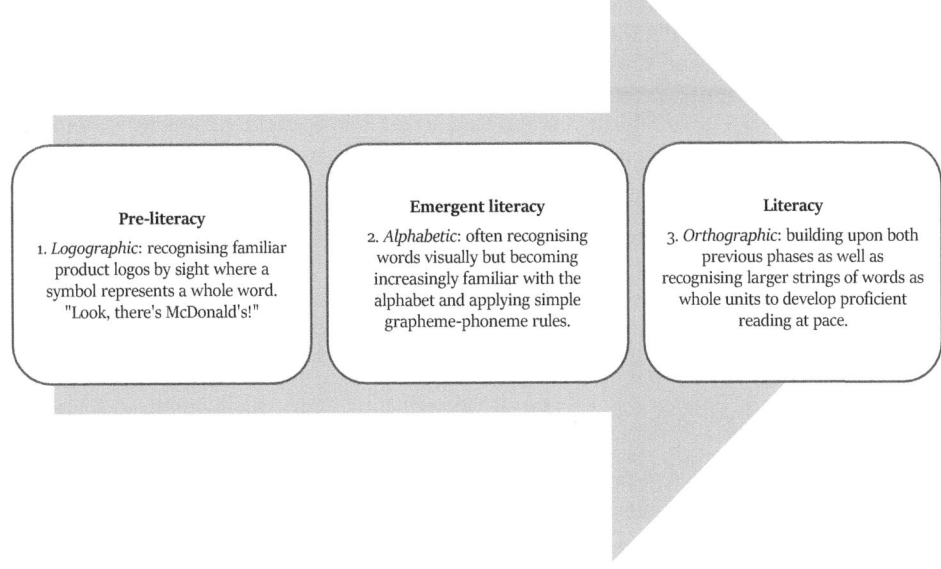

*Figure 4.2* The three stages of reading development

A review of early reading found that the teaching of phonics is essential in instruction of reading[14,15] and this case continues to be made in the USA and Australia, too.[16] Tests of phonological awareness predict future reading ability, but reading ability also predicts a child's future phonological awareness.[17] Reading is therefore both the result of and improves good phonological awareness. The more sophisticated a pupil's phonological awareness, the more able they are to manipulate sound which then develops their written literacy skills. Whatever a pupil's initial level of phonological awareness it is *always* worth working to improve it. More reading helps, of course, but so too does training the ear through music and singing to develop pitch and rhythm, as argued by Sally Goddard Blythe in *The Well-Balanced Child*;[18] and as evidenced by the inspiring *Feversham Primary Academy*. This school, in a deprived area of England, provided up to six hours a week of music for every child, and alongside this, their results went from being below- to above-national average in reading, writing and maths, including results for disadvantaged pupils which were well above average.[19]

---

### No Child is Missed – Action Point 4.2: Screen Phonological Awareness

Whether you're a fan of it or not, the annual *Phonics Screening Check* in Year One (England) is a quick indicator of phonics skill and any child who underperforms in this will certainly need additional support. However, it is definitely not a catch all. There will be children who pass this fairly blunt test and still struggle to develop secure reading and spelling skills, which may impact on them showing their underlying potential. The reason is that phonological awareness and phonics are different skillsets and also that phonological awareness is layered and more complex than simply grapheme–phoneme correspondence.

In terms of evaluating phonological awareness, there are actually five areas, as identified by Professor Marilyn Jager Adams, each increasing in difficulty, which indicate level of skill.

- Awareness of *rhyme and alliteration*, usually developing in pre-school
- Explicit awareness of *shared sounds* within words – being able to hear and compare/contrast simplistic onset (*tin*, *tap*, *toe*) and rime sounds (m*op*, sh*op*, p*op*).
- *Dividing and blending syllables* – foghorn *(fog-horn)* and more complex onset and rimes *(f-oghorn)* and then blending (What word do these sounds make? Fog – Horn = *foghorn*)
- *Segmenting phonemes* – separating popcorn into its constituent parts *(f,o,g,h,o,r,n)*
- *Manipulating phonemes* – adding sounds, deleting sounds, swapping sounds (what word do you get if you remove 'horn" from foghorn? What word do you get if you add "-iest" to it? Or what word do you get if swap the first sound in "fog" for "b"?)

If you are concerned about a child's ability to read or spell, or that they're not making the progress you think they should, it is worth assessing their phonological awareness, in addition to any phonics screening check, which can help you work out where they are getting stuck and then deliver a targeted intervention. If you would like to look further into this, there are some brilliant (free) resources by *Hertfordshire Specific Learning Difficulties* team in their *Phonological Awareness Pack*. They provide screening tools and intervention ideas for both primary and secondary. There is also the *WESFORD (Wiltshire Early Screening for Dyslexia)* which is equally helpful. Have a look at them both and decide which suits you better. A costed assessment of phonological processing is the *Comprehensive Test of Phonological Processing (CTOPP)*.

When it comes to placing meaning on those sounds, children must combine their vocabulary knowledge, their decoding skills and their wider background knowledge. As they engage with texts, they learn to make inferences, connect ideas, and monitor their understanding by asking questions or rereading passages. Learning to read and to understand is a complex multi-faceted process and, given the requirement of wider knowledge, it demonstrates the importance not just of a complex soundscape for phonological awareness but stimulating and varied life experiences, too, to connect complex sounds to myriad meanings.

## No Child is Missed – Action Point 4.3: Screen Reading Comprehension

Reading comprehension can be quite time consuming to evaluate, so it pays to be as strategic as you can to make your screening efficient. It is however, really important.

You can either assess reading comprehension in person, or in class tests. In terms of class tests, *ReadWorks* and the *ROAR (Rapid Online Reading Assessment)* are US based online resources which are research-driven and well-developed. *Twinkl* provide standardised reading assessments. Another quick way to create reading comprehension resources is to use AI to help you. ChatGPT is able to create texts and questions which you can target to different levels of difficulty. You will need to think carefully about your prompts so you get exactly what you're looking for. Whilst not all of these options will give you a standardised score, you will be able to compare children against the class as a whole and gain a sense of their overall comprehension ability.

If you would like to explore paid-for options which test and standardise at scale, the *NFER reading tests* are assessments designed to monitor pupils' reading comprehension across different age groups and can be used to track progress over time.

Another alternative is *Literacy Assessment Online*, which offers a range of whole class or year group, standardised reading comprehension tests. *Lucid EXACT* is very useful for access arrangements. *Hodder Group Reading Test* is also worth looking into.

If you are keen to add in an in-person reading comprehension into your test battery, there are tests you can purchase, such as the *Salford Sentence Reading and Comprehension Test* and the *Wechsler Individual Achievement Test (WIAT)*. You will also find example in person reading tests on www.nochildismissed.org

## Spelling

Speech sounds, vocabulary and reading comprehension may be age-appropriate and yet phonological awareness may still need development for spelling accuracy. That ability to distinguish the individual units of sound may not (yet) be sensitive enough to segment whole words into their sounds and may still need some work. This is a classic indicator of what assessors look for when testing for dyslexia. Even a simple game of challenging a child to create a new pair of words by switching initial sounds (spoonerisms) will give you an idea about their phonological awareness skills for spelling words (or should I say *"welling spurds"*?!) Listening to them singing will tell you more about their awareness of pitch – as you might now predict, there is a strong correlation between singing out of tune and poor phonological awareness affecting spelling.[20]

Like reading, there is a general pattern of development which children tend to experience. It is not uncommon for reading to outpace spelling to start with and for children to read words they cannot spell (and equally, sometimes spell words they cannot read!) Knowledge of phonic sounds is critical for secure spelling development and whilst a sight word approach (such as look-say-cover-write-check) can be very helpful, it is ultimately a time-consuming way to teach spelling. As the famous saying goes, "give a man a fish and he will eat for a day; give a man a fishing rod and he will eat for life". The same is true for spelling.

By the time they are seven, when pupils sit their national curriculum assessments in spelling (England), most pupils will be in the full alphabetic stage but there will be considerable variation within it, and depending on both the pupil's phonological awareness (sensation) and their classroom learning experience and home support (perception) a class of students' spellings will continue to be quite varied over time. The challenge with spelling, as with maths, is that it is a skillset built layer upon layer and so any deficit early on cements as a gap or insecurity unless specifically targeted judiciously by a very alert classroom teacher, teaching assistant, specialist teacher or tutor. The harder that a pupil finds spelling, the more likely a more multi-sensory approach is required to support the development of phonological awareness and phoneme–grapheme correspondence. If spellings aren't consolidated regularly and with conscious and targeted repetition, it is likely that it will continue to be an area of weakness.

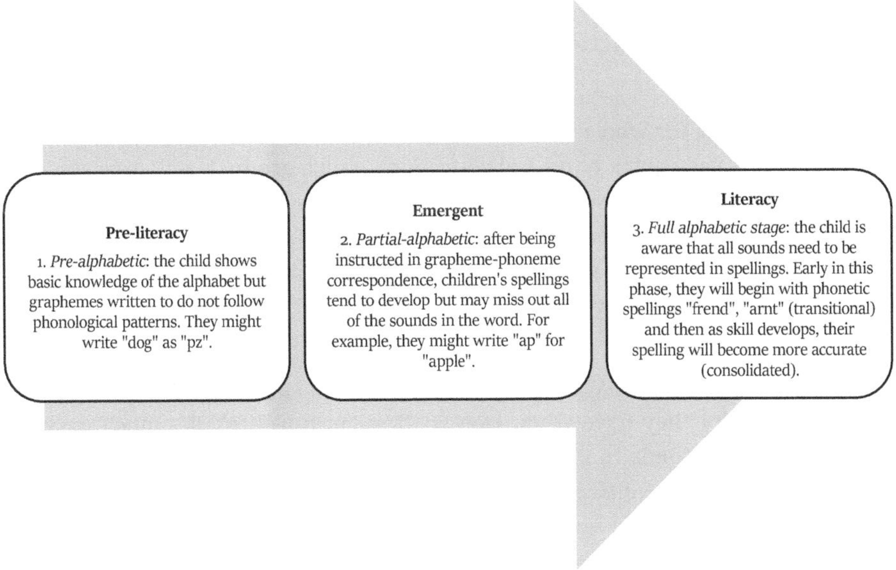

**Pre-literacy**

1. *Pre-alphabetic*: the child shows basic knowledge of the alphabet but graphemes written to do not follow phonological patterns. They might write "dog" as "pz".

**Emergent**

2. *Partial-alphabetic*: after being instructed in grapheme-phoneme correspondence, children's spellings tend to develop but may miss out all of the sounds in the word. For example, they might write "ap" for "apple".

**Literacy**

3. *Full alphabetic stage*: the child is aware that all sounds need to be represented in spellings. Early in this phase, they will begin with phonetic spellings "frend", "arnt" (transitional) and then as skill develops, their spelling will become more accurate (consolidated).

*Figure 4.3* The three stages of spelling development

In my experience, as they age some poor spellers work *very* hard to disguise their difficulties and, I think, ultimately to their own disadvantage actually. I notice this more often with girls than boys, but it affects both sexes. What some children do is choose to *use words that they know how to spell* (simple, basic words) in their written work so their spelling accuracy is high, *rather than use more complex words which they might get wrong* (but would improve the overall quality of their written expression) and get them a higher mark. It also means that they rarely practice using more complex language in their written work and so it doesn't just disguise their difficulties in the moment, it impedes their literacy progress over time, too.

A red flag comment from teachers in terms of their feedback will tend to be about the limited quality of content, rather than that spelling is a problem, which shows how deceptive this can type of presentation can be. You'll be very familiar with another classic comment from teachers everywhere: "they respond well to questions in class but they don't get it down onto paper". If you hear these types of comments, this is a sure-fire indicator that a more detailed analysis of a pupil's oracy and literacy skills would be helpful.

**Top Tip:** Limited range of vocabulary in written content can often flag a spelling difficulty – particularly if there is a mismatch between oracy and written work.

## No Child is Missed – Action Point 4.4: Screen for Spelling Accuracy (Core)

Assessing spelling for whole word accuracy has its merits. For a start, a traditional test like this is very quick to do and you can do it as a group. It will give you comparative data so you can see whose spelling appears to be weaker.

Spelling, like maths, is either right or wrong and as a result it can provoke anxiety. There are some health warnings which come with assessing spelling as a result and it's worth keeping these in mind.

1. Some children find that they can do quite well in spelling tests but this masks the difficulty they have when free writing "in real life". It's much easier to have a few seconds to think about how to spell one word, and perhaps even write it out a few different ways to choose which one looks right, than it is to spell at pace when writing a sentence. Don't be lulled into a false sense of security by average spelling scores, particularly if extended writing is a less rosy picture.

2. Most spelling tests don't tell you what to work on next in terms of improving spelling ability, they just tell you how a child is performing on a small group of words. If you want to learn which spelling patterns to target to develop spelling competence more widely then you need to use a spelling test which gives you onward steps into a spelling programme. See No Child is Missed Action Point 4.5.

3. For young learners and those who struggle with spelling, spelling tests can feel "high stakes" with the risk of triggering both public and personal shaming, through revealing something intrinsic about themselves and their value as a learner. Marking sensitively and supportively can help, by marking letter placement accuracy as well as whole word accuracy. For example:

✓ ✓ ✓ ✓ ✓ ✗ ✓

Rather than: Kitchin ✗ = 100% wrong          Instead: K i t c h i n  =  87% right

If you simply want to know how their spelling ability ranks for their class or age, compared to a national sample as a summative assessment, then a standardised single word spelling test is the way to go. Examples to look at are the *Wide Range Achievement Test (WRAT)*, *Vernon Graded Word Spelling Test*, *NFER Spelling Test*, or if you're looking to test through computerised assessment, there are tests such as *Literacy Assessment Online, LUCID Exact*.

**No Child is Missed - Action Point 4.5: Screen for Spelling for Intervention (Additional)**

If you've tested a pupil's spelling and their standardised score is low, or their spelling in free writing is "consistently inconsistent" then you may want to know more about their spelling difficulties in order to put together an intervention for them.

a) If you want to unpick what specific areas for spelling development there are for a pupil for intervention purposes, as a formative assessment, then doing a test which helps you to format an intervention plan is more helpful. Examples of tests to look at for intervention are *Helen Arkell Spelling Test, Alpha to Omega, Apples and Pears, Toe by Toe*.

b) If you want to evaluate transference of spelling difficulties into free writing then comparing spelling test results with extended writing may be useful. Looking at error rates and types of spelling errors will help you to evaluate what might be worth targeting in any support. You will be able to put together a list of words which need learning and securing.

It is worth saying that if a pupil has poor spelling as well as handwriting that is difficult to read, then it is worth investing in supporting handwriting *first* (see Chapter Six) because once you take away or reduce those challenges, it frees up the brain to focus on spelling. Your spelling intervention will have greater effect then.

**Top Tip:** If a pupil has poor handwriting and spelling, focus on improving handwriting first, to reduce the number of barriers to accurate spelling.

## No Child Misses Out: What to do next. . . .

**First of all: Rule out a Hearing Difficulty**

If you have identified a possible difficulty in any area of phonological processing – oracy, reading or spelling – it is prudent to advise parents-carers to contact their Health Visitor or GP to book their child in for a hearing test. It is worth being assertive about this suggestion to raise its importance and to follow up with parents-carers to check in on progress towards this action if you are concerned. It might seem excessive – surely if they can hear, they can "hear", but research by Carroll and Breadmore (2018)[21] showed that about a third of children with a history of repeated ear infections show literacy difficulties, and a significant minority (25%) of the poor readers they tested had some degree of undiagnosed mild or very mild hearing loss. Personally, I have known a small number of children who have had foreign objects deeply embedded in ears, sometimes unbeknownst to parents, affecting hearing and phonological awareness. Children also don't tend to complain of a hearing difficulty as they don't necessarily know how little they can hear compared to others. Hearing difficulties can easily be missed by all of the adults around a child. In short, a hearing test can make a critical difference.

---

**No Child Misses Out – Response Point 4.1: Supporting Development of Speech, Language and Communication**

---

- *Attention and listening*
  Visual orienting (turning the head to help locate the sound) and maintaining focus on the sound are important facets of effective communication. This particular aspect of communication is linked to executive function which we'll look at in Chapter Seven.
  In-class strategies to support may include:
  o   Careful seating (taking into account pupil preference and any specific auditory needs)
  o   Ensuring a child is able to see the speaker's mouth clearly
  o   Having visual stimuli to support comprehension and retention of information through dual-coding
  o   Shorter, chunked instructions to reduce the length of time required for focus
  o   Opportunities to review the instructions through repetition of instructions orally and through task boards or check lists
  o   Helping children to focus on the main features through pointing, or limiting choices between two choices
  o   Regular circulation by the adult(s) in the room, to re-encourage and re-focus
  o   Use of ear defenders or ear plugs for extended independent work

  Individual support may require:
  o   Further assessment for hearing difficulties
  o   Further assessment by a Speech and Language Therapist
  o   Further assessment of executive function
  o   Use of a sensory room to reduce stress, supporting concentration
  o   Considering trying pioneering therapies such as the *Listening Program®, Forbrain, The Sound Therapy Site* (www.soundtherapy.co.uk)

- *Understanding (receptive language)*
  In-class strategies to support may include:
  o   Giving thinking time for speech to be processed and a response considered
  o   Speak a little more slowly, and make breaks between words clear, emphasising key words that you want students to focus in on
  o   Repeating the question and/or re-phrasing

o    Simplifying language to improve comprehension

o    Having key words on the board and/or access to a glossary

o    Extending vocabulary with conscious intent – giving visual cues, using the word in several examples to support comprehension and retention, providing it in written/visual form, relating it to known concepts to develop their schema

o    Using gestures or actions

o    Using visual aids to support communication such as *Widgit* symbols

Small group intervention may involve:

o    Pre-teaching of vocabulary and concepts, particularly Tier 2 & 3

o    Pre-reading a simpler version of the text to support initial comprehension before being exposed to more challenging age-appropriate text. AI is useful here as you can ask it to simplify a text to a certain level

o    Post-teaching review and small group discussions

o    Post-reading summaries of concepts or narrative covered

Individual support may require:

o    Further assessment for hearing difficulties

o    Further assessment by a Speech and Language Therapist

o    Further assessment of English as an Additional Language

o    Further assessment of executive function

o    Consider trying pioneering therapies such as the *Listening Program®, Forbrain, The Sound Therapy Site* (as before)

o    Consider your evidence for exam support such as modified language papers; live speaker; extra time

- *Talking (expressive language)*
  In-class strategies to support may include low-cost, high-impact strategies like those proposed by the Education Endowment Foundation (EEF) review of oracy:[22]

  o    targeted reading aloud and discussion with pupils

  o    explicit approaches to extending spoken vocabulary

  o    modelling inference through the use of structured questioning to develop reading comprehension

  o    purposeful, curriculum-focused dialogue and interaction

  o    group or paired work to allow pupils to share thought processes (metacognition)

Alongside this:

o    wearing lanyards with key word and visual prompts such as *Widgit* symbols

o    and/or, putting key words on the board or word mat and regularly pointing to them when speaking; even better, adding their meanings or a visual prompt

Small group intervention:

o    If you are looking for a specifically tailored and evidence-based approach, the *Word Aware* series of resources are well-regarded by Speech and Language Therapists and education practitioners alike

o    *Elklan* provides highly rated resources

o    *Thunks* can be used with thought stems to promote discussions

Individual support may require:

o   Working with parents-carers to develop vocabulary awareness during 1:1 reading at home

o   Further assessment for hearing difficulties

o   Further assessment by a Speech and Language Therapist

o   Further assessment of English as an Additional Language

o   Consider trying pioneering therapies such as the *Listening Program®, Forbrain, The Sound Therapy Site*

• *Social communication and use of language*

Whilst "social skills" groups and interventions are well-embedded into many schools' SEND provision, and there are some highly respected resources (such as the *Talkabout* series) it is worth noting that some people are beginning to question the extent to which they prioritise certain, more conventional, communication styles – for example, encouraging eye contact and training children to practice small talk. Advocates for avoiding these practices suggest that it places the need for change on the individual child rather than considering how the environment could be more supportive and inclusive in the way it is structured. In practice, I think we need to take a balanced approach.

Wherever you sit on this continuum, and whatever the individual child's unique profile, a focus on building self-awareness to support an increase in self-confidence in social communication, and an awareness of other types of communication styles, is likely to be really helpful for all children – just as it is for colleagues in the workplace! It's also going to be beneficial to consider how the environment might need to be adapted so all can thrive.

In-class strategies to support may include:

o   Thoughtful pairing and grouping

o   Having clear classroom rules and expectations for inclusive behaviours

o   Designating roles and responsibilities for group work (e.g. *De Bono's Thinking Hats*, being the timer or the monitor/noticer)

o   Giving sentence starters for speaking ideas aloud

o   Find ways for pupils to share ideas even if they don't feel confident to speak out loud (e.g. pointing, writing ideas down for someone else to read)

Small group or individualised intervention may involve:

o   Helping children to identify their emotions and the corresponding physical sensations and feelings are crucial for developing interoceptive skills. You may already use something like *Zones of Regulation* to help pupils identify their different emotional states. As an individualised approach, I personally really like the *"How We Feel"* App, which has been developed by Dr Marc Brackett, the founder of the Yale Center for Emotional Intelligence and author of *Permission to Feel*.[23] It encourages participants to "check in" by thinking about whether they are feeling high or low energy, unpleasant or pleasant feelings, and then from there, honing in on exactly what emotion it might be. It also gives tools to help people "move on".

As this field develops, newer approaches (or perhaps, not so new, really) to building **interoception** might also take more creative pathways, such as spending time listening to music and identifying physical feelings triggered by different music types to support greater self-awareness.[24]

Individual support may require:

o  Further assessment for hearing difficulties

o  Further assessment by a Speech and Language Therapist

o  Further work with a psychotherapist to help reconnect mind and body and build emotional self-awareness if high stress is, or has been, present.

o  Consider your evidence for exam support strategies

> **Interoception:** The awareness of internal sensations in the body, including heart rate, respiration, hunger, fullness, temperature, pain as well as emotions.

- *Play*

  It is worth watching and considering how children play during unstructured times to learn both about individuals and their style of play, as well as the terrain and use of space on the playground and other areas of the school itself. This will enable you to see where barriers and supports for group play can be developed. Playground duties are invaluable as these give opportunities to monitor what's going on and to think and review provision. Most schools will feel that the main social issues arise during unstructured times and therefore it is worth spending time seriously considering how to help pupils feel confident, safe and supported during these times of day.

  Play is a vital channel to enable pupils to build their flexibility and adaptability, as well as their social communication skills. Play is important in helping children to make sense of the world through taking on different roles and perspectives; re-enacting social situations; coping with feelings of competitiveness, including learning to win and lose graciously; and testing boundaries and learning from them. When we support the healthy development of play, we are also enabling pupils to connect positively with each other and to reduce loneliness, which can have serious impact on people's emotional and physical wellbeing across a lifespan.[25]

  It's also worth evaluating the amount of time your setting dedicates to play, too. Research by Nuffield in 2017[26] showed that primary settings had, on average, 45 minutes less play per week than in 1995 and in secondary the situation was even worse, with 65 minutes less play each week. In some cases, pupils barely had enough time to eat lunch, let alone chat and play with friends or participate in a club, which is a risk to both mental but also physical health and wellbeing, given the rises in teenage anxiety and obesity.

It might be that you could introduce a "trim trail" or painted games for children to play together; for older children, perhaps you could introduce table tennis tables, stocks of balls of differing sizes, board games club, for example. It might be that adults on duty are specifically directed to model play, by inviting children to join in games with them, and are also trained in diffusing situations quickly to avoid escalation. This might involve being given scripts or approaches that help with consistency. You might also be able to review your extra-curricular provision in light of demand and pupil preferences to support friendships and play, such as hosting Lego Club (or even Lego Therapy), particularly for those who are lower in social confidence and benefit from a more structured approach.

If you want particular specific activities, you might like to purchase *Why Play Matters – 101 Activities for Developmental Play to Support Young Children* by Caroline Essame which looks at building emotional wellbeing, social skills, school readiness, physical skills and sensory processing skills. You might also be interested in learning more about play, through organisations that focus on *Play Therapy*.

---

**No Child Misses Out – Response Point 4.2 & 4.3: Supporting the Development of Phonological Awareness & Reading Comprehension**

---

- Awareness of rhyme and alliteration
- Explicit awareness of shared sounds within words
- Dividing (segmenting) and blending syllables
- Segmenting phonemes
- Manipulating phonemes

The younger a child, the more phonological awareness skills will be embedded into general classroom teaching and learning and so a focus on improving the quality of early years provision will help all children. However, if a child has a slower development of phonological awareness skills, whilst small group work can help if it's well-structured and pupils have similar gaps, really improving phonological deficits takes time and individualised support.

Further practical guidance and strategies can be found in:
o   Phase One of *Letters and Sounds*
o   *Nuffield Early Language Intervention (NELI)*
o   *Elkonin Boxes*
o   Teaching phoneme–grapheme correspondence in a personalised format (e.g. starting with their name to build interest and a sense of purpose) rather than a prescriptive order from a programme.

The older a child is, the harder it is to find age-appropriate resources to develop literacy. It may still be entirely appropriate to look at developing skills within the levels of phonological awareness as part of your overall approach, in which case using the resources above may help. Alongside this, however, you are likely to want to focus more heavily on active reading development. Look for resources which are often entitled "high-interest" but are targeted to less developed readers. And, of course, providing opportunities to engage with music and rhythm – playing instruments, singing etc. This might seem a challenge to a grumpy teenager but is really worth investing in.

Instructional strategies such as guided reading, questioning, and summarising can significantly enhance comprehension skills.[27] Using explicit instruction in comprehension strategies – such as identifying the main idea, making predictions, and visualising content – helps children process texts more effectively.[28] Having access to vocabulary, either known or in a glossary, also plays a critical role, so encourage your staff to focus on this, too.[29]

Further literacy resources and strategies can be found in:

o   *That Reading Thing*
o   Ruth Miskin, *Fresh Start*
o   Barrington Stoke and Rising Stars are UK publishers who target some of their resources at this group of children
o   Christopher Such, *The Art and Science of Teaching Primary Reading* (worth reading for secondary colleagues, too!)

---

**No Child Misses Out – Response Point 4.4 & 4.5: Supporting the Development of Spelling Accuracy**

---

In-class strategies to support may include:

o   Explicit teaching of synthetic phonics, following a well-designed programme including games, flashcards, songs and mnemonics
o   Teaching spelling rules and patterns, regular practice using interactive activities
o   Word or Spelling pattern of the Week to help pupils build spelling knowledge through writing exercises, discussions, and vocabulary-building activities
o   Spelling in context. Provide dictation exercises, writing prompts, or creative writing tasks where they have to use their weekly spelling words
o   Multisensory learning. Use multisensory techniques to teach spelling, such as air writing, tracing words in sand, or using manipulatives like magnetic letters

Small group or individualised intervention may involve:
Similar activities to whole class spelling. In addition, adults may wish to use further practical guidance and strategies in resources, such as:

o   *Anyone Can Spell It*
o   *Alpha to Omega*
o   *Apples and Pears*
o   *Nessy*
o   *Precision Teaching*
o   *Morph Mastery*

### How do you know all your hard work is "making a difference"?

Assessment is both a summative and a formative process and just like classroom teachers, SEND teams need to be approaching screening in a similar way. In fact, if you've come across the work of Dylan Wiliam in terms of his research into the importance of formative assessment,[1] you'll know that it has its roots in the field of SEND. In England, we often use the summary *Assess-Plan-Do-Review* as a way to capture this cyclical process.

Screening with a standardised tool is really helpful and important, if we want to group pupils and understand the overall pattern of needs within our class, year or setting. However, a standardised score can only tell you so much. It is important to learn other data about a child's learning to structure a plan for their next steps, if you want to design teaching that targets a pupil's *"Zone of Proximal Development (ZPD)"*.[30]

When we understand *next steps* (the "what I can do with help") and target those, we provide a *pathway of progress,* we can then administer a further assessment to measure how far the pupil has come and whether the learning has "stuck" by considering the development that a pupil is able to demonstrate independently in relation to their previous scores. This is the territory of both classroom teachers and intervention teachers. Sometimes, measuring this progress is hard with blunt tools which are standardised to a particular psychological or educational **dimension** and so we need more sensitive tools to capture this more nuanced picture.

If you're looking to find a way to capture progress in a more granular way, obviously you can look carefully at the curriculum and compare outcomes in relation to this, but you can also use tools such as the *Engagement Model, The Toolkit Progress Tracker*

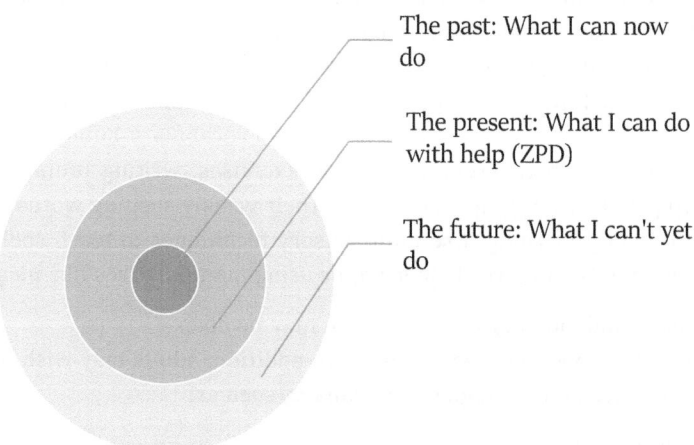

The past: What I can now do

The present: What I can do with help (ZPD)

The future: What I can't yet do

*Figure 4.4* Vygotsky's Zone of Proximal Development

---

1   Wiliam, D., & Leahy, S. (2015). *Embedding formative assessment: Practical techniques for classrooms* (UK ed.). Learning Sciences International

through Access to Education or any of the holistic *Step* assessment tools designed by *B-Squared* – whatever your pupils and your setting needs.

---

**Dimension:** An attribute or construct that we value and seek to measure.

---

## Final thoughts: shaping the narrative

*"If a tree falls in a forest and no one is around to hear it,*
*does it make a sound?"*

You might have come across this philosophical musing before. According to quantum mechanics the answer is "no", because no perceiver is there to "hear" it. Subjective idealism would take it one step further: "to be is to be perceived".[31] Here the issue is not whether there is noise to hear but whether the sound event even happened. If we define sound as existing in the ear and mind of the beholder, then being able to use your voice and be heard is pretty fundamental to your perceived existence.

Writing this chapter has caused me to think a lot about the importance of sound in survival. And it has also made me think a lot about privilege and power. If you speak and someone is close enough to hear you, you make a sound. You exist in their mind. But what if you're not allowed to get near them? What if you're not invited into "the room where it happens"? What if your voice never even gets heard?

Miranda Fricker, a British philosopher, explores the idea of **testimonial injustice** where statements by members of particular groups are "unheard"; systematically neglected or discredited.[32] She cites the example of the case of Stephen Lawrence, a black teenager murdered in London in a racially motivated attack, whereby his friend, fellow victim and chief witness of the crime was not properly listened to by the investigating police officers. This led to the perpetrators remaining at large for nineteen years before their eventual conviction, despite their names being known to the Police within hours of the crime. A public inquiry into the handling of the case concluded that the investigation was incompetently handled and the Metropolitan Police was institutionally racist.[33]

Fricker also talks about another form of injustice, which she calls **hermeneutical injustice:** when someone is unable to make sense of their own traumatic experiences because these occurrences have never been acknowledged as problematic in the first place. The issues have not been widely experienced, particularly by those in positions of power, so they don't formally exist in our collective mind. This is increasingly relevant when we think about what constitutes sexual abuse. Behaviours which were perhaps blindly accepted and culturally tolerated as "normal" or "unproblematic", or undermined through denial, have since been reframed for the abusive behaviour that they are. For a sobering reality check, in the late 1970s and early 1980s, the standard American text book of psychiatry at that time stated that incest was extremely rare, occurring once in every million women.[34] Furthermore, this same text book stated that father-daughter incest[2] "diminishes the subject's chances of psychosis and allows for a better adjustment to the external world" – essentially endorsing child sexual abuse. Its estimation was also wildly out.[35] Although really difficult to quantify accurately, a recent report puts it at 10.6% in the USA[35] and UK data suggests it's likely to be between one in 5–16%[37] – far greater than originally assumed. Culture was shaped by these accepted norms and assumptions.

As a result of identifying and accepting that barriers to communication exist for certain groups of people and that our systems need to better allow for diverse voices to come through and be valued, we reduce testimonial injustice. As we listen to and engage with these voiced experiences, we are then better able to understand our own experiences of injustice, thereby reducing hermeneutical injustice. The #MeToo movement is a really good example of this.

Being heard is a condition of our freedom and of our power, both for ourselves and for those whom we represent. And yet, some people regularly experience testimonial and hermeneutical injustice. I think those living the realities of fighting for special educational needs provision often do, particularly those groups who have less privilege. In our settings we need to continue to find ways to ensure all voices are equally represented in all aspects of our community life and decision-making. Through listening to the testimonies of the children, young people and families we work with in schools, we help to reduce injustice: we prevent the silence of the unheard and we get to re-shape the narrative.

**Top Tip:** Review your student council demographics and consider what you can do to facilitate greater diversity within it. Screening everyone also means all voices are captured.

**Testimonial injustice:** Unfairness in trusting someone's word – being ignored or disbelieved due to their personal characteristics (age, gender, sexuality, race, disability, care status etc.)

**Hermeneutical injustice:** Caused by people not being able to make sense of their own life experiences because they have not been captured and conceptually framed. This is most common with those who have historically wielded less power to shape the narrative and the categories through which people understand the world.

---

2   NB. I'm conscious here of the specificity of the gender and wonder about an even greater hermeneutical injustice for male victims of child sexual abuse, who don't even get a thoughtful mention, let alone an estimated statistic.

## Chapter Summary: Phonological Processing

- *Phonological processing is crucial for learning speech, reading, and writing, starting from infancy with sound perception.*
- *Accurate perception of sounds builds vocabulary, which is heavily influenced by the complexity of one's sound environment and exposure to language.*
- *Research highlights a word gap illustrating differences in word exposure across socio-economic groups and its impact on language development.*
- *Phonological awareness, the ability to distinguish and manipulate sounds, is critical for literacy, particularly in developing reading and spelling skills.*
- *Reading development involves both phonological skills and sight word recognition, helping children decode words and comprehend meaning.*
- *Phonological awareness, vocabulary, and reading comprehension are interconnected, and strengthening one can improve the others.*
- *Spelling relies on phonological awareness and the ability to segment words into sounds, with a gradual developmental pattern that varies by child.*

# 5  Visual Processing

We don't really think much about our eyes, often taking vision for granted. We aren't taught much, if anything, during our teaching training about how children see. So long as a student is not bumping into things, squinting at the clock on the wall or peering at a book from an acute angle, we might assume that the vision in our classroom is "fine"; that the visual experience within those thirty pairs of eyes staring back at us is fairly homogenous. It won't come as a surprise to you, given that I'm about to write a chapter on it and that nothing biological is ever that simple, that the reality is often quite different. In fact, this lack of understanding of visual processing and its potential barriers to learning is a really significant awareness gap affecting education, health and care support systems around children and young people. It's a cavernous **lacuna** which needs closing.

Because of this gap, the content in this chapter might seem very new and a bit technical and science-y, at times. We'll use terms and explore perspectives that you haven't met before, but stick with me – you'll learn a lot. I think future research in this field will be game-changing.

## Understanding good vision: light, eyes, brain

Just like our auditory system, our visual system **transduces** energy in the world around us into neural signals in the brain. We have sensory receptors in our eyes which respond to wavelengths of light energy. When we look around the classroom or at an exercise book in front of us, patterns of light give us information about where one surface stops and another begins. This is how we tell the difference between our students at a glance, or interpret the different shapes which make up written text, for example. The properties of light waves which are visible to humans can be measured on their length, their amplitude, and their purity – or in layman's terms: their colour, their brightness and their saturation or richness. And it is these properties of light which the photoreceptors in our eyes detect.

> **Lacuna:** An unfilled space, a gap. (I love this word by the way and mention it a few times throughout this book because we've got a lot of gaps in our field.)
> **Transduce:** To convert something (such as nerve energy or a message) into another form.

DOI: 10.4324/9781032663968-7

Half of the nerve fibres in our brains are linked to our vision, which makes it a phenomenally important source of information for learning. It accounts for two-thirds of the electrical activity in the brain, taking just 150 milliseconds for a brain to recognise an image and a mere 100 milliseconds more to attach a meaning to it (on average, of course!).[1] *Efficient* vision, however, is complex and in this chapter we're going to look at four key areas we can review to ensure children make progress in the classroom:

1. **Visual acuity** – that's to say, how far down the test chart you can get, unaided. It's about the clarity of our vision – how clear the pathway is for the light to reach the back of our eye. This is critical for the obvious factors like reading, writing and accurate movement.
2. **Effective and efficient processing of light**, so we can understand colour, shape, size, depth and speed – how easily the photoreceptors in the back of our eye can transduce this light energy. Here, we look at colour blindness, as well as other colour perception profiles, to explore how the world around us can appear differently.
3. **Efficient connection between our eyes and our brain**, so we can process and understand a continuous stream of information as we move our eyes and as new scenes come upon us. As you know, time plays an important role in school and in this section, we'll explore the significance of speed of visual processing in the classroom.
4. And, **previous experience and regular exposure** of the stimulus itself to be able to "know" what it is we're looking at. Finally, here we look at the encoding of visual memory and its impact on advancing knowledge and skill.

Of course, particularly with reading, all of the above needs to align synchronously with our **phonological processing**, as we've just covered in Chapter Four.

Within these four areas above there are many, many variables – some of which are driven by our DNA, and some of which are driven by our lived experiences. Understanding a child or young person's visual processing is not only vital for good learning, reading and mental wellbeing especially, but it can also help us to understand factors which may also impact on overall social, emotional, physical and mental health, too. But because vision issues are silent and not immediately obvious to the child concerned, or to the observer, we very often haven't even considered it. And yet, vision concerns more than half the nerve fibres in the brain. . . .

> **Visual acuity:** A clinical measurement of vision over distance. Accurate vision which needs no correction is called 20/20 vision.
> **Phonological processing:** The efficiency of sound travelling along the auditory pathways from ear to brain (sensation) and then, where relevant, from brain to action (perception)

## 1 Exploring visual acuity and how our "useful field of view" affects reading fluency and concentration

When you go to the opticians, the optometrist measures your visual acuity. If objects in the distance are blurred, you are short-sighted (myopic); if you have to put more effort in to see objects up close, to see things clearly, then you are likely to be long-sighted (hyperopic); and if you're creeping past forty-five and can't find where you put your reading glasses, you're presbyopic (old!)

Optometrists also look at eye teaming skills, which means how efficiently both eyes work together to produce comfortable single vision. This is known as **binocular vision** and it has a number of benefits, including depth perception to support good hand-eye co-ordination, which is vital in fine- and gross-motor skills, like handwriting and eating.

Alongside this they will also be reviewing the physical health of your eyes, considering if there are indicators of disease or ill-health. This point is particularly important to understand in relation to education. Optometrists are trained to assess medically – they are looking to remediate **pathology** within the eye and correct poor visual acuity, they are not looking to evaluate vision in relation to efficient and fluent reading. Successful reading of singular letters on a test chart isn't necessarily a good indicator of how well your eyes will function reading streams of small letters at pace in day-to-day reading tasks. This means that a standard eye test does not always lead to an optometrist having concerns about a child's visual processing, even if *you* do. This is something to be alert to.

> **Top Tip:** If you're recommending a child go to the opticians for an eye check then ask their adult to mention that their teacher has concerns about their reading efficiency and visual processing skills in the appointment.

Let me explain a bit more. If you've been to have your eyes checked, you might be familiar with **"field of view"** tests which measure how wide your vision field is. They tend to ask you to stare into a machine and flash lights in different places, asking you to respond when you see one. Testing your field of view is an important indicator of overall health. However, just because you *can* perceive a wide range of visual information, doesn't mean you always *notice* this wide range of information at pace in an everyday, functional way. As such, these optometry tests are not particularly sensitive enough to evaluate the *functional* field of your vision or as some researchers call it, your "useful field of view". Have a look at the next set of images.

> **Binocular vision:** A type of vision in which two eyes face the same direction to perceive a single 3D image.
> **Pathology:** The study and diagnosis of disease.
> **Field of view:** This is the range or angle of the world you can see clearly without moving your eye.
> **Functional field** also known as **useful field of view:** The actual details you notice and attend to within your field of view.
> **Saccade:** A rapid movement of the eye between one fixation and the next.

*Figure 5.1* Examples of different functional fields of view
© Posit Science

Within the four images, you can see two central circles. The outer circle indicates the extent of the fields of view that four different individuals have (what optometrists test) – how far they can see when they move their eyes. The inner circle indicates their *functional* or *useful* field of view – what they are likely to focus on and draw information from. When you compare the two, if you're child A, you are going to fare far better than child D in the classroom. Here's why.

- *How a functional field of view affects reading*

Amongst other things, a reduced functional field of view is essentially a bottleneck to our ability to quickly and accurately read. It's a bit like looking through binoculars and trying to find a bird: you have to keep moving your head to work out where the object is that you're looking for. If you observe a student carefully whilst they're looking at a page, notice how they position themselves in relation to the text and how much they need to move their head and/or eyes to read it.

Successful and fluent readers don't need to move their head or their eyes as much to move along the sentence, which really helps with speed. When we move our eyes, making a **saccade**, we bring the next bit of text into our functional field of view. If this functional field of view is reduced, we have to make more saccades, which increases the number of times we have to search for the next word, slowing us down. It also increases the likelihood of making mistakes because we are more likely to struggle to locate the correct next word, jumping a line, skipping or misreading a word.

It makes sense doesn't it, that just like leg length which affects how many strides it takes to walk ten metres, so too the size of our functional field of view affects the number of saccades it takes to read a sentence. The current research suggests that we need to be able to see about 7–9 letters to our right before moving our eyes for fluent reading, but that the number of letters we can all individually read varies considerably. In fact, some people can even see up to 15 characters to their right.[2] For those with a reduced functional field, they may see fewer than seven letters to their right, which is likely to cause reading difficulties.

What I think is *especially* interesting about this is that research is also beginning to tentatively show that when our body takes a micropause from converting a physical environmental signal into a neural signal, such as making a saccade or breathing out, our brain also takes a micropause.[3] These tiny moments are how we regulate ourselves. In reading stakes then, not only is a reduced functional field likely to be impeding accuracy and speed because of the higher number of saccades someone is having to make, their brain is also having more mini rests from processing the in-coming visual information. This might lead to greater fatigue from the increased time it takes from stopping and starting, and also be further compounded by whether someone can hold on to that information in their memory for that long, affecting overall comprehension.

- *How a functional field of view affects concentration*

The size of your functional field also has quite profound effects on learning and task success more broadly, too, in terms of focus and attention. Research has started to show that the further away information is from our useful field of view, the slower our reaction time and the more errors we make with interpreting visual information,[4] including facial expressions.[5] This can affect someone's social skills and their efficiency at "reading the room". If you can't see what's going on clearly without moving your eyes and/or your head, you're at risk of losing track of what's going on and you might not pick up on all of the important details for confident perception.

If we think about a student who gets easily distracted in the classroom, they are often unable to tune out from background noise because they haven't learnt to understand and manage a complex soundscape. Many are then compelled to move their eyes or head away from the primary and important learning stimulus (their work, or the teacher) in order to find out what it is. This leads not only to disruption in learning for the student in the moment but it then also takes a while to relax back into the task at hand, leading to a perpetual cycle of distraction and disruption. Whilst field of view and visual attention develops with age and experience, gradually increasing the amount of attention we can give to something without losing focus,[6] our lived experience plays a large part in this development, too.

Regardless of our baseline useful field of view, it is dynamic for all of us. In moments of acute stress, our vision changes. We do not need to spend time processing everything that is going on around us, we only need to focus on being ready to get ourselves out of danger if we need to. Our muscles tighten, like a coiled spring ready to go; our breathing shallows and quickens, to flood our body with oxygen;[1] and our useful field of view reduces. When this state of stress becomes chronic - from a relentlessly stressful daily life or a major traumatic life event - every sound outside of our useful field of view can then come to be perceived as a potential threat. We live in a state of hypervigilance. This chronic stress and anxiety might also lead us to experience light sensitivity and eye strain,[7] leading to increased blinking to lubricate and relax the eye. This is another way that the body tries to micropause from the world around it; like a computer fan, trying to cool itself down.

> **Top Tip:** Increased blinking is a sign of visual stress. Be aware that if a student you are working with is blinking a lot, they might need a break.

What's also interesting is that stress can impact upon depth perception and grasp efficiency causing us to be clumsier and more accident-prone. This explains why we tend to drop things or become careless when we're in a rush or feeling under pressure: more haste, less speed. It probably explains why just before I had to give an important presentation to some parents a couple of years ago, I misplaced my laptop on the stand and when it fell, the corner landed on my foot! Excruciating. By the time I'd finished talking, my foot was puffed up like a balloon. When you notice ongoing clumsiness in a student who seems to have poor balance and gross motor difficulties, this can be an indicator of trauma and/or chronic stress within the body.[8]

A reduced functional field of view can therefore prevent fluent and accurate reading, reduce overall speed of working, impair visual recall, prevent accurate interpretations of social situations and cause clumsiness and increased risk of accidents. It can also be cyclical, both causing and leading to higher levels of anxiety. The extent of impact on daily living is pretty significant, isn't it? And most optometrists aren't trained to evaluate or help remediate this at all. . .

## No Child is Missed – Action Point 5.1: Screen for Symptoms of Visual Stress

1.   Complete a visual stress checklist

The *British Association of Behavioural Optometry* have a checklist on their website which gives a list of symptoms present when someone's visual system would benefit from review, many of which I have mentioned in this chapter already. These symptoms include regular headaches, getting very tired, missing out words when reading, losing their place easily in the text.

---

1   This can actually lead to reduced levels of oxygen over time however so is only a short-term emergency response.

2.   Visit a behavioural optometrist, or an optometrist who looks at functional vision as well as eye health

If a student is regularly jumping lines, missing out words, mirror-reversing words, misinterpreting social communication, learning more slowly, has poor handwriting or is struggling to concentrate, then a trip to the optometrist is important to explore their visual processing, in terms of visual acuity *and* binocular vision. However, it is worth finding out if a local optometrist would measure a child's functional field of view and support with specialist lenses. (Make sure to ask parents to mention their reading, handwriting and/or concentration difficulties to the optometrists so they can explore the cause of these phenomena more specifically. Remind them that standard optometrists may not be expecting this and that it's not normal practice under the NHS.)

To support this, it's helpful to build relationships with local optometrists, particularly those who have additional qualifications in behavioural optometry, so a reciprocal relationship can develop. A trusted eco-system of specialists around the children in your school is a really helpful resource. (I have one of my local optometrists, Katrina Turnbull, to thank for being expert eyes checking the acuity of this chapter!)

3.   Evaluate symptoms of perceived stress in someone's life

Alongside visual support, a careful evaluation of the wider stresses in someone's life may also be important to consider. We will learn more about this in Chapter 8.

### 2 *Exploring efficiency of luminance and colour processing, and their impact on learning and wellbeing*

The back of the eye is known as the retina. It is full of *magnocells* (big cells), *parvocells* (little cells) and *koniocells* (dust-like cells) and they transmit visual information about light from the eye to the brain. These cells pack quite the punch.

The role of the 120 million magnocells, which form the rods in our eyes, is to help us locate and transmit black and white information at speed. The **magnocellular pathway** cannot provide fine detailed information or colour; its role is to detect high contrast, simple information, quickly picking up on changes of luminance and allowing us to react quickly. We don't need to know exactly what it is that is flying towards us at great pace, we just need to remove ourselves from its flightpath as quickly as we can to avoid harm. Magnocells are also excellent at helping us interpret luminance off a page at speed – in other words, they're vital to reading.

In contrast, the **parvocellular pathway** carries the colour information: the hues and the saturation, the marvellous detail, the beauty. Parvocells are dotted across the retina but they are concentrated on a part of the eye called the fovea, giving us the full HD experience of incredible technicolour and detail. Parvocells may be small but they are mighty. Their information processing capacity dwarfs that of the magnocells and so, given the limited space in our eyeballs, we have fewer of them: only about 6 million in each eye. They form the cones in our eyes, which communicate colour. As such, for large parts of our eye we compromise detail for speed (more **rods** than **cones**), which supports our peripheral vision.

Research has paid far less attention to **koniocells** – probably because they're so small that when we named them "dust" we simply considered them clutter: a few tiny cells which weren't really doing very much and not worth studying. However, recent research is reviewing this and wondering whether koniocells are better at transmitting blues and yellows, whereas parvocells are better at transmitting reds and greens.[9] Time will tell as research helps to explain more.

Whilst we estimate that on average each eye has approximately 120 million magnocells and 6 million parvocells, we haven't tested enough people to determine this with great accuracy. The probable reality is that, like other body parts, everyone is actually quite different and this means we all likely to see colour and luminance in our own genetically unique way. Those of us who have a greater ratio of magnocells to parvocells, or some form of colour vision deficiency affecting the parvocellular pathway, are more likely to be sensitive or responsive to changes in luminance signals. Those of us who favour colour and beauty over speed may well have a different ratio.

> **Magnocellular pathway:** Transduces black and white information at speed so we can react quickly if we need to i.e. light and its absence.
>
> **Parvocellular pathway:** Transduces information about colour and detail, processing more slowly than black and white.
>
> **Rods and cones:** Rods communicate black and white information quickly (the absence and presence of light); cones communicate the colour.
>
> **Koniocells:** Not much is known about koniocells as they are very small and there has been little research. They *might* transduce blues and yellows.
>
> **Colour vision deficiency (CVD)/colour blindness:** Is present when colours are perceived differently by the majority of people due to the genetic make-up of their cones. Most commonly, those who experience CVD are red-green deficient, but some can experience blue-yellow deficiency and very rarely some people only experience the world in black and white. If you'd like to learn more about CVD in schools, do read: Difolco, M. (2025). *Supporting colour blindness in education and beyond: A practical guide for teachers and families.* Routledge.

Having an efficient magnocellular pathway can be to our advantage: we may find learning to read comes more naturally and that we are able to process the visual world around us very quickly, noticing details and changes, spotting patterns and subtle changes –

a great advantage in the classroom, enhancing our levels of stimulation. But at times, it may also lead to our detriment if we continually process information quickly and absorb so much information that our brains cannot cope with the high level of processing required – we're at risk of being "over" stimulated. Just like a computer gets tired from processing and needs to be switched off and back on again, so too we also need a reset through sleep and rest. Without taking conscious steps to slow down, appreciate colour, to breathe deeply, to close our eyes and to restore our energies through rest and relaxation, it might mean we are more photosensitive,[10] particularly to visual disturbance such as flickering or strobe lighting, and more at risk of stress, anxiety, overwhelm and exhaustion through cognitive overload.

Certainly, there is evidence to suggest that **colour vision deficiency** (CVD) - more commonly referred to as colour blindness - is seen with higher prevalence amongst children and young people with autism and/or inattention and hyperactivity, and with other learning difficulties more broadly, which seems to add to this thinking.[11] There is also evidence to suggest that exposure to alcohol and/or cocaine use can affect colour processing[12] so children who have been exposed to this in utero, may well find colour perception more difficult, too.

But it also makes me wonder about the impact of increasing use of digital technology, and even our addiction to the stimulation of it, in terms of the amount of visual energy being transduced by our eyes into our central nervous system? This, against a backdrop of less time outdoors, less physical activity, less human social interaction, which leads to fewer opportunities for decompression, genuine bonding and relaxation, and goes against our body's need to maintain balance. As well as stress and long-term risks which come from the permanency of digital information encoded and freely shared online, it is likely that visual overstimulation and a cumulative build-up of nervous energy within our bodies may well indeed be adding fuel the fire of the anxiety and mental health epidemic we seem to now be living through.

In contrast, those of us who have fewer magnocells or a more sensitive and powerful parvocellular pathway may find that visually processing the world in front of us takes slightly more time. Whilst we might enjoy colour and detail in a way which others simply don't take the time to appreciate or have the visual tools to do, this might also make us slower to notice details and changes in luminance signals – in other words, we might be slower and less accurate readers. Less productive under timed conditions.

Our natural preference and strengths centre in a slower, richer, more colourful view of life, which might be at odds with the faster paced visual processors who are whizzing around reading everything in sight, responding to the slightest change. Just like the faster visual processors however, we all need rest and recuperation, so we might find ourselves more readily overwhelmed by the intensity and pace of visual processing required from a visually stimulating day. As such, we may thrive in and prefer subjects, careers and ways of living which focus more on valuing colour and detail, and less on speed. Wherever a child falls on this genetic colour spectrum and whatever their lived experiences have been and continue to be, helping a child to understand and manage their visual experiences will be empowering for them and good for your results.

**No Child is Missed – Action Point 5.2: Screen for Colour Blindness (CVD)**

Statistically speaking, one child in every class will have a colour vision deficiency. It affects more boys than girls (1 in 12 versus 1 in 200) and because it is not routinely part of any early years testing or standard vision tests, a whopping 80% of children will go undiagnosed into secondary school*. It's such a gap in medical and educational practice that it is not uncommon for people to find out well into their adulthood – I kid you not! In fact, I know of two fully-grown men to whom this has happened. One discovered that he was colour blind in a random conversation over a pint with his friends when he could not see the same number in the circle as they could. And similarly, a colleague recently took his daughter to the opticians for an eye test and *he* identified *himself* through the test she had to do. I also have a friend who is really passionate about colour-vision deficiency being screened for when young, commenting regularly in the press about it. He was picked up through in-school screening back in the 1980s, and he feels it is every child's right to know and to be supported, and also for society to recognise colour vision deficiency in its approach to design to enable all to fully participate and enjoy life with confidence.

Sharing his resolve and bucking the national trend, Dame Allan's School in Newcastle (UK) has implemented whole year group screening for colour vision deficiency from early years to seniors, to make sure that no child is missed. Using the *Ishihara Test* (a series of circular plates with two different numbers and patterns encoded into the coloured circles within), they are able to make recommendations to parents-carers about visiting the optometrist for further testing, significantly improving the number of children who have been identified and better supported in their school. Working individually with little ones and in groups (using a digital version) when they are more independent, students with a full range of colour vision will see one number or shape, those with some type of colour vision deficiency will see another, taking less than five minutes to administer. The results are then gathered and evaluated by the SEND team and school nurse, recommendations to parents-carers are made and staff are updated through the SEND database. They've been thoughtful about their inclusive teaching strategies and support for colour vision deficiency, too, given that research suggests CVD can impact upon confidence in the classroom. I have recently introduced their approach to our screening battery too and we have been amazed by its impact. I'll share more about their simple but effective approaches in the section on No Child Misses Out as a way to make a difference.

*According to the CIC Colour Blind Awareness

### 3 & 4 *Exploring efficient connection (binding) and regular exposure (perception)*

As we know, vision is the sum of its photoreceptor parts. In order to see the world around us, we must first have visual acuity and a reasonably-sized field of view to see things clearly; and we must also transduce the visual energy through our magno-, parvo- and konio-cellular pathways to take it to the brain for processing. The third and fourth stages require that somehow these incoming streams of information must come together - "binding" them into one single image - before we're then able to add meaning into the mix and "perceive" it as a whole. This is known as the **binding problem**. How on earth does such a complex process happen, not just once, but *constantly*? The reason we call it a "problem" is because we don't have a definitive working model yet - we've still got a lot more to learn.

What we do know though is that vision is unbelievably complex. Part of what makes vision so complicated is that within the whole image are many, many parts. As well as binding the visual information together – bringing the brightness, colour and saturation from the three cellular pathways to form a whole coherent image in our mind, we must also simultaneously separate out the shapes within the image, by looking for edges, dividing it into regions, groups and objects to know where something ends and where something else begins. This is made even more challenging because we also may not see the whole item clearly or fully if part of it is occluded, which means assumptions also need to be made.

**Binding:** The mechanics of how sensory information such as colour, shape, texture is dynamically brought together in the brain, creating the visual image in the mind.
**To occlude:** To close up or block off.

Perception is nuanced and it relies heavily on previous experience and prior knowledge. How do I know that that is a chair poking out from behind the door? Because I've seen so many chairs in my life that I can recognise one even from catching sight of its leg. And I know that it's a chair, even though I may not have seen *that particular* design of chair before, because I know and understand what chairs are; I appreciate their purpose and their design. I have a conceptual understanding of them.

Research suggests that if there is disruption in the timing of this binding process, where information does not come together synchronously from the three pathways, it can also impact on visual processing efficiency, delaying speed of perception.[13] As we learnt in Chapter Two, when we considered that IQ is a product of the speed of sensory information travelling throughout the body, perception is also not a light-bulb moment, even if we often talk about it as though it is. That's to say, when this bound image reaches our brain, the speed at which we are able to recognise what it is, is not a binary moment in time. Biologists and psychophysicists who measure these phenomena, increasingly agree that our ability to sense and then perceive a signal from our external or internal worlds is *gradual*.

It might seem immediate to you and me ("ooh, there's a chair!") but forming a confident perception actually takes measurable time. It's also deeply personal – it's only when *you* decide *at some point* that you've detected *enough* of that signal that you're confident in it to make a response. Recognising the sensation, and connecting it to a meaning, is critical to perception. Above all, it takes *exposure*. The more we're exposed to something, the quicker we recognise what it is. Experienced radiographers can confidently detect cancerous shadows on x-rays which, to you or I, might look like innocuous shades of grey. Experienced readers can confidently detect tiny nuances of difference between letter formations with a quick glance, whereas early readers have to grapple with each and every letter to really decode what they're reading, often struggling with mirror-reversals, too.

Practicing reading accurately and at increasing speed is vital for reading fluency, which we're pretty good at testing for and supporting. But by evaluating visual processing speed specifically, we can get a sense of how efficiently the visual binding and perception process is for a student. Whilst research indicates that *everyone* needs to learn the phonic code - regardless of how difficult they might find it - in teaching reading terms, some pupils may benefit from a more analytical approach to support reading development (whole sight words) as well as a synthetic phonics approach (its constituent parts) because of their binding difficulties.

The debate around synthetic versus analytic reading is often polarised. I can feel some of us gently bristling as I type this. But perhaps it's also interesting to know that this debate actually has roots in psychology from its earliest days. Do we know something because we learn it as a whole and can then segment it down into its parts, or do we learn something because we learn its parts and then blend it to form a whole? This debate influences the discussions around diagnosis, as well.

Wherever you land on the learning to reading continuum, one of the very best ways to see a binding difficulty at its clearest, is to measure a pupil's *Rapid Automatic Naming* speed or RAN for short.[14] Honestly, if I tell you that this test is without doubt the most powerful and simple test I have ever come across, I would still be underselling it. It is fascinating to watch and the results are critical to supporting children in the classroom. Whilst developing vocabulary and cultural capital is vital for reading comprehension, accuracy and fluency are the gatekeepers. Without accurate and fluent word reading, comprehension is significantly impaired. The stakes are high with RAN. Children need their visual processing identified and supported.

## No Child is Missed – Action Point 5.3: Screen Rapid Automatic Naming Speed

Testing Rapid Automatic Naming (RAN) speed is very simple and is a well-established indicator of reading performance. Sadly, despite the fact that it is achingly simple, there aren't many free resources which are standardised to give an indication of the efficiency of a child's RAN. The tests themselves however are very straightforward, commonly requiring someone to name very familiar symbols, such as letters, numbers, colours, and simple objects, as fast as they can. For example, if you use the *Comprehensive Test of Phonological Processing (CTOPP)*, it requires the pupil to name a list of 32 numbers and then 32 letters as quickly as possible. In total, the test takes less than two minutes to administer. What is really fascinating however is just how much you can learn about someone from such a simple test.

Tests assessors tend to use are:

- *CTOPP*
- *RAN/RAS*
- a subtest in the *Phonological Assessment Battery (PhAB)*

Although I would recommend you invest in one, you may not have the budget to purchase anything expensive so the next best thing is to download a *Rapid Naming Drills* tool by *Bonnie Terry* on her website which will give you the test stimulus of arrows facing different directions for pupils to say "up", "down", "left", "right", but no scoring table to compare data with. She also has a book. What I suggest you do is to screen the whole class and rank them top to bottom on speed. (It really won't take you long.) You'll then work out who needs your attention. Over time you will be able to build up your own table of data to compare a single test score to, to give you an idea. It'll be worth it.

**Top Tips:** These are the observations from RAN testing that we've collected over time:

- Pupils often read letters more slowly than numbers – sometimes the difference is quite stark. The slower the reading of letters, the harder reading tends to be, too. Numbers can also demonstrate insecurity with numeracy.
- Pupils sometimes group letters into patterns (couplets, triplets etc.) which might give an indication of their functional field limitation or a coping strategy to manage and support working memory.
- Pupils sometimes seem to miss the same letter or number in the pattern along one or two lines in the test, which somehow suggests a disturbance in their visual field or weakness in distinguishing between certain letters, e.g. c and k.
- There is a huge variation in the time it can take someone to complete a short task. It can range from less than ten seconds to more than forty. This kind of lag between two comparable pupils proves that the playing field is definitely not level. It's not uncommon for a slow visual processing speed to be masked as it can affect your hardest working pupils, too.

With screening multiple dimensions, it then becomes possible to combine observations across them. For example, we've noted that:

- Sometimes our fastest visual processors are also affected by anxiety and/or difficulty maintaining focus indicating a tendency for sensory overstimulation.
- Sometimes clarification of instructions is needed, despite the simplicity of the task, which indicates that there is a level of anxiety, or difficulty with comprehension more generally.

Tiny observations are unbelievably valuable. Don't ever discredit the fleeting details you notice and what you might be able to learn or infer from them. But, *always write them down immediately* – you *think* you'll remember them at the end, but trust me, with all the other things you need to think about, you probably won't.

## No Child is Missed – Action Point 5.4: Screen for Reading Efficiency

Testing reading efficiency is quick and simple. You're testing how many words can be read accurately in a fixed period of time. The *Test of Word Reading Efficiency (TOWRE)** is one of my favourites. It takes just 45 seconds to administer and is excellent for access arrangements. The *WIAT (T version)* also covers reading fluency and is worth considering because it comes as part of good range of tests. Another test to consider is the *Wide Range Achievement Test (WRAT)** – although, this only measures reading accuracy not speed as well. When you're looking to purchase a reading test, your time is valuable and limited. Long tests, however informative, are resource intensive. Avoid.

*These tests require a higher level of qualification to administer.

Purchasing a test isn't always necessary. You can conduct a *Miscue Analysis.*

1. Choose a short, age-appropriate text. (As a rough guide, age x 10 = number of words if you're screening a lot of pupils.) They shouldn't have read it before.
2. Have a copy for them and a (double-spaced) photocopy for you.
3. Name and date the paperwork with the pupil's name. Critical!
4. Follow ethical guidelines from Chapter Three about how to screen pupils.
5. Ask pupil to put their glasses on, if they need them.
6. Ask the pupil to read this text aloud to you at a normal pace, whilst you time them, listen and observe.

Listen out for:

- **Self-correction** – I write s/c above the word when a pupil does this.
- **Insertion** – a word added by the pupil, not in the text. I write ^ and the word.
- **Omission** – a word in the text, missed out by the pupil. I cross the word out.

- **Repetition** – a word said more than once. I underline it however many times.
- **Reversal** – words are read out of order. I draw an arrow to show word order.
- **Substitution** – a word is changed. I cross the correct word through and write what they said instead, above it (omission and Insertion combined).
- **Pause** – if a pupil is taking longer to decode than expected, I write an ellipsis.
- **If a pupil skips a line** – I will redirect them to the correct line, but I will also make a note on the text to show that this happened.

Observe:

- **Discomfort** – proximity to text, wriggling, frowning, blinking, rubbing eyes.

7. Stop the timer. Write down the total time taken to read the text. Also any observations.
8. Ask comprehension questions if you wish. Note answers and a comment about speed of response.
9. Count their errors, divide this number by the total number of words in the passage. This is their error percentage.
10. Take their total time (in seconds) and divide this by the total number of words in the passage. This is their word per second rate.
11. Ask, "how did you find that?", noting anything they say and acting ethically.

## No Child Misses Out: What to do next. . .

**No Child Misses Out – Response Point 5.1: Supporting the Visual System – Increasing a Functional Field and Reducing Visual Stress**

*Supporting the visual system through the use of specialist lenses*

A behavioural optometry assessment can improve the efficiency of the visual system in a number of ways, including the prescription of specialist lenses. Specialist lenses look, to all intents and purposes, just like regular lenses. They are crafted to reduce the demand on the eyes and reduce tiredness, by opening up the functional field. Another approach behavioural optometrists often focus on is vision training, which are exercises designed to improve eye tracking by strengthening the ocular muscles. Both lenses and/or exercises can help the eye to move more efficiently when reading, reducing errors and improving fluency.

You can go on to the British Association of Behavioural Optometrists website to identify a practitioner close to you. This is an email I received from a parent not so long ago after I advised they took their child to see a behavioural optometrist: "I cannot thank you enough for advising us to book in to see the optometrist – the results were quite honestly jaw dropping – a 52% uplift in reading speed." My hairdresser's younger brother finds such benefit from his specialist lenses, too, that he's reluctant to take them off – even after school.

There is an alternative to behavioural optometry, which is a rather different approach. Helen Irlen, an American educational psychologist and therapeutic counsellor, is credited with discovering that a subgroup of children showed a marked improvement in their reading ability when material was covered by coloured acetate sheets.[15] She then went on to develop coloured lenses for glasses as well. The Irlen® Institute has a large number of assessors globally and you can go onto the Irlen® website to identify an assessor close to you. The way most assessors work is that they like you to see a regular optometrist first and if you need lenses to purchase them without any coating on so an Irlen®® filter can be added to the lens. Coloured overlays and tinted lenses serve to reduce stress in the visual system, making text look clearer and eyes feel more relaxed.

Whilst having a coloured lens may feel odd (and look unusual) to some, for those who find visual processing stressful, the use of colour can significantly reduce neural overactivity in the brain, resulting in a calmer state. Plenty of people's anecdotal experiences shared in social media platforms such as Facebook groups[16] suggest that Irlen® lenses are really helpful. Their anecdotal experiences seem to be evidenced here in the brain scans in Figure 5.2.

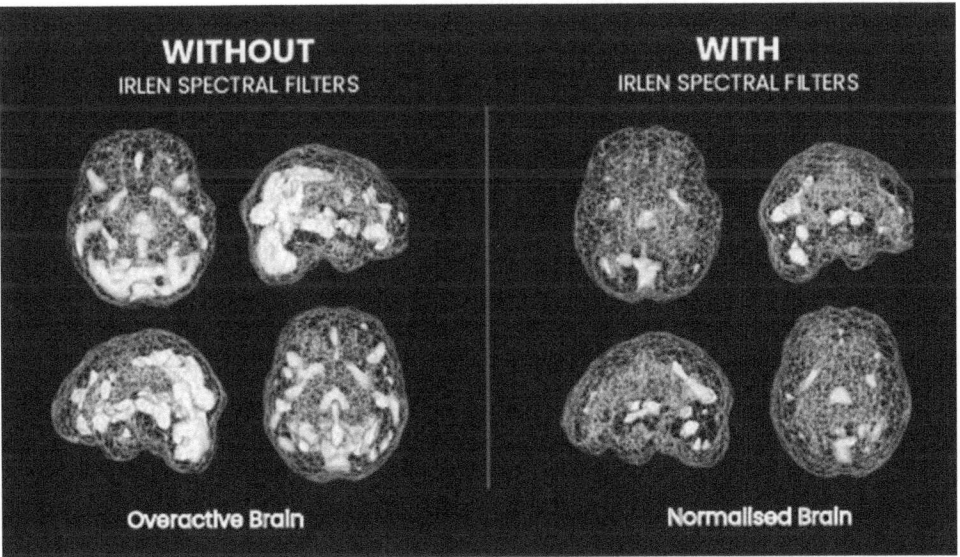

*Figure 5.2* SPECT scans by Dr Daniel Amen, showing brain activity without and then with Irlen® filters

©Amen Clinics www.amenclinics.com

Both approaches offer valuable support and have made a difference to many, many people. Having been trained in assessing for Irlen® Syndrome and hearing about the powerful relief people experience from their lenses, I believe it is a credible alternative, once visual acuity and eye health have been assessed by a standard optician.

### Supporting the visual system through the use of coloured overlays and paper

It is fair to say that exploring the functional aspects of vision by seeing a behavioural optometrist, and/or using coloured overlays and exercise books has come under scrutiny and criticism in recent years. The NHS do not recognise behavioural optometry within their services, which may seem to undermine its credibility. It is also true to say that the evidence base is unclear for using colour[17] and others criticise the use of glasses or overlays as a tool educators use *instead of* additional tuition (which it shouldn't be).

The SpLD Assessment Standards Committee (SASC) take a slightly different approach, acknowledging the need to test for visual stress, but advising caution regarding schools determining visual stress without specialist optician involvement.[18] However, some reading difficulties can be persistent in spite of ongoing intervention and you may wish to consider the idea of looking at other supports alongside reading intervention. If you do not have a specialist near you, or a parent-carer is not able to afford this service, it may still be worth trying in school.

My professional view is that whilst there is certainly a lot more research to do and it is by no means a panacea, there are two key reasons why trialling a behavioural optometry or colour approach shouldn't be dismissed.

1.  There is scientific evidence that people have different numbers of magno-, parvo- and koniocells, different visual perception abilities, different responses to light variation and different colour contrast sensitivity, affecting their experience of luminance and colour. We cannot rule these variations out when considering reading difficulties.
2.  People's opinion and perception is also evidence that it works for some. I firmly believe that it is important not to deny someone their personal lived experience. Otherwise, this is a form of testimonial injustice. If someone perceives an improvement in their visual system with a coloured overlay, then they perceive an improvement in their visual system with a coloured overlay. Even if it is a placebo effect, placebos can be enormously powerful.

I take an honest and pragmatic approach with students and their parents-carers, explaining that this is an area which still needs a lot more research and so they should consider whether they want to try it or not. If they do, there are two key questions to consider when trying out different coloured overlays in school with a student:

*   Does it make the text look clearer?
*   Do your eyes feel more comfortable?

Keep trying different colours until you find one that works – or not.

In-class strategies to support a visual system may include:

- ○ Seating a pupil with visual processing difficulties carefully: centrally, either at the back or the front, depending on their attention levels.
- ○ Designing worksheets with simple and well-spaced layouts and a clear font.
- ○ Highlighting or drawing attention to the most important information that pupils need to know so they have quick visual prompts for scanning and finding information.
- ○ Giving enough time for pupils to process complex visual information (i.e. lots of text), particularly in timed assessments.

---

**No Child Misses Out – Response Point 5.2: Supporting Pupils Experiencing Colour Vision Deficiency (Colour Blindness)**

---

There is currently no "cure" for colour vision deficiency, although specialist lenses have been developed making colours appear more vibrant and distinct, which some find helpful. This means that in-school support is really important for children and young people, which is what Dame Allan's School has been exploring.

Colour Blind Awareness CIC have information on their website which details ways teachers can help and who also offer in-school training. And you can also read their book, *Supporting colour blindness in education and beyond: A practical guide for teachers and families.*[19] Once you know just how many pupils on roll who have some form of colour vision deficiency, you may feel you want to train people specifically. In the meantime, here are some recommended strategies.

In-class strategies to support a visual system may include:

- ○ Being mindful of traffic light systems where children have to interpret by colour (whether that's marking or level of difficulty).
- ○ Labelling coloured pencils, pens and crayons. Crayola are so good at this, especially with their crayons!
- ○ Being mindful of how you code reading book levels if children need to choose levels themselves.
- ○ Dual coding information where colour is important for understanding. For example in early years counting, map reading in geography, interpreting information on a table in science. Use patterns to separate information, or labels to guide colour awareness.
- ○ Avoiding red and green in PE. Dame Allan's school has thought carefully about their sports bibs (they're patterned) and cones (they're yellow and blue) so that vision doesn't prevent enjoyment and engagement of sport.
- ○ Ensuring pupils with a colour vision deficiency can access help to identify a colour in a test scenario if no guide has been given.

> **No Child Misses Out – Response Point 5.3 & 5.4: Supporting Rapid Automatic Naming and Reading Efficiency Difficulties**

In-class strategies to support reading inefficiency may include:

o   Giving pupils more time to complete a reading task (in external examinations, you may be able to apply for additional time too).

o   Consider investing in assistive technology for reading support in external examinations. Pupils in my setting who use it speak about the confidence they feel being able to double-check a word or sentence, and the increase in speed and accuracy of working because of it.

Individual support may require:

o   Thinking about a pupil's reading profile.

o   Carrying out reading efficiency interventions, as detailed in the following section.

Figure 5.3 will help you to consider a child's reading profile to support your thinking about what the next steps might be.

What this could mean for next steps:

A.   Pupil appears to be reading well.
B.   Pupil needs more intensive support for mastering phonic knowledge and common exception words.
C.   Pupil needs to be consider specialist lenses and/or colour.
D.   Pupil needs both more intensive reading mastery support *and* specialist lenses and/or colour.

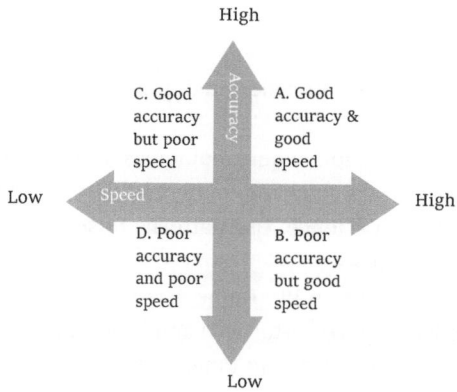

*Figure 5.3* A diagram to help you consider a child's reading profile

With all of these however, but particularly for Students A and C, if there are issues with comprehension, evaluating and supporting working memory (which we'll look at in Chapter Seven) and vocabulary (which we looked at in Chapter Four) will also be important.

The following advice should not override your current multi-sensory approaches and reading schemes, which will be based on heavily researched practice in teaching reading through synthetic phonics, as we discussed in Chapter Four. This advice is about improving automaticity and, for this, intensive repetition can be very powerful. What's brilliant about it too, is that it is not limited to primary schools. So many reading resources and schemes are just not age-appropriate for secondary aged pupils. This is an excellent approach because:

1.  It's quick and it's cheap to run.
2.  Progress is measurable and very encouraging for each pupil.
3.  You can do it with any graphemes, syllables or whole words – it's totally flexible and takes very little planning.
4.  You do not need to take children out for long intervention sessions where they miss other learning going on.
5.  You can train individual parents how to do it and support learning at home (especially with flashcards.)

*Bonnie Terry* demonstrates how to do this well. She has recorded a video called *Reading Fluency Training: How to Improve Reading Fluency (5 minutes to Better Reading Skills)*. You'll see, she asks pupils to read a list of words (which are very prescriptive and similar e.g. brag, rag, sag, nag, rag, sag, brag, nag etc.) and notes how many they are able to do in 60 seconds – errors are corrected. They record this on a score sheet. This is regularly repeated and the pupil can see their progress over time. You may have come across an intervention called *precision teaching* and this is an example of it in practice.

The same concept can be used with flash cards because they're easy to grab on the go and do anywhere in a moment. Take a list of words which are needed (e.g. Common Exception Words for the year group) and, depending on the pupil's current accuracy and fluency, take a handful and repeatedly go through them. As they get better, you can increase the number in the pile, keeping familiar words as well as new words to keep confidence levels growing. A neat way to mark as you go is to put the cards into two piles: on your right if they're right, on the left if they're not there yet. Check which ones are wrong at the end and go through them to overlearn corrections. Alternatively, you can just stick an error back somewhere into the pack so they meet it again going round. (Make sure you tell them the correct pronunciation each time so they overlearn correctly it as they go.) Do this until they've got all the words right. It's important to end on a positive!

NB. Don't be tempted to take on too many words at a time. Remember in Chapter Four, we covered the Zone of Proximal Development (ZPD). Those who know a child well – at home or at school, will be able to pitch this well. It just takes a combination of ability-appropriate resources and learning from observation so each session matches the learner and where they're at.

If a child is struggling with the regular phonics programme, it is important to reflect and adapt. Reading efficiency has real-world economic and generational impact on a child in school and on their future prospects. This is known as the Matthew Effect:[20] the rich get richer and the poor get poorer. In reading, not only do we see the progressive decline of slow starters, but a widening gap between the slow and the fast starters. Or to quote James Clear from his NY Times Bestseller *Atomic Habits*, "what starts as a small win or a minor setback accumulates into something much more. . . as time goes on, these small improvements or declines compound and you suddenly find a very big gap between people."[21]

This is the cold, hard truth about the socio-economic discrimination built into a system where reading ability is considered an indicator of intellect and therefore of high value to the human race. If you can't read comfortably and efficiently, your career choices are fewer; often you either don't have the academic desire or skillset to support at home, and/or the time because your job requires you to commit many hours for a low wage to just keep the family afloat. You're less likely to have a good knowledge and understanding of the world: your cultural capital will be more limited; your vocabulary less expansive. Illiteracy trickles down the generations to grave effect. If we, as educators, are not fully aware of the internal noise distracting our children from becoming fluent readers, we risk short-changing their life chances and future earnings considerably. We cement in that socio-economic discrimination rather than breaking it.

## Final thoughts: seeing the world differently

Before the industrial revolution, most people were illiterate and unlikely to travel particularly far or fast. Our eyes just didn't need to interpret information at such speed. Since then, our lives have changed significantly. In evolutionary terms, our visual system is still catching up. Only ten generations ago, the demand for perceiving changing luminance at high speed was not a biological necessity like it is now; and not necessarily more important than other functions of vision. Instead, monitoring sheep grazing on a hill, or observing and appreciating a greater range of colours and their richness, to assess the ripeness of crops or the health of a family member were really valued skill-sets. Speed of visual processing has really only been prioritised above the others in the last century.

Likewise, we tend to consider colour vision deficiency as a disadvantage. And there are certainly frustrations with the "normal sighted" world that people with colour blindness experience, as we've discussed. However, we also know that those who experience CVD are often able to see better in low-light and potentially under water too (many marine life animals see through a reduced colour spectrum). Many can also see a greater variation of greens than average. Those with CVD may have provided an advantage for hunter-gatherers. In fact, there are several stories of colour-blind soldiers in World War Two, highly valued because they spotted the enemy's camouflaged uniforms, when others couldn't, and helped their platoons to victory.

It goes without saying that the gene pool needs eyes that can quickly transmit black and white information to the brain. We like them in the classroom because they're often fast learners. They may well process a lot of information quickly. But we also really need eyes whose strength is to process the colourful information more slowly, helping us engage in the joys of a technicolour world – expression which often communicates to our deepest, wordless selves, stimulating emotion, self-awareness and need to feel connected to something bigger than ourselves.

Perhaps, then, an evolutionary consideration of these genes being reproduced freely within the gene pool, is that although a *risk factor* for reading they are in fact a *protective factor* for the health and wellbeing of humanity. Maybe without people exploring and celebrating colour in our lives, who champion us to slow down a bit and take stock of our world in high-definition technicolour, life might become very much more fast-paced and monochrome? And undoubtedly we'd all be a lot more stressed because of it.

This idea that we value one way of being over another can significantly affect the way we perceive people and the way they perceive themselves. Seeing the strengths of different types of visual processing, as well as other conditions, can help us to encourage the children and young people with whom we work. We need variety in the global gene pool. And we need those who see themselves as "stupid" or "less than" to perceive the value they bring to the world, too. In short, we need to revise our perspective.

---

### Chapter Summary: Visual Processing

- *We can often overlook hidden visual challenges in children, which can affect learning, health, and wellbeing.*
- *Vision is a complex process involving light conversion, clarity, and brain-eye connections for continuous information processing.*
- *Visual acuity tests by optometrists assess clarity but may miss functional reading issues that impact classroom performance.*
- *A reduced functional field of view slows reading fluency and comprehension due to the need for more eye movements.*
- *A smaller functional field of view can cause distractions in the classroom, making it hard for students to focus on important information.*
- *Chronic stress narrows the functional field of view, leading to perception problems, clumsiness, and learning difficulties.*
- *Magnocellular and parvocellular pathways process brightness and colour, and imbalances between them can lead to different experiences of colour. In particular, many children experiencing colour vision deficiency go undetected.*
- *Speed and accuracy of visual perception depends on experience and exposure.*

# 6 Handwriting and Sensory Integration

Where are you right now? That's a question which could be taken in many metaphorical ways, and this book is definitely about helping you to chart new territory, but I mean literally. Where are you right now?

Me? I'm perching on my kitchen bar stool, typing into my laptop, which is placed on the kitchen island. It's early on a Sunday morning, my children are watching TV a few feet away within my peripheral vision and I've got my ear phones in listening to some music. I quite like sitting up here: I'm simultaneously aware of what's going on, high up enough to check everyone is ok with a quick glance, and also distanced enough to be able to shut myself off from the world, so I can concentrate on writing this for you. I've got my legs crossed – not great for those varicose veins – but necessary because my kitchen barstool is narrow and back-less and actually it is quite hard to sit on comfortably. After children my core stability needs some improvement which means I am using little tactics, often subconsciously, in my body positioning to keep strong and stable for writing.

All of this is going on whilst I am also thinking about what I want to say, how I'm going to say it, putting those words into the written form, ensuring spelling is accurate, that punctuation and grammar pass muster and that this thought I'm having leads you and me onto the next. I'm regularly checking in with my sense of hunger (I need breakfast) and that time is passing too (we're due at ParkRun shortly and we've all got to leave the house dressed and ready – no mean feat, because we are all still in pyjamas). And then deeper buried, I'm aware that there's the rest of the day and it's school tomorrow . . . Typing a paragraph with all this going on is certainly a task for my body and mind. So, imagine then how difficult learning and refining handwriting in a busy classroom actually is? Especially if you're not that keen on the people sitting near you, you can't get comfy, it's a bit noisy, you're hungry, it's PE next, which you really dislike because you struggle with catching the ball, and you're always last to be picked.

Mastering the skill of accurate and fluent handwriting is challenging. In fact, it's one of the most complex skills a child can learn.

## Understanding efficient handwriting and motor co-ordination

Handwriting is known as a **sensorimotor** skill. Whereas our ability to hear and to see the world around us and then form perceptions requires purely sensing nerves, handwriting

DOI: 10.4324/9781032663968-8

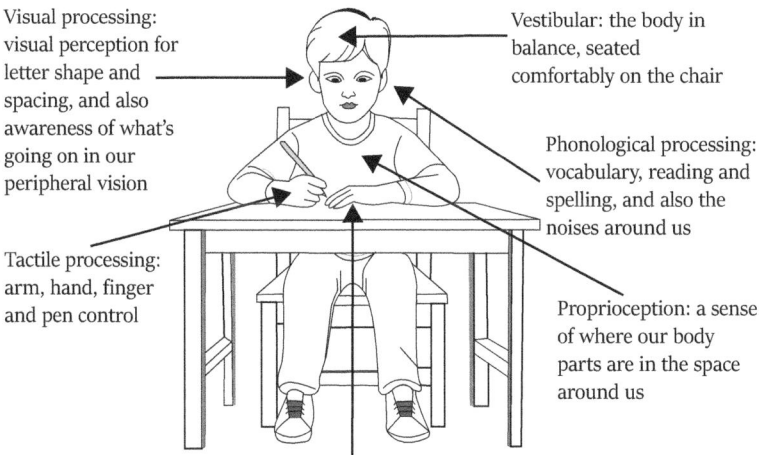

Visual processing: visual perception for letter shape and spacing, and also awareness of what's going on in our peripheral vision

Vestibular: the body in balance, seated comfortably on the chair

Phonological processing: vocabulary, reading and spelling, and also the noises around us

Tactile processing: arm, hand, finger and pen control

Proprioception: a sense of where our body parts are in the space around us

Crossing the midline: moving our hand from one side of the page to the other, sensing and perceiving information from the other side of the body

*Figure 6.1* The sensorimotor processes involved in handwriting

necessitates sensing and moving simultaneously, drawing upon and communicating to multiple senses in order to write accurately. Being able to move sets animals apart from plants, which is why animals have a brain.[1] Brains are designed for movement. Our brains function to develop movement skills and, in return, movement develops our brain. The more automatised and unconscious our movements, the more space is freed up in our conscious brain for increasingly complex tasks and thoughts. Let's have a look at some of the different sensorimotor processes involved.

**Sensorimotor:** Having or involving both sensory (input) and motor (output) functions or pathways.
**Vestibular System:** Provides feedback about our state of balance.
**Binding:** The mechanics of how sensory information is dynamically brought together in the brain to enable perception.
**Proprioception:** Our ability to sense where our body is in space by understanding the movement (speed, direction resistance, beginnings and endings) of our body parts to help us with pinpointing location.
**Tactile:** This is related to anything which touches the skin, sharing information about type of touch, pain, temperature and vibration.
**Somatic Sensation:** sensation within the body.

---

1   A minute number of animals don't, such as jellyfish and anemones, but these don't move on their own.

## The senses and practicalities for handwriting

- *Vestibular sense*

A pupil needs to be seated in balance to be steady enough so that their writing flows and is well-shaped. Maintaining balance depends primarily on our **vestibular system**, which comprises three fluid-filled semi-circular canals next to the cochlea in each inner ear. These canals are perpendicular and are studded with hair cells which detect the movement of fluid when the head moves or accelerates. Detecting movement enables us to maintain our balance, or the position of our body relative to gravity. The movements of the hair cells encode these **somatic sensations**.[1] When we are unable to efficiently detect and respond to the somatic sensations from these hair cells, balance can be compromised. It's why when we're dizzy, we need to sit down to let the fluid return to normal again.

Being able to remain in balance frees up a pupil's central nervous system to allow the flow of other information so they don't have to concentrate on re-balancing all the time, as well as thinking about and constructing what it is they actually want to write. Our vestibular system also affects our muscle tone which supports the development of our fine- and gross-motor skills. As a result, a well-developed vestibular system gives stamina to write for longer.

Strong muscles in the torso enable good posture and balance. A strong core helps to keep the spine flexible and to prevent injury to our vital organs. When we have good core stability, we are able to support our body during movement. For example, when writing, instead of resting our heavy head in our hands or crossing our legs or wrapping our feet around the chair legs to keep us stable, we're able to use our stomach muscles to bear the weight of our body parts. This enables our fingers, hand and arm to move without restriction of extra weight. Pupils who complain of pain when writing (finger, hand, wrist, shoulder, neck) and/or who find sitting still difficult would greatly benefit from developing their core stability to support handwriting, and also develop finger and hand strength.

- *Visual perception/ocular motor skills*

Balance is also supported by vision. If you see that you are swaying relative to something stable and vertical, you will amend your position accordingly to remain in balance and avoid falling over. When there is a mismatch in sensory information processing such that the vestibular information and the visual information do not integrate together to make perfect sense to the brain, motion sickness can result.

As we've just learnt in Chapter Five, vision requires acuity, a decent functional field and the **binding** of three different information pathways to enable perception. It also requires good muscle movement to be able to direct the eye where it is needed. Visual perception is therefore really important in writing because it tells you where to place your pen, how your letter shape is developing in relation to itself and those around it, and where you need to go next. Good visual perception skills allow us to draw appropriately sized ascenders and descenders. We are more likely to start a new line close to the margin, not increasingly further away from it. We will remember what a letter looks like, not mirror-reverse it unwittingly, and when we look back at our work, we will be able to "see" any errors. We are skilled noticers. Difficulties with visual perception will lead to some difficulties with all or any of the above.

• *Proprioception*

Handwriting requires proprioception. **Proprioception** results from the efficient sensing of where our body is in space, by understanding how our body parts are moving, the speed and direction of movement, any resistance or weight which is added to it which needs accounting for and the beginnings and endings of each move which enable us to pinpoint location. Good proprioception means we don't need to look at our feet when we're walking – unless it's new and unpredictable terrain, of course. Proprioception helps us to distribute energy and focus to stay in balance and to execute the desired movement effectively.

It's as relevant to how our eyes move, as how our hand moves. In fact, it's present in every muscle movement you make. Like other senses, it requires experience to develop the accuracy of this perception so that each time you repeat a movement, particularly when you have constructive feedback either through someone encouraging and guiding or through self-recognition of successful completion of the action itself, you become increasingly accurate in future executions of the action. If you want to keep the ball within the lines when playing tennis, you have to practice, practice, practice.

In terms of writing, good proprioception allows us to judge the amount of pressure we need to apply on a writing surface so that our handwriting flows. Slow, heavy and forced handwriting is a sign that there may be proprioception difficulties. This might be because of a lack of handwriting experience (a pupil is concentrating hard on letter formation and not thinking about the amount of pressure being applied) but more likely it suggests that their seating position, posture and foot placement need review. Pupils with good proprioception sit on their chairs calmly, without fidgeting, rocking, kneeling on the chair, constantly changing position, or falling off.

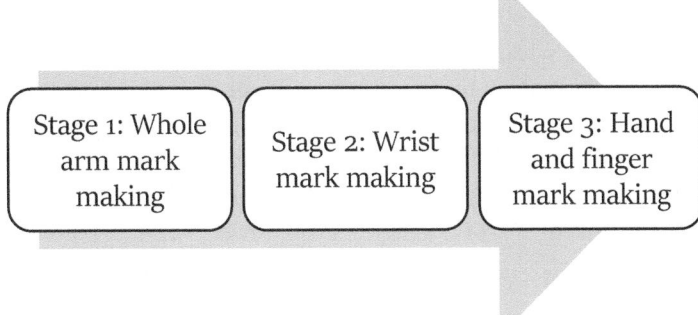

Stage 1: Whole arm mark making

Stage 2: Wrist mark making

Stage 3: Hand and finger mark making

*Figure 6.2* Stages of handwriting development

- *Tactile senses including hand strength and the feel of the pen*

When we write, we touch the desk, the paper and the pen. We touch the chair we're sitting on. We touch the floor with our feet. **Tactile** sensory feedback is critical for efficient handwriting, too.

Pen hold can be a complex issue in handwriting and there are three stages of development. You can gauge the level of development by observing which stage they're at.

*Stage 1:* Developed in early years, the first stage of handwriting is mark making by moving the arm, often with paint and crayons. Not only does this encourage the movement skills necessary for writing, but it also develops the child's awareness of the world around them. It enables them to visualise scenes or objects and encode memories.

*Stage 2:* When arm movement is increasingly accurate, our mark making will develop by manipulation of the wrist. If a pupil is struggling with clarity of handwriting, have a look at the angle of their wrist. If the pupil rests their hand too on edge or too flat to the page, this may cause the slant of the writing to obstruct clarity. Using squared paper can help giving the writer vertical support with which to gauge their slant, and adjust the angle of their wrist.

*Stage 3:* Reaching this stage means development is such that the fingers now manipulate the shaft of the pen. At this microlevel, the fingers are responsible for the size and proportion of the letters. If letter shape, size and proportion is an issue then finger and hand muscle strength and sensitivity should be considered.

All pens are not created equal however (said all stationery lovers, ever!) Some pens can be difficult to hold, too. Appearance and cost-effectiveness are major factors in pen design, so they are not (ironically) always well designed for writing. Too smooth a barrel and they force us to either squeeze very tightly or move the thumb further around to clamp on top of fingers, which limits movements for letter formation. Alternatively, we might increase our grip by pushing in the opposite direction with the thumb bending the knuckle back on itself, which leads to a very stiff, inefficient and, eventually, painful grip. Reviewing a child's grip can be helpful – noting that the tripod grip is not the only way to hold a pen or pencil. Instead, many occupational therapists look for efficiency and comfort, as well as supporting this with a pen grip to improve the ergonomics of the desired pen, or to choose a different pen altogether. One with a fibre tip nib or a gel is all the better for writing with, too.

It is also worth thinking about the type of paper pupils are writing on. For some, the feel of it can be off-putting. Others need to rest on several sheets of paper to help with their sensory feedback. Still others benefit from different size and colour lines to guide their visual perception. If a child is struggling to write, have a think about the paper quality, as well as the pen, and any other tactile sensory experiences they are having simultaneously.

- *Crossing the midline*

The midline is an imaginary line down the centre of the body. In order to be able to operate speedily we need our limbs to be able to cross the midline and operate effectively as if it were on its normal side. For example, crossing the midline allows us to write fluently from left to right. Regardless of handedness, being able to cross the midline requires one of our hands and both of our eyes moving to sense and perceive information from the other side of our body so that letters are formed correctly, in the correct sequence and at pace. If we cannot do this well, you may notice a pupil moving their whole body along the line, left to right, as a compensatory strategy.

On the cricket pitch, we might need to quickly reach for a ball coming slightly to our right that requires us to catch with both hands. We should be able to bring our left hand across our body to catch it, rather than moving our whole trunk to the right and even taking a step, to be able to catch the ball. We might even be *really good* at catching by using this compensatory strategy but it is still a compensatory strategy nonetheless: we *should* be able to cross the midline.

Our ability to cross the midline also links to the interconnectedness of our thoughts and actions. Whilst there is still a lot more to learn about what happens and where within the brain, good connectivity between the left and right hemispheres is important. Too few connections between the two hemispheres can lead to developmental delays and barriers emerging, which can be observed beyond physical movement.

- *Oracy, phonological awareness and representational thought*

Once the writing process is enabled, then we need to consider what it is we want to say, how to organise those thoughts through the flow of our writing, which words to select and then how to spell them. Handwriting deity Rosemary Sassoon, of the famous typing font, explains that in her experience poor spelling and grammar can cause hesitation and lack of confidence in handwriting but that spelling often improves as writing becomes more relaxed. "Repetitive letter patterns separate the spelling element from skill training. Get your handwriting to flow and you relieve one urgent worry. Then you can tackle the other problems."[2] Planning and executing extended writing skills also develop with intentional modelling in teaching and plenty of practice. This is absolutely true from an occupational therapist point of view because handwriting is an example of *praxis*, otherwise known as motor planning, which we'll look at in the next section.

Given that writing is fundamental to learning success and especially in timed conditions, I think it is odd that we don't tend to test handwriting efficiency like we do words per minute in reading. I think it's vital to test handwriting efficiency regularly, building up an evidence base over time to identify strengths and areas of difficulty in terms of sensory development and test efficiency more generally.

**Top Tips:**

- If you notice a pupil wrapping their feet around chair legs or moving restlessly on a chair, it is likely they are struggling to remain in balance.
- Listen out for pupils talking about feeling motion sickness. It is one of those common symptoms often associated with visual-perception difficulties; a contextual flag that I'm always interested to know if someone experiences.

- Writing that moves further away from the margin, mirror-reversals and inappropriately sized ascenders or descenders indicate visual-perception difficulties.
- If a pupil is resting their head, crossing their legs, or wrapping legs around a chair, they are seeking stability. This might suggest core muscles would benefit from strengthening exercises.
- Finger or hand pain might improve with hand strengthening exercises. Wrist pain might improve with greater core stability, to reduce weight bearing.
- Pupils who fidget, rock or kneel on their chair are likely to have proprioceptive difficulties.
- If writing is very slanted and difficult to read, consider supporting the rotation of the wrist. Writing on squared paper can help train the motion.
- If letter shape, size or proportion is an issue, consider strengthening the hand and finger muscles.
- Consider moving away from the Pen Licence. Children who are last to progress often carry a sense of shame. Try working on their handwriting instead, and giving them a better pen.
- If a pupil has an awkward or painful grip, consider them using a pen grip or an ergonomically designed pen with a fibre nib or gel ink.
- Think about the paper a pupil is writing on, too. Do they need softer paper, more sheets underneath, or to see the lines more clearly?
- If you have a pupil with handwriting *and* spelling difficulties, focus on improving their handwriting first.
- Test handwriting regularly and hold evidence on file to monitor improvement over time.

### No Child is Missed – Action Point 6.1: Screen Handwriting Efficiency

In terms of assessing how well each child has developed with their handwriting efficiency, there are key areas to look at and think about:

- letter shape, letter and word placement
- flow and pen pressure
- spelling and punctuation
- getting started, planning and executing a piece of work with an age-appropriate level of coherence
- fluency and speed

1  Ask them to write for ten minutes on a topic they feel knowledgeable about, rather than an assessment piece. You want to be assessing handwriting, not

their progress on a topic (e.g. something about themselves, a pet, favourite food, a person they admire, which doesn't matter if it's true or accurate).

2   As the children write, notice if anyone zones out or stops writing for any length of time. For any children whom you particularly want to consider, you may want to do an additional observation about their posture and body movement when writing, too. See **Appendix 6** for help with this.

3   After their time is up, if they're able, ask the pupils to count their words into groups of ten, making a mark after each tenth word as they go. Then total their number of words on the page before handing it in. (You can double check this when reviewing but it tends to save you a bigger counting job. Or, you can use ChatGPT to do the hard work for you!) The words per minute score gives you an indication of their sensory integration and flow. You can find more detailed guidance on handwriting speed on the website – www. nochildismissed.org

NB. Do scan the text for content. This activity can trigger children to make a disclosure, particularly if you've selected a topic like "family". You need to liaise with your Safeguarding team about anything which concerns you.

If you're keen to purchase a test, the *Detailed Assessment of Speed of Handwriting (DASH)* can be used to establish evidence for extra time in examinations.

NB. Another helpful test, if handwriting is proving very difficult, is to assess typing speed and error rate. Monitoring both current ability and progress over time. You can easily and quickly do this by asking a child to complete a test of typing efficiency, such as the one I really rate on *TypingTest.com*

## Praxis

**Praxis** is known as motor-planning and handwriting is a good example of a praxis task in action. Significant difficulties with this can lead to a diagnosis of dyspraxia from continued poor planning and execution of desired movements. Successful praxis, therefore, is the ability of the brain to conceive of, organise and carry out a sequence of unfamiliar actions.[3] It requires three stages.

The more practiced and skilled we are at completing a motor activity, the less we need to think about these stages and the more automatic our movements become, which is important because when we're writing in school we need to be thinking about the topic at hand and demonstrating our understanding of it, not how to sit on the chair and hold the pen.

Turning it into a three-stage process rather diminishes the complexity of praxis, however, because motor planning relies upon *multisensory* information streams which must combine together simultaneously to form a clear perception and successful execution.

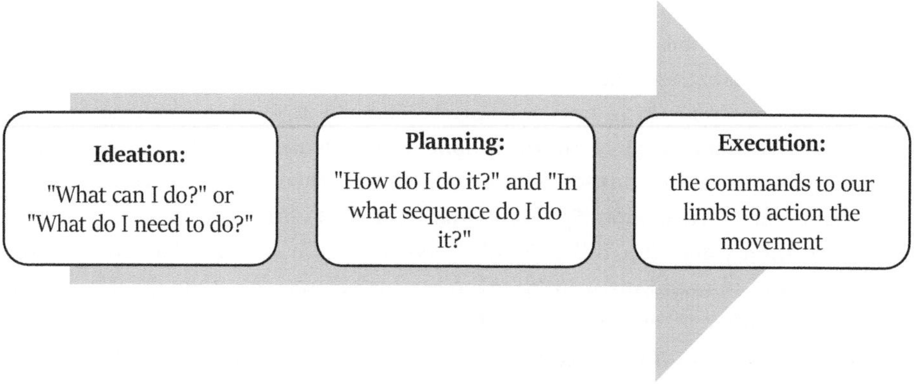

| Ideation: | Planning: | Execution: |
|---|---|---|
| "What can I do?" or "What do I need to do?" | "How do I do it?" and "In what sequence do I do it?" | the commands to our limbs to action the movement |

*Figure 6.3* The motor planning process (Praxis)

This is known as *sensory integration* and it's similar to the concept of **binding** that we came across with vision.[2] In order to complete a movement task, we must interpret information from several sensory pathways in a concert of stimulation, which we must then perceive and act upon in a physically, socially coherent way, which requires excellent precision and timing.

> **Praxis:** Praxis or motor planning is the ability to conceive of, organise, and execute a novel or new task.
>
> **Affordances:** require knowledge of our body and what it can do in relation to the environment we find ourselves in.
>
> **Exteroception:** perception of stimuli outside the body, like hearing a fire alarm and knowing we need to leave the building.
>
> **Interoception:** the awareness of internal sensations in the body, including heart rate, respiration, hunger, fullness, temperature, pain as well as emotions.

## Movement planning and physical co-ordination

In order to complete a physical action – whatever it may be – we need to know four key pieces of information.

1.   We need to know our own body and what it is capable of
2.   We need to know how we can move it
3.   We need to know the features of the environment we're in
4.   We need to know its "demands and invitations"

---

2   The difference is that binding refers to the bringing together of information from multiple information pathways within *one* sense whereas sensory integration refers to the bringing together of information from multiple sensory pathways at the same time. If you dig a bit deeper into these fields however, you'll see that there are similarities and therefore there is a need for greater clarity around this binding/sensory integration problem. Another lacuna!

For example, if you've ever seen me ice-skating (after you've got over your fit of giggles, obvs) you'll know that, to begin with, I cling helplessly to the side of the rink. I do know how to skate but those particular tactile, vestibular and proprioceptive requirements are not automated to start with. I have to consciously remind myself how to ice-skate which takes time and more than a little bravery. I must remember how to move my body on the ice – sliding rather than stepping; that the ice is cold and slippery; that there are indentations from previous skaters and their icy scrapes and slides, which could cause me to topple; that other skaters could come at me at high speed, or crash into me and cause a pile up. I need to prepare for this by making sure I've put on a waterproof, padded coat, warm trousers and my gloves, in case I fall. In letting go of the side, it demands planning, balance and spatial awareness beyond that of walking or running. It invites me to have fun, but it requires complex co-ordination and higher risks. Physically, I need to be able to cope with all of this.

Even from the earliest moments of life, as embryos and as babies, children are exploring their environment, categorising their experiences and developing **affordances**, just like I did about ice-skating. They are working out what their body can do within their physical environment and what opportunities and demands are around them. They are primed for growth and development but this doesn't mean they can just get up and walk. There are layers of sensory development that must happen first; milestones to meet. Through this ongoing interaction with the environment, thinking and cognitive processes begin to develop. Brains are designed for movement, remember. So when we move, we learn through this sensory feedback loop where our body engages with the outside world. We call this growing knowledge from the external world **exteroceptions**.

These physical experiences become encoded as mental representations, which help us both with the task at hand, and also with future decision making. We might know and understand the physical properties of the environment, but when it comes to deciding if we're going to let go of the side of the ice-rink or not, perception of our own capabilities in relation to the task ahead will influence what we decide to do. If the last time I went ice-skating I broke my arm, I might be much less inclined. These are known as **interoceptions** and they are very powerful in forming our choices and actions for movement.

What this means for children and young people is that tasks which require complex multisensory interactions in an organised and co-ordinated approach (anything from running on the football pitch to writing an essay) need to go through this process. Children need to know their body and what it is capable of; know how to move it to complete the action; know the environment and the demands that accompany it. Success comes from practice and a sense of competence, enough to give it a go. Although there is a healthy dose of truth to the old adage, "whether you think you can, or you think you can't, you're right", we need modelling, practice, positive reinforcement and a sense that we're getting better, otherwise progress is likely to take much longer, or worse, atrophy. Depending on a child's genetic makeup and early years' experiences, motor planning can take varying amounts of time to learn for each new unfamiliar action.

If you're worried about the development of a child's co-ordination and movement skills, it is worth carrying out a motor screening. It's also worth thinking about skill development in school more generally, looking at introducing novel and complex skills through the four stages mentioned.

---

### No Child is Missed – Action Point 6.2: Screen Motor Planning (Praxis)

In order to reflect on praxis difficulties, there are lots of short checklists online. If you want a more detailed one, search for the *Developmental Co-ordination Disorder Questionnaire (DCD-Q)*, which can be scored for children aged 5–15. There is a version for children aged 3–4 however there is a small cost to purchasing this. Alternatively, there is a less detailed one on *Twinkl* if you have an account.

If you'd like to invest in a test, the *Peabody Developmental Motor Scales (PDMS)* covers preschool children, whereas the *Movement Assessment Battery for Children (Checklist)* provides a standardised measure of everyday gross and fine motor co-ordination difficulties (ages 3–25) which can be used across a whole class.

---

## Hypo- and hypersensitivities

For some children and young people in our schools, it is not the co-ordination of move-ment that is challenging, but the intensity of the sensory stimulation in their bodies. Or, it might be both.

Jean Ayers, one of the most famous researchers in this field describes: "Sensations flow into the brain like streams flowing into a lake . . . The brain must organise all of these sensations if a person is to move and behave normally".[4] For example, the inte-gration of our auditory (phonological) and vestibular (body movement) senses help us to learn to speak. The integration of our vestibular, proprioceptive, tactile and visual senses enables us to move precisely and purposefully. "All of the senses together are required for the end products – concentration, organisation, self-esteem, self-control, self-confidence, academic learning, abstract thought and reasoning, and specialisation of each side of the body and the brain."[5]

We notice problems with learning when a child's senses have not integrated fully such that they are in a state of regular imbalance or asynchrony; sensation and perception are somehow still disorganised, causing dysregulation inconsistent with their developmen-tal stage. As a result of this disorganisation, confusion and stress can arise, particularly within a busy and sometimes unpredictable environment with lots of sensory stimula-tion through multiple channels at the same time, like a classroom.

We often then observe sensory seeking and sensory avoiding behaviours as a way to restore a sense of calm within the body. If it's too noisy to think, a child will cover their ears or tell someone to stop talking. If that work is too difficult, a child will do something else instead like look out the window or put their head on the desk or draw their favourite dinosaur. Or, for some, there may be a delayed response where they appear fine in school, but when they get home, a lot of regulating behaviours are required to restore balance and calm, such as spinning, jumping, shouting.

It is completely normal for any of us to use compensatory strategies to help us cope when we feel our senses are over- or under-stimulated. We might choose to pound it out on the streets by going for a run; curl up under a duvet and watch the raindrops trickling down the windowpane; or pour ourselves a glass of something after a hectic day. Problems can arise however when our perception of the stimulation is regularly disproportionate to its reality, known as a **registration difficulty** (e.g. we experience the sound of the computer whirring nearby like a chainsaw next to our head.) Registration difficulties can cause hyperarousal: overwhelming flooding within our body leading to shutdown or an extreme desire to flee or to fight for survival. Likewise, registration difficulties can also lead to under-arousal if we can't regularly sense feelings from our body parts, or imagine what touching something might feel like. For example, we may regularly or even seemingly obsessively touch surfaces or people for feedback, or we might want to keep a woolly jumper on even if it's 30°C.

To put it simply:

### Stimulus (too much) → Response (avoid)

### Stimulus (not enough) → Response (seek/crave)

But let's have a look at the smaller steps within this stimulus-response arc because if we want to support a child to modulate their behaviours then we need to know what's going on at a cellular level.

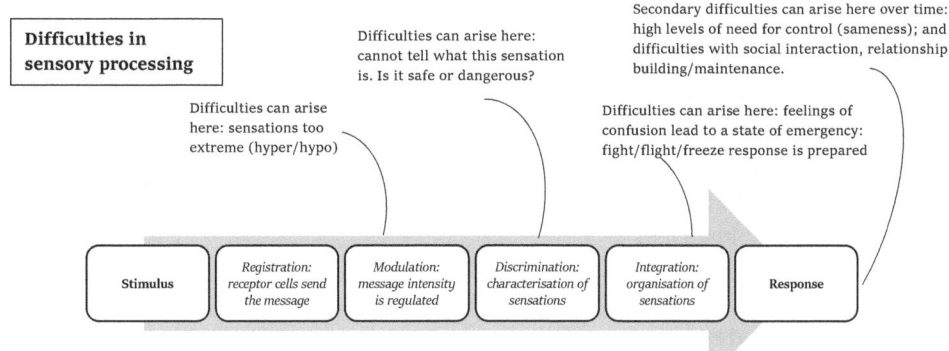

*Figure 6.4* A diagram showing the four steps required for processing sensory information and where difficulties can arise

> **Registration difficulty:** A difficulty in identifying the nature of the sensation (too much/too little). Sensory information travels through the reticular formation, integrating it together to transfer on to the midbrain and thalamus, in order to co-ordinate bodily functions in response. Too much sensory information perceived and it will trigger the fight/flight response; too little and it will continue to seek sensory stimulation.
>
> **Cerebellum:** Known as the "little brain", it co-ordinates movement, vital in language and attention too.

## Sensory integration in action

Sensation starts with the receptor cells all over and within our body *registering* input. These receptor cells detect a stimulus (change) and communicate this through our nerves along our spinal cord to the brain. For example, if we put on a woolly jumper because we are cold, the receptor cells in our skin will identify this change and release a chemical to let the rest of the body know. The chemical will be detected by other cells around them and the message will be transmitted via neurones (nerve cells) onwards until it arrives at our **cerebellum** for onward direction within the brain.

The greater the number of receptor cells detecting a stimulus, the more quickly and more powerfully the message will travel to our brain. In order not to be overwhelmed by the message however, our body regulates its intensity through a process known as *modulation*. We then *discriminate* the characteristics and specific qualities of the input (scratchy but soft, enabling warmth, smells pleasant, isn't constricting vital airways or blood supply etc.) to be able to *integrate* them together and form a response (keep it on or take it off).

In education, we tend to talk about this as "processing" information; and we also tend to think that *fast* is "good" and *slow* is "bad" as it implies a desired level of automaticity. And it is absolutely true that being able to do something with a level of skill at speed is important for lots of reasons. We would struggle to read, write or drive a car if we couldn't. Occupational therapists however are also interested in how levels or intensities of stimulation and response, from multiple channels simultaneously, can affect someone in living their daily lives. And this is a crucial point because it is not quite as simple as fast being good and slow being bad. Actually, in order for us to function well in the classroom, or indeed anywhere, it is about the balance of sensory stimulation being "just right".

## The just right state

Maintaining the just right state is important to our overall health and learning, and the more demands upon our sensory system at any one time, the more challenging it can be. It can be especially difficult to remain calm and relaxed, managing multisensory input and responding appropriately to the situation, if our body is feeling in need of replenishment, perhaps through tiredness, illness, hunger. (It's exactly why my friends and family have all learnt never to go out for an evening meal with me if we haven't booked the restaurant beforehand . . .!)

As we mature, we can cope with complexity and stimulation better and for longer. Experience and knowledge about the type of situation helps us to stay calm through any low-level negative sensory stimulations that we face. For example, whist we may still find the sound of someone chewing their food incredibly irritating, we can override the internal cues we experience telling us to shout at them – or worse, and still carry on anyway knowing that it will be over soon and our just right state will resume. The same is not necessarily going to be true for a child if someone at their table does something irritating however. As a teacher, you might find you have a situation to deal with.

## When things aren't "just right"

It is much harder to remain within a just right state and to carry out tasks which are important for living a normal daily life when we are regularly flooded or underwhelmed by stimulation. What we often see as a result of this theory are recommendations from occupational therapists, in particular, advising on strategies to maintain and/or repair a "just right" state through therapeutic strategies targeting the central nervous system, such as swinging, vibrating, rotating, deep pressure. Whilst a unique and detailed assessment and plan is essential for children experiencing high levels

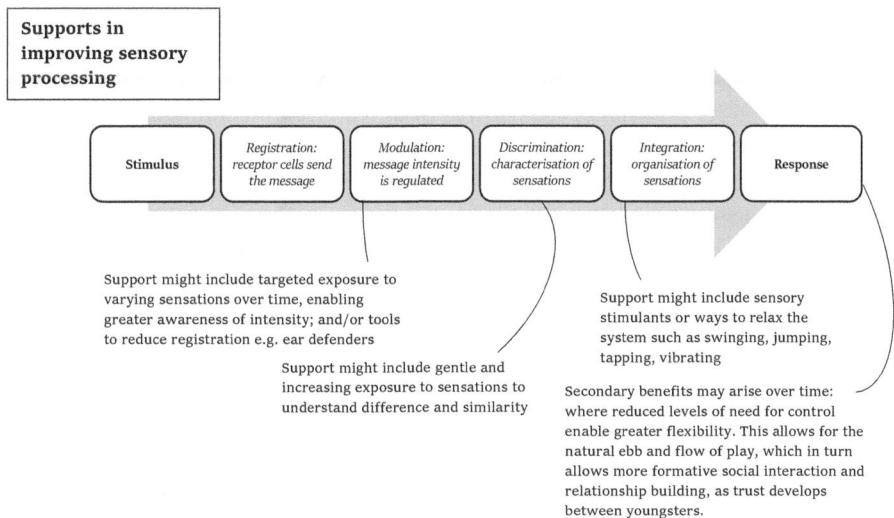

*Figure 6.5* A diagram showing the four steps required for processing sensory information and where supporting strategies can help

of hyper- and hypoarousal, which will require referral to an occupational therapist, schools can carry out their own basic screening through observation to put together some simple and personalised support plans for home and school with resources detailed in this section.

### No Child is Missed – Action Point 6.3: Screen for Sensory Integration (Processing)

In terms of reviewing a child's sensory integration, it is worthwhile considering how a child behaves in both the home and school environments. A screening checklist for schools to use, which I think broadly covers both primary and secondary education, is the *South Warwickshire NHS Foundation Trust Sensory Checklist*. It gives you clear examples of the different activities to observe and consider, broken down into the key senses, and a summary evaluation page at the end to help you consider the patterns emerging from your reflections. This, in turn, should help you to identify ways to help a child with any sensory processing difficulties. Other ways to gather information about the impact of the environment on sensory experiences is to complete the *School Stress Survey*; and to traffic light a pupil's timetable (red = problematic, amber = ok, green = positive).

A screening checklist for, or with, Home that I really like is the *Sensory Smarts* checklist. It also gives an easy-to-follow list, broken down into the key senses. If you have a child who is struggling at home and at school, this is a way you can have a supportive and structured conversation about how both Home and School can help.

Some practitioners advocate considering whether primitive reflexes have been retained as a way to integrate the senses. This isn't a practice that I have engaged with, but given its prevalence in the field of SEND, I am including it here, in case *you* want to. To get around the fact that babies are pretty helpless when they're born, nature equips us with reflexes. These are stimulus-response survival mechanisms which are the foundation of our nervous system. When we're too little to be conscious, our bodies do the "thinking" for us by responding unconsciously to our needs. They help us develop in utero, and they help us to move our bodies enough to get out nine months later. Parents and early years colleagues will know that by about six months old, those primitive reflexes will have integrated and disappeared. What this means is that instead of being impulsive, involuntary movements which respond to the environment, they come under cognitive control, responding to the command of the brain.

There are free questionnaires online but the best I have found are in books. I've read both *The Symphony of Reflexes* by *Bonnie L. Brandes* and *The Well Balanced Child* by *Sally Goddard Blythe*. Both of these books also provide exercises to practice to help integrate retained reflexes. Whilst this type of practice could be helpful at all stages of education, this particular focus might be most helpful for colleagues in early years and the first few years of school.

## The known limitations of sensory integration and retained reflexes

There is no debate about the existence of reflexes and that primitive reflexes should disappear. There is debate, however, about whether these primitive reflexes can be "retained" or not, which essentially means that those initial survival mechanisms are not cognitively controlled, leading to ongoing impulsive and involuntary behaviours. Those who advocate for the existence of retained reflexes argue that they can result in overly-reactive fear responses, poor impulse control, attention-deficits, postural issues, poor muscle tone, W-sitting, poor hand–eye co-ordination, toe walking and poor spatial awareness. Interestingly, professionals working in neurological health-care often notice these primitive reflexes *return*, in conditions such as Parkinson's. The exact manifestation depends upon the specific reflex(es) retained (or returned), of which there are six.

Those who promote **retained reflexes** as a key to explaining learning difficulties suggest that factors in the environment such as maternal stress during pregnancy, the diet and general health of the mother affecting the prenatal environment and any traumatic birth events (including forceps and caesarean section) can disrupt sensory development. Early years' advocates champion sufficient movement opportunities like tummy time, encouraging rolling over, sitting, crawling, side-walking, standing independently and walking etc. which can help sensory integration, brain organisation and motor development.

Likewise, theories of sensory integration are still a focus for debate. Whilst the concept of sensory processing, and associated difficulties, is commonplace within occupational and speech and language therapy currently, it is important to know that evidence justifying approaches like using **a sensory diet** to reduce symptoms of hyper- or hypoarousal, is limited[6] and therefore the impact of these approaches is still unclear. Likewise, the impact of repetitive movements to integrate retained reflexes is also still unclear.

Partly this is because there is a range of different terms used in research papers, which makes it difficult to compare evidence bases like-for-like; partly it is because the types of research conducted so far are not immune to bias and confounding factors (such as other factors in a child's life or within the intervention event itself which have not been fully accounted for). As with research around the impact of different approaches to therapy or teaching, the role of the unique practitioner (their person-ality, values, the precise nature of the environment of practice) is very difficult to separate away from the practice itself in terms of evaluating its impact. But another significant reason is that funding and research simply hasn't been directed towards running gold-standard research trials, despite calls in the literature for more than two decades. An absence of data in terms of evidence of impact does not mean that this theory is weak. It just means that any impact it might have has not been rigorously identified and quantified.[7]

Whatever the cause of sensory integration difficulties, retained reflexes or not, enabling the body to build confident motor movements through practiced routines allows for good cognitive development. What we are aiming for is healthy development where an increasing number of movement sequences are well-rehearsed and embedded for mastery and fluency.

**Retained reflexes:** the idea that infantile movements and reactions fail to integrate into conscious control.

**Sensory diet:** a set of activities, and/or accommodations that can help someone to regulate their sensory system. For example, doing star jumps, bouncing on a therapy ball, wearing a weighted vest. These activities/accommodations can be used both in a proactive way to maintain sensory regulation, and in a reactive way, to help restore the nervous system to its "just right" state.

### No Child Misses Out: What to do next. . . .

**No Child Misses Out – Response Point 6.1: Have a School Wide Approach to Teaching and Supporting Handwriting**

Recent findings from a meta-analysis showed handwriting interventions are worthwhile, helping all students, regardless of difficulties, with noticeable improvements.[9] The information below is specific to school settings. At EYFS, handwriting skills should be developed through play and developing balance, proprioception, tactile and visual perception skills which are explored in NCMO Response Point 6.3.

- *Teaching handwriting systematically and consistently through a whole school policy*
  In-class strategies to support may include:
  - A consistent script for letter formation, for both lower- and upper-case letters. There are several handwriting specialists who can guide you with your choice of script and style of handwriting who have resources for purchase and training.

- A description of some key grips for teachers to support pupils to test out to see which works for them. The dynamic tripod is most popular but there are also the dynamic quadruple or the alternative tripod grips.
- Awareness of hand positioning. The wrist should not rise off the page or bend inwards. The hand should not rest on its edge or fall flat: both of these positions indicate difficulties with core stability or visual perception.
- The importance of correct posture which supports writing at pace, reducing the chance of overstressing weaker joints and causing pain.
- Repetition, repetition, repetition with a focus on pupil practice, regular adult feedback and self-checking, avoiding too much time on teacher instruction demonstrating: how, how often, when, where, order of letter learning.
- Guidance about letter spacing, the importance of automaticity for writing fluency and also recognition that jotting notes and handwriting for best require different levels of effort, time and care. A recognition of register and flexibility of approach.

- *Ensuring appropriate posture and equipment for writing*

  In-class strategies to support may include:

  - Posture and equipment checks
  - Good light
  - Comfortable seating with feet flat on the floor (find a box if legs are too short to reach the floor)
  - A helpful posture: back almost straight; head upright without neck poking forwards; weight evenly distributed on feet and forearms
  - A flexible surface such as several sheets of paper underneath
  - Paper placed at an angle, 11 to 5 o'clock if right-handed, or 7 to 1 o'clock if left-handed
  - Holding the paper in the top corner with the non-dominant hand
  - Writing on an incline surface (if stability is unsteady) – a ring binder will do but you can also get handwriting slopes
  - Feeling relaxed – uncrossed knees, relaxed shoulders, relaxed grip
  - A comfortable pen with a flexible tip and a good grip – such as a fibre tip pen, or a hexagonal/triangular shaft
  - Using a pencil weight (some blu-tac stuck on the end) helps gravity to encourage the pencil into the crook of the thumb and hand.
  - Using age-appropriate line sizes. 15mm for Reception and Year One, 10mm in Years Two and Three, and then 8mm for Years Four upwards.[10]
  - Left-handers should hold the shaft of the pencil about 2cm higher then right handers. Wrapping a rubber band around the pencil can help left-handers judge this better. Particular care to keep their hand below the line upon which they are writing.[11] Watch out particularly for lefties gripping pens too tightly. Pen grips are likely to be particularly helpful to support this.

A helpful acronym and mnemonic for your school:

**S**traight back
**T**uck chair in
**R**est forearms on the table
**O**rganise equipment
**N**inety-degree angles
**G**rounded flat feet

> *With thanks to Andrew Percival of Stanley Road*
> *Primary School for sharing their strategies.*[12]

Whole class and/or individual support may require:

- *Exercises to develop hand-eye co-ordination, eye muscle-strength and crossing the midline, handwriting, such as:*
  - Dot-to-dots
  - Spot the difference
  - Copying shapes: rectangle, oval, triangle, straight cross and diagonal cross. Older children can also do a diamond shape and a percentage sign without taking pen off page, going both anti- and clockwise for the circles.
  - Use tracing paper to trace line pictures
  - Jigsaw puzzles
  - Tying shoelaces and putting on socks
  - Lego building, Jenga, Chess, Draughts, counter games which involve counting and moving spaces, e.g. Snakes and Ladders (encourage verbalising number and distance)

Parents-carers and/or Teaching Assistants can carry out daily eye tracking exercises:

  - Hold a pencil about a metre away from their eyes and move it purposefully, but not too fast, left to right to left so that their eyes must follow. Try to ensure that their eyes cross the midline. This can be tiring on eyes and arms, so should only be done in short, sharp bursts.
  - Slowly bring the pencil in close to the point at which they feel their vision go blurred or double. Gradually pull back, encouraging them to refocus onto the pencil quickly again. Repeat a few times.

Crossing the midline:

  - Reaching an arm across the other side of the body
  - Put hands on hips, rotate upper body from left to right and back
  - The *Saturday Night Fever* dance moves

Handwriting activities:

  - Do a pages-full of downstrokes all the same height, with some level of slant – what comes naturally to you. Be consistent over time.
  - Then try uuuuuuuuuuu. Then nnnnnnnnnn. (joined up).

- ○ Then try 3s paired like butterfly wings. A full page at a time.[13]
- ○ Draw sideways infinity loops in varying sizes: on paper, in a sand tray, seated correctly (as above).

- *Supporting and developing pen hold*
  - ○ Use a grip or ergonomic pen
  - ○ Put elastic band on the pen shaft to help keep the hand in one place
  - ○ Write on squared paper to help directionality
- *Supporting spelling, oracy and planning for writing*
  - ○ See Chapters Four and Seven
- *Alternative tools for writing*
  - ○ Touch-typing support for older children whose handwriting is simply not legible or fast enough to work effectively under timed conditions. *TypingTest.com* is great for this but there are lots of other ones out there. *BBC Dance Mat* is well-loved, too.

    N.B. Recent research showed that handwriting is better than typing for encoding memories because of the increased connectivity within the brain (it is more demanding on our senses) and therefore gives us more opportunity to hold onto these sensations as memories – vital in the classroom then.[14] However, in terms of typing as an examination arrangement, there is very little research about the difference (positive or negative) that typing can have on children with literacy difficulties in this environment. A small research study suggested the positive impact of typing in examinations for those with dyslexia.[15]

Further handwriting support can be found:

*Morrells handwriting* – Sue Smits
*Kinetic letters* – Margaret Williamson
*Write from the start* – Ion Teodorescu (LDA learning)
*Pegs to paper* - Angela Webb, National Handwriting Association

> **No Child Misses Out – Response Point 6.2: Supporting Praxis Development**

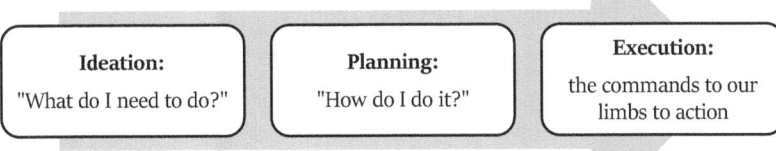

| Ideation: | Planning: | Execution: |
|---|---|---|
| "What do I need to do?" | "How do I do it?" | the commands to our limbs to action |

If you want to understand praxis in more detail, I recommend you watch the training by Teresa May-Benton "Ideation in Praxis: A New and Evolving Perspective" on YouTube.

In essence however, it involves active participation to develop movement (more complex awareness of the body within its environment) and using language to label (more specific language terms to support interoception.)

Whilst it is closely enmeshed with chunking and breaking things down to support executive function, there is a subtle distinction to be made with ideation in praxis and that is to use visual imagery *created by the pupil* to support their own conceptual development of the specific praxis you want them to master.

Whole class and/or individual support may require:

- *Improving active participation and language to label*
  - Ask pupil to draw the process in images (representation) and label (combining movement with language).
  - Explore the sequences involved, gradually working on greater complexity.
  - Make sure language is specific and highly descriptive to support mental imagery.
  - Repetition is crucial. If it's an immediate physical action, it needs to be practiced at least five times. Pupils may push back on the number of repetitions. The fourth time may look worse than before but this is part of the disorganisation/organisation process. By the fifth time, the actions should be more secure. If it's a complex written task, take it a step at a time and offer models, attempts with positive feedback to support accuracy and interoception.

---

**No Child Misses Out – Response Point 6.3: Supporting Sensory Integration (Hyper- and Hypoarousal)**

---

- *Improving visual perception skills (at home and at school)*

There are plenty of suggestions online for how to support sensory development so I will only note a few here as examples. The *Sensory Smarts* website and book with Lindsey Biel are both excellent and well-regarded. She also does webinars for schools.

Whole class and/or individual support may require:

- *Improving vestibular and proprioceptive skills*

  Building core stability and strength for balance

  - Kneeling on all fours, kicking out one leg backwards at a time
  - Press-ups against the wall
  - Pouring water from one cup to another
  - Wheelbarrow walking – walking on hands
  - Kicking a ball

- Jumping and hopping
- Crab walking
- Running
- Racket and ball games
- Throwing and catching
- Invest in play equipment for play spaces: climbing frames, balancing equipment, and a "trim trail" to build muscle strength.

Building Proprioceptive awareness of space

- Hanging from a bar
- Playing football
- Climbing ladders, wall ropes or bars
- Resistance training
- Games (jigsaws, board games) lying on tummy
- Trampolining
- Heavy work/muscle building activities (carrying piles of books)

Building hand and finger strength

- Playing with dough (knead, squeeze, roll, cut)
- Scrunch soft balls, squeezy toys, newspaper into balls
- Sharpen pencils
- Get dressed independently
- Cut up food with knife and fork
- Use pincers or chop sticks to pick up small items

- *Improving auditory and visual processing skills*
  This is covered in more detail in the chapters on phonological and visual processing, but don't forget that you could:

  - Consider trying pioneering therapies such as the Listening Program®, Forbrain, The Sound Therapy Site
  - Refer a child to a behavioural optometrist to explore ways to improve functional vision

- *Improving gustatory and olfactory processing skills*
  - See Chapter Nine where this is briefly covered.

If in doubt or if a child is in increasing distress, involve specialists:

- Refer to an Occupational Therapist to explore praxis (motor skills) and sensory integration in more detail.
- Refer to a Speech and Language Therapist and/or a Nutritionist if a child is struggling with food.
- Refer to a Clinical Psychologist or Mental Health specialist and consider the need social services involvement, if concerned.

- *Improving retained reflexes*

  Both *The Symphony of Reflexes* by *Bonnie L. Brandes* and *The Well Balanced Child* by *Sally Goddard Blythe* include physical activities and routines which have been developed to integrate the retained reflex. If you are interested in learning more about this, then please go to these books for their advice.

## Final thoughts: hypersensitivities, exceptional capabilities

There is an interesting parallel between exceptional intelligence and sensory hypersensitivity. If we think about some of the greatest talents in the world, we notice unusually perceptive senses. Alan Turing is known both for being the father of computing technology after cracking the impossibly complex German Enigma Code (saving fourteen million lives and reducing the length of World War by two years)[16] and also for his unusual behaviours, routines and personal preferences, which were not typical for the time. Temple Grandin, with hypersensitivities that led to challenging behaviours and being rejected from mainstream education, has gone on to become a hugely sought after animal behaviourist and livestock consultant, with global influence in the meat trade.

There is even emerging research to suggest that high intelligence is a *risk factor* for "psychological and physiological overexcitabilities",[17] highlighting that there is a potential association between a hyperbrain (high IQ) and a hyperbody (hypersensitivities); placing those with extraordinary sensory perceptions at higher risk for psychological "disorders" and "disease". Perhaps this corroborates Sir Francis Galton's observation of his own significant intellect and the reflections of "insanity" that he saw within it?

Even though, in adulthood, we might be able to recognise hypersensitivities as enormous strengths offering great potential, in school, with the rigidity of curriculum and timetables, sensory hypo- and hypersensitivities can pose significant learning and behavioural challenges. These we turn to next.

### Chapter Summary: Handwriting and Sensory Integration

- *Handwriting is a complex sensorimotor skill requiring coordination of multiple senses for accuracy and fluency.*
- *Good posture and balance, controlled by the vestibular system, are essential for sustained handwriting without constant rebalancing.*
- *Visual perception guides letter formation, spacing, and alignment, with difficulties leading to errors in handwriting.*
- *Proprioception helps regulate movement, pressure, and hand position, ensuring smooth and efficient handwriting.*
- *Proper pen grip and tactile feedback are crucial for comfortable, efficient handwriting, and pen choice can influence writing quality.*

- *The ability to cross the body's midline is vital for fluent writing, with limitations potentially causing compensatory body movements.*
- *Motor planning, or praxis, is necessary for coordinating movements during handwriting, with difficulties leading to issues like dyspraxia.*
- *Sensory integration combines input from multiple senses to perform coordinated actions like handwriting, requiring precision and timing.*
- *Children with sensory processing issues may experience hyper- or hyposensitivity, affecting their ability to regulate behaviour and complete tasks.*
- *Theories of sensory integration and retained reflexes are still debated, with limited evidence supporting their effectiveness in therapy.*

# 7 Executive Function

Eyes bulging, face contorted, mouth locked and loaded before I could intercede. Suddenly, my visiting parent deluged their son in a spray of vitriol and spittle: words weaponised to do maximum damage. The rifle burst lasted a handful of moments, perhaps only one breath, but it ended in a phrase I shall hear for the rest of my life: "Why are you such a frrrreeeak?!" The final word seemed to hang in the air, reverberating around the room like a gong.

Shock and panic flooded my brain and body. I couldn't reach out and catch those words midair; I couldn't edit them out of anyone's memories. Worse than expletives which can roll meaninglessly off the tongue, this felt so personal, so destructive; and all I'd got in my dumbstruck toolkit was a rather feeble but passionately meant recourse. "He is *not* a freak!" Then I paused, unsure of my next line; breathed, and thought "how on earth am I going to get everyone through to the end of this meeting safely, and out of my cupboard-now-office unscathed . . .?"

*

I expect you've sat in some very intense meetings in your role in education and have managed cases which stretch you to the limits of your emotional capacity at times. People behave in destructive and combative ways for many reasons; parents as well as pupils. As you'll know from the previous chapter, one possible cause of dysregulation comes from a lack of sensory integration through hyper- or hypoarousal, and difficulties with the tactile, vestibular and proprioceptive senses. In this chapter, we're going to focus on what's happening in the brain and its impact on both behaviour and learning. We're going to focus on what's called our *executive function*.

It is in fact the very same skillset which, when it is underdeveloped, or when it temporarily lapses, that can lead to human behaviour that breaks social and moral boundaries; when our rational calm brain is dysregulated and destructive primal instincts take control. It is also the same skillset that helps us to retain and organise information in the classroom. In fact, some argue that executive function is *more important than IQ* in terms of influencing academic outcomes, although in practice they are very closely related. Because of the depth and breadth of academic, social and emotional behaviours that it covers, I'm inclined to agree. As such, we're going to go a bit deeper into the context for development before looking at the presentation of EF in children and young people.

DOI: 10.4324/9781032663968-9

Before we begin though, I will start with a word of caution. This chapter is an uncomfortable read, at times. We will touch on research that might feel reductive and even discriminative. This is because our current understanding of executive function is heavily embedded within those themes we met in Chapter One: race, gender, socioeconomic status. And of all the dimensions we will cover in this book, I feel we still have a long way to go in understanding the complexity of this particular aspect of psychology. We need much more nuanced research and understanding into the impact of our biopsychosocial worlds on our executive function development, which is worth bearing in mind as we travel together through the next few pages. But we are where we are, with the map that we've currently got . . . so, let's jump in.

## What is executive function?

**Executive function (EF)** is an umbrella term which describes a whole host of processes which are "future focussed" – helping us to think about and prepare for what's next. It supports our overall level of success in life, covering the top-down regulation of our thoughts and behaviours. Schacter et al. (2020) compare it to our own personal Senior Leadership Team: managing our resources (time & energy), taking stock of what's going on, estimating what might be required in the near future, monitoring what is currently available, planning and executing a strategy and – very importantly – regulating subdivisions of our brains (some of which might be quite demanding at times) to run our bodies efficiently and competitively.[1] It's not dissimilar to *praxis* that we covered in the last chapter, although that is more focussed on carrying out the immediate task at hand, whereas executive function covers longer term strategy as well as immediate action. In practice however, it is likely that the two get confused easily because of such overlap. Whether it is coined executive function or praxis will likely depend on the experience of the observer.

That aside, it won't surprise you that better EF is linked to positive outcomes related to education, health and overall quality of life. In contrast, deficits in aspects of EF very often lead to poor progress in school, difficult peer relationships, reduced career prospects and engagement with the criminal justice system. In short, anything we can do to support the development of executive function is going to be helpful for pupils for the rest of their lives, affecting not just their personal future wellbeing, but generationally into their own children's futures, too.

Due to its obvious significance, executive function is increasingly a hotly researched topic, rapidly shifting and growing all the time as we continue to understand what it is and how it can be fostered. We've actually been studying and measuring it for about the last hundred years and, for now at least, researchers have begun to sub-divide it into two groups of functions: *hot* and *cool* (sometimes referred to as cold.)

Hot functions are those which swing into action to protect us. They interrupt something we're doing to make us switch priorities. Hot functions are biological imperatives or emotionally charged drives in-built for our own safety.[2] In a school context, pupils who have hot EF strategies in alignment with their age expectations will increasingly be able to sustain attention on a task without being distracted by something or someone else; switching focus[5] only when it's appropriate to context, like when the fire alarm goes off. They will also increasingly be able to refrain from calling out or from speaking too bluntly, by predicting its impact on others. Keeping their emotions under control, they stay calm under pressure. With developing empathy for peers, they use strategies to support themselves or others if they are feeling a bit wobbly or stressed. Finding increasing autonomy and physical control, they are able to protect themselves when they need to, but otherwise navigate play and social interactions successfully.

Conversely, cool functions enable us to keep focussed on the current problem. We use them to help us make logical choices, to remember what we need to do, to plan and execute a strategy.[3] We see these developing in pupils through their awareness and understanding of what they're reading or the step-by-step instructions of what they're doing. Pupils with age-appropriate cool EF will increasingly be able to plan out and manage the complex processes involved with handwriting a piece of extended work, to follow multi-step mathematical processes successfully, to hold several facts in mind and draw from long-term memory in order to complete a task well. They will be able to keep an answer in mind whilst calmly waiting with their hand up to be asked for their response. Pupils with well-developing cool EFs will increasingly have a sense of purpose, of competence, of growing independence and security within the world, using mistakes as ground for learning and seeing their trajectory as one of growth.

They're both really important skillsets, fundamental to our survival and life successes, but when facets of someone's EF are out of kilter or underdeveloped, they can lead to underachievement in school or worse. You can imagine that under-developed hot functions can cause children to be impulsive, hyperactive, and overly emotional; vulnerable in the classroom but especially so in less structured times like the playground. Underdeveloped cool functions are visible when completed work lacks structure or organisation; recall is insecure; that their maths is behind;[4] when they become easily deflated at small setbacks.

## How does executive function develop?

Given the complexity of the processes involved, there isn't an easy answer to how EF develops. Some say that hot and cool functions are separate entities from birth and develop at different rates;[5] others say that they are one construct in early childhood up until about age six, after which they then separate and develop at different rates (cold faster than hot).[6] Whichever side of the tracks psychologists find themselves, a widely held view is that they develop throughout childhood, with two peak times of intense development: *pre-school years and adolescence.*[7] The relevance of distinguishing these important developmental periods is because research is centring on how we can capitalise on these periods of plasticity to improve skillsets within school through targeted teaching and intervention.

This is a really important focus because research suggests that EF is largely stable across someone's life: that's to say, it's very hard to change its trajectory. However, we also don't know enough about why that might be, as the complexity of EF and their heterogenous origin and presentation in individuals can make it difficult to support precisely or to spot patterns. In short, there's more research to do and much more to learn.

There are however, some known factors about the optimum environmental context for their development and some functions which seem to have more influence on outcomes than others, which we'll explore together throughout the chapter.

## The context for development

Erik Erikson was an eminent psychologist who identified eight stages of psychosocial growth throughout our lives.[8] He believed in **the epigenetic principle** – that people grow in a sequence that occurs over time and within the context of a larger community. Erikson's theory of psychosocial development outlines eight stages, each marked by a central conflict that individuals must resolve to develop a healthy personality. These stages range from infancy to old age, addressing challenges like trust v. mistrust in early childhood, identity v. role confusion in adolescence, and integrity v. despair in later life. He argued that a sense of positive resolution in each stage comes from successful resolution of each conflict. Psychological growth would result. A negative resolution, on the other hand, may result in difficulties that continue to impact across the lifespan and affect later development.

> **Executive function:** Describes thoughts and behaviours which are future focussed, managing resources, being conscious of our surroundings, estimating needs, executing strategy and regulating the different parts of the brain.
>
> **The epigenetic principle:** People grow in a sequence that occurs over time and within the context of a larger community.

Paramount from the very start, infants must feel a sense of trust in their care-giver; that they will respond to their needs in a timely manner and that they are safe in their care. Once this is established, or not, the next phases (early childhood and pre-school) are where children should begin to gain a sense of autonomy and initiative; a growing sense that they are able to survive in the world. Barriers to the development of these positive feelings instead promote a sense of **shame**, self-doubt, excessive dependence on others leading to a sense of feeling like they're a problem. In particular, Erikson identifies toilet training and bladder and bowel control as a key indicator for a child's

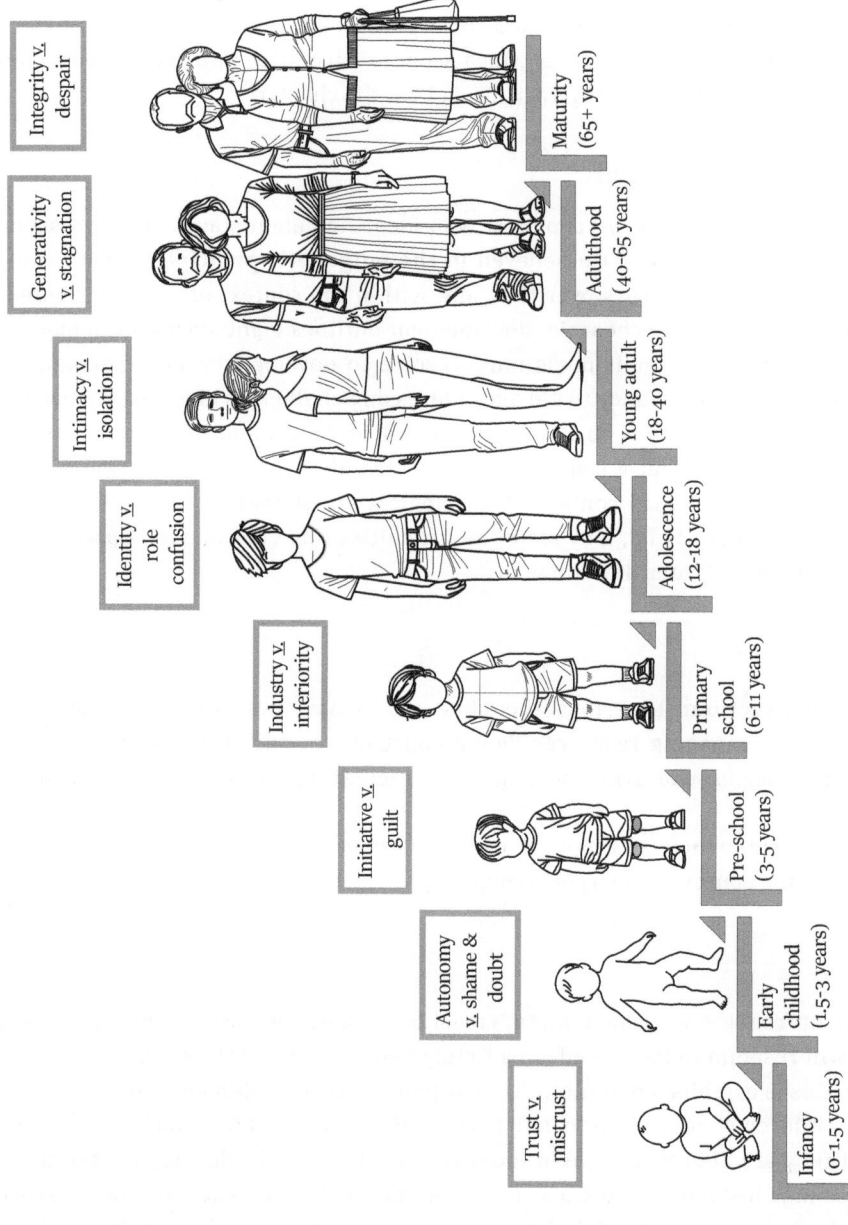

*Figure 7.1* A brief summary of Erikson's Stages of Psychosocial Growth[9]

| Stage | Successful completion of stage means: | Lack of progression means: |
| --- | --- | --- |
| Infancy | A warm, stable, loving and nurturing world. It is reliable and predictable. Trust. Hope. | A frightening, stressful, unreliable world. Emotional detachment. Distrust. Despair. |
| Early Childhood | Sense of personal choice and control (e.g. potty training). Increasing sense of survival chances. | Little sense of personal control. High criticism. Shame. Excessive dependence. Survival fears. |
| Pre-School | Feeling capable, secure and able to use initiative. A sense of purpose. | Feeling a nuisance to others, when criticised, controlled or questioned, preventing social ability. |
| Primary School | Displaying competencies admired by peers: literacy, numeracy and problem-solving. | Unable to perform specific skills. Low confidence in self to handle complex and novel situations. |
| Adolescence | Searching for personal identity, of future self. Beliefs, values, goals, personal power. | Inability to resolve questions about identity. Confusion, insecurity of where and how we fit. |
| Young Adult | Well-formed identity. Major relational conflicts but ultimately finding meaningful, lasting love. | Poor sense of self. Avoidance of or failure to form long-lasting bonds. Isolation. Depression. |
| Adulthood | Productive, of value. Making our mark on the world. Nurturing and pride in offspring. | Failure to "make a dent in the universe". Unproductive. Disillusioned. Disconnected. |
| Maturity | Wisdom of a life well lived. Integrity. Wholeness. Peace. | Despair. Regret over opportunities not taken. Incompleteness. Bitter. Frightened. |

own sense of self-perception and capacity at this stage. Success in this phase is largely in parent territory, supported by early years' providers, if children attend.

Given the notable developments of EF during the preschool years, research focus has been targeted towards understanding the effect of parenting practices. Lucasson et al. (2015)[10] have built upon the work of others to identify that parenting practice *does* have a significant impact on the development of children's execution function development; specifically in *updating* abilities to plan and organise, as well as to employ *inhibition* strategies. In particular, they have identified that *lower levels of maternal sensitivity* and a *harsher paternal parenting* style are risk factors for developmental delays in executive function.

To many of us, this perhaps won't come as a surprise. We have all met children whose behaviour was a concern and we have often seen these traits in their parent figures, too. As I mentioned at the start, there seem to be genetic components to executive function so it is likely that if a child struggles with impulsivity (hitting, shouting verbal abuse), then one or both of their parents did, or do, too. EF development therefore is likely to be cyclical and generational, which may go some way to explaining why change is so difficult because it'll be influenced both by genetics and by the home environment in which a child grows up.

**Shame:** Brené Brown describes shame as "the intensely painful feeling or experience of believing that we are flawed and therefore unworthy of love and belonging – something we've experienced, done, or failed to do makes us unworthy of connection." Brown, B. (2013, January 15). Shame v. guilt [Blog post]. Retrieved July 10, 2024, from https://brenebrown.com/articles/2013/01/15/shame-v-guilt/

**Attachment theory:** Coined by John Bowlby, it asserts that young children need to develop a relationship with at least one primary caregiver for their survival, and for healthy social and emotional functioning. Practitioners today consider there to be four different *styles* of attachment: secure, ambivalent, avoidant or disorganised-insecure. These are the result of research conducted by Mary Ainsworth, Mary Main and Judith Solomon.

## Parental investment

At this point, I think it's worth checking in with our animal cousins and having a look at parenting in the animal kingdom to review any parallels. In 1974, an evolutionary biologist Robert Trivers defined the term "parental investment" which he described as "any investment by the parent in an individual offspring that increases the offspring's chance of surviving"[11] In effect, you can only give what you have; you can only invest in something if you have the capital to invest in it in the first place. Motherhood in a baboon troop is a good example of this in practice.

In the baboon tribe, not all mothers are born equal. Status is immutable, inherited, and "laced with privilege",[12] with direct implication for the survivability of offspring. Children of higher-ranking baboons have mothers who are able to let them roam, safe in the knowledge that they are protected by their rank. Their privilege confers independence and safety upon them, allowing them to grow up in a relatively risk-reduced environment. Conversely, low ranking females have little social standing to protect their babies from threats within and beyond the troop; employing restrictive parenting styles which might result in a higher likelihood of survival through early childhood but that ultimately delay independence, placing more demand on the mother's own resources, for longer.[13] As zoologist Lucy Cooke, puts it: "Faced with a non-stop stress-fest of potential threats, low-ranking mums live life on perpetual high alert."[14]

This relationship between status, parental stress and child-rearing practice is relevant to the development of executive function in humans, too. What we also know about the development of EF is that you are more likely to have poor EF if you have been born to a mother with more of these risk factors: unmarried, on a low household income, young, has a low education level, uses or has used cigarettes, alcohol or drugs, did not breastfeed, or had the baby prematurely;[15] clearly demonstrating a socioeconomic influence within this list. This does not mean that executive function difficulties, or any other barriers to learning for that matter, affect *only* those with fewer economic and social resources, but they become *risk factors;* highlighting the cumulative impact of disadvantage on psychosocial development. (Feels a bit uncomfortable, doesn't it . . .?)

**No Child is Missed – Action Point 7.1: Screen for Social and Economic Risk Factors**

In terms of identifying which children may be exposed to visible and invisible social and economic risk factors, it is worth reviewing the following list, and any other local factors relevant to your setting. (To be clear, in noting these factors I am indicating that they can lead to children's educational needs being missed or misidentified, not making a value judgement on these as personal characteristics.)

- *Children born at the last four months of the academic year, which makes them younger and perpetually less developed than their peers*
- *Those born prematurely*
- *Children in foster care or who have been adopted*
- *Children with parents with significant chronic physical or mental health conditions*
- *Gender (female/questioning)*
- *Families with social care involvement*
- *Children flagged for safeguarding*
- *Single parent families, especially young mothers*
- *Multilingual learners*
- *Black, Minority Ethnic, Gypsy Roma Traveller children*
- *Children displaying challenging behaviours, at risk of exclusion*
- *Children with poor attendance*
- *Children who appear withdrawn*
- *Children with medical conditions*
- *Children of low socioeconomic status*

As well as socioeconomic status, what also stands out for me is that it shows how gender-specific the research has been to date. In genetic and developmental terms, maternal relationships are more measurable given this relationship pattern requires far greater investment into their offspring from the very start. Besides, it is obviously more difficult to observe and measure the impact of absent or transient parent figures. There is clearly more to do in this research arena however, thinking more closely about the context for maternal health and support which enables healthy child development and how barriers beyond a parent's control are strongly influencing the situation. Dr Katriona O'Sullivan writes a gripping autobiography about growing up in poverty and becoming pregnant during her GCSEs – it's well worth a read. She states, "There is a pervasive attitude that young mothers do not feel real love for their babies. That we have them to get flats or money or because we are lazy or vindictive. It's framed that way to dehumanise us because dehumanising the most vulnerable is a great way to excuse yourself from helping them."[16]

Both with humans and in the animal kingdom, twenty-first century researchers are trying to extract Victorian values and gender stereotypes from previous and current findings; to discover, as yet uncaptured, narratives influencing child development. Much needed. For now, however, we will consider some highly relevant and influential mother–child research from the 1960s: **attachment theory**.

Mary Ainsworth was a developmental psychologist who has been instrumental in early childhood research. Her Maternal Sensitivity Scales identified four areas which are impactful in a flourishing mother–child relationship. These are:

- *awareness of the child's signals* (learning their non-verbal cues)
- *accurate interpretation of these signals* (what those non-verbal cues mean)
- *an appropriate response* (acknowledging those cues and supporting the need)
- *in a timely manner* (being present, not distracted)

Her view of a "good mum" then was someone who can read body language and understand the different cries of their baby (hunger, tiredness, discomfort, loneliness) and who is able to provide for those needs appropriately and in good time. Conversely, lower maternal sensitivity might mean a young child is left without food or touch for long periods of time, in a dirty nappy, with little to look at or explore. In later childhood, when a child is more able and perhaps increasingly desperate to advocate for themselves, the resultant distrust from early experiences is likely to mean more fractured relationships with others as they seek to have their wellbeing needs met by trying to control the situations around them – and not always with success.

Further exploring EF in early childhood, Fay-Stambach (2014)[17] built upon our understanding of maternal–child relationships to identify three more areas which are fundamental to its successful development:

- *scaffolding* (giving support to develop independence, alongside verbal and physical prompts, praise and elaboration, and redirecting attention back to a task)
- *stimulation* (an engaging and interesting home environment with things to play with and do)
- *allowing a sense of control* (safe boundaries, allowing of mistakes and supporting measured risk)

In essence then, executive function develops well when a child is given interesting tasks to learn, think about and do which are appropriate to their level of current achievement (within their **ZPD**); they're not just left alone to get on with it, but instead prompted, encouraged, kept on task. They are not shouted at or ridiculed for making mistakes, they are encouraged to do new things and "fail forward". (It sounds just like a great classroom environment, too.)

What's clear is that the children who most need consistency in scaffolding, stimulation, sensitivity and a sense of personal control from parental investment are often the ones who have the greatest barriers to it; or as John D'Abbro, an experienced school leader in a challenging London school, puts it, "the ones who are hardest to love are often the ones who need your love the most".[18] It is easy to judge those in poverty, finding them as "undeserving" as they did in nineteenth-century Dickensian Britain. The reality of poverty is much more complex and multi-dimensional; and consequently, children who have had very little parental investment, of social and emotional as well as financial resources, need extra from someone else instead, or they'll be left behind. In reality then, where gaps of vulnerability exist, this means others have to fill them; people in public services like teachers, social workers, foster carers, healthcare providers.

To quote Rita Pierson, "Every child deserves a champion."[19] (And if you haven't watched her amazing TED talk, go and play it now!)

> **Zone of Proximal Development (ZPD):** A key construct in Vygotsky's theory of learning and development, it is the space between what a learner can do without assistance and what a learner can do with adult or peer guidance.

## Investment throughout childhood

At primary school, although decreasing over time, it is the classroom teacher and (if you're lucky to have one) the class teaching assistant who have a significant level of influence over children's development alongside their parents-carers. The same children with limited capital however, are also likely to have less investment at school through exclusion from social and academic learning as well as at home; risk factors start to mount up.

In many ways, it's understandable. Just like with their mothers, children with delayed or impaired executive function will be the ones who use up a lot of staff energy, often needing help to get started, to keep going, to access the curriculum and to avoid conflict. It is also really hard to invest more into a child or group of children in your classroom when resources are stretched, and especially when the evidence suggests returns are limited and that our highly limited teaching time could have more impact elsewhere. The challenge, of course, is that if we *don't* prioritise classroom investment into children at risk, then we definitely won't engage with the levers which could lead to change and growth. Given the impact of underdeveloped executive function is devastating for individuals and for society as a whole, at a group level it is a false economy. At the most extreme end, children who are permanently excluded from school each year will go on to cost the state an extra £2.1 billion in education, health, benefits and criminal justice costs.[20]

At the top end of primary and beyond into adolescence, influence on child development shifts quite considerably to that of peers, as future survival becomes dependent on acceptance and approval of others.[21] Therefore, it is our peers from whom we need most investment. We need to be validated and included into the pack where we will be sustained and developed through our inclusion: our acceptance will enable us to flourish academically and socially, with less fear of rejection. This is as true of us as it is baboons. Even amongst low-ranking baboons, females who have friends live longer and their offspring survive better.[22] And yet, if we haven't had a lot of parental or classroom investment, so we're operating below our age expectations in both (but particularly hot) EFs, we are less likely to be invested in by our peers as well; and almost certainly by those who have greater capital than us. It is an entirely understandable and judicious use of a child's personal resources to want to maximise their own return on investment by spending time with those who can offer them the greatest symbiotic relationship of growth and survival. The power of who you know and awareness of the potential of social connection begins very early.

The problem of course is that, as adults, we know that life isn't fair: barriers are often well beyond our own individual control. Many of us shun the unfairness of "the old boys' network", preferring to work towards a world which is more equitable; predicated on what you can offer, rather than who you know. Yet, this unconscious awareness of the cultural and social network starts really early and if we want to get on top of it, to develop executive function levels across the school and to cultivate a sense of belonging for all at the same time, we also need to engage meaningfully with the societal levers which are influencing it.

## What types of executive function difficulties are faced by pupils?

Earlier on, we met the idea of hot and cool functions which, together, make up what we understand as executive function. In particular, of the whole range of dimensions that make up hot and cool functions, three stand out in terms of enabling us to succeed more readily when completing tasks, and it's these we will focus on for screening.

- *Updating (working memory)*

Updating skills require strong **working memory** for tasks such as comprehension, planning, and organizing. Working memory is critical for academic success, as it allows us to hold and manipulate information over short periods of time, helping us to respond to questions methodically and accurately, because we can hold different pieces of information in our mind simultaneously and order them as needed for the task at hand.

Pupils with weak working memory will have barriers in doing this, particularly affecting their ability to sustain focus and attention, which is likely to impact upon their work completion rate. Interestingly, in echoes of the Alpha and Beta tests we met in Chapter One, research into working memory became of paramount importance during World

War Two. Psychologists at the University of Cambridge, such as Donald Broadbent, were set to evaluate the human ability to focus, attend to and process information in order to direct those with higher levels of focus and attention to become their newly trained RAF pilots. War creates an urgency to measure and maximise the mind.

The reason it is important to test for working memory is that inattention is often a silent barrier to learning. Pupils' needs can easily get missed. A weak working memory contributes to slower productivity, with greater need for checking and stopping, increasing the likelihood of forgetting, too. As a result, pupils with weak working memory may produce written work that is briefer or less well developed than others, affecting progress. More recently, psychologists in the CALM study, led by the University of Cambridge, identified that inattention poses the greatest risk to academic outcomes and future educational success.[23]

Weak working memory can cause particularly pronounced difficulties with maths, such as poor confidence in maths vocabulary, weak retention of maths facts, poor number sense and place value. Small but significant errors which carry through their workings, leading to the wrong answer. This can then affect student self-perception around maths confidence, leading to feelings of maths anxiety, too.

Pupils with poor working memory are likely to get very tired from school because of the sustained pressure on their memory, resulting in higher levels of stress from the school environment. Parents might describe them as having a limited range of subjects they enjoy, often more practical subjects which involve less intensive cognitive load. Whilst generally good natured, and having some friends, they may present as shy and lacking in confidence, perhaps less likely to put their hands up and draw attention to themselves, in case they're wrong or in case, when chosen to answer, they've forgotten what they wanted to say.

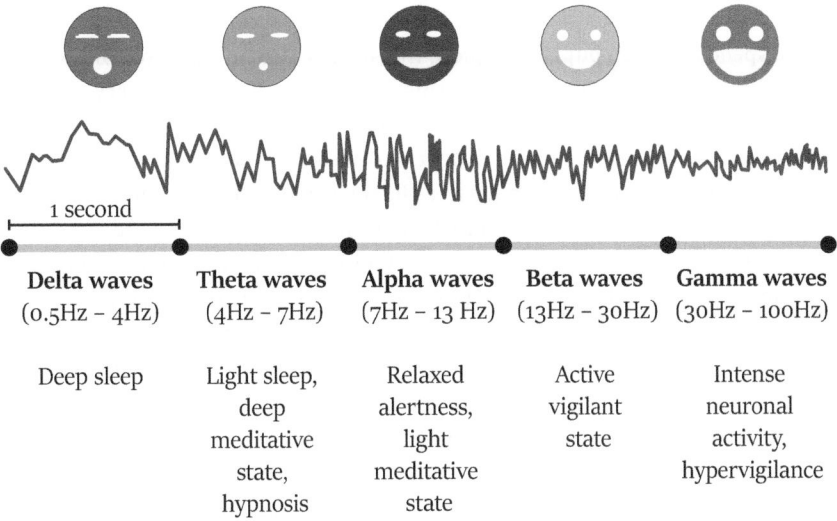

*Figure 7.2* The frequency of different brainwaves

From a neurological perspective, this type of pupil, whose attention and focus is affected by limited working memory, is likely to find it harder to get into and experience longer periods within "the learning zone" of *alpha* brainwave lengths – the frequency of brain waves pulsing through the brain optimum for relaxed but focussed learning. Instead, pupils with poor working memory may well have brainwaves found in a very relaxed state, more like that of a meditative state (the *theta* waves of being "zoned out"). This means less engagement with stimulation from the classroom; less learning.

In NCIM Action Point 7.2 you will learn more about testing for working memory. Below are my top tips when assessing for it.

**Working memory:** The ability we have to hold in mind and mentally manipulate information over short periods of time.

**Top Tips:**

- When a child is taking this test, you may notice a pattern emerging. We regularly see some children doing really well on one prompt and then getting the following one wrong. This seems to indicate difficulties maintaining attention and focus: zoning in and out. This can be particularly relevant if a pupil is naturally well-mannered and calm in class: their frequent inattention is invisible.
- You can also see evidence of impulsivity in this test, too. Listen out for the pupils who interrupt you before you've got to the end of the string of numbers. This is their inhibition getting the better of them. I always make a note of it by writing an "i" in a circle (like the © sign but with an i) each time it happens.
- The speed at which pupils complete this task is also an indicator of their speed of working. Some whizz through this test, others scrape the very crevices of their mind to recall information. Speed is not always an indicator of their level of accuracy, however. Some are fast and wrong, others can be slow and correct. I think the speed can sometimes be more indicative of their mental health and ability to cope with discomfort, than their memory competence.
- This test can occasionally provoke an emotional reaction in pupils. Although it seems quite a fun challenge to most, be mindful that for those with underlying anxiety or heightened stress responses, this task can be triggering. Noticing how a pupil is finding this test is important and using your professional instinct to judge whether to continue or to end the test early, perhaps trying again another day, is something to keep in mind.
- Hopefully what the above has taught you is to notice the pupil as well as their responses. You can learn a huge amount from just watching and observing *how* they complete a task.

## No Child is Missed – Action Point 7.2: Screen Working Memory (Updating)

In terms of assessing the size of a child's working memory, there are two key areas to look at. I tend to prioritise one over the other in a screening, purely for efficiency, but you can do both if you're keen to. How well does this young person perform in:

- Auditory recall
- Visual recall

**Appendix 5** directs you to a free working memory test and includes guidance for how to conduct two other relevant tests to assess executive function. The first is the *Turner Ridsdale Digit Memory Test* (you might also hear this kind of test referred to as a "digit span".) It is very simple to do and requires a pupil to recite numbers back to an assessor in the order that they heard them. It starts very easy with recalling just two numbers in the same order as the assessor says them, but steadily increases in difficulty as the strings of numbers lengthen. In the second test it gets a little trickier again, where pupils must recite the numbers back to an assessor in the *reverse* order. The more a child can hold in mind, the better they will be able to function in the classroom and the better they will do in their exams in the future.

The second test looks at visuo-motor memory and is based on *Luria's Theory* (1966, 1973). Again, the test itself is incredibly simple – although it needs a bit of practice. The assessor moves their hands through a series of sequences of either fist, edge or palm movements and the pupil's ability to follow these movements in order will guide you about their visual memory, physical control and general ability to follow a sequence. You may see a correlation between a weaker outcome in this test and a pupil's handwriting ability, too.

There are paid-for screening tools which you can use, too. One that we use regularly is a better version of the simple tests I have linked you to, above. The test we prefer for working memory is called the *Test of Memory and Learning (TOMAL)*. However, the *CTOPP*, which I have signposted in other chapters too, also has a sub-test which looks at auditory recall so you can access a memory test in the *CTOPP*, too. These are both specialist tests, however, so you'd need to have an additional qualification to purchase and use.

- *Inhibition*

Inhibition skills require being able to deliberately override dominant responses that conflict with an overall aim or goal, in particular resisting temptation. High self-control in toddlers and pre-schoolers is positively associated with a range of later outcomes including better academic skills, physical health, behavioural regulation, social competence and prosocial behaviour. Children whose inhibition control is more limited will struggle due to the more obvious "externalising" nature of their difficulties. These are the children who are more likely to get up and wander around the classroom when they're bored; to call out even when a teacher has asked for "hands up"; to be off-task communicating with people in the room during class discussions or focused work. In short, they're more likely to underachieve academically and also to get into trouble.

A more impulsive pupil will also have barriers to sustained focus and attention which are likely to impact upon their work completion rate. As such, their written work and maths skills are likely to be impacted in a similar way to those with purely weak working memory. Where you may start to see differences, however, is in the level of disorganisation of self and work; the poor punctuality to lessons, especially after a break or lunch, and to school itself. During lessons, they call out, particularly in higher-stakes and tense situations like an inter-class competition or quiz, and seek out constant stimulation from what's going on around them. They fidget. Sitting still for too long is difficult to cope with.

Thinking about the frequency of their brain waves, pupils whose attention and focus is affected by limited working memory and who display impulsive behaviours are also likely to find it harder to get into and remain within "the learning zone" of *alpha* brainwave lengths. They are, however, also too readily at risk of accelerating beyond the alpha zone into *beta* and *gamma* states, which we associate with excitement, heightened perception and increased speed of response. There are benefits to this state for all of us, most often in time-pressured situations which are critical to survival. We gain heightened perception through hypervigilance; our muscles contract ready to spring into action and our visual field narrows so we can focus on the threat at hand. Heightened perception is important at certain times, but it is not helpful as a normative state for learning. T*oo alert* and we'll find our pupils *too* quick to respond, *too* quick to judge, not thinking deeply enough. A person who operates regularly in a beta or gamma state is more likely to "feel alive" and purposed but they're also more likely to find it difficult to relax back down again, too, finding themselves in a vicious cycle of over- and under-stimulation. Long term states of hyperarousal can lead to poor mental and physical health – it's called chronic stress.

Socially, children who readily experience overstimulation can get themselves into scrapes too, because they are also likely to be the children who speak before they think. This means they have a tendency to interrupt or offend people, and unchecked, this can be perceived as dominance and unkindness. They disrupt the flow of conversation and a sense of safety. Children may become wary over time of this unpredictable classmate. We often see cases of bullying arise around pupils with impulsive behaviour – both because they are vulnerable to manipulation (why get told off for disrupting the boring lesson you're in when you can just nudge your impulsive classmate and he'll do it for you?) and also because they're vulnerable to their own speed and lack of sensitivity in social communication. It can be difficult to work out the underlying influences in a situation of bullying because of this seemingly symbiotic relationship.

What also tends to happen, because we're hard-wired for connection, is some children who are impulsive may adapt their behaviours to become the "class clown". If they cannot have a meaningful friendship like most others seem to be able to master naturally just by being themselves, then goofing around to get a laugh or two is the next best thing. This may make them more popular, which is a really positive coping mechanism (or as psychologists would say, an "adaptive response"), but it may also continue to be a risk factor for being perceived as attention-seeking by pupils and staff alike. We are all dopamine hunters – we enjoy doing things that make us feel good and we seek them out. Negative attention is still better than no attention at all. Rewarding behaviour patterns, adaptive or not, can easily become entrenched.

Parents might describe them as having a limited range of subjects they enjoy – they love the ones they love and can focus in (the stimulation boost they're looking for) and the rest they are much less inspired by. Pastoral or Key Stage leaders might see this too, looking at how a pupil's behaviour or progress shifts across the topics or the timetable. Whilst generally good natured, and having some friends, they may occasionally get into conflict in unstructured times because their impulses get the better of them from name-calling or getting themselves into social scrapes. At home, parents-carers may notice that they regularly struggle with insomnia (taking longer than an hour to get to sleep).

---

### No Child is Missed – Action Point 7.3: Screen for Impulsivity (Inhibition)

Maladaptive impulsivity is quite easy to sense, especially if you know a group of children well, and often even when carrying out a short observation. If you are in the latter camp, it is better to observe a pupil in several different lessons otherwise you risk being influenced by the level of interest they have in the task they happen to be doing and/or the time of day. (It's much easier to resist temptation and override a dominant response if you're enjoying what you're doing, or if you've just had a snack.) It is often helpful to take a look at their classwork in terms of work completion and organisation.

In order to assess impulsivity, **Appendices 7 & 8: Observation Forms (EYFS & Early Primary; Upper Primary & Secondary)** are helpful in guiding you about what to look for and to note down relevant information for any future referrals you might make. You can also consider asking young people, parents and/or teachers to complete the *Strengths and Difficulties Questionnaire (SDQ)* which can give you some guidance about how elevated certain behaviours are within someone's profile. If you are completing formal paperwork for an assessment, you may be asked to complete the *Vanderbilt* or the *Connors* questionnaires. These can be helpful for internal monitoring too although scoring is not available unless you purchase the tests, which are restricted. It is worth exploring sleep habits in your conversations with pupils and parents as this can be enlightening, too.

There are a couple of quite fun tests you can do to assess impulse control but I am not advocating adding them to your screening battery for ethical and practical reasons. However, because I think you'll enjoy them I thought I would introduce you nonetheless so you can have a go for yourself, reflecting on how hard you find them.

The first is the *Colour-Word Stroop Task* – a classic test from 1935, well established as a measure of executive function. It requires the participant to say the *colour* of the word rather than the word itself. E.g. imagine the word "yellow" but printed in the colour blue. The challenge is to say "blue" not "yellow". There are plenty of versions online if you want to have a go. They're tricky but fun! Have a look at Neuroscience For Kids - stroop effect (https://faculty.washington.edu/chudler/words.html).

The second is a test that has been used with pre-schoolers is the *Marshmallow test*. A child is offered a smaller reward now (a marshmallow) or a bigger reward fifteen minutes later, testing whether they can delay their gratification. The adult then leaves the room and waits, returning to assess whether they've decided to eat the marshmallow or not. A follow-up study identified that those children who held out for the greater reward were more successful academically in later years. I'd like to think I'd be able to hold out – but I'm not so sure in the final weeks of another busy term. What about you? Finally, there is the Go-No Go test which I've included in **Appendix 5** if you want to try.

- *Shift*

Children who can adapt to the needs of the moment, who are flexible and can cope with change to ordinary routines and expectations, are more likely to feel relaxed in a classroom or the playground. They can manage the internal noise which is naturally elevated in all of us during novel and unexpected experiences; they can self-soothe and reassure, helping to navigate the situation. These children are able to shift focus and demeanour as required by the situation, with cognitive flexibility. Conversely, challenges we will observe in children who struggle with *shift* can be seen in their rigidity of thinking. For example, being less able to consider alternative approaches, strategies or views, and often insisting on their own preferred method or opinion – whether it is correct or not. You will also notice a preference for sameness over change, which will come to the fore at transitions between tasks, or lessons and breaks. Just because the clock says we should move on, does not necessarily mean someone with shift difficulties will be happy or ready do so.

This need for sameness can also be observed in a desire to persevere with a conversational topic, even when it is no longer of interest to the listener. The fascination for particular topics can lead to exceptional knowledge; and this same intensity of focus can also be seen in all-consuming maladaptive rumination about situations, either past or future, at times leaving little space for anything else. For example, you might notice a pupil is obsessively concerned about what others would perceive to be a mildly stressful situation taking place later in the day (a class recital or an unknown visitor) which domineers their every thought, leaving them unable to move on. In pupils who internalise their emotions, these all-encompassing feelings can lead to overwhelm and avoidance. In pupils who externalise their emotions, the largeness of these feelings can lead to outbursts, when frustration or panic occurs if expectations are not met.

Difficulties with cognitive flexibility can result in reluctance to try something new or in difficulty transferring skills from one context to another. Because of the need for high levels of control within the environment, often as a result of the anxiety which comes from unpredictability or risk of the unknown, children may experience social communication difficulties, struggling with the flow, turn-taking, asking questions to explore other people's views. Playing games on the playground, particularly ones which adapt in free-flow, like shoals of fish changing direction, are confusing and can therefore seem threatening. Likewise, someone "not sticking to the rules" of play, can quickly instigate emotional outbursts and overwhelm. Without interoception and opportunities to calm, situations can quickly escalate between classmates and between child and teacher. The unchanging nature both in the rigidity of the situation and their frequency can make these cases very complex to navigate.

Struggling with interpreting social cues, change and being flexible, their journey through school(s) can be punctuated by absconding during the day and absence from school – whether by overwhelm or exclusion. Without really careful handling, relationships between school and home risk becoming both fraught and/or unresponsive, too; trust eroding, sometimes beyond repair. In terms of brain waves, these pupils are more likely to experience extremes of hypo- and hyperarousal states. Sometimes it might mean pupils self-stimulate (known as "stimming") to help them access a calm and ready state. It also means we need to help them access this state through the classroom and school environment: spaces that are calm, focused, warm and safe, with minimal additional distractions.

Of the three presentations, this is perhaps the most challenging to support – highly demanding for both teachers and pastoral teams. Practitioners may choose to use sensory integration techniques discussed in the previous chapter, and/or to use standard **behaviourist principles**, and this is likely to be dependent on the overall resources, approaches and policies within the setting. Despite best endeavours, practitioner time in education is extremely limited and the regular and high demand on resources that difficulties with cognitive inflexibility can present, can quickly take professionals into deficits of time and resource. The limited time and flexibility we have can directly influence the level of empathy and compassion we are able to demonstrate.[24] Behaviours that are either a risk to the health and safety of the community, or that require significant staff intervention and resolution are often too high-stakes to allow for long, given their impact on the resources available to everyone else. The older the child, and the more physical risk they present to others, the smaller the window of opportunity.

Research suggests that the most aggressive pupils are often filled with shame and self-doubt.[25] Years before, they would likely have been Erikson's little pre-schoolers struggling to progress through his psychosocial stages, with few social opportunities to build trusting and safe relationships. If we can identify vulnerabilities through screening before the risks increase through age and stage, we stand a chance of improving some-one's future life chances and experiences. When I think back to the traumatic meeting that we opened the chapter with, and beyond the memory of that moment, I can see the shadows of this parent's early childhood: feelings of shame, worries for the future, insecurity, failure. I wonder what might have happened if someone had tested and then invested in them sooner? I wonder if that meeting would have happened at all . . . In screening for executive function skills, we give ourselves opportunities to try.

One thing is for sure: there is still plenty more to learn in terms of executive function and how we can support its development, both in educational settings, and in societal support structures for reducing vulnerability. Let's take a look at what you can imple-ment in your setting to try and make a difference.

**Behaviourism** (also known as **operant conditioning**): A method of teaching and learning that uses rewards and punishment to modify behaviour. This is a typical approach used in schools globally. It works on the principle of stimulus–response, where an unpleasant response (e.g. detention) should reduce an unwanted behaviour (e.g. disobedience); and likewise, a pleasant response following a desirable behaviour (e.g. a commendation after an excellent piece of work.).

### No Child is Missed - Action Point 7.4: Screen Shift

Shift, or rather, inflexibility is quite easy to sense and observe too. Again, talking to class teachers and using **Appendices 7 & 8: Observation Forms (EYFS & early Primary; Upper Primary & Secondary)** as well as asking young people, parents and/or teachers to complete the *Strengths and Difficulties Questionnaire (SDQ)* will give you some guidance about how elevated certain behaviours are within someone's profile. If you are completing formal paperwork for an assessment, you may be asked to complete the *Vanderbilt* or the *Connors* questionnaires. These can be helpful for internal monitoring too although scoring is not available unless you purchase the tests, which are restricted.

There are two others you might have come across, regularly used in schools, and these are the *Boxall Profile* and the *Pupil Attitudes to Self and School (PASS)*.

Whichever tool you use, analysing what might be going on will help you plan a strategy going forward.

There are other ways to gather this information, such as playing board games or working as a team to build Lego® construction kits. I would particularly recommend playing the card game UNO, which is both really good fun and simple to learn, but is also designed to stimulate intense emotional responses that require pupils to cope with changing directions, unpredictable card play and tricky social situations. Clearly, putting any child into a potentially stressful situation needs to be really carefully considered, but you are likely to notice which children struggle more with shift when you play a game like this.

## No Child Misses Out: What to do next . . .

> **No Child Misses Out – Response Point 7.1: Supporting Socioeconomic Risk Factors**

Thinking about the risk factors which can lead to vulnerability doesn't necessarily afford simple and easy solutions to try. Given the complexity of context associated with these risk factors, it is important to engage with these vulnerabilities within their context, looking to underpin or engage wider support structures with advice, guidance or resources to support. Accessing advice and guidance from your local social care services will be a good place to start. Broadly though, this is a complex and wide-reaching field of focus. Reducing socioeconomic risk factors is a topic we'll return to in greater detail in Chapter Eleven.

> **No Child Misses Out – Response Point 7.2: Supporting Working Memory (Updating)**

In terms of supporting weaker updating skills, the adults in the classroom need to become an external source of executive function, modelling cold functions in practice.

Classroom distractions can severely impact working memory, especially for children with limited cognitive capacity. Minor noises or movements can rapidly overwhelm their attention, leading to deficits in focus and learning. This is why a well-managed classroom, with clear behaviour expectations and minimal distractions, is essential for those with the most learning barriers. However, it's equally important for teachers to show compassion, acknowledging that maintaining focus is harder for some students than others. Balancing high behavioural expectations with empathy is key to fostering a supportive learning environment. A culture of high expectations as well as warm and encouraging relationships can seem paradoxical. It *is* possible but it is challenging to get that balance right, too. With the high number of relationships in any given classroom, under the constraints of a fast-paced and challenging curriculum, especially in a stressed education sector, getting the balance right takes a great deal of skill.

Internal distractions also play a role in limiting working memory. Noise from our internal senses, our interoception, can disrupt short-term recall, especially when tasks are too difficult or when there is time pressure. Faced with overwhelming tasks, students may struggle to break problems into manageable parts, leading to mistakes and mental blocks. Similarly, when multiple tasks demand attention simultaneously, such as in handwriting, cognitive overload can reduce the ability to recall important information. As we'll explore in the next chapters physical and mental health also contribute to the internal noise that affects working memory and executive function.

Strategic, whole class and/or individual support may require:

- *Scaffolding: supporting autonomy and growth*
    - ○ Regular reminders and instructions available to check
    - ○ Visual examples of work to be achieved (e.g. model answers)
    - ○ Curriculum architecture: context, design, structure and sequence of a curriculum which builds upon prior learning and connects schemas
    - ○ Mixed-ability grouping and seating for opportunities to share capital outside of social and academic norms, improving the chances of peer investment
    - ○ Balancing cognitive load – scaffolding tasks so that success is carefully carved into consciously designed steps, supporting limited working memory.
- *Stimulation: enabling focus and fostering self-confidence in learning*
    - ○ Regular prompts to help someone stay in the alpha zone, e.g. seated at the front of the class
    - ○ Knowledge-rich curriculum to support cultural capital
    - ○ Questioning for understanding and for engagement
    - ○ Retrieval practice, spaced practice and interleaving so that long-term memory is capitalised to underpin working memory limitations
    - ○ Desirable difficulties – finding and capitalising upon pupils' Zone of Proximal Development
    - ○ Fostering a love of learning – building in opportunities for celebration, recognition and self-confidence to grow motivation
- *Sensitivity: appropriately responding to pupil need in a timely way*
    - ○ Assessment for learning – heightened sensitivity to the learning needed for the next lesson – who got it, who didn't, and what to do to help change that
    - ○ Providing access arrangements for learning and application, e.g. rest breaks and/or extra time to complete work to the standard, typing instead of handwriting
    - ○ Quality feedback which moves learning forward
    - ○ Sensitive and safe teacher-pupil relationships – consciously building psychological safety
- *Sense of control: emotional safety, measured risk, clear and consistent boundaries*
    - ○ Clear and practiced organisational and behavioural routines which determine expectations for all, whilst also investing social capital into those whose executive functions are underdeveloped

- ○ Clear expectations for the lesson in terms of tasks, as age-appropriate – Now & Next/visual timetable/sharing a brief plan for the lesson at the start
- ○ Fostering sensitive and safe peer-to-peer relationships
- ○ Opportunities and emotional safety for reflection, remorse and restoration, not ongoing and unresolved resentment

Those working with children and families in a pastoral capacity, may also help by trialling the following:

- *In-school additional support*
  - ○ Storing and accessibility of equipment, e.g. in a locker
  - ○ Spare correct uniform and PE Kit
  - ○ Readily accessible lesson and homework timetables wherever is commonly visible e.g. laminated in pocket or saved as a screensaver on their phone
  - ○ Access to homework club
- *Advice and support for parents-carers*
  - ○ Have a school timetable on the fridge and a Bring-to-School list on the front door
  - ○ Pack bags the night before
  - ○ Have a homework timetable
  - ○ Have access to a quiet workspace (at home or nearby)
  - ○ Have a place to hang uniform and keep shoes
  - ○ Have a morning and an evening routine which has times and tasks to follow
  - ○ Listening to binaural beats on YouTube or Spotify to support focus in independent work (music which aims to regulate the brain waves into an alpha state) – this one is new advice and there's still a lack of strong evidence for it but it's worth trying I reckon (listening to music on Spotify isn't going to harm)
  - ○ Consider seeking medical assessment for inattention and using stimulant medication to support, e.g. Ritalin
  - ○ Have medication in school and someone to go to who can manage and administer medication
  - ○ Encourage parents-carers to explore sleep hygiene as there is plenty of research which overwhelmingly indicates a link between poor sleep and attention deficit[26]

---

**No Child Misses Out – Response Point 7.3: Supporting Impulsivity (Inhibition)**

---

Just like with updating skills, the adults in the classroom must also be the external source for executive function, modelling the hot functions that children with impulsivity do not have so well developed.

Although measuring brainwaves, as I introduced earlier (see Fig. 7.2), might seem very far from current classroom practice, I believe the future of interventions for this profile will increasingly involve this, because the frequency of someone's brainwaves is a clear indicator of what's going on in the brain. The more we can do to support brain-wave patterns to stabilise and regulate, the better we are likely to be able to support the growth of executive function.

Strategic planning, whole class or individual support may require:

- *Scaffolding: supporting autonomy and growth*
    - A diverse curriculum with opportunities to demonstrate physical and creative skills
    - Teaching to support regulation emotions by naming the physical feeling in the body ("my throat feels tight"); breathing three slow deep breaths; pausing and accepting ("I feel upset right now and it's ok for me to be upset"); moving (walk/star jumps/bounce); pausing until in a better frame of mind to make decisions[27]
    - Opportunities for deep relaxation: yoga, art club, mindfulness, choir, running club
- *Stimulation enabling focus and fostering self-confidence in learning*
    - Seated away from distractions (windows, noises, people) with enough space around them
    - Careful positioning of pupil in class and exam hall if impulses (tics) distract others or cause the individual shame and embarrassment, reducing their focus during exams
- *Support: appropriately responding to pupil need in a timely way*
    - Keep the window open where possible for greater access to oxygen
    - Support for regulating emotions using co-regulation tools
- *Sense of control: emotional safety, measured risk, clear and consistent boundaries*
    - Opportunities to be able to leave the classroom for a mini-break to help calm the body if over-stimulated (e.g. a toilet break) or if not a safe option, given a responsibility for a role in the class which involves movement.

Those working with children and families in a pastoral capacity, may also help by trialling the following:

- *In-school additional support*
    - As working memory support, and
    - A safe space to escape to in school when feeling stressed/overwhelmed
    - Exploring trigger points in the day and thinking about adaptations and supports (Red/Amber/Green days/times/subjects to understand patterns of behavioural challenge)
    - An opportunity to have a mini 1:1 check-in and review with the class teacher or pastoral lead regularly throughout the day (metacognition and direct feedback)
- *Advice and support for parents-carers*
    - Have a school timetable on the fridge and a Bring-to-School list on the front door
    - Trying neurofeedback: a tool to improve brain regulation, measuring brainwave

activity through EEG and then engaging the brain in tasks which enable the brain to self-regulate into more natural brain rhythms

- o   Putting restrictions onto phone to avoid digital disruptions (e.g. Engross App, change the phone's interface to black and white rather than colour etc.)
- o   Using Pomodoro Technique for homework
- o   Support for sleep: regular routine, reading or listening to an audiobook, lavender pillow spray, white noise, head stroking, Melatonin (see GP) – reference ADHD report advice
- o   Support regular exercise to support concentration
- o   Keep the home environment supportive and encouraging.
- o   Keep time on digital devices to a minimum, particularly before bed and overnight (no phones or gaming in bedroom)
- o   Reduce in-take of caffeine, sugar and other stimulants several hours before bed
- o   Consider seeking medical assessment for hyperactivity and using stimulant medication to support e.g. Ritalin
- o   Having medication in school and someone to go to who can manage and administer medication

---

**No Child Misses Out – Response Point 7.4: Supporting Cognitive Inflexibility (Rigidity, Aggression, Problematic Peer Relationships)**

---

In terms of supporting cognitive flexibility skills, the adults in the classroom need to model the shift skills, that children do not have so well developed. This takes conscious effort to fight natural instinct because when a child or young person is being aggressive, it is only natural to engage our own self-defence strategies by mirroring the behaviours we are encountering, to square up and begin a power struggle. This, however, only risks escalating the situation. What adults *actually* need to do is employ de-escalating strategies to reduce the risk of further conflict which could cause significant harm.

Strategic, whole class and/or individual support may include strategies like those proposed by the Education Endowment Foundation (EEF) review of improving behaviour (2019) in schools:[28]

- • *Scaffolding: supporting autonomy and growth*
  - o   Extended transition opportunities (additional to the normal plans for most pupils) such as meeting new teachers before the academic year begins, having a tour of the school campus, spending time really understanding what a timetable looks like, including timings and safe places to go during unstructured times, where to go if you need help
  - o   Having access to a new timetable as early as possible to prepare for change

- o   Being alerted to possible changes in the day (especially cover teachers) and planning for support in the disruption where possible. Cover teachers also need a brief update about these pupils prior to taking on a class.
- o   Careful planning of group and paired work, with psychologically safe peers
- o   Really clear and consistent structures to a lesson, including how the lesson will progress and what will signal the end is coming
- o   Teaching and modelling how to behave and the behavioural norms you want to foster in class
- *Stimulation: enabling focus and fostering self-confidence in learning*
  - o   Regular and plenty of genuine praise and support
  - o   Knowledge and use of a pupil's name with conscious warmth directed towards the pupil (**unconditional positive regard,**[29,30])

> **Unconditional positive regard:** Initially developed by Stanley Standal (1954) and then expanded upon and embedded by Carl Rogers (1956), it is a person-centred approach which centres on the basic acceptance and support of a person regardless of what they say or do. This is because this humanist approach is founded on the principle that in order to have a facilitative and reciprocal relationship, the practitioner (teacher) must consider the individual (pupil) to have within them "vast resources for self-understanding, for altering [their] self-concept, attitudes, and self-directed behaviour" – that they have what it takes to understand and to adapt.

- *Sensitivity: appropriately responding to pupil need in a timely way*
  - o   Circulating the classroom to check in on pupils, anticipating problems in advance and resolving difficulties and frustrations early to avoid escalation.
- *Sense of control: emotional safety, measured risk, clear and consistent boundaries*
  - o   Enabling a limited and structured choice within a lesson so that tasks are not too loose but a pupil can also navigate through anything they perceive to be difficult with a sense of control.
  - o   Having a key person to check in with regularly throughout the day, who is psychologically safe, allowing for mistakes, enabling reflection and facilitating restoration
  - o   Establish-Maintain–Restore method
  - o   Consistently applying the school's behaviour policy
  - o   Reflecting on the Incredible Years Teaching Pyramid® – to review the frequency of your individual or school approaches and their impact on pupil behaviours
  - o   Reinforcing positive behaviours through recognition
  - o   Building relationships through simple actions of friendliness and warmth, e.g. greeting pupils at the door
  - o   Maintain a far higher ratio of praise to criticism (5:1)

Those working with children and families in a pastoral capacity, may also help by trialling the following:

- *In-school additional support*
    - Asking how school can help with life at home (advice, practical support)
    - Having a safe space for pupils to go to regain self-control, so if they need to run, they have somewhere safe to run to. This also reduces the time that staff might spend searching the school site.
    - Additional curriculum spaces and courses to enable life skills, such as, a girls' groups to support secure friendships and positive behaviours towards each other, try *Girls on Board*
    - Boys' groups to support the development of identity and safe behaviours, try *10 Dialogues* created by *Men At Work cic* or *YES Matters UK*
    - Social skills groups, using resources like *Talkabout*
    - Emotional regulation support, using resources like *Zones of Regulation*

*A word about gender and small group interventions . . .*

The concept of gender is an area of global transition. Each school will be on their own journey with this, along with the pupils themselves. Some schools feel they need and want separate groups to meet a specific need, but you may want to avoid gender stereotyping through having separately gendered-groups and focus on the needs specifically. Only you will know what you feel is right for your setting.

Individual support may require:

- An individualised course with the group resources mentioned above
- Working with parents-carers to develop vocabulary awareness and practicing scenario work at home
- Further assessment by an Occupational Therapist
- Further assessment by a Speech and Language Therapist
- Further assessment by an Educational Psychologist
- Considering trying pioneering therapies such as the Listening Program®, Forbrain, The Sound Therapy Site
- *Advice and support for parents-carers*
    - Nutritional support (signposting to cost-effective and healthier recipes; you might even be able to develop a relationship with a local supermarket to give away unsold produce or have a local foodbank nearby which can help)
    - Signposting to/host parenting support programmes targeting troublesome areas (e.g. bedtimes, disagreements, sibling rivalry, managing split households, relationships with step-parents etc.). I particularly like Dr Siggie on Instagram.
    - Conversations at home exploring the Five Love Languages and personal preferences
    - Conversations about personal space and sense of control at home: what works, what's problematic

- o   External Agency Referral for Family Support: social services, youth offending, third sector youth workers
- o   When trust between school and home is deteriorating, exploring parental aspirations and hopes for their child, shared values and use of Brené Brown's BRAVING inventory
- o   Encouraging mental health access for parents-carers who are struggling
- *Supporting the growth and maintenance of prosocial behaviours within our school communities*

There are important actions to take at whole school level such as reflecting on school policies, systems, expertise and practice:

- o   Anti-bullying
- o   Positive behaviour (staff as well as pupils)
- o   Mental health
- o   Effective safeguarding and child protection
- o   Multi-agency working
- o   Approaches to relieving the effects of poverty on families
- o   Personal, social, health, sex and relationships policies

## Final thoughts: How's the water?

> *Two young fish are swimming along and they happen to meet an older fish swimming the other way. "Morning, boys, how's the water?"*
> *The two young fish swim on for a bit, and then eventually one turns to the other and says, "What the hell is water?"*[31]

We've talked a lot about environment and its influence on child development in this book, and in this chapter especially. But what do we really mean by it? What should we be noticing or thinking about?

American psychologist Urie Bronfenbrenner described our environment as "a set of nested structures, each inside the next"[32] and that a child is affected by these many interconnected systems which revolve around them. At the centre is their individual family, their school, their friendships and immediate care providers (including doctors, dentists and wraparound care). This microsystem is bi-directional (the parts influence each other). Beyond this, we see wider influences impacting upon the child (mass and social media, the opportunities provided by the local area, parent workplace cultures) and beyond that, the macrosystem (gender, cultural norms and identities, education, health and social care systems, socioeconomic factors). The outside structure of our environment is affected by time, both in terms of a child's lived experiences (getting a phone or a gaming device, losing a relative, puberty) but also the time in which they live (global pandemic, war, change of government etc.).[33] All of these systems can affect child development to greater or lesser extents, which makes discerning the influence of any individual environmental factors very challenging. Are we looking at correlation or causation?

Bronfenbrenner was clear: these environmental systems are often more influential than the innate potential within a child. Tying that down precisely with a child you are working with might feel much more convoluted, however. Nevertheless, this should cause us as educationalists to pause and reflect. What are we really trying to change when we're working with a child who is struggling?

As teachers, we like to think we are in the "growth" business, fostering and maximising potential. This sense of purpose and development is critical to maintaining confidence in our everyday practice in education. After all, if growth isn't possible, we might as well give up and go home. But, when a child is struggling – particularly with something like hyperactivity or shift difficulties, which can be so hard to manage in a classroom of thirty – sometimes it is really hard not to conflate growth with "fixing" people. But is it the child or the environment that actually needs "fixing"? Medicating for executive function problems may help in the short-term, but is it ethically appropriate to focus solely on the child's problems when there is considerable evidence to suggest that they are closely linked to a child's environment?

Being aware of this environment – the water in which we're swimming – can help us to look beyond the child to the systems which might also be at play. This broader perspective can help us to recognise that growth is often about supporting the structures around a child, not just the child themselves. When we think about the power of investment and its generational implications on executive function, for example, we may feel compelled to think about how we can channel better investment into children and families as part of our in-school approaches. After all, if we have invested properly and understood the risks affecting our future generations, we are protecting their growth. Education then becomes about fertilising and pruning healthy children. But if, as a society, we have not sufficiently invested in child development by preventing known risks and building structures that support healthy growth, then we are forced to try and fix what has inevitably gone wrong – with far less success. Education then becomes about "closing gaps" and "restoration", which has a distinctly "fixy", child-centred focus about it.

If children's outcomes and behaviours are the result of their complex biopsychosocial environment, then when we think about executive function, we must stop to notice the water around us.

*

*This chapter covers huge ground and many vast concepts I have named only in passing. If you would like to engage in further reading, research and reflection, here are some resources to look at. You may also wish to refer to research explored in the previous chapter around sensory integration, too.*

- *Childhood and society*; and *Identity: Youth and crisis*, Erik Erikson
- *Cognitive Load Theory*, John Sweller
- *Cleverlands: The secrets behind the success of the world's education superpowers*, Lucy Crehan
- *Making kids cleverer: A manifesto for closing the advantage gap*, David Didau

- *Memorable teaching,* Peps Mccrae
- *Retrieval practice,* Kate Jones
- *Desirable difficulties*, Robert Bjork
- *Powerful questioning,* Michael Chiles
- *Embedded formative assessment, 2nd Edition (2018),* Dylan Wiliam
- *Rosenshine's Principles in action,* Tom Sherrington
- *The fearless organization: Creating psychological safety in the workplace for learning, innovation and growth,* Amy C. Edmondson
- *The Excludables,* Kat Stern
- *They don't behave for me,* Sam Strickland
- *Better behaviour/leading better behaviour,* Jarlath O'Brien
- *When the adults change, everything changes,* Paul Dix
- *Dare to lead* and *Braving the wilderness,* Brené Brown (and any of her other books and talks)
- *Belonging, behaviour and inclusion in schools: What does research tell us?* Dr Tracey Allen, Professor Kathryn Riley, Dr Max Coates (NEU publication)

---

### Chapter Summary: Executive Function

- *EF refers to cognitive processes that help regulate thoughts and behaviours*
- *Hot EF involves managing emotional, impulsive responses, while cool EF helps with logical decision-making, planning, and memory.*
- *EF skills develop from early childhood through adolescence, with critical periods of development during preschool and teenage years.*
- *Parenting practices, such as sensitivity, scaffolding, and providing a stimulating environment, significantly impact the development of EF in children.*
- *Children from disadvantaged backgrounds, with factors like poverty or maternal stress, are at higher risk of underdeveloped EF, making early intervention crucial.*
- *A key aspect of EF, working memory allows children to hold and manipulate information, aiding comprehension, problem-solving, and task completion.*
- *The ability to control impulses and resist distractions is crucial for academic success and social interaction, with deficits leading to impulsive behaviour and difficulties in school.*
- *Cognitive flexibility allows children to adapt to change and think creatively, while rigid thinking leads to challenges in social interactions and problem-solving.*

# 8 Social, Emotional and Mental Health

There are moments in our lives that deeply change us: some loud and unexpected; some almost imperceptible or mundane at the time, but which turn out to be profound nonetheless. One of mine happened whilst on playground duty, having just been told that my SENCO time was being reduced due to budget constraints. Feeling the kind of stress and anger about the injustice of SEND that knocks a few years off your life, I fumed: "what I need is research that shows how much time is needed to be a SENCO. This can't just be an issue for me!" Imagining that if the army of SENCOs, fighting valiantly for the rights of children and young people, could down tools for just a few minutes and capture their individual experiences into a survey, then it could provide the kind of data about the realities of time for SENCOs in schools that might enable change. "Oof, that's a job for someone", I thought. And then the bell rang, the playground emptied and I didn't think about it again for another few months.

Nearly two years later on a crisp autumn day, the National SENCO Workload Survey team sat in an ultra-modern seminar room at Bath Spa University, looking at the data from the two thousand SENCOs who'd just participated in our research.[1] My own frustrations about the role had been tough enough to carry, but reading about the collective lived experience of SENCOs was even worse. I could just feel the emotions bursting out of the spreadsheet: deep sadness and desperation rising off the table and infiltrating my whole being. When I got home, I sobbed big, ugly tears. The following day, I sat with a counsellor, haunted by what I'd read. Feelings of SENCO isolation, powerlessness, distress, responsibility and complicity; statistics which evidenced the stress and strain within the education system; trauma being experienced by SENCOs watching pupils and families suffer and not being able to help. With resolve, I gathered up my sprawling feelings and channelled them back into representing those experiences as loudly as I could.

*

## Emotions and their impact on SENCOs and pupils in school

Emotions are powerful. Chemicals influence the function of our body and those sensations lead us to perceive feelings which can influence our mood. They change the way we behave, the choices we make. When it comes to school, and all the people that

DOI: 10.4324/9781032663968-10

exist within those walls, there are a lot of different feelings impacting on a lot of different behaviours and choices. Some of those behaviours and choices directly impact upon our workload.

When we asked SENCOs how they felt about the role and why, there were some clear trends which stood out. Despite voluminous stress, more than two thirds enjoyed and felt passionate about the role. Determination and indignation on behalf of our children and young people. SENCOs gathering up their own sprawling feelings and channelling them back into making a difference. That said, a shelf life emerged from the data – people seemed to imply that they could only do so much. "I love being a SENCO, but I just don't know if I can cope with the level of stress for a long period of time. It's a very frustrating, upsetting role."[2]

Digging deeper, themes emerged. "I rarely get my allocated SENCO time as it gets used . . . dealing with behaviour management." This was echoed by other SENCOs explaining that they spent a lot of time managing crises, particularly around challenging and disruptive behaviour and safeguarding concerns.[3] We collected this data before the pandemic, and I suspect if we gathered SENCO voice again now, we'd also have more comments about the significant impact of school avoidance on workload, too, given that it is high on the national agenda.[4] Additionally, what came through, however, was the concern about how difficult it is to monitor and support other children whose needs weren't so immediately demanding leading to "long periods of time where they are not having their needs met".[5]

This chapter is written to help you identify emotions and mental health needs to support pupils but I've started with the mental health of educators because I think it serves to show just how interconnected we all are. Undoubtedly, there is more to say about mental health than we can cover here – this is simply a whistlestop tour of small focus areas – and I will signpost some further reading and resources at the end, too. My hope, however, is that better data about the emotions and feelings affecting the children in your setting will enable us all to make significant inroads into understanding the complex landscape that children and young people are navigating at the moment. My hope is that with better data we can intervene before feelings escalate to crisis point, and we can think more strategically about our environment in school.

In particular, this chapter will cover screening for and supporting:

- Low self-confidence for learning in the classroom, including maths anxiety
- Trauma and quality of life leading to complex behaviours
- Anxiety and feelings of not fitting in

## Low self-confidence for learning

How you feel about yourself and your capabilities "to organise and execute the courses of action required to manage prospective situations" is known as **self-efficacy**;[6] and it can significantly affect a pupil's confidence and academic outcomes. Boosting confidence for learning, a healthy sense of self-efficacy can lead to a child developing a sense of mastery, encouraging children to take risks and to push themselves to take on more challenging tasks. Self-efficacy can become self-fulfilling, as children who believe they can complete a task well tend to work harder, weather setbacks more confidently and with resolve, and feel less anxiety about new tasks or getting work done. A healthy sense of self-efficacy seems to influence outcomes particularly in maths and sciences, indicating that there are links between self-efficacy and executive function skills, too.[7]

A child's sense of self-efficacy is heavily dependent on their perceived abilities in the classroom. This is why low self-efficacy often goes hand-in-hand with learning difficulties and disengagement from learning. A loss of confidence early on can have long-term consequences, as we learnt when we considered the work of Erik Erikson in the previous chapter. Self-fulfilling prophesies are also powerful both for the child and their teacher. Research from 1968 into teacher beliefs about their pupils' potential influenced how they interacted with them – from their body language to the amount of attention and encouragement given.[8] So which comes first? Is this loss of confidence as a result of learning difficulties or as a result of insufficient support in the first place? In contrast, the greater a child's self-efficacy, the more likely they are to be independent learners, to achieve well and to have good mental health. Is this confidence as a result of timely adult investment into the child when they've needed it?

> **Self-efficacy:** The belief in one's capabilities to organize and execute the courses of action required to manage prospective situations (Bandura, 1977).
>
> **Zone of Proximal Development**: The space between what a learner can do without assistance and what they can do with guidance or support.

The great misperception about independent learning is that, fundamentally, it requires dependency on an adult or more advanced learner in order to develop. Hendrick and Macpherson (2017) state that independent learning only works for "experts who already know what they know, know what they don't know, and know what they need to know in order to solve the problem at hand. And by definition, that's not a student."[9] In essence then, we can only foster independent learning in pupils when we've specifically *encouraged* them to recognise what they already know, when we've *helped* them to recognise what they don't yet know and when we've *guided* them to take supported steps towards increasing academic maturity. The onus is on us to provide support, not to leave them to it. These metacognitive processes are critical to progress and require positive and trusting relationships with knowledge of the pupil's **Zone of Proximal Development** (ZPD) to help foster growing independence.

Self-efficacy can impact differently across different domains. We've all taught a pupil with low self-efficacy in academic skills but who shines on the sports field, for example. The main areas to consider for academic confidence however are:

- A sense that teachers can and want to help them
- Capacity to focus when studying despite distractions

- Confidence in revision for a test
- Completing homework
- A sense of understanding of what's been studied in lessons
- Parental pride and recognition of progress
- Positive test scores

Where there is a sense of lack in any one of these areas, confidence for learning is likely to be comparatively lower. This is where the power of cognitive science really comes into its own, and particularly when it is both used to inform teaching practice as well as to train pupils in metacognitive strategies which enable them to become better learners. Bradley Busch from Inner Drive is brilliant at explaining strategies to capitalise upon cognitive science in lessons.

Taking a holistic approach to evaluating pupil self-efficacy will enable you to be really strategic about how you use your teaching opportunities in school to maximise outcomes. When you know how an individual pupil is feeling about themselves, and specifically which areas are lower and higher in confidence, you can target those and advise parents-carers about how to target them, very specifically. When you have year group data which shows trends across the group, you can use this data to inform strategies in class, teacher training, use of tutor time and personal, social, health and economic (PSHE) education lessons, supporting the whole. This kind of data is invaluable.

You might however want to look more broadly than academic self-efficacy and consider social and emotional self-efficacy, or pupil wellbeing in general. The important point is, choose something and measure it so that you have a good grasp of what seems to be affecting your pupils' wellbeing and who is in need. Knowledge is power. Once you know, you can think about what you can do to help pupils well before it reaches crisis point. And even when it does, you have opportunities to target needs proactively and supportively, reducing the likelihood of pupil behaviour or school avoidance taking up disproportionate amounts of time.

**Top Tip:** If you are assessing self-perceptions at scale, you may wish to digitise these questionnaires. This is useful for lots of reasons: data is saved in one place; data is scored by the computer, saving time; data can be reviewed holistically for year group trends, not just individually, allowing you to think strategically.

### No Child is Missed – Action Point 8.1: Screen for Self-Efficacy, Pupil Wellbeing, Maths Anxiety

Questioning children on their self-perception can be a powerful way to capture their voice. For many children, this might be enough. For others, you may wish to dig deeper and have a fuller conversation with them, to explore their views and experiences. There are several tests you could use to evaluate children's sense of wellbeing or self-efficacy: some free, some costed.

The Children's Society has been measuring wellbeing for a decade with a simple questionnaire called *The Good Childhood Index* which you can use to capture children's wellbeing in your school. What's great about this questionnaire is that it is comparable to children nationwide. Whilst you will want to focus on your own data, sometimes – particularly with a low result – you might want to see how it might compare with the national picture.

Alternatively, you might want to consider using *The Self-efficacy Questionnaire for Children (SEC-Q)* which looks at three areas of self-efficacy (academic, social and emotional). It's directed towards older learners but you could adapt it for younger learners. This will give you a sense of areas of strength and areas for development within your school or an individual pupil profile. The *Perceived Scale of Stress* may also be illuminating.

If you notice that a pupil is struggling with mathematics specifically, you might want to explore feelings in relation to this. Maths anxiety triggers the same activity in the brain as a fear response. It is a real phenomenon and is linked to the fear of being wrong. (Alongside this, a pupil might also experience difficulties associated with number, sequencing and subitising - being able to visually estimate.) Steve Chinn, a specialist in this area has written a book on maths difficulties which includes a maths anxiety questionnaire, and is worth investing in if you want to work on maths development in your school, but he has a website which has lots of helpful free information, too.

There are other paid-for tests such as:

- *Myself as a Learner* which explores aspects associated with learning in the classroom and is accessible for children aged 8–16. It is very reasonably priced and gives you some indication for how a child might be scoring compared to peers.
- *Steve Chinn's Maths Anxiety questionnaire for children* found in *More Trouble with Maths, 3rd Edition* (2023).

## Social, emotional and mental health in relation to trauma

This book is about questioning what might be getting in the way of learning and there is no doubt that schools are facing unprecedented challenge when it comes to children's mental health and **externalising behaviours**, significantly impacting upon learning. Increasing numbers of children lashing out, absconding from lessons and being verbally and physically abusive to staff. Previously, we have looked at challenging behaviours through the prism of sensory hypersensitivities and through executive function, now we will view it through a perspective of mental health difficulties in response to trauma and what we might be able to do in terms of identifying need and support.

Having taught in a variety of contexts over the last twenty years, I've worked with a lot of children and experienced a wide range of different situations and contexts, from privilege to poverty. What I can tell you is that trauma happens at both ends of the spectrum: addiction, grief, loss, abuse and neglect can happen in any family. The cost of trauma plays out in school classrooms and offices across the land, stealing opportunities for academic, social and emotional confidence, grasping at any sense of personal control and safety.

A landmark piece of research into this field is that of The **Adverse Childhood Experiences (ACEs)** study carried out in 1998[10] which identified ten potentially traumatic events or experiences that can occur when we are young, and can have lasting impact. Long-term toxic levels of stress which are often at the root of common, serious and resource-demanding situations in education, health and social care. ACEs can impact upon everyone regardless of gender, socioeconomic status, race, ethnicity or location; and they're common. Recent UK studies revealed that about 50% of the population had experienced at least one ACE, with 12% experiencing four or more.[11] The impact of ACEs is cumulative: the more we have experienced, the more at risk we are of life-long negative consequences. For example, the life expectancy of someone with six or more ACEs is nineteen years shorter than for someone with none.[12]

The ten areas identified in the study on adverse childhood experiences are shown in the following diagram. When you look at it, you will see just how many of your pupils are likely to have been affected by at least one of these experiences.

**Externalising behaviours:** These are directed outwards and include problematic behaviours like physical aggression, disobedience, theft, destruction of property. Externalising behaviours are normal in children as they learn boundaries and mature. Generally externalising behaviours can be seen as problematic through extremity (how serious the behaviours are), prevalence (how often a child externalises their feelings), and how long it can take for the episode to conclude.

**Adverse Childhood Experiences (ACEs):** Ten traumatic events or experiences from childhood which can have lasting impact. The more of the ten a child experiences cumulatively in childhood, the more profound a negative effect on their long-term life chances and overall wellbeing.

**Epigenetics:** A field which explores the heritable changes in gene function that occur without a change in the sequence of the DNA. Chromosomal DNA transmits physical traits and noncoding DNA is responsible for emotional, behavioural and personality traits. Noncoding DNA is known to be affected by environmental stressors, toxins, nutrition, stress. It is this aspect of our DNA which allows us to adapt and change as the situation requires.

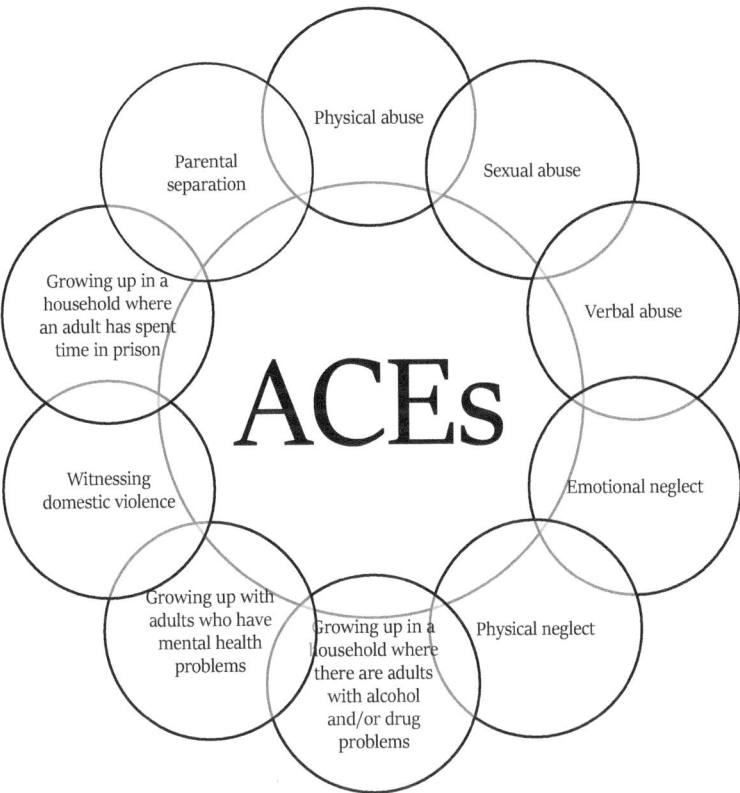

Physical abuse

Parental separation

Sexual abuse

Growing up in a household where an adult has spent time in prison

Verbal abuse

ACEs

Witnessing domestic violence

Emotional neglect

Growing up with adults who have mental health problems

Growing up in a household where there are adults with alcohol and/or drug problems

Physical neglect

*Figure 8.1* A visual representation of the ten Adverse Childhood Experiences

What's interesting is that since this study, so much more has been learnt about the biopsychosocial impacts of trauma, particularly in the field of **epigenetics**. In 1961, the Swiss psychiatrist Carl Jung wondered about the subconscious influences of previous generations on his life.[13] When you think about it, this isn't a particularly bizarre thought given that part of you has existed since your mother was conceived. As an historian, it intrigues me to think that I have been around in some form or other, and even the earliest traces of my children, too, since my mother was in my grandmother's womb.[14] What intrigues me even more however is the impact of those lived experiences of my previous generations in history and how they play out in my emotions, feelings, moods, behaviours and even health, in the current time.

Research indicates that these "epigenetic changes biologically prepare future generations to cope with the traumas that our parents experienced".[15] This can be clearly seen in two pieces of research by Rachel Yahuda, professor of psychiatry and neuroscience. The first, in 2005, identified abnormal levels of cortisol and increased distress to new stimuli in babies born to mothers who had experienced the 9/11 attacks on the World Trade Center in New York City in 2001, suggesting that the mother's terrifying experiences had profoundly shaped her gene expression in the longer-term. The second, in

2015, identified specific epigenetic "tags" on a certain gene in Jewish descendants of families who had experienced the Holocaust, as opposed to children of Jewish families who had not. It seems increasingly clear that our bodies keep score, not just for us, but for generations to come. What we can take from this is that ACEs in a child's life in your setting may be significant in the *now*, but so too might their parents' ACEs – about which you may never know. This is where viewing the observable behaviours in a pupil through a biopsychosocial and environmental systems lens can be illuminating.

Context is critical. And as trauma specialist Kate Cairns says, "we are living in a time of profound social chaos and collective trauma in the UK".[16] Disrupted attachments between parents who would normally be able to absorb the stresses of their little ones, struggling to maintain their own mental health within a sea of relentless threat, from public service cuts and job insecurity, to the threat to health and wellbeing from the pandemic, unregulated social media, and limited food access through inflation. Life is tough. No wonder we are seeing challenging behaviours within our pupil and parent body. No wonder we are seeing an increasing number of assessments and diagnoses as we seek to understand what has happened and what is happening to us.

As you consider the impact of trauma on your children, it can be both helpful to think about the ACEs a child might have experienced and put in support for those; but also it will be helpful to think to their familial context and what you might be able to do to signpost or engage wider support or multi-agency services for the family, too. It might be helpful for you to reflect on your own experiences, too, as you learn more about who you are, what affects you and what helps you to stay safe and well.

### No Child is Missed – Action Point 8.2: Screen for Social, Emotional and Mental Health in Relation to Trauma

In terms of evaluating the possible impact of trauma, it is important to work with your safeguarding lead, or with other senior colleagues if you are the DSL, to establish whether it is appropriate to screen for ACEs for a particular child, and how best to approach it. Equally, seeking expert clinical help is also best practice to ensure you are not putting anyone at risk. That said, you may not have access to regular mental health specialist support or you may already be a "trauma informed" school and already have systems in place: only you will know what is right for your setting and your children. The purpose of adding in this screening tool is to help you help a child or young person, not to harm them, so it is critical that empathy and respect are central, placing the child and their needs at the centre of any work you do. With that in mind, it might be appropriate to explore possible trauma in a child through parental report or professional discussion using a tool like the *Adverse Childhood Experiences International Questionnaire (ACE-IQ)*. Alternatively, you may wish to prioritise having a conversation with a child of concern, to capture their voice and find out exactly what life is like for them. Pupil voice can be very powerful. The *Perceived Scale of Stress* may also be helpful here, too.

Alongside this, if a child is involved with or exposed to antisocial behaviours outside of school and is at risk of involvement with gangs or criminal activity, it might be appropriate to liaise with your local policing service and/or Youth Offending Team (YOT); and/or to engage in the types of evaluative thinking that the YOT would when looking to rehabilitate a child's behaviours if support is not readily available. This would typically include considering aspects which we cover in this book, including:

- Mental and physical health (Chapters 8 & 9)
- Speech, language and communication needs (Chapter 4)

And also:

- Stability and support in the home environment
- Consideration of use of possible illicit or harmful substances
- Reducing opportunities and risks of offending

You might want to consider using the *PedsQL™ Measurement Model* which you can find online which explores aspects of a child or young person's quality of life.

The purpose of these suggestions here is for you to feel you have tools to use and options to explore when you are at a loss as to what to do or how to move forward with a particular child or young person in helping them to cope in school.

## Social, emotional and mental health in relation to anxiety and feelings of not fitting in

For some children and young people, struggling in school looks very different to the disruptive behaviours we've just considered. This next section will look at **internalising** behaviours: those which are barely visible and yet can have significant and lasting impact.

### Masking the real me: learning how to fit in

Children and young people interviewed through research conducted by Brené Brown and her team around their experiences of belonging, made some profound statements; statements which make me catch my breath. "If I get to be me, I belong. If I have to be like you, I fit in."; "Not belonging at school is really hard. But it's NOTHING compared to what it feels like when you don't belong at HOME."[17] Shame is often described as the sense that we are "not ____ enough"; that our identity is somehow flawed.

Not cool enough, not sporty enough, not popular enough, not normal enough, not clever enough. Or as a parent, not good enough, not tough enough, not soft enough, not around enough, not successful enough, not loving enough, not interested enough, not energised enough, or simply sometimes just "not enough enough". Whatever the cause of our "not enough-ness", the sense of having to hide that pain or protect it with a heavy armour is a common response. No one wants their sore spots noticed and prodded by others. Sometimes, as we've just explored, armour can be very obvious for others to see when emotions are externalised; at other times, that armour is heavy for the wearer but not always obvious to the rest of the world. We might consider this to be **"masking"**.

It is normal to adapt aspects of our behaviour, to "fit in" with the appropriateness of context. This is commonly called **impression management** and the theory goes that "like actors on a stage, people in society are constantly engaged in managing the impressions they give to other people by putting on performances or a 'show'"[18] to try to convince them of the identities they wish to assert. With this in mind, we learn from an early age what is ok to do in public and what's not ok to do in public. For example, we might feel a great sense of relief when breaking wind in private, but we will avoid letting rip loudly and publicly on a first date (especially if we want a second one!). This is normal *adaptive* behaviour. It is social camouflaging; copying what others do and avoiding what they don't; consciously and unconsciously imitating to strengthen social bonds, which is an important tool we use to avoid the pain of being rejected.

Research by Sebastian et al. (2010) found that perceived inclusion or exclusion in an online game of catch significantly affected mood in both adolescents and adults alike – although it was more pronounced in teenagers.[19] Exclusion hurts. In fact, we feel it like a threat to life – because it is. Loneliness has the equivalent health risk of smoking fifteen cigarettes a day.[20] In response, we work hard to avoid being excluded and to mitigate the circumstances where it might occur, but that can also come at a cost. It can be tiring to be on best behaviour all the time, particularly if fitting in requires a lot of social camouflaging away from your desired and most comfortable state. Social camouflaging is common in close proximity to others, when identities are fragile and still forming, and where not being included in the pack feels like a life-or-death situation. In other words, it's common at school.

When a pupil actively identifies core aspects about themselves which they feel are or are likely to be rejected or stigmatised by the majority around them, they will often take steps to suppress, hide or change their presentation, for self-protection. The extent to which someone needs to suppress a part of themselves is often indicative of the sense of freedom and safety within the environment. The less safe the environment and the higher the risk of rejection, the more likely and more frequently someone will mask their identity. Given it is an act of concealment, masking can be very difficult to spot.

It can start really early: children have been known to try to bleach their skin;[21] change their hair;[22] conceal their sexuality;[23] publicly distance themselves from their intense interests or pastimes, or their need to **stim**.[24] Adults reflecting on their masking in childhood talk about needing to be "more like everyone else" to avoid being made fun of, practicing phrases and behaviours in private in order to become less of an outsider.[25] We know that internal stress can impact upon learning and outcomes.[26] We also know this splintering of public and private identity leads to an increase in risk for self-harm and suicidal ideation.[27]

Different student communities experience "**minority stress**"[28] and identify with these self-protective behaviours, including the autistic community who tend to refer to this need to conceal and to camouflage as "masking"; and similarly it is common amongst the **LGBTQ** communities to hide one's sexuality until ready to "come out". Whether it is referred to as "camouflaging", "compensation", "adaptive morphing" or "masking" across the research, it speaks of the need to conceal aspects of oneself in order to avoid rejection, othering, judgement and blame. Hiding one's true identity can be a painful necessity but changing an environment to become more inclusive takes conscious and concerted effort, social risk, bravery, and the actions of a number of people taking pride in their identity over a considerable period of time. This can be hard to engender when those who are camouflaging are doing everything possible to not stand out. As such, schools with high levels of masking may not even know it.

> **Internalising behaviours:** and stress result from negativity that is focused inwards. When someone has difficulty coping with a negative emotion or situation, they will direct their feelings inside and the symptoms or experiences will be mainly felt internally, in that person's body and mind. People who internalise their anxiety are more likely to want to withdraw from the world around them.
>
> **Impression management/masking:** is the way that people try to influence how others view their identity often through visible choices for example, around clothing or music.
>
> **Stim/stimming:** is short for "self-stimulation" and refers to repetitive movements, speech or use of objects to calm oneself down. It is a form of self-soothing.
>
> **Minority stress:** excess stress to which individuals from stigmatised social categories are exposed as a result of their social (minority) position.
>
> **LGBTQ:** Lesbian, Gay, Bisexual, Transgender, Queer

## Emotional based school avoidance (EBSA)

"Belonging" is a word commonly used in education at the moment, not least because the data around attendance in school suggests there is a lack of it. In this post-Covid world, emotional based school avoidance (EBSA) is a high priority for many schools as children who once went to school regularly have now struggled to return. School avoidance is not new however. Equally common amongst boys as girls, there are three key risk points in a child's education for it to take hold.

School avoidance has existed since the inception of formalised schooling. Back in the nineteenth century it was called "mitching" and until quite recently it was often referred

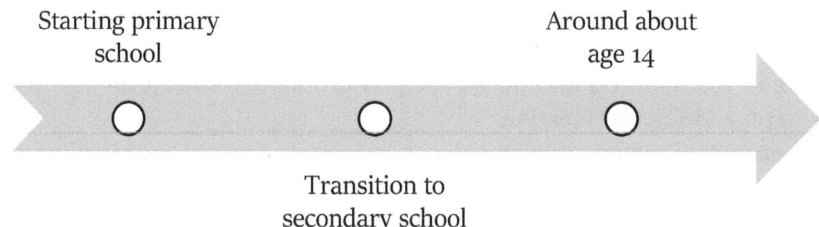

*Figure 8.2* A diagram indicating the most common times with elevated risk of school avoidance developing

to as "school refusal". Now re-framed as "emotional-based school avoidance", it can be deeply challenging for professionals, parents and the pupils themselves. It is not a situation that anyone initially wants but what makes it particularly difficult to resolve is that each case can be very different: there is no one-size-fits-all cause or approach to support. This can often leave everyone feeling powerless, unsure what to do for the best, wondering if they're ever going to return.

Some children feel unsafe: hypervigilant to what upsetting experiences they may meet in school. Some children feel completely or increasingly overwhelmed from the sensory stimulation (light, sound, touch etc.) or the ongoing demands drawing upon complex sensory integration. Some might be struggling with the rigidity of the academic curriculum, having to engage with subject areas which are triggering either by content or by skillset (e.g. reading texts they find distressing such as gothic horror, or having to read aloud). Some may avoid school due to insecure or negative social relationships with both pupils and staff, including bullying or stereotyping/discrimination. Some may avoid due to sanctions owed. Some may avoid school because of worries outside of school, such as separation anxiety about leaving family members, not having the correct uniform, insecure housing arrangements. Some may have no choice and absence is the result of neglect. And, to add further complexity into the mix, the reasons for avoidance in any one child might be different on different days.

What is a very common characteristic across children and young people who avoid school, however, is their over-estimation of the perceived threat and their underestimation of their ability to cope.[29] And as we now know, perception *really* matters. This can lead to diverse and sometimes opposing views about an individual. In frustration, some adults make reductive and simplistic assumptions about how to resolve an attendance situation, such as "parents just need to get them in", or "schools just need to put more support in place", or "we just need to refer on to external agency support". The reality is that "justs" under-estimate the complexity of what we're dealing with and the need for a more nuanced understanding of the situation.

Another factor which can make dealing with school absence more challenging is the speed at which it can escalate. One minute, attendance is ok and bobbing along, and the next, it has been three weeks since they were last in. This is because school avoidance is a vicious cycle that is very difficult to get out of once it has begun.

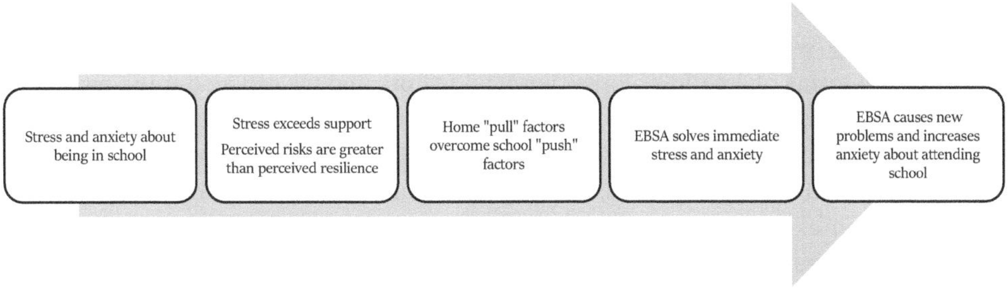

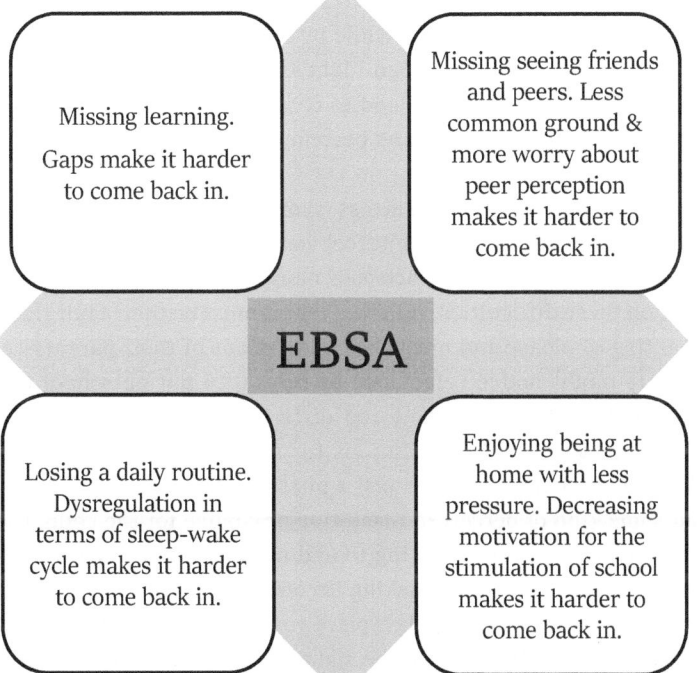

*Figure 8.3* A diagram based on the work of Thambirajah et al. 2008[30] showing a common school avoidance trajectory

*Figure 8.4* A diagram showing the secondary risks associated with prolonged school absence

Prolonged school absence then engenders new problems in addition to the ones that had already developed, that are summarised in *Figure 8.4*.

In many cases, the loss of social interaction, daily routine and a sense of achievement in school can lead to severe social anxiety which can cause difficulties even leaving the house. This can have life-long consequences in terms of mental health and wellbeing, employment, independence.[31]

Wherever someone is in their school avoidance journey, improvement may come when engaging with the different factors in someone's life. We can, of course, think about this in terms of a child's biopsychosocial factors and we can also think about it in terms of the policies and practices which influence the child's school and home. Taking this more systemic approach allows us to reflect upon many more options for action to reduce a child's stress levels across several domains: in school, at home, and with involvement of external agency support. There is a joint responsibility for improving attendance; the earlier, the better.

## What internalising stress looks and feels like from early red flags to crisis point

As we know from masking, concealing aspects of ourselves is common for survival. In order to flourish, however, we need to live in a state of balance, of homeostasis. We can live slightly out of kilter for a while by utilising coping strategies to help us get by – going to bed early if we had a bad night's sleep, for example, but consistent dysregulation of our bodily systems can lead to considerable stress within the body: stress which accumulates to chronic levels and becomes increasingly difficult to resolve with a simple strategy or two.

In the early stages of internalising stress, symptoms are subtle – easy to miss and are relatively common. Some children might feel very tired or very grumpy at the end of the day; they might complain of tummy aches or nausea before school. Some children might not even mention these difficulties, thinking that it must be their fault that they're struggling, and wanting to please and meet the expectations of their parents-carers.

Parents-carers might notice reluctance or refusal to put on school uniform – shoes going missing or PE kit unexpectedly too dirty to wear. Given the legality of school attendance and pressures and expectations for parents-carers to work, children often get sent in regardless, hoping that it's just a phase or it will get sorted. Insidiously however, without some kind of perceived resolution or change for the child, the stress inside their body builds as they keep adjusting to and normalising the sensations within their body. The required coping and/or masking becomes ever more demanding.

As Gabor Maté explains, when the last place you want to be is in your body, you start to live in your head and stop listening to the signals within your body. Where interoception is a neurobiological experience of identifying signals within the body and attaching meaning, **alexithymia** is a difficulty attaching emotional meaning to these physical experiences. Lacking self-awareness to understand how an experience is affecting you emotionally can mean continuing on with actions or behaviours which might actually be harmful. "Not knowing how or what one feels . . . is a sure sign of disconnect from the body."[32] This can even manifest as a strength – putting in incredible hours of work, for example, but at the cost of not eating or drinking enough (and then not being able to listen to the signals of satiation when at last you do stop to eat and drink). The "enough" signal just doesn't get through or is ignored. But often the underlying reality is this sense of "never enough-ness", the need to fight for connection with others at the cost of connection with ourselves.

Red flags turn into loud warning signals where exhaustion and fatigue are prominent. The additional **allostatic load** on the body means it tires more easily. Coping with regularly changing environments – different teachers, different classrooms, different expectations, different temperatures, different soundscapes, different sensations, different foods, becomes ever more a struggle. Memory function reduces to keep focus on the simple act of living; less important functions to life might begin to falter – speech slows or reduces given its demands upon the body; high energy movements reduce significantly. Choices become increasingly restricted to help manage perceived ability to cope.

**Alexithymia:** "No words for emotion", when someone struggles to identify and connect physical sensations (feelings) with emotions.

**Allostatic load:** Coined by Bruce McEwen, it means "staying the same amid change", which is the body's stress response to help maintain life in the face of threat.

**Cellular clocks:** These are known as telomeres which are a measure of biological age, rather than chronological age.

**HPA axis:** The HPA axis links the hypothalamus, the pituitary gland and the adrenal gland, vital in the interactions between nerves and hormones. The infrastructure of the HPA axis is set early in life (in utero and early childhood) and is the hub of the body and brain stress management system.

As the symptoms develop and become more consistently apparent, these coping mechanisms increasingly become a person's daily lived experience. The people inside these bodies might deeply desire to return to a previous iteration of themselves or to engage in an experience of life that others seem to have access to, but for whom physiologically it is currently not possible. As the situation worsens over time, relationships between the individual and their support network are likely to feel strain or begin to fragment. The adults around the child might begin to despair as a child or young person is less easy going, less responsive to support and help, more rigid in their choices. In essence, we see the body closing down on itself to protect its vital organs, but at great cost to its engagement with the wider environment, causing stress within its significant relationships, too. The family unit begins to fracture. And so we see stress pass between loved ones like a contagious disease. It is so powerful it actually ages people,[33] evidenced by their "**cellular clocks**".

This emergency response maintaining homeostasis in the face of stress, whether that is an infection, an injury, a challenging context or a traumatic life event, places chronic strain on our body's **HPA axis**, which "leads to an excessive and prolonged release of the stress hormones adrenaline and cortisol, nervous tension, immune dysfunction, and, in many cases, exhaustion of the stress apparatus itself."[34] The resources required for school attendance are beyond that which a child's body and mind can cope with.

In this context, a letter home encouraging attendance from the school with some data about the relationship between attendance and life outcomes, or even a penalty notice, is not going to cut it. As former headteacher and now campaigner, encouraging fellow teachers to see school non-attendance for the physical and mental health issue it is, Steve Bladon says, "behind every child's attendance data, there's a unique set of circumstances . . . We improve their individual attendance by addressing the issues causing them to be absent from school. The right way to do this is with understanding and compassion, not judgement and punitive measures."[35]

This way of viewing attendance allows for opportunities for children and young people to reconnect with school and to thrive again. And it goes without saying that when we work to improve attendance in a single case, we are really working to improve collective attendance in our school as a whole. The details matter.

**Top Tip:** In, thankfully rare, Serious Case Reviews, non-attendance is often highlighted as a notable factor leading up to a child's significant harm or death. Understanding the reasons behind school non-attendance is a critical part of our duty to safeguard children and young people. If your data shows a high number of contextual risk factors – biological, psychological and social – and their attendance is low, this should be cause to seek external advice, guidance or intervention as a priority. This child is likely to need you more than you might realise.

## No Child is Missed – Action Point 8.3: Screen for Feelings of Not Fitting In

### Masking

Whilst we need to take great care when screening children to avoid harm, when it comes to assessing mental health, it is just as important to seek expert advice and guidance as it is for physical health. We are education rather than health professionals. That said, for some pupils, further exploring identity might be helpful – vital even, especially if the wait for an assessment for autism is very long and specialist help seems very far away. In this sense, working with the pupil's parent-carer to ensure consent, and with the pupil themselves to ensure assent, you may want to consider exploring masking through the *Camouflaging Autistic Traits Questionnaire* (CAT-Q) created by Hull et al. (2019) at UCL, which is freely available online. This type of testing in relation to understanding identity is a very fragile process which needs time, care and attention. Rather than screening, it might be worth simply reading through the test criteria and reflecting with parents-carers and staff who know the pupil well as to whether this might be something they are often doing, and then approaching support as if they are. The more mature the pupil, the more they wish to explore their identity privately and as they find their own way. There is a very useful guide about masking which I will signpost you to in the No Child Misses Out section in this chapter.

In addition, or alternatively, exploring potential anxiety and depression may also be indicative of children's confidence in themselves and at school. The *Revised Children's Anxiety and Depression Scale (RCADS)* measures the reported frequency of various symptoms of anxiety and low mood. It is freely available and easy to score.

### Emotional Based School Avoidance

Gathering information about why someone might be avoiding school is a nuanced process which will involve multiple pieces of data from the types of tests included earlier on in this book, including their physical health. There is however a free questionnaire which you can use to specifically evaluate the impact of potential causes of school avoidance, from four common causes, namely:

- Avoiding sensory or physical sensations of stress
- Avoiding social or academic stresses
- Avoiding separation anxiety from caregivers
- Having more fun outside of school than in it

The questionnaire is called the *School Refusal Assessment Scale – Revised* and there are free versions online for both child and parent. Again, it might be more appropriate to have a gentle conversation with a child rather than put them through the formality of a questionnaire. You will know your context and your pupil and what might be best. It is however a tool which you can use to guide you as to what might be contributing to a child's difficulty in attending school.

## No Child Misses Out: What to do next . . .

> **No Child Misses Out – Response Point 8.1: Supporting Low Self-Confidence for Learning and Pupil Wellbeing**

Whole class and/or individual support may require:

- *Prioritising quality pupil-teacher relationships to give pupils with low confidence the courage to speak up and seek support*
  - Train teachers to operate with "unconditional positive regard"

- o   Encourage teachers to build relationships with pupils and remember little details about their lives – like which football team they support, or their pet's name
- *Enabling clear focus and attention in lessons*
  - o   Keep distractions to a minimum in class
  - o   Consider careful seating for pupils who need support with focus and attention (this may be either at the front or the back – one is often better than the other)
- *Improving lesson recall and building revision, metacognition and study skills into the curriculum to "develop independent learners"*
  - o   Knowledge organisers
  - o   Reading for meaning strategies
  - o   Flashcards
  - o   Self-quizzing
  - o   Mindmaps
  - o   "Brain Dumps"
  - o   Time management – including the Pomodoro Method
  - o   The Leitner System as a revision tool
  - o   Retrieval practice and spaced retrieval
  - o   Interleaving and dual coding
  - o   Managing distractions and fostering "healthy habits"
  - o   Seeking out some expert training:

    Bradley Busch from Inner Drive is an excellent communicator about teaching practice which uses cognitive science for maximum impact. He's worth searching out.

    Peps McCrea is also an inspiring researcher-communicator who offers weekly research "snacks" through his emails which are free to receive. He also tweets regularly so is worth a follow.
- *Discussing barriers and supports for getting homework done*
  - o   Consider time of day
  - o   Ask about the help a pupil might need in terms of resources, e.g. a desk, peace, sustenance, time
- *Communicating positively with parents-carers*
  - o   Call home and share positive news even if there are negatives to discuss, too
  - o   Start every meeting or phonecall with an area of progress so that parents can have positive conversations at home and build a sense of pride as a motivating factor for children and young people to respond to
  - o   Mark using positive language to give pupils something to be proud about – avoid critical terms at all costs

---

**No Child Misses Out – Response Point 8.2: Supporting Social, Emotional and Mental Health in Relation to Trauma**

Whole class and/or individual support may require:

- *Prioritising quality pupil-teacher relationships which focus on teacher behaviours first as a way to de-escalate situations*
  - Train teachers to take a "low arousal", calm approach in challenging situations, giving pupils as much control of the situation as you can, to help them feel safe
  - Gareth Morewood and Professor Andrew McDonnell from Studio 3 deliver great training on this and there are some free training vidoes on YouTube to get you started. E.g. the Low Arousal Approach (25.03.2024)
  - Paul Dix takes a more relational approach to his methods of improving behaviour, too. His book is called *When the Adults change, everything changes: Seismic shifts in school behaviour*
- *Preparing for crises – be ready for when they happen*
  - Enable children who are in a state of heightened stress to escape the classroom or playground in a controlled way to a safe space
  - Think about behaviour change in terms of months and years, not hours, days and weeks – and recognise the micro steps of positive change, rather than the lack of progress.
  - Provide children at risk of exclusion with daily access to at least one named and emotionally available adult who can co-regulate with them when crisis strikes. It makes it more difficult and potentially compromises the safety of the relationship if this person is both "carrot" and "stick", providing both the support and the sanction. Avoid this role confusion, if you can.
  - Timetable regular opportunities for children to have time with their named adult in a proactive way, so that not all conversations are reactive and problem-solving but are opportunities to learn what a safe and happy relationship can feel like where they are valued for who they are.
  - Build trusting relationships with family at home – make a point of calling home to celebrate the progress and successes that have happened so that they know you have their child's best interests at heart and want them to succeed, rather than just pointing out their challenges.
  - Keep the final weeks of term as a calm and safe time where you can, and prepare for targeted pupil support in these final weeks where you can't, as tiredness and potential change can often lead to increased stress – particularly if home isn't as safe or as happy as we would want it to be.
  - Have enough training for all staff and specifically employ adults on site who are able to work with pupils in crisis, e.g. a school psychotherapist.
- *Preparing to avoid crises – predicting what might cause stress and putting safety nets in place*
  - Having and sharing a clear plan for the day – especially important at EYFS and primary when children are less able to understand what is going to happen and when timetables can be less structured than secondary school. Visuals on lanyards and on the board are great for this.

- ○ Thinking ahead about who might need a specific conversation or plan about an unusual school activity – for example a school trip, an unknown visitor.
- ○ Recognising that transitions – beginnings and endings can often be harder for pupils: starts and ends of terms, Fridays.
- ○ Build good links with previous settings and deliver an extended transition programme for pupils who need safe relationships in a new setting from before they join. SEND specialists, such as Gary Aubin, regularly write about this and have some excellent suggestions, as do national advisory bodies such as Whole School SEND and nasen.
- ○ Offer small group sessions and safe spaces for practicing social skills and growing in social confidence, such as Lego Club, Jigsaw Club, Board Games Club. My team and I have set up "Pit Stops" in different schools, comfy rooms where a few named children can come in to feel safe instead of going out onto the playground which they find more hostile and stressful.
- ○ Work with families to consider approaching external agencies for early help to reduce stresses at home, and in school.
- ○ Help parents to access good parenting advice and support by hosting parenting courses on site. Alongside this, I particularly recommend Dr Siggie Cohen who has a strong social media presence and has practical tools from toddlers to teens. She is great! (I'm often taking tips for myself, too.)
- ○ Beacon House is also a great source of support. Their website has useful resources you might wish to try. https://beaconhouse.org.uk/resources/

> **No Child Misses Out – Response Point 8.3: Supporting Social, Emotional and Mental Health in Relation to Anxiety and Feelings of Not Fitting In**

Whole school/year group support may require:

- *Monitoring school attendance with a fine-tooth comb*
  - ○ The best predictor of elevated absence is previous absence. With known pupils and families, act quickly when any miss days in the first week or two of term.
  - ○ Get to know families and children who have early absence and build relationships with them quickly.
- *Working on strategies to improve belonging and inclusion*
  - ○ Have clear policies on bullying. You might want to consider working towards *The Diana Award*, for example, and develop student ambassadors and structured approaches to reducing stigma and exclusion.
  - ○ Having safe spaces across the school and staff consciously monitoring who is drawn to these spaces and the frequency of their attendance.
  - ○ Hold assemblies and events which celebrate difference – for example, different religious festivals, awareness weeks or days.

- ○ Celebrate pupils for achievements outside of school and also for achievements in school which are oriented towards recognising "progress" as well as "excellence".
- ○ Provide extended and structured transition experiences for pupils with elevated anxiety, particularly around attendance and social confidence.
- ○ Have key named adults who are able to provide a warm welcome to school, quickly resolving any small issues (things forgotten, homework not done etc.) to help to pupils enter the school site knowing that their attendance is more important and more valued than any smaller easily resolvable issue.

Individual support will require:

- • *Engaging with the more subtle and nuanced causes of absence*
  - ○ Carrying out more detailed screening to explore school avoidance, including listening to the pupil's own perceptions about their attendance difficulties, demonstrating care rather than judgement and asking for their input to any planning
  - ○ Responding to needs which are identified through this process with a careful, strategic and potentially wide-reaching approach, which might include:
    - ▪ Looking at a pupil's day or week by subject/topic/teacher and thinking about times which are more and less stressful to help problem-solve
    - ▪ A flexible timetable which allows for an extended return to school, building up little by little, to overcome anxiety
    - ▪ Involving multi-agency support to look at support outside of school, e.g. referral to mental health specialists, social services, alternative provision opportunities
    - ▪ Using resources designed by specialists in Local Authorities excelling in this area, for example Tower Hamlets, West Sussex
    - ▪ Working to develop dialogue between school and any health provider involved with a pupil, to explore barriers from a health perspective (see advice from the INSCHOOL research project in Chapter Nine)
  - ○ Seeking out some expert training:
    - ▪ Pooky Knightsmith is an excellent communicator in this area.
    - ▪ *Belonging, behaviour & inclusion in schools: What does research tell us?* Dr Tracey Allen, Professor Kathryn Riley, Dr Max Coates (NEU publication)
    - ▪ Brené Brown, Daring Classrooms

## Final thoughts: Is my child normal?

People often ask me, "Is it that there is just more autism/dyslexia/ADHD/ [insert diagnosis here] nowadays or that it's always been there and we've not identified it before?" I think the answer to this is somewhere in the middle. Medical developments have increased significantly so survival rates of babies have too, increasing the number of children entering schools with complex needs. Child health has deteriorated over the last few decades, too, as we'll cover in the next chapter. Alongside this, there are simply more children than there were years ago; we have more need by number, not just by prevalence.

However, I also think we are more aware of children's needs because of the growth of social media and the power that you and I now have to publish our innermost thoughts freely and anonymously at the click of a button. Where, perhaps previously, we might have asked ourselves privately: "Is my child normal?" or "Am I normal?"; or, "Is it ok to feel anxious about meeting new people and talking to myself out loud to practice what I'm going to say?"; or, "Should I/they enjoy talking about dinosaurs *this* much?" Now, we talk publicly instead, and "find our tribe" through social media groups which helps us to feel connected and included in this increasingly disjointed world. We find strength in number.

Disconnection can make us feel extraordinarily vulnerable. As trauma specialist Kate Cairns wrote, we are living through difficult times politically, socially, financially. Like we considered at the end of the previous chapter, the micro- and macrosystems at play, including the digital age and its impact on physical and cognitive development and overall health, cannot be ignored. So, is there a higher prevalence? The data about assessment and diagnosis and the level of conversation about it would indicate that there is. Yes. But can it be explained by our environment?

If we look at the research into epigenetics – the idea that DNA is not our destiny – our lived experiences are as powerful in our development as our genes – if not more so. Epigenetic research therefore suggests that the rampant increase in demand for paediatric assessment and diagnoses *cannot* be genetic. Genes do not change in such a short period of time. Instead, we must look around us at what is changing our environment, and therefore, us.

The fact is, focussing so heavily on the need for gene-dependent diagnosis actually serves a deeply conservative function (one which benefits the status quo). When we identify the difficulty within the child rather than acknowledging the environmental factors around them, we become increasingly complicit in justifying inequalities which cause significant distress in childhood.

As trauma specialist Gabor Maté says, "if phenomena like addiction or mental distress are determined mostly by biological heredity, we are spared from having to look at how our social environment supports, or does not support, the parents of young children, and at how social attitudes, prejudices, and policies burden, stress, and exclude certain segments of the population, thereby increasing their propensity for suffering."

We'll catch up with a clinical geneticist in Chapter Ten to see if she agrees . . .

\*

*Like the previous chapter, this chapter covers huge ground and many vast concepts I have named only in passing. If you would like to engage in further reading, research and reflection about mental health within the context of childhood and schools, then the following may be helpful to look at. These are listed in addition to those mentioned in Chapter Seven which are also relevant in relation to low confidence for learning.*

- *Social Learning Theory (1977)* and *Self-efficacy: The exercise of control (1997)*, Albert Bandura
- *The body keeps score*, Bessel Van der Kolk
- *The myth of normal*, Gabor Maté
- *It didn't start with you*, Mark Wolynn
- *Taking off the mask: Practical exercises to help understand and minimise the effects of autistic camouflaging*, Dr Hanna Louise Belcher

## Chapter Summary: Social, Emotional and Mental Health

- *Understanding and addressing the emotional and mental health needs of students is crucial for preventing issues from escalating into crises.*
- *Students with strong self-efficacy are more likely to take risks, overcome challenges, and succeed academically, while low self-efficacy often leads to disengagement and poor outcomes.*
- *Trauma, including adverse childhood experiences (ACEs), has long-term effects on students' emotional, social, and academic development, affecting behaviour and learning in school.*
- *Trauma can be passed down through generations, influencing students' emotional and mental health, even if they haven't directly experienced traumatic events themselves.*
- *Students can mask their true identities to fit in, which often leads to internalised stress, anxiety, and a sense of not belonging, further impacting mental health and wellbeing.*
- *School avoidance is a growing issue, which can be triggered by anxiety, sensory overwhelm, or social challenges, and requires early intervention to prevent long-term disengagement from education.*
- *Prolonged internal stress can manifest in physical symptoms, such as exhaustion and withdrawal from school environments.*
- *Addressing school avoidance and attendance issues requires understanding, compassion, and support rather than punitive measures to help students reconnect with education.*

# 9 Physical Health

Our results were in and they were good. I breathed the annual collective sigh of relief with teachers everywhere, and celebrated with pupils and colleagues. This year's hard work had paid off. Wanting to get underneath the surface of the headlines however, I wandered back to my office and sat down to ask some more nuanced questions. I was definitely pleased, but there were still some stories I wanted to better understand.

Given my ongoing research, I decided to collate the biopsychosocial data I had about each pupil to see if there was anything else to learn. In terms of biological data, I listed: their gender; their date of birth; their medical conditions. For psychological data, I considered: their IQ data; their processing skills from the screening tests discussed in this book; their access arrangements for external exams; any known diagnoses of SEND; their level of perceived motivation; their behaviour record; any engagement with mental health professionals. Within the social factors, I noted: their attendance for Year Eleven; what we knew of their familial context including involvement with our Designated Safeguarding Lead; their network and security of friendships; their sexuality or gender identity if we had any awareness of this; their ethnicity.

I paused for a moment, reflecting and questioning my motives. Was it ethically appropriate to gather our pupils' data in this way? It felt deeply personal information in such a cold and clinical spreadsheet. And yet I couldn't ignore the niggle that there might be hidden patterns of underachievement, which none of us were seeing through our usual lens; invisible barriers which needed detecting. With resolve, I turned back to my laptop, conditionally formatted the columns and sorted them from greatest to least progress. I removed everyone's names to hide their identity, even from myself.

I let my eyes wander over the spreadsheet. I expected the usual trends to jump out – those with poor attendance and/or behaviour to have made the least progress. I wasn't wrong in that assumption (although I was interested to see that some of our best performers weren't always great attenders!) And it was also clear, not unsurprisingly perhaps, that those with an overall slowness in processing (and therefore with comparatively more access arrangements to compensate) were also at greater risk for underachievement within a context of an exam system which prizes speed of working and accuracy of recall. Gender flagged, given the national picture, too. But my blood ran cold when my eyes clocked the column of medical data. . . In our lowest performers by progress (not attainment), the rate of asthma was *four times* that of our overall school average. *Four times!*

DOI: 10.4324/9781032663968-11

In a bit of a panic and to check I wasn't imagining things, my fingers raced over the keys as I searched the internet to see whether this was unique to my little dataset or whether there was something more pernicious afoot.

It wasn't anomalous. Asthma *is* a risk factor for educational underachievement.[1] Asthma: not one of the conditions we might immediately trill when naming a special educational need, and yet operating exactly like one. And if asthma requires us to think and act differently to avoid underachievement, then what about other chronic and acute health conditions?

And if *that's* the case, then why *aren't* we routinely talking about the impact of our pupils' physical health on their educational achievement in the way we talk about autism, dyslexia, ADHD . . .?

Mind ruminating, I closed my laptop and wandered back across the now empty campus. The sun was still high in the late summer sky but a cooling breeze reminded me that September, and another cohort of Year Elevens, was just around the corner. It was time to dig a bit deeper. And quickly.


## What do we mean by "health"?

In 1948 the World Health Organization (WHO) defined health as "a state of complete physical, mental and social well-being and not merely the absence of disease or infirmity."[2] Thinking about health as "a state" places us within the **medical model** we are familiar with; that health (or its antitheses, disease and disability) is a within-person entity. Since the 1970s and particularly in the field of disability rights[3] however, the medical model has increasingly come under heavy criticism for stigmatising the individual, rather than recognising that elements of society actively disable people, fostering systemic exclusion and discrimination. For example, it does not matter how much money a wheelchair user has in their pocket if they cannot get into the shop to spend it because of a step. A 1976 report birthing the **social model** of disability promulgated, "it is society which disables physically impaired people".[4] And from this seminal conceptual shift, we see the growth of societal supports, such as accessible toilets, parking spaces, hearing loops, ramps, to name but a few.

But arguably even the social model is of its time. As sociologist and bioethicist Tom Shakespeare points out "a theory which addresses only external barriers is an incomplete response to the challenge of disability".[5] This is a view which is shared by others in the field globally, too, who advocate that it is vital to see the individual and their (medical) impairments *within* the context of society and the (social) systems of support around them, to be able to determine or produce ill-health or disability.[6] In other words, children and young people with medical conditions and/or disabilities need both personalised supports and more inclusive societal design to manage their conditions and to thrive.

This balanced approach, which some call **"whole health"** is better represented in the WHO update (1984), which acknowledged that health exists within a context, enabling us to engage with the world – coping with and adapting to differing environments.[7] This view of health and wellbeing as a resource for living is increasingly widely accepted.

In fact, it's become big business. Social media, the internet and TV streaming services are awash with self-made experts (of all calibres) capitalising on the happiness industry[8] showing us how to look healthy (exercise and diet advice), wealthy (careers, finance, clothing, interiors, garden design) and wise (parenting, politics, education). Like me, I expect you already follow a few.

Thinking about health as multi-faceted and the interaction of both individual and society together requires us to reflect on what the influencing factors might be. This is where the biopsychosocial model is a helpful framework for analysis as it requires us to be more expansive in our considerations of someone's life, thinking about factors in combination that serve to elevate or reduce risk. The greater the number of risk factors across a person's biopsychosocial context, the more likely they are to be interacting with each other and contributing to someone's ability to live and to cope with the different environments in which they exist. Health, or ill-health is then the outcome of these constant and dynamic interactions: some days will be good days, others less so.

> **The medical model (of health):** situates illness or disability as intrinsic to the individual; that it is part of that individual's body. Treatment is therefore related to the illness or disability.
>
> **The social model (of health):** situates the barriers to health outside of the individual's body and within society itself. It argues that society itself should be inclusive by design, rather than stigmatising the individual.
>
> **Whole health:** this approach looks at all the factors which contribute to health such as access to food and drink, opportunities for purposeful work, the wider family and social networks, quality of sleep and rest, the quality of the accommodation etc.

## Health in the context of school

If we think about this in our school context, it means that we need to see the aspects of the lives of our pupils, both at home and in school, which may be affecting them in terms of their health and wellbeing. At an individual level, this might be recommending that a parent-carer takes their child to the GP for a check-up, giving a pupil permission to use the accessible toilet or to leave quickly and quietly to check their blood sugars. In more complex cases, especially where you might have particular concerns about a pupil's learning and/or wellbeing, too; it might be that you monitor and follow-up on any health check recommendations and also discuss broader factors about hygiene, nutrition and keeping children safe at home, for example. If still concerned, you may offer to attend a medical appointment with the family as an advocate or refer the family for further external agency support. At a whole school leadership level, you may think about supporting health and wellbeing by reviewing your toilet provision, considering how safe and accessible they really are for all different pupils, for example, or how you use your school nurse hours, in support of the health of your whole school community.

These practices are not unfamiliar. Those involved in inclusion and safeguarding will routinely have these types of conversations and reviews, but we don't often have them in such a conscious way that directly links known physical health risk factors to academic outcomes. It might be intuitive to link good health with good achievement but somehow an acute allergic reaction to nuts seems quite separate and different to the general and ongoing skills required for learning. I don't know about you but I have yet to attend a routine EpiPen training that includes reference to progress and achievement trends of those who experience anaphylaxis. Given this, we would be entirely forgiven for thinking that so long as we know exactly which quadrant of the thigh to inject, that we champion being a "nut-free" school and our canteen staff carefully monitor allergens, we're fully supporting our pupils with overly reactive histaminic responses. We have covered off both the medical- and the social-models there, nicely. Great job. But what if, like for allergies as for asthma, there are hidden links between chronic conditions and underachievement that we've not been trained to be aware of from an educational point of view?

## The state of children's health in England

In 2018–19, there were 1.7 million children and young people in England who had a long-term condition. The big three affecting the most children are asthma, diabetes and epilepsy.[9] Data from the January census of that academic year, showed that the total number of pupils in England during a similar timeframe was about 8.7 million children and young people.[10] This means that the percentage of the school population with a chronic health condition stands at a whopping 20% of pupils. Broad statistics like this can hide a multitude of truths however. Children with lower socioeconomic status are more likely to experience poorer health[11] so schools in different areas will have relative overall percentages depending on their catchment demographic: the more deprived the catchment area, the worse the states of pupil health overall.

If chronic health conditions are risk factors for underachievement, as we're beginning to explore, then schools' outcomes are also likely to be affected by the capacities of the wider, local ecosystem that fosters good health: access to health services, quality housing, efficient and reliable transport, stable employment, quality food. These factors also impact upon parent-carers' capacity to provide for their children, tying in with the development of executive function that we met in Chapter Seven. If pupils are living in accommodation which is damp and mouldy, their health is likely to be compromised.[12] If public transport is costly and schedules limited, their health could be affected through poor access to health services and long waiting lists for reappointments.[13] If parents are not healthy and well themselves, their children's health risks also being compromised.[14] Good health is the result of the complementary and complex interaction of structures which support each other. This is potentially exacerbated further by the complex philosophical dilemma I watch play out in the grey area between education, health and social care: our differing ethical practices.

Up until the latter part of the twentieth century, many medical practitioners were trained in a paternalistic approach; the premise of which is that the doctor's knowledge of medical procedures and practices is superior than a patient's, and therefore professional knowledge should override patient wishes or choices, to determine the course of treatment. Nowadays, many medical practitioners prefer to work to a shared care model (where both medical expertise and patient preferences are combined to determine a course of action). As such, **paternalism** in its purest form is now considered ethically unsupportable by the General Medical Council.[15]

This shift towards a more "**patient-centred**" approach, which focuses on the "best interests" of the patient, is undoubtedly more ethically sound. In practice, however, it also enables a patient to *not* engage in a course of treatment if it is their wish to do so. That's to say, current ethical guidelines work on the premise that *not* attending appointments, *not* having treatment, *not* staying healthy is everyone's individual right, whether their doctor agrees with it or not. This is slightly more complex with children because children under a certain age are too young to give (or remove) consent and therefore it becomes parental choice.

However, this more humanistic model is where the ethics of education and health butt heads because as teachers we still operate in a strongly paternalistic model where we very much *do* expect children and young people to come to school, to stay in lessons and to take qualifications, regardless of their wishes or choices, regardless of their autonomy or their consent. And we do this because we believe that we are protecting their futures by legally enforcing education until the age of eighteen on the presumption that children and young people are not yet able to make sound decisions about their lives. After all, qualifications offer access to the world of work.

This places children in a paradoxical situation where depending on the context, not attending can be seen both as an individual right that doesn't need challenge and as an infringement of the law. In my own experience of these positionalities in practice, they both rely heavily on the adults in health, school and home to respect and protect the rights of the child or young person, by ensuring they attend appointments and by listening to their views as part of the process of determining the course of action. Experience however also tells me that the children and young people most at risk of being negatively affected by these paradoxical extremities, are those who fall between the gaps: children who perhaps haven't even been asked, and whose health is very much in the hands of people who are struggling to manage their own responsibilities, whether ill-health, disadvantage or workload.

**Top Tip:** In Serious Case Reviews, non-attendance is often highlighted as a notable factor leading up to a child's significant harm or death. Neglect is cumulative and there is a correlation between poor parental management of chronic health conditions causing extended school absences, for example, and neglect. If your data shows a high number of contextual risk factors – biological, psychological and social – and their attendance is low, this should be cause to seek external advice, guidance or intervention as a priority. This child needs you more than you may realise.

The reality then is that schools exist within an ecosystem much greater and more impactful than we perhaps realise when it comes to pupil progress rates and outcomes. The quality of teaching and learning within the classroom is vital, of course, but we shouldn't underestimate the pupils' whole lived experiences in terms of their access to good healthcare, the quality of their living accommodation and safety of their local area, their access to healthy foods, in also determining their outcomes.

What we also know is that overall figures for all types of children's health conditions are increasing, year on year, both because of a growth in the child population but also relative to the total – our children are comparatively less healthy, and less well, than children used to be.[16] We see this in education in the strain within the system for mental health support and SEND assessments; and in school attendance figures. However, it can also be seen in indicators such as the uptake of immunisations, levels of obesity and poor oral health; through rates of smoking and now the rampant growth of vaping; mis-use of alcohol or drugs; and suicide rates; many of which, unfortunately, are heading in the wrong direction;[17] not to mention the engagement with toxic social media and pornography, which can have catastrophic impact on the development of healthy minds and healthy relationships.[18,19]

Perhaps the most eye-opening example of just how little we have been concentrating on children's health and wellbeing is the fact that we've only really just started to monitor and report on it. You are likely to be as gobsmacked as I was that the **inaugural** State of Child Health report was only published in. . . 2017.[20] Yes, you read that right. Not even a decade ago. The only hope I take from this is that it demonstrates an increasing desire to think differently about child health. Given that it is the most decisively formative period of our lives, focusing on it is likely to benefit people for the remaining decades that follow, in myriad ways.

This growing focus on monitoring, understanding and improving child health is also likely to require a shift in educational practices as a fundamental part of child health. Uncomfortable though it might feel for us all based on our previous training and lived experiences, I think we're beginning to see a radical review of childhood: a questioning of children's rights for protection (and our investment in services and practices which enable that), and their rights for autonomy (and our wrestle with that in relation to shifting tides in adult power). Whatever the outcomes and changes over the coming years as we put childhood under the spotlight, as adults we will likely all have some learning and reflecting to do.

---

**Paternalism:** the approach that prioritises the medical practitioner's knowledge and experience over patient autonomy and choice in terms of determining a course of treatment.

**Patient-centred:** we see here a reference to the work of Carl Rogers and the humanist movement that we met in Chapter Three.

**Inaugural:** the first ever, marking the beginning of an institution, activity or period in office.

## Underachievement risk: Asthma, the quality of our breath and related factors

Asthma is a chronic condition characterised by inflammation and narrowing of the airways, making it difficult to breathe. This can lead to serious and even life-threatening situations. Common symptoms include coughing, wheezing (a whistling sound when breathing), chest tightness, shortness of breath, and occasionally chest pain. Asthma attacks can be triggered by various factors such as allergens, smoke, air pollution, cold air, exercise, and respiratory infections like colds or the flu. In some cases, particularly chronic ones, children may experience persistent coughing, or you may notice them breathing louder or faster than usual.

While asthma is a serious condition, it can be managed with appropriate treatment and care. It is crucial for children with asthma to have a treatment plan, follow it carefully, and attend regular check-ups to monitor their condition. Poorly controlled asthma can lead to fatigue, poor performance at school, stress, anxiety, depression, absenteeism, pneumonia, stunted growth and even death.[21]

A 2020 study on the impact of asthma control on school attendance, academic performance, and overall school life for children aged 9 to 14 revealed some concerning findings.[22] Children who missed more than nine school days due to asthma were often from low socioeconomic backgrounds or had parents with lower levels of education. However, the study also uncovered other, less obvious, school-related factors contributing to asthma-related absenteeism. Crowded, damp classrooms increase exposure to respiratory infections and fungal spores, both of which can exacerbate asthma symptoms. The condition of school buildings, their maintenance, and class sizes can also influence asthma-related school absences. Furthermore, asthma can impact children's social lives, as those who avoid exercise to prevent discomfort from asthma symptoms may miss out on forming friendships through play, leading to feelings of isolation.

In addition to missing school, poor asthma management can affect children's ability to concentrate and keep up in class. Research has shown a clear link between asthma and attention deficit,[23] suggesting that medical and educational professionals should be more proactive in identifying and addressing both conditions. There are social implications, too. Children with asthma who struggle socially or academically may hesitate to take their medication for fear of being stigmatised, which can further impact their health. Physical education (PE) classes, in particular, can be stressful for asthmatic children due to the increased physical exertion, which can lead to chest pain and tightening.

Breathing difficulties, such as during an asthma attack, happen when the airways narrow, restricting the flow of oxygen in and out of the lungs. This leads to hyperventilation, where individuals breathe rapidly to take in more oxygen. Acute airway narrowing is treated with a blue inhaler (salbutamol). Longer term inflammation of the airways is treated with the brown inhaler (steroid inhaler). Asthma can also be exacerbated by lower overall fitness levels because better health enables the body to use the oxygen it already has more efficiently. This oxygen efficiency can be measured through **VO² max**, as keen athletes will know.

The way we breathe can significantly affect our health. You might have seen a finger clip used in hospitals to measure blood oxygen levels, called **SpO²**. When oxygen levels drop below 96%, the body starts to experience stress and increasing inflammation. For asthmatics, who often breathe more frequently than non-asthmatics, this can exacerbate health problems by reducing oxygen efficiency. And, if you remember back in Chapter Five, we covered interesting research suggesting that when our bodies take a micropause such as when we breathe out or blink, our brain also takes a mini pause, too.[24] Those asthmatics who are breathing faster and taking micropauses more often may well be at risk for taking in less information in a lesson as a result. A 2014 study showed that training asthmatics to breathe less, under clinical supervision, led to significant improvements in their health.[25] In addition, a Japanese study from 2013 found that breathing through the mouth, rather than the nose, reduced the oxygen reaching the brain's prefrontal cortex, which is essential for attention, concentration, and working speed.[26] Nasal breathing, on the other hand, heats, cleans, and pressurises the air, allowing the lungs to extract more oxygen with each breath. Asking parents about whether their child sleeps open-mouthed, can be illuminating.

Breathing efficiency is crucial, but it isn't just about how we breathe. Oxygen uptake can also be affected by nutrient deficiencies, such as iron deficiency. A recent study that followed girls and young women aged 12 to 21 over eight years found that 38.6% were iron deficient, with higher rates among those from lower socioeconomic backgrounds or non-white ethnicities.[27] Food scarcity, whether due to poverty or disordered eating, was linked to iron-deficiency anaemia, a condition that can severely impact oxygen transport in the body and, by extension, brain function. Despite the availability of treatment, iron deficiency and anaemia remain under-recognised conditions with significant health consequences. Imagine if, in secondary schools, we were aware that between 16–33% of our year groups were iron-deficient, getting less oxygen around their body impacting upon healthy brain function and potential outcomes? We'd certainly be more proactive around questioning the impact of health on outcomes, particularly in higher-risk groups.

Asthma, as well as other health conditions like iron deficiency, can significantly affect children's lives, particularly in school settings. And it's not only a physical condition but one that interacts with a child's psychological and social environment, highlighting the complex relationship between a biological condition and its broader effects on a child's life.

> **VO² Max:** measures the rate of oxygen consumption during physical exertion which is an indicator of cardiovascular fitness and aerobic endurance.
>
> **SpO²:** is a measurement of oxygen saturation; how much oxygen your blood is carrying as a percentage of the maximum it could carry.

**No Child is Missed – Action Point 9.1: Screen for Asthma and Indicators of Impaired Oxygen Efficiency**

In terms of monitoring medical conditions, we are not medically trained practitioners but the evidence is clear that the links between health and education are not yet effective enough to prevent children's needs being missed and therefore children missing out on important formative experiences and outcomes at school. What this means for us is that we need to be better skilled in noticing indicators of ill-health and being conscious of the impact of known risk factors, proactively signposting parents-carers on for medical review and building better working relationships between education and health.

When assessing, gather background information about a pupil including *their health and attendance data. If you don't see this pupil regularly and already know, ask them about their perceptions of their health and wellbeing – what helps them to feel well, what doesn't. Talk to the PE staff about their observations of pupil fitness or look at report data about effort in PE.*

Make sure to gather wider data about attention and concentration too through the *Strengths and Difficulties Questionnaire (SDQ)* and also include questions at the start of your screening and in parent-carer conversations. **Appendix 4: Starter Questions** and **Appendices 9 & 10** will help. If you have additional questions, you could also carry out an observation of the pupil in class or at playtime.

## Underachievement risk: Diabetes and the quality of our food

Diabetes mellitus is a condition in which the body has difficulty processing food into energy, especially sugars from carbohydrates, leading to high blood glucose levels. Raised blood sugar causes proteins in the blood vessel walls to become stiff and inflexible, leading to scar tissue that blocks oxygen flow to nerves and vital organs. This can result in long-term damage to the heart, kidneys, and eyes if diabetes is poorly managed.

Type 1 diabetes is caused by the body's inability to produce enough insulin, while Type 2 results from the body's increasing resistance to insulin. Long term blood sugar control is measured through **HbA1c**. Both forms can be dangerous and reduce life expectancy if not properly controlled. Type 1 diabetes can occur at any age, but it most commonly develops between ages 4 to 7 and 10 to 14. Type 2 diabetes, once considered an "adult-onset" disease, is now increasingly affecting children as young as 10 due to rising rates of childhood obesity. Excess sugar in the blood that the body cannot use is excreted through urine, leading to dehydration. Common symptoms include bed-wetting, increased thirst, and fatigue. In adults, poorly controlled diabetes can cause severe consequences such as nerve damage, blindness, and an increased risk of heart attack or stroke.[28]

Impaired blood sugar control is a risk factor for poorer health outcomes, adding to the body's overall stress load. Raised sugars throughout the day can affect focus and concentration in class. Though well-controlled Type 1 diabetes does not typically affect academic achievement, poorly managed blood sugar, even if it doesn't meet the threshold for diabetes, is linked to underachievement in children and young people. The body's ability to efficiently metabolise food for energy, like its capacity to process oxygen, is crucial for academic performance. A recent study found that higher blood sugar levels correlated with lower academic attainment.[29] This suggests that the broader biopsychosocial environment of a pupil can impact their blood sugar levels, which in turn affects their academic success.

The role of diet in managing blood sugar and overall health is significant. Celebrity chef Jamie Oliver's campaign to improve school meals highlighted the importance of quality nutrition, especially for children who may rely on school lunches as their primary meal.[30] However, it's not just school meals that matter — what children eat for breakfast, snacks, and dinner also plays a critical role in their academic and physical health. The contents of a parent's shopping trolley can have a direct impact on a child's academic performance, too. There is more that supermarkets need to do, too, to help families eat healthily.

Processed foods, which are often soft and easy to eat, pose long-term risks. Over time, the lack of chewing weakens the tongue, leading to crowded teeth and a smaller palate, which can cause speech problems like lisps.[31] It can also contribute to inefficient breathing, especially during sleep, as the tongue relaxes back further into the mouth. Soft, ultra-processed foods also digest quickly, causing blood sugar spikes and subsequent energy crashes. Over time, ultra processed foods expose the body to increasing levels of harmful chemicals, including those found in processed meats, which have now been linked to cancer.[32]

Getting children to eat healthier options can be difficult, in many ways. A child's relationship with food is complex and influenced by physical, sensory, and emotional factors. Developing proper feeding skills is not unlike learning to handwrite. It requires those efficient sensory feedback systems to enable gross motor coordination to sit properly and fine motor skills to handle utensils. It also requires oral motor skills, such as muscle tone and a strong palate, to manage the social demands of a mealtime, like switching between conversation and eating. This can be made harder through the unpredictability of natural foods.

As Natalie Raven Morris, CEO and founder of The Feeding Trust, explains, ultra-processed foods offer safety through consistency. Whole foods, like blueberries, vary in size, texture, and flavour, which can make eating stressful for some children, especially those with sensory sensitivities or previous traumatic eating experiences, such as choking or allergic reactions.[33] This unpredictability can lead to anxiety and a limited diet, further complicating their relationship with food, leading to diagnoses like **ARFID** and **Paediatric Feeding Disorder**.[34,35]

In addition to emotional and sensory challenges, issues like constipation or the inability to use the bathroom flexibly can also influence what and when a child chooses to eat, limiting their food choices and intake. All of these factors contribute to broader difficulties with food and nutrition.

Ensuring children have access to healthy, unprocessed foods and helping them develop a healthy relationship with food is essential. What we eat significantly affects our overall health, brain function, speech, breathing, sleep quality, and obesity risk. Proper nutrition not only affects blood sugar control but also plays a crucial role in a child's overall wellbeing and academic success. If we want better outcomes for our children, we need to look beyond the classroom and consider their food consumption, too.

**HbA1c:** is a blood tests which is used to monitor blood glucose control. It measures the protein in red blood cells (haemoglobin) which carry oxygen through the body and the level of glucose which has fused to it.

**Feeding difficulties:** There are two major presentations you are likely to come across with feeding difficulties in children. These are: **Paediatric Feeding Disorder (PFD)**, which is associated with medical, nutritional, feeding skill, and/or psychosocial dysfunction (Goday et al., 2019).[36]And **Avoidant Restrictive Food Intake Disorder (ARFID)** which is motivated by a lack of interest in eating or food, sensory sensitivities and/or a fear of aversive consequences, like choking or vomiting (DSM-5). They are different, with PFD more associated with the functional aspects of eating, and ARFID centred more around the impact on mental health from food and eating.

### No Child is Missed – Action Point 9.2: Screen for Difficult Relationships with Food (including, diabetes and indicators of impaired blood sugar levels)

Medical testing for blood sugar is not something we can reasonably conduct but we can evaluate likely blood sugars and indicators of overall health and wellbeing by exploring food consumption with pupils or parents-carers, or simply noticing what types of foods we see children and young people eating. Nutritionists use various questionnaires and evaluation techniques in this way, including the *Screening Tool for the Assessment of Malnutrition in Paediatrics (STAMP)*.

*STAMP* is a tool developed by the Royal Manchester Children's Hospitals and the University of Ulster to support early identification of nutrition risk and reduce malnutrition. Whilst I am not advocating carrying out a full nutritional screening, which should be left to the specialists who are trained, I have begun to explore embedding part of the STAMP questionnaire with parents-carers, based upon advice I've taken from a nutritionist, as a way to help us to think more proactively about a child's nutrition and its effects on their wellbeing in school. If you have additional questions, you could also carry out an observation of the pupil at lunch time if you are particularly concerned.

## Underachievement risk: Epilepsy, autoimmune conditions and other contributing factors

- *Epilepsy*

Epilepsy is a common neurological condition where bursts of electrical activity temporarily disrupt normal brain function, resulting in seizures. These seizures, ranging from noticeable symptoms like uncontrollable jerking, stiffness, or collapsing to subtler signs like staring blankly (absence seizures) or experiencing unusual sensations, can significantly impact energy levels, memory, and concentration.[37] In turn, these effects can hinder academic performance. Epilepsy and learning difficulties are closely linked because it is also true to say that structural brain abnormalities affect learning, which can lead to seizures.

Epilepsy, like asthma and diabetes, can have severe long-term consequences if not properly managed. Studies have shown that children hospitalised for epilepsy are less likely to achieve basic numeracy and literacy skills and are 78% less likely to complete compulsory education.[38] This research highlights the need for better collaboration between healthcare professionals and schools to ensure earlier intervention and improved seizure control, minimising the negative impact on educational progress.

- *Anaphylaxis*

**Anaphylaxis** is a life-threatening allergic reaction that can escalate quickly without treatment, much like a severe epileptic seizure. The distinction between intolerance, allergies, and anaphylactic reactions lies in the intensity and speed of response to allergens, as indicated by **tryptase** enzyme levels in the blood. The severity of an allergic response can fluctuate based on exposure to allergens, general health, and seasonal factors. Common allergens include certain foods, venom, and environmental triggers such as pollen or chemicals, with food allergens posing the greatest risk of fatal reactions in childhood and adolescence. Symptoms of anaphylaxis include a runny nose, sneezing, sinus pain, coughing, wheezing, swelling (especially around the eyes, lips, mouth, and throat), as well as gastrointestinal distress.

Despite the serious nature of anaphylaxis, I cannot find any real research which explores its impact on educational outcomes. No wonder we never hear about it in our EpiPen training. Drawing parallels to other chronic illnesses, however, it seems reasonable to hypothesise that higher baseline tryptase levels from allergies, could pose risks to a child's educational attainment. It suggests to me that anaphylaxis may well be a risk factor for underachievement, we just haven't identified this through research yet. There is growing indication of this.

- *Hay fever*

Seasonal allergic rhinitis, or hay fever, although less dangerous than anaphylaxis, still has significant effects on cognitive function. Hay fever can impair concentration, problem-solving, and mood, affecting academic performance.[39] Research from 2007 revealed that hay fever symptoms, along with the medication used to treat them, are associated with a greater likelihood of unexpectedly dropping a grade in summer exams compared to winter mock exams.[40] Moreover, a recent study showed that high pollen levels in the weeks leading up to exams negatively affected student performance and outcomes in Maths and English Language.[41] It is staggering to consider that a few days of high pollen could potentially alter a student's entire career trajectory.

Whilst hay fever *is* a **special consideration**, for which a pupil might be lucky enough to get a compensatory, and perhaps rather arbitrary, percentage point extra if your school applies on your behalf, pupils will never know if they actually did or not, because the exam boards will not share this information. Whether this is the correct approach or whether we should take a more dynamic approach to assessments in terms of when a pupil can sit them is a question for another day, but I wonder about the pupils affected by hay fever whose schools didn't apply on their behalf; and I wonder too about the pupils whose schools didn't *even know*?

**Top Tip:** Make sure your Examinations Officer knows who has hay fever and someone monitors the Met Office pollen forecast, applying for special consideration on behalf of those who are affected.

- *Other contributing factors*

In addition to pollen, food consumption and environmental pollutants can also impede students' educational performance. For example, gluten allergy, causing Coeliac disease, can lead to inflammation of the gut, malabsorption of nutrients and reduced immunity. And, a large-scale study found that children attending schools located within 250 meters of busy roads, where chemical pollutants are more prevalent, are less likely to perform as well as their peers in less polluted areas.[42] In a landmark case in 2020, a court found that pollution "made a material contribution" to the death of nine-year-old who lived twenty-five metres from an arterial road around London.[43] Research also indicates that allergies in children and young people are on the rise, further complicating the relationship between environmental factors and health.[44]

These findings highlight the need to consider not just the physical environment inside classrooms but also the broader environmental context in which students live and learn. External factors such as food consumption, pollution and pollen levels meaningfully affect students' wellbeing and academic outcomes, raising questions about the equity of educational opportunities when it comes to the level of environmental stressors they are exposed to within the different domains of their lives.

Pollution rates, for example, are directly tied to the number of vehicles on the road. More cars mean higher pollution levels, which in turn increases the **allostatic load** within the body. Disadvantaged children are more likely to live in more polluted areas, breathing greater amounts of unsafe air. In fact, of the 43,000 playgrounds in Britain, only 1% comply with World Health Organization recommended limits on air pollution, but the more urban the school, the worse the air likely is. "Toxic air takes a heavy toll on children and young people – it stunts the growth of their lungs which can damage their health for the rest of their lives."[45]

As systemic stress builds, internal noise and distraction increase, making it harder for students to perform at their best. For me, this raises serious questions about the validity of using labels like "children with special educational needs and disabilities" (SEND), which often imply that the issue lies solely within the child. In reality, many of the barriers students face – such as exposure to environmental pollutants which aggravate and cause chronic health conditions – are beyond their control and not a result of personal or family choices. It crystallises the concept that the health of our environment is not just about issues which seem relatively removed from education, like rising sea levels and increased global temperatures, but that when we talk about the climate crisis, we're actually talking about immediate factors like the toxic fumes affecting pupils' walk to school and playtimes, and the chemicals found in many ultra processed foods.

Addressing these issues related to chronic health conditions require a concerted effort between us all: not just healthcare providers and schools, but businesses, policymakers, global leaders, to improve the health of our environments, to help mitigate the effects of chronic illness and environmental stressors on children's academic success. The long-term survival of humanity depends upon it.

**Anaphylaxis:** is caused by an allergic reaction. Symptoms of anaphylaxis include feeling faint, finding it hard to breathe, an elevated heartbeat and high anxiety.

**Tryptase:** is an enzyme found in mast cells. Enzymes help to speed up reactions in the body and mast cells are white blood cells that are part of the body's immune system, which are activated during an allergic reaction. Tryptase therefore speeds up our body's response to fighting something it perceives to be a threat. The more tryptase, the faster the response.

**Special consideration:** If a student is disadvantaged during exams by unforeseen circumstances such as illness, injury or bereavement, or if there is a disruptive incident which takes place during an exam itself, schools can apply to the exam boards to adjust the mark as a "special consideration". The maximum allowance given will be up to 5% of the raw marks available in the test concerned.

**Allostatic load:** coined by Bruce McEwen, it means "staying the same amid change", which is the body's stress response to help maintain life in the face of threat.

**No Child is Missed – Action Point 9.3: Screen for and Monitor Other Common Conditions which May Affect Outcomes**

The current picture, particularly around autoimmune conditions, seems to indicate that the links between health and education are not yet effective enough to prevent children's needs being missed, causing them to miss out on important formative experiences and outcomes at school. What this means for us is that we need to be better skilled in noticing indicators of ill-health and being conscious of the impact of known risk factors, proactively signposting parents-carers on for medical review and building better working relationships between education and health, and proactively applying access arrangements and special consideration on behalf of our pupils as a way to ameliorate disadvantage.

When assessing, make sure you have access to children's medical diagnosis information and you may also wish to include questions at the start of your screening about allergies or medication needs. You can find these indicator questions in **Appendix 4: Starter Questions** and **Appendices 9 & 10**. If you have additional questions, you could also carry out an observation of the pupil using **Appendices 7 or 8**.

## No Child Misses Out: What to do next . . .

**First of All: Consider a Pupil's Physical Health**

### Known health needs

We have skimmed the surface of only a few key areas of children's health and there are, of course, many, other conditions that children and young people experience. As a result, you will need to work specifically with parents-carers and a child's medical professionals to establish precise needs for pupils experiencing less common chronic health conditions. That said, recent research, by the INSCHOOL project, explored commonalities of how children's health needs can impact their educational experiences, regardless of the specific medical condition and what we can do.[46] These were:

o   The need to safely manage their health in school
    e.g. being allowed to go to the toilet or check blood sugars immediately when needed.

o   The need for a formalised yet flexible education pathway
    e.g. formally structured approaches to extensions for work submission when poorly, adjusted and adjustable curriculums, opportunities to trial access arrangements before examinations, thinking proactively about enabling children and young people to keep/catch up.

o   The need to be acknowledged and listened to by staff
    e.g. being sensitive when asking questions, like not staring at physical symptoms and not talking about personal medical information in front of others.

o   The need to be included in and supported by the school community
    e.g. attending social opportunities and school activities, staff and peers "checking in", not being stigmatised for low attendance and missing out on rewards.

o   The need to build towards key transition points to support positive feelings about the future
    e.g. even in spite of life-threatening or life-limiting conditions. NB. some pupils still want to have choices and career goals; others may not prioritise this over other opportunities to enjoy what time they have left. Respect and support for their choices is important.

o   The need to develop attitudes and approaches to help children and young people cope in school and with any mental health challenges which come with being ill
    e.g. the level of maturity developed through coping with a chronic health condition can make pupils very independent, but this both a positive trait and a risk factor for less support being given.

**Top Tip:** There are robots which can be used to help children in hospital attend lessons remotely – e.g. AV1. Teachers can also consider creating an online meeting so that children can attend remotely.

### Exploring support for complex health conditions

If you recall when we looked at the practice of optometrists, medical practitioners are trained to look for signs of pathology – signs of illness or disease. This means that research is often pointed at remediating disease, especially through pharmacology, and less about how to improve symptoms when you have a disease through living well.

This has come starkly into focus with Covid-19 and its longer-term effects because there is still so much to learn about it. Dr Ben Sinclair, a leading UK expert on Long Covid in children and young people, explained to me recently:[47] a lack of research and knowledge leads to understandable caution, but as medical practitioners "we need to be functional rather than just pharmaceutical", re-purposing medicines for alternative benefits, using nutritional and other therapies to optimise health, and continuing to explore the causes for someone's suffering. This is because traditional Western medicine offers lots of tests but very few treatment options beyond the standard advice about exercise, rest and counselling.

Through that lens and knowing that children's health, particularly within an educational context is under-researched, you might feel the recommendations below are pretty obvious. However, just like trying to maintain a healthy weight – sometimes even though we know what we should be eating, the best options are not always a high enough priority, and we perhaps underestimate the impact of every day consistency over occasional, big gestures. In that sense, it is worth engaging with the suggestions below as a way to improve long-term outcomes for the children and young people in your care. Let's do the best we can, until we know better.

> **Top Tip:** If you're looking for further advice and support relating to Covid, Dr Ben Sinclair recommends the charity Long Covid Kids (www.longcovidkids.org) who have an educational toolkit which can help us manage cases in school.

---

**No Child Misses Out – Response Point 9.1: Supporting Better Asthma Support and Oxygen Efficiency Rates in Pupils**

---

In terms of what we can do in schools to improve the environment for pupils with asthma and improving oxygen efficiency, there are a range of factors we can consider. The following advice comes from various asthma support services but medical advice can change, so do check advice with a recognised advisory service. One I particularly like is Asthma and Lung UK.

- *Supporting asthma in schools*

Group strategies may include:

   o   reducing exposure to allergens (such as mould)
   o   reducing humidity/dampness in the classrooms
   o   keeping exposure to chemicals in practical lessons to a minimum

o   avoiding crowded classrooms

o   keeping windows open – especially after lunch

o   better training for teachers in asthma and its management – and especially PE teachers

o   encouraging regular physical activity

o   encourage appropriate use of inhalers

Individual approaches may include:

o   monitoring a child's breathing rate – does it seem fast compared to others? Do they appear to be struggling for breath at times? Advise parents to monitor mouth breathing at night and to seek medical advice if this is occurring.

o   review the number of risk factors within a pupil's biopsychosocial experience and see where you can do small things to bring improvements

o   actively checking in with parents-carers about asthma appointments and encouraging/monitoring attendance

o   writing to a child's GP, and social worker if they have one, if you continue to be concerned about their health and wellbeing

---

**No Child Misses Out – Response Point 9.2: Supporting Better Blood Sugar/ Insulin Control and Eating Habits in Pupils**

---

Helping children to manage their diabetes well takes effort and training. Similarly, developing healthy habits and relationships with food takes effort from influences at home and school, and when problematic, a multidisciplinary approach. The following advice comes from various diabetes support services but medical advice can change, so do check advice with a recognised advisory service for updates and additional recommendations.

•   *Supporting diabetes and healthy eating in schools*

Group strategies may include:

o   working with catering services to review the food options in the school canteen

o   having clear and consistently applied rules about foods that are not permitted on site (e.g. high energy drinks)

o   adults modelling eating skills at lunchtimes and sitting with pupils when they're little and just learning table skills (especially important if sitting eating at a table is unlikely to be happening at home)

o   opportunities to explore different foods within the curriculum

o   having access to a school nurse

o   having whole school training to raise diabetes awareness

Individual approaches may include:

- o  monitoring a child's food intake – does it seem restricted or unhealthy? Do they appear to be struggling to eat? If so, recommending a parent-carer seeks professional advice from a multidisciplinary service such as *The Feeding Trust* in the UK, or *Feeding Matters* in the USA.
- o  review the number of risk factors within a pupil's biopsychosocial experience and see where you can do small things to bring improvements, for example food vouchers for fresh foods, if access to healthy foods is prevented through poverty
- o  actively checking in with parents-carers about diabetes appointments and encouraging/monitoring attendance
- o  writing to a child's GP, and social worker if they have one, if you continue to be concerned about their health and wellbeing

---

**No Child Misses Out – Response Point 9.3: Supporting Epilepsy and Autoimmune Conditions**

---

The following advice comes from various epilepsy and allergy advice and support services but medical practice can change, so do check advice with a recognised advisory service for any updates or additional recommendations.

- • *Supporting healthy management of allergies and allergic reactions in schools*

Group strategies may include:

- o  being conscious of flickering lights or blinds and geometric patterns, aware that a small number of pupils with epilepsy may have photosensitivity
- o  being clear about health and safety in practical lessons (especially swimming), extra-curricular activities and trips, particularly for those with epilepsy, and what to do in an emergency detailed in any risk assessments
- o  allowing a pupil to seek medical help in a lesson if needed
- o  talking about epilepsy to help pupils understand it and what to do if someone has a seizure
- o  For more information, seek out advice from *The Epilepsy Society* and *Epilepsy Action.*

Individual approaches may include:

- o  ensuring teachers know what to do when a seizure happens
- o  considering a pupil's need for extra time in assessments

- making notes available for pupils who miss out on key information unintentionally through absence seizures in lessons
- space and time to recover after a seizure
- recognising that anti-seizure medication can cause side effects including tiredness and problems with memory and concentration
- For more personalised support advice, seek support from a pupil's epilepsy specialist
- Encourage parents-carers to keep to appointments and update school if risks or medications change.

## Final thoughts: the implications of research gaps

If the last decade of practice has taught me anything, it is that educational attainment, or lack of it, is complex. Far more complex than we've given credit to; and focussing on classroom practice is only one part of a much bigger picture. Moreover, the knowledge gaps in the intersectionality between education and health suggest that there is still much more to learn about the short- and long-term implications of children's health and wellbeing on education.

This criticism is often levied at the research into women's health, too, leaving fifty percent of the world's population "chronically misunderstood, mistreated and misdiagnosed."[48]

These lacunas are leading to really live issues that we're grappling with in schools, often alone, often very much in the dark. Issues like the burgeoning of challenging behaviours and the growing gender identity "epidemic", particularly in girls and young women, which brings the interwoven nature of brain, body and environment sharply into frame.

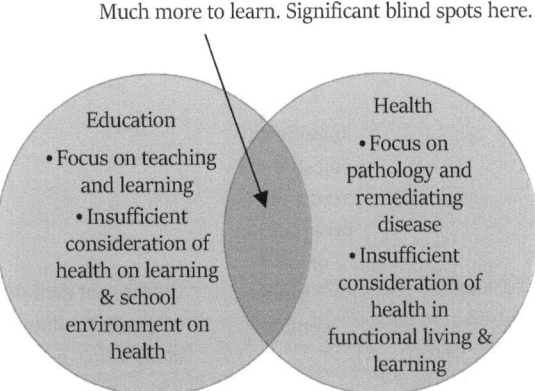

*Figure 9.1* The gaps between education and health research

The Cass Report (2024)[49], reviewing the healthcare for children and young people with **gender dysphoria** and those identifying as transgender, raised some important questions about the risks to health and wellbeing that come from "unquestioning" cultures not taking into consideration wider contexts and comorbidities. We see this in affirmative cultures, as Dr Hilary Cass explored with the Gender Identity Development Service clinics, where children and young people were given life-changing medication without robust enough multi-disciplinary care monitoring the individual ethical considerations. (I can also see a time in the next decade where a similar review of the rise in medicating for ADHD finds similar.) We also see this in cultures of disregard, denial and whitewashing, where children's needs are ignored or quashed with little or no support at all.

> **Gender dysphoria:** the feeling of discomfort or distress occurring in people whose gender identity differs from their sex assigned at birth or sex-related physical characteristics

These polar approaches are, however, rooted in the same soil: a lack of critical engagement with complex data and too much emphasis on relativity of personal experience and opinion. As we've touched on before in this book, we need *better sensitivity and specificity* of data in order to identify children's needs accurately and determine safe and child-focussed support in response.

With regard to gender, as ever, evolutionary biology gives us some clues. Darwin may have straight-jacketed sex into a binary concept, but this view is increasingly coming under heavy scrutiny in the animal kingdom. It's coming to light that there is a continuum, with males at one end and females at the other, and variability is continuous

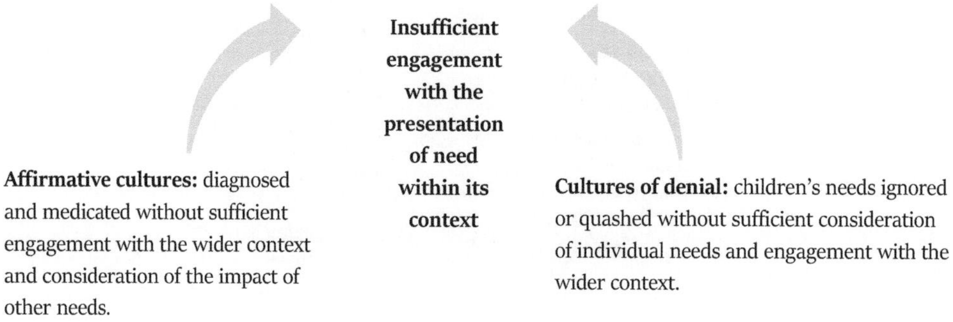

**Insufficient engagement with the presentation of need within its context**

**Affirmative cultures:** diagnosed and medicated without sufficient engagement with the wider context and consideration of the impact of other needs.

**Cultures of denial:** children's needs ignored or quashed without sufficient consideration of individual needs and engagement with the wider context.

*Figure 9.2* Affirmative cultures versus cultures of denial

between those two types;[50] a spectrum of continuous variation in sexual characteristics with many kinds of intersex between the masculine and feminine extremes.[51] If biology is only just beginning to grapple with some deeply entrenched assumptions about gender, then medical and educational practice is several steps behind.

Underfunding, under-resourcing and pervasive lack of desire to truly engage with implications about the biological, psychological and social causes of health, and illhealth, are not just a stresser for educational practitioners today but a risk for the future wellbeing of humanity as a whole.

## Chapter Summary: Physical Health

- *Analysing students' biological, psychological, and social data can reveal significant patterns of underachievement.*
- *Chronic health conditions such as asthma, diabetes, and epilepsy are risk factors for underachievement in school and should be considered similarly to other conditions like autism or ADHD.*
- *Students from lower socioeconomic backgrounds often experience poorer health, such as higher rates of asthma and diabetes, which contribute to underachievement in school.*
- *Poorly managed asthma can lead to issues with concentration and learning, while efficient breathing and proper oxygen uptake are crucial for cognitive performance in children.*
- *The quality of food, including school meals and home diet, directly impacts students' blood sugar levels, cognitive function, and overall academic performance.*
- *External environmental factors such as pollution, pollen levels, and living conditions can exacerbate health issues like allergies and asthma, affecting students' academic outcomes.*
- *Conditions like epilepsy and anaphylaxis have significant social and academic implications, yet they are often under-researched in terms of their impact on educational achievement.*
- *Addressing chronic health conditions and improving environmental factors in schools and society requires collaboration across healthcare, education, and policymaking to support better outcomes for children.*

# PART 3
# Be The Change

PART 5
The Change

# 10 All's Well that Ends Well

You're here at this chapter because you're now beginning to think about bringing all that knowledge together from the previous chapters to work with a child or young person. First of all, let's high five! This is a really exciting moment of anticipation, hope and opportunity. You're going to put this new found knowledge to the test and begin to think deeply and with confidence about how you might help this child or young person. I wonder what you are going to learn? What strategies you'll be able to consider from your results?

Secondly, it can also be a time when you might feel a bit nervous too. This is because you really care and you want to get it right, which is a good thing, but it might also be because it feels new and relatively high stakes. Don't worry if you're doubting yourself a little bit. Will you get the process muddled? Will you forget to do something? Will you get something wrong? Yes, you probably will. I have, too. But I've yet to cause a disaster when screening, even if I have had to see the child again to do something that I've forgotten, or rectify an error I've unwittingly made. As long as you take the process seriously and respectfully, honouring your values as you go, making little mistakes is part of the learning process. As the late, great Maya Angelou once said, "Do the best you can until you know better. Then when you know better, do better."

Thirdly, we've covered a lot of ground in this book and so the idea of the screening process might now feel quite complex and big. In practice, it really isn't that complicated to do, but of course, I've had to give you options for all different scenarios and children and I've had to assume all different levels of previous experience and knowledge. Trust me, you can absolutely do this.

What we're going to cover in this chapter is a protocol that I recommend and a step-by-step process to help you do it as efficiently and as successfully as possible. Put it this way – I've constructed, refined and simplified the process through my own trial, error

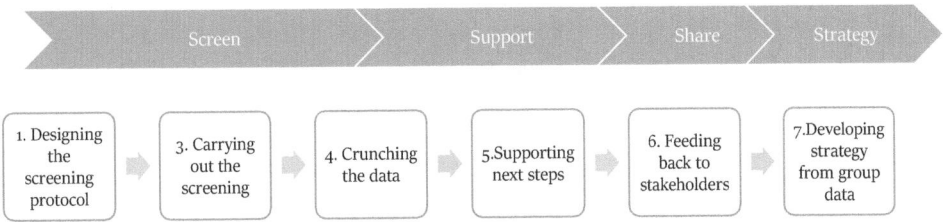

*Figure 10.1* An overview of the later steps to consider

DOI: 10.4324/9781032663968-13

and experience, so you've got a massive head start. You're already way more efficient, skilled and knowledgeable than I was when I first started!

This chapter is also a sibling to Chapter Three, where we explored how to get started: thinking about our values; the ethics of screening and reporting; and, how we inform, guide and respect stakeholders (step number 2). This chapter will now take you through the more practical steps to help you be as efficient as possible and to finish well. We will cover the following.

- How to **Screen:** We will cover the practical steps to designing your screening proto-col: what tests to use and when. Using the **No Child is Missed** guidance throughout the chapters and the Appendices at the back of the book (and hosted on the website), you will bring together the tools you need to answer the first important screening question: **What can we learn about [name]?**
- How to **Support:** We will cover the types of supports you might recommend or put in place, both in the setting and at home, and any external, specialist assessments you might want to recommend to parents-carers as a result of the screening. Using the **No Child Misses Out** recommendations and following information, you will answer the second important question: **What support might make a difference to [name]?**
- How to **Share:** We will then cover how to bring your results and recommendations together and the channels you'll need to have ready to share your findings about each pupil with staff, their parents-carers and even the children themselves.
- And finally, how to build a **Strategy:** This step will become more important as you screen whole year groups because you can then think about how you can use this screening data as a whole, and over time, to develop your whole school and SEND pro-vision. It will also prompt you to consider what investments you might want to make as a result of the emerging trends.

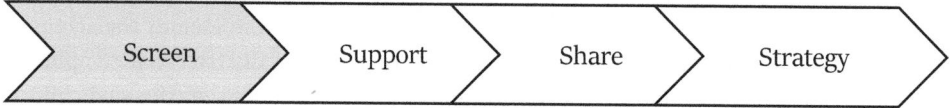

## 1   Designing the screening protocol

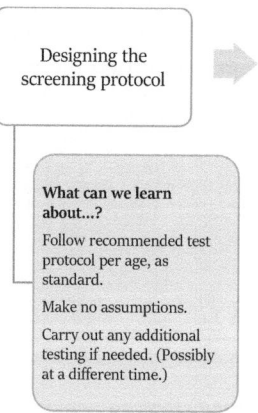

This first section will take you through the face-to-face part of the screening process, considering what tests to use and when. Using the **No Child is Missed** guidance, you will bring together the tools you need to answer the first important screening question: **What can we learn about [name]?**

Over the following pages, I'll introduce you to the plans for each age and stage. The screening protocol guides have been written as standalone sections so you do not need to read about an earlier or later stage to understand the one or two you want to focus on today.

> **Education Health and Care Plan:** (England only) This is for children and young people aged up to 25 who need more support than is ordinarily available. It is a legal document which requires provision to be made by the educational setting and is reviewed annually by professionals and parents-carers on behalf of, and often with, the pupil.

- *Screening early years: up to age five*

It's no secret that supporting children well in their early years can lead to improved longer-term outcomes. If you're reading this section then I expect you are passionate about it! Thank you for the work you do, helping children get the best start in life – my own included. I also want to acknowledge and apologise that I haven't always been able to use early years specific language in the book. In that respect, this book isn't as inclusive as a separate standalone guide for this age group. I hope you've been able to transpose terms and references as you've gone along.

At the time of writing, the Nuffield Foundation has just released research indicating the importance of quality early years provision. It concluded that the Sure Start initiative in England launched in 1999 under the Labour government to provide health, parenting and family support services to new families in areas of disadvantage, enabled children to obtain nearly a grade better in their examinations at age sixteen, compared to similar profile children who did not have the same access to Sure Start centres. Likewise, Sure Start centres enabled earlier identification of special needs leading to an *increase in SEND data at age five, but an overall decrease in SEND levels by age eleven and sixteen*, and a 9% reduction in the need for **Education Health and Care Plans**. Gordon Brown, former Labour Prime Minister and Chancellor of the Exchequer, said "These results tell us in detail what most parents already know. That if you provide a supportive environment to children in their early years and invest in their futures, the results will be life-transforming."[1]

Identifying and supporting needs changes lives.

By now you'll have a really good understanding of the areas which are critical to child development, but what are we looking for in the early years? In screening children at the start of their educational journey, we're looking to evaluate the *risk and protective factors* which may affect their ongoing healthy development over time. The screening plan therefore looks at phonological processing (Chapter Four), colour vision deficiency (Chapter Five), physical development (Chapter Six), executive function (Chapter Seven) and mental and physical health (Chapters Eight and Nine), by considering:

o   *How safe and capable does this child feel?*
o   *How well can this child understand and express themselves?*
o   *How well can this child sustain attention and control impulses?*

These three areas of safety, connection to others and being able to focus, are critical throughout life, not just childhood, but experience leads me to believe they are strongly linked to outcomes later on in the educational journey, too. This is why we need to capture this information now and improve any difficulties emerging through targeted work, both in setting and through family support, where we can. When children are really little, we can ignore the warning signs hoping they might *"catch up"* or *"grow out of it"* because *"they're only little"*. And whilst there is a healthy dose of truth in this, risks left unchecked can become bigger and bigger, sometimes becoming serious and life-limiting. The evidence proves it: identifying and supporting needs in the early years changes lives.

## No Child is Missed Action Point 10.1: Core Screening Protocol – Pre-School to Age Five

| Risk/Protective Factors | Screening Focus | NCIM Action Points/Data to Gather |
|---|---|---|
| **Sense of safety and capacity** | Basic health checks: hearing (4) and vision (5) | 5.2 Colour Vision Deficiency |
| | Relationship with food (8 & 9) | Appendix 9: EYFS and Primary Parent-Carer Conversation Form |
| | Bladder and bowel control Parenting support and child social and economic risk factors Social and emotional development (7) | 7.1: Social and Economic Risk Factors |
| | Physical and sensory development: (6) | 6.2 & 3: Praxis and Sensory Integration |

| Ability to express themselves and be heard | Attention and listening Receptive and expressive language Social communication Speech sounds Play (4) | 4.1: Speech, Language and Communication |
| --- | --- | --- |
| Ability to sustain attention and delay gratification Developing independence | Impulse control Remaining focused Thinking ahead (7) | Appendix 7: Observations in Setting (EYFS & Early Primary) |

- *Screening: ages five to seven*

The first stage of formal education is a transition phase. Early skill development moves towards a more mature skill development. In this way, the tests for ages five to seven are also a transition approach, capturing elements of both the earlier and later screening protocols.

Teachers of this age range will know well that each group of children entering into formal education will arrive with a wide range of experiences and skillsets. There are challenges that come with a single structured and pacy curriculum, and a higher ratio of pupils to teachers, when there are so many *risk factors* which can affect progress: developmental gaps between the youngest August birthdays learning alongside oldest September birthdays; differences in their early years experiences around their sense of safety and capacity; differences around speech and language and phonological awareness; differences in self-awareness, attention, concentration and impulse control; differences in previous life experience that we might call "cultural capital".

Enabling children to feel a sense of purpose and competence is critical for success further down the line, and yet, ushering all children through to achieve readiness for the next phase of learning is incredibly challenging. Understanding the needs of each child and meeting them individually is juxtaposed against the uniformity of expectations within the curriculum. This is often where the gaps really start to widen between those who have developed the "sensations and perceptions" to cope with the increasing independence that is required of them for success, and those whose experiences leave them with gaps, misperceptions and dysfluency and increasing dependence upon the adults around them to avoid overwhelm.

According to Erik Erikson,[2] who we met in Chapter Seven, at this stage individual feelings of success come from the approval of others through competencies in skills like letter formation, phonics, counting, playing. Children beam when a teacher or peer acknowledges their progress and conveys competence and growing industry, feeling pride and self-esteem. Conversely, the children who have a strong dependence on others, who feel unable to display skills like more industrious peers, will increasingly struggle with new situations and new learning challenges, and are likely to feel shame and inferiority.

Identifying and supporting needs changes lives.

Like the previous screening plan, we consider those key risk factors around a sense of safety and capacity, communication ability, physical skill development, and focus/impulse control. Alongside these however we also want to start seeing growing confidence in a sense of self and in reading and handwriting skills. The five-to-seven screening plan looks at all aspects within the book, specifically phonological processing (Chapter Four), visual processing (Chapter Five), handwriting and sensory integration (Chapter Six), executive function (Chapter Seven) and mental and physical health (Chapters Eight and Nine), by considering each child, asking:

o   *How safe and capable does this child feel?*
o   *How well can this child understand and express themselves?*
o   *How efficiently can this child process visual information?*
o   *How well can this child hold a pencil and make accurate letters and numbers?*
o   *How well can this child remember, sustain attention and control impulses?*

These five areas are critical throughout later childhood, positively and negatively influencing a huge range of factors in a child's life and well beyond into adulthood.

### No Child is Missed Action Point 10.2: Core Screening Protocol – Ages Five to Seven

| Risk/Protective Factors | Screening Focus | NCIM Action Points/Data to Gather |
|---|---|---|
| **Sense of safety and capacity** | Basic health checks: hearing (4) and vision (5) Relationship with food (8 & 9) Bladder and bowel control (7) Parenting support, child social and economic risk factors Social and emotional development (7) | Appendix 9: EYFS and Primary Parent-Carer Conversation Form 7.1: Social and Economic Risk Factors |

| Ability to under-stand and express themselves | Phonological aware-ness (4) | 4.2: Phonics Screen-ing Test/Non-Word Test Evaluating Phonemic Decoding |
|---|---|---|
| | Reading comprehen-sion (4) | 4.4: Spelling 4.3: Reading Comprehension |
| Ability to correctly interpret visual information at speed | Colour processing (5) Speed of sight-sound correspondence (5) | 5.2: Colour Vision Deficiency 5.3: Rapid Automatic Naming (RAN) Speed |
| Pencil hold and early writing skills | Handwriting grip and hand strength and visuo-motor skills (6) | 6.1–2: Early Handwrit-ing and Praxis Skills |
| Ability to sustain attention and delay gratification Developing independence | Updating (working memory) Focus and attention (7) | 7.2 Appendix 5: Execu-tive Function (core only; additional if needed) |

- *Screening: ages seven to eighteen*

There are challenges that come with one structured and pacy curriculum and a higher ratio of pupils to teachers, when there are so many *risk factors* which can affect progress: developmental gaps between the youngest August birthdays learning alongside oldest September birthdays; differences in their experiences of personal safety, capacity, inclusion; differences around vocabulary knowledge and oracy; differences social skills and emotional reactivity; differences in attention, concentration and impulse control; differences in hormone regulation; differences in attendance; differences in previous life experience that we might call "cultural capital" and differences in a more traditional measure, IQ. Ushering all children through the same curriculum in a fixed timeframe with limited resources is an extraordinarily difficult task.

When underlying skills are not well developed enough, divisions widen between those who have developed the "sensations and perceptions" to cope with the increasing independence that is required of them for success, and those whose experiences leave them with gaps, misperceptions and dysfluency and increasing dependence upon the adults around them to avoid overwhelm.

The two previous screening plans measure these early building blocks of formal education, evaluating speech and language and the development of phonological awareness as critical foundations to literacy, for example. For some pupils whose needs continue to be unmet as they move through school, it might be appropriate to take a step back to an earlier stage of screening to get to the heart of what's going on. For most settings and pupils however, we can evaluate a pupil's profile quite speedily, from age seven upwards, directly exploring more obvious indicators like reading and spelling, rather than underlying skills for example. According to Erik Erikson,[3] who we met in Chapter Seven, during these stages of life individual feelings of success come from a sense of purpose; firstly through competence and feeling of self-worth in typical academic skills which he called "industry"; and then during the teenage years, a growing sense of clarity around who they are, what they want from their life and the things that are important to them, which he called "identity". We'll be looking to evaluate aspects of these stages to help us identify how a pupil is developing.

Once you have completed the standard battery of tests, you may find you still have some questions. At this point, you may feel you'd like to dip into additional tests to tailor your approach and further substantiate information about a pupil.

There is no doubt however: identifying and supporting needs changes lives.

The seven-to-eighteen screening plan looks at all aspects within the book, specifically phonological processing (Chapter Four), visual processing (Chapter Five), handwriting and sensory integration (Chapter Six), executive function (Chapter Seven) mental and physical health (Chapters Eight and Nine), but as the pupils become more self-aware and competent, the emphasis moves towards more direct dialogue through the assessing process, requiring pupil self-assessment. Tests seek to answer:

o   *How physically and mentally well does this child feel?*
o   *How confident does this child feel academically, socially and emotionally?*
o   *How are this child's literacy skills developing?*
o   *How efficiently can this child process visual information?*
o   *How well can this child sustain attention, recall information and control impulses?*
o   *What does their cognitive profile indicate about their current performance?*

These six areas are critical to better understand risk and protective factors for success in the classroom, and well beyond into adulthood.

---

**No Child is Missed Action Point 10.3: Core Screening Protocol – Ages Seven to Eighteen**

| *Risk/Protective Factors* | *Screening Focus* | *NCIM Action Points/ Data to Gather* |
| --- | --- | --- |
| **Sense of mental and physical health** | Basic health checks Safeguarding checks | Appendix 4: Starter Questions Known Health data (use Appendix 10 if needed) |

| Sense of academic, emotional and social confidence | Self-efficacy (8) Impulsivity and shift (7) | 8.1: Self-efficacy questionnaire 7.4 Strengths and Difficulties question- naire (Age 11+) |
| --- | --- | --- |
| Literacy skills: accu- racy and speed of working | Reading efficiency Reading comprehen- sion (4) Spelling (4) Handwriting effi- ciency (6) | 5.4 Reading efficiency 4.3 Reading comprehension 4.4 Spelling accuracy 6.1 Handwriting efficiency |
| Visual processing speed and colour accuracy | Colour processing (5) Speed of sight-sound correspondence (5) | 5.2 Colour vision deficiency 5.3 Rapid Automatic Naming (RAN) speed |
| Ability to sustain attention and delay gratification | Updating (working memory) Focus and attention (7) | 7.1: Social and eco- nomic risk factors 7.2 Appendix 5 Execu- tive function (core only; additional if needed) |
| Cognitive profile | Cognitive ability/ intelligence (2) | 2.1 Cognitive ability |

- *Screening: what else to collate (all ages)*

Alongside the basic screening data you've collated from pupils, I would advise you to download other known data about pupils from your setting's database.

o   Date of birth
o   Gender
o   Known medical conditions
o   Known SEND diagnoses
o   Additional information about family and home circumstances which may be relevant

- *Screening: additional and specific tests (non-core tests)*

The core battery seeks to answer the question, "What can we learn about [name]?" which is a really useful question in terms of gathering proactive data, catching children at risk before they fall. But you might also have some cases at the moment which are taking up a lot of time and which you need a better understanding of.

This next section is an overview of the optional tests you might want to run, in addition to the core tests, to help you think more deeply about what a pupil might be experiencing which is leading to their distress in school.

In some of these cases, even your in-school screening might be insufficient for what you need and you will want to refer on to external specialists as well. However, with waiting lists as long as they are, these additional screening tools can be used in the interim to try and make a difference whilst you are waiting for specialist support.

Again, these tools are not suggested as part of a diagnostic process, but without a shadow of a doubt, any external specialist will be glad of your diligence in gathering this additional information because their conclusions and advice will be much the better for it.

- *Additional Screening: complex behaviours and mental health*

## No Child is Missed Action Point 10.4: Additional Protocol – Complex Behaviours, Trauma, Mental Health

| Risk/Protective Factors | Screening Focus | NCIM Action Points/ Data to Gather |
|---|---|---|
| **Speech, language and communication skills** | Attention and listening Receptive and expressive language Social communication Speech sounds Play (4) | 4.1 Speech, language and communication |
| **Stress in the school day** | Visual stress (5) Sensory integration (6) | 5.1 Visual stress 6.3 Sensory Integration |
| **Quality of life** | Basic health checks Safeguarding checks Relationship with food Bladder and bowel control (8 & 9) | 8.2 Quality of life, ACES Appendix 9 or 10: Age-appropriate Parent-Carer Conversation Form |
| **Typical behaviours observed in school** | Profile of common behaviours and challenges inside school (7) | 7.3 & 7.4 Impulsivity, shift, strengths and difficulties |

| | | Appendix 7 or 8: Age-appropriate observations in setting |
|---|---|---|
| **Influences and choices outside of school** | Profile of risk exposure outside of school (8) | 8.2 Consider local Youth Offending resources |

- *Additional Screening: school avoidance*

### No Child is Missed Action Point 10.5: Additional Protocol – Complex Behaviours, Masking, School Avoidance, Mental Health

| *Risk/Protective Factors* | *Screening Focus* | *NCIM Action Points/ Data to Gather* |
|---|---|---|
| **Speech, language and communication skills** | Attention and Listening Receptive and expressive language Social communication Speech sounds Play (4) | 4.1 Speech, language and communication |
| **Stress in the school day** | Visual stress (5) Sensory integration (6) | 5.1 Visual stress 6.3 Sensory integration |
| **Quality of life** | Basic health checks Safeguarding checks Relationship with food Bladder and bowel control (8 & 9) | 8.2 Quality of life, ACES Appendix 9 or 10: Age-appropriate Parent-Carer Conversation Form |
| **Barriers to attendance, including sense of belonging and identity** | Social, emotional and mental health (8) | 8.3 School avoidance and perceived stress |

- *Additional screening: learning delays*

Sometimes, there doesn't seem to be an obvious cause emerging from the Core screening battery. If you still have unanswered questions, consider adding in some or all of these tests, too, including a numeracy screener.

**No Child is Missed Action Point 10.6: Additional Protocol – Learning Delays**

| Risk/Protective Factors | Screening Focus | NCIM Action Points/Data to Gather |
|---|---|---|
| **Speech, language and communication skills** | Attention and listening Receptive and expressive language Social communication speech sounds Play (4) | 4.1 Speech, language and communication |
| **Handwriting and Spelling Difficulties** | Rhyme and alliteration Shared sounds Dividing and blending syllables Segmenting phonemes Manipulating phonemes (4) Handwriting and praxis (6) | 4.2 Phonological Awareness 4.5 Spelling accuracy (additional) 6.1 & 6.2 Appendix 6: Handwriting and Praxis Checklist |
| **Stress in the school day** | Visual stress (5) Sensory integration (6) | 5.1 Visual stress 6.3 Sensory integration 8.3 Perceived stress |
| **Quality of life** | Basic health checks Safeguarding checks Relationship with food Bladder and bowel control (8 & 9) | 8.2 Quality of life, ACES Appendix 9 or 10: Age-appropriate Parent-Carer Conversation Form |

## A word about maths and early numeracy development . . .

You might be wondering why I haven't included numeracy in any of these lists? It is, *of course*, a vital skillset and one you might wish to measure. But what I've concluded – through trial and error – is that I haven't yet learnt *enough* from putting every child through a maths screening, given the time it adds to the process, to make it worth including into the core battery of tests. But that's not to say doing an additional maths screening for some children isn't worth it – it may be if a child is really struggling with numeracy.

However, as we learned in Chapter Seven, experience and research suggests that maths difficulties commonly occur as a result of executive function difficulties[4] (which you're already testing anyway). As such, if the pupil has difficulties with attention and concentration or accurate short-term recall, these difficulties are likely to affect maths ability. You also probably already know if a child is struggling with maths and what their areas for development are. It's likely that targeting support to executive function skills, reducing maths anxiety and focusing on developing competency in basic maths facts is going to be the best course of action anyway. In early years, research suggests that working on a concept called **finger gnosis** is an important strategy to support early maths development,[5] improving knowledge of ordinal and cardinal numbers. Finger training may also be a really helpful approach to improving cognitive and quantitative skills.

**Finger gnosis:** recognising and understanding the difference between our fingers. For example, knowing that our thumb represents number one and our little finger, number five.

### No Child is Missed – Action Point 10.7: Screening for Numeracy and Maths Skills

If you do want to do additional numeracy testing, the best way to do this is to evaluate speed and accuracy of basic numeracy skills (place value and maths facts) as well as maths anxiety. If you have got significant issues with numeracy in your setting however, feel free to add numeracy screening to your core battery of tests. You might want some further reading. In which case, I recommend Steve Chinn's *More Trouble with Maths, 3rd edition (2023)* to help you dissect what might be going on and to support pupils with their numeracy development. You might also like to read more about finger gnosis strategies.

 **Top Tip:** An important strategy to support early maths development is improving knowledge of ordinal and cardinal numbers. Finger training may also be a really helpful approach to improving cognitive and quantitative skills.

**2 Carrying out the screening**

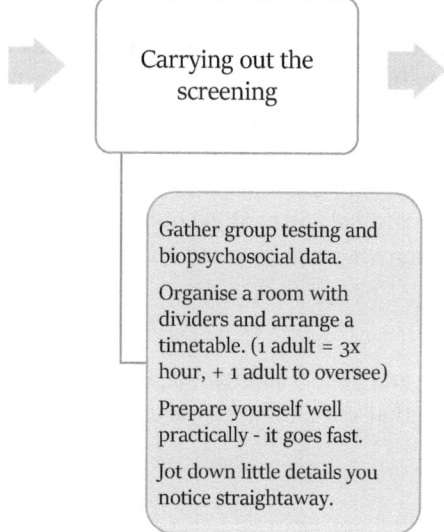

Carrying out the screening

Gather group testing and biopsychosocial data.

Organise a room with dividers and arrange a timetable. (1 adult = 3x hour, + 1 adult to oversee)

Prepare yourself well practically - it goes fast.

Jot down little details you notice straightaway.

### Part A Running the process: example classroom information gathering – ages seven to eighteen

If you are running this process on an individual child, you could carry out the plan at a time of your choosing, although you may decide to break up the process into chunks to avoid overwhelm or removing them from too much of a lesson. The complexity comes with running the screening process at scale. Below, I will provide a suggestion for how you might want to plan it if you are running this process with a whole class or year group within a short period of time.

- *Gather examples of literacy skills*

1. During a selected lesson – e.g. English – total 15 minutes
   Minutes 1–5:
   - **Group spelling test**
     - *Suggested marking approach:*
     - *Class teacher marks spelling test raw score*
     - *Or, use AI to mark spelling tests*

Minutes 6–15:
- ○ **Handwriting test: ten minutes free writing about a topic of their choice (e.g. their life, a trip they went on etc.)**

Suggested marking approach:
*Pupils count and mark every 10 words (ease of counting)*
*Pupils total their scores to work out total number of words in ten minutes.*
*Or, use AI to count total words*

- *Gather pupil sense of self-efficacy*

2. During a selected pastoral time – e.g. form – total 15 minutes
   Minutes 1–15:
   - ○ **Self-efficacy assessment e.g. Myself as a Learner**
   - ○ **Health and wellbeing check e.g. Strengths and Difficulties Questionnaire**
   - ○ **Ishihara Colour Blind Screening***

   *Suggested marking approach:*
   *Either digitise onto a Google Form/other survey tool*
   *Or, create an overlay for speed scoring*
   *\*This needs to be digitised within this context*

- *Gather pupil biopsychosocial data from your school database*

You will want to collect as much as you can. Talk with your colleagues about the type of data you hold which might be useful, such as:

- ○ **Date of birth**
- ○ **Sex**
- ○ **Known medical conditions & diagnoses**
- ○ **Family circumstances**
- ○ **Race/ethnicity**

Use No Child is Missed Action Point 7.1 (Social and Economic Risk Factors) to help you decide what you want to know; and what else is pertinent to your setting right now.

## Part B Running the process: example face to face screening – ages seven to eighteen

3. With a member of the SEND team, within the school day – total 20 minutes

   Remember:
   - ○ Remind yourself of your values and the importance of a safe experience for everyone (Chapter Three).
   - ○ Prepare as well as you can beforehand – a screening goes *fast*

    o   Note down anything you observe – any little thing that might be important, like "regularly touches hair"; "head in hands"; "leans back"; "seems anxious" etc. And do it immediately, don't think "I'll add that in a minute/at the end". You won't. You'll have forgotten it within seconds.

    o   Make no assumptions, just observe and gather information.

    o   The more you do, the easier it'll get and the more interesting it'll become. Do the best you can until you know better. Then when you know better, do better.

Minutes 1–5:

- *Sense of health and wellbeing*
  - **Appendix 4: Starter questions**

| | |
|---|---|
| **Pupil Name:**_____Date of Birth: _____ | |
| **Date of Assessment:** _____ Assessor: _____ | |
| How are you feeling right now? | 1  2  3  4  5 |
| 1-2 Pupil Voice questions | 1  2  3  4  5 |
| Wearing glasses? Y /N    Last eye test within 2 years? Y / N | |
| When is bed time? _____ How easy is sleep? 10-20 / 45 mins+ | |
| How many hours on tech after school? | 1  2  3  4  5 |
| What food do you enjoy? _____ | |
| How much water do you drink a day?  500ml   1l   1.5l   2l | |
| Are you on any regular medication? Y / N If so, what?_____ | |
| If you could be an animal, what would you be and why?_____ | |

*Figure 10.2*  An image of Appendix 4, showing the types of starter questions you may wish to begin with

Minutes 6–10:

- *Evaluation of reading comprehension and oracy*
  - **Reading comprehension evaluation: brief questioning on passage**

Minutes 11–15:

- *Evaluation of focus, attention and impulse control*
  - **Appendix 5: Executive function core tests**

Minutes 16–20:

- *Evaluation of visual processing*
  - **Rapid automatic naming test**
  - **Reading fluency test**
- *Closing checks on wellbeing and signposting*

4.  Optional additional screening testing: with a member of the SEND/pastoral teams, within the school day – total minutes as needed

*

> **Top Tip:** In terms of in-person screening, using the previous plan as a guide, we have found that we can complete three pupils per assessor per hour, and a total of twelve pupils a day, leaving the afternoon for scoring and consolidation. (Check out www.nochildismissed.org for a spreadsheet which will help you to store and analyse your pupil data.) You'll need a large enough space with enough dividers to muffle sound. And, like immunisations, you will need class teachers on board and someone to manage and direct pupil flow. Pre-screening video explainers played in class or assemblies help pupils to feel more relaxed about their upcoming screening experience. When everyone is being screened it is normalised.

## An overall screening plan

I really value having regular data on pupils to see how each child is developing over time. It allows you to identify earlier and notice changes, separately from any pastoral, class- or intervention data you might gather in school. Figure 10.3 is a flow diagram showing an overall plan for screening at different stages,[1] and how it can all come together. This might be particularly relevant for a through-school or a multi academy trust. You can, of course, screen at any time, as a need presents, too.

## A word about computer screeners . . .

You might be wondering why I haven't really mentioned computer screeners. I think there are genuinely amazing opportunities with using technology to support the screening process, however if screening technology alone was enough currently, you wouldn't have invested time and energy into reading this book. You can, of course, use a computer screener for a whole year group and they're fine. But this book has shown you that the basic screeners are just that – they're not as nuanced or broad. You will miss way more than you learn. There is much more data you can gather and use. In addition, I also remain somewhat concerned about the commercial use of children's data. So, other than time, in-person screening is very low cost to run and is infinitely more flexible, nuanced and protected. For any number of reasons, however, you may want to take a both-and approach, which can also help to balance the many demands on your time. Do what works for you.

*

Now that you've got your screening data, you can look at it as a whole and begin to see areas which might need support. Using the **No Child Misses Out** recommendations and following information, you will answer the second important question: **What support might make a difference to [name]?** If you need a reminder about interpreting

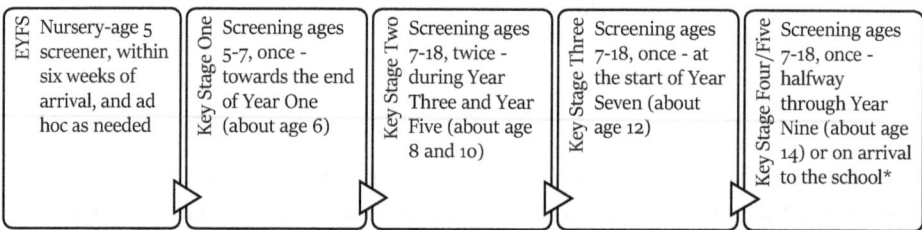

*Figure 10.3* An overview of the screening process across a child's journey through education

standardised scores, have a look at the diagram, Figure 2.1, of the bell curve in Chapter Two (page 19). All tests will also give you some guidance as to how to interpret the data. It is critical that you refer to these for analysing individual outcomes.

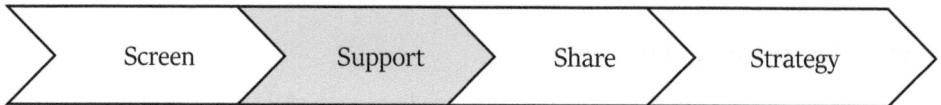

3  **Crunching the data,** *and*
4  **Supporting next steps**

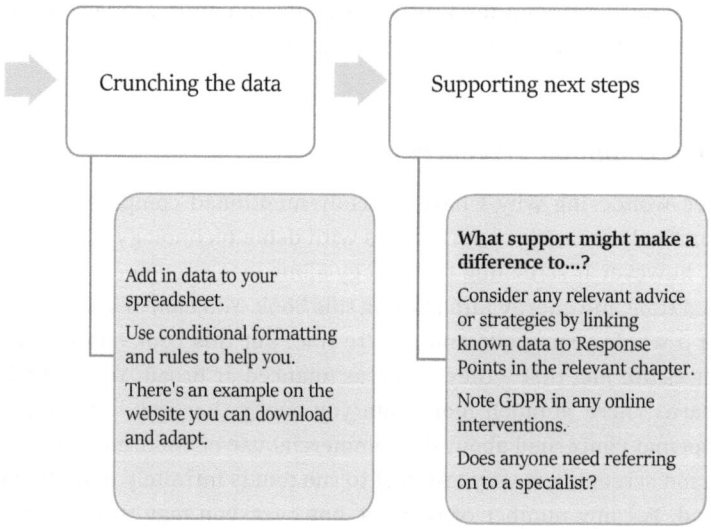

---

*   This testing needs to be carried out by someone qualified to assess for Access Arrangements (England) to be eligible for evidence for external examinations. If you'd like to learn more about getting qualified to assess formally, seek out providers offering the Certificate of Competence in Educational Testing (CCET) or universities offering Level 7 specific learning difficulties qualifications. I listed some at the end of Chapter Three. It's a great qualification to have.

One of the first barriers we have come across is suddenly being aware of the level of need and not feeling like there are systems and staffing to manage and support all of it. This is an issue, but it's not yours alone. And it's an issue whether you know about the level of need or not. Education is simply not funded well enough. We know that. And we're going to dig into that a bit more in the final chapter. What I would say is, if you've screened a whole year group, this doesn't suddenly mean you have to overload the curriculum with intervention groups and wear yourself out. Actioning from whole year group trends is a *strategic* long-term approach and we'll look at that later on in this chapter. What it will do however, is give you information you can feel empowered by.

You're going to be able to support children because:

*You've got knowledge and advice to give*
> Go back to the relevant section(s) of the chapter and remind yourself of the knowledge and training points you can share with staff in your setting and parents-carers in any meetings.
> o   What does the research say about this dimension or need?

*You've got strategies to try*
> Go back to the relevant section(s) of the chapters and find their equivalent Response Points. Also, look at the JCQ (or your equivalent body) regulations for examination support in terms of access arrangements.
> o   For example, if you've discovered that a pupil has a speech, language and communication need (Chapter 4, Action Point 4.1) then you can now look at Chapter 4, Response Point 4.1 to explore a whole host of strategies to try.
> o   What in-class and assessment access arrangements can you put in place to help a child or young person succeed more readily?

*You've got clarity over which external professionals you might need to refer on to, if you need additional support*
> o   Have a look at this flow diagram (Figure 10.4) which will help you to signpost with confidence. (It's not a catch-all but it'll help)

## A word about diagnosis as a next step. . .

As we've covered the different dimensions and tools to assess, I've very deliberately avoided using diagnostic terms. For a start, we're not looking to diagnose through this process because we lack the qualifications, so that would have defeated the object. But there is also another reason why I've been cautious about using diagnostic terms too liberally. Following on from our consideration of epigenetic changes at the end of Chapter Eight, with our world of cheaper genetic testing and the hugely augmented opportunities for analysis offered by machine learning, diagnoses are increasingly coming under scrutiny.

Assessments for ADHD and autism follow a medical model – an either/or approach – which leads clinicians to look for the cause. Genetic research however shows that, while

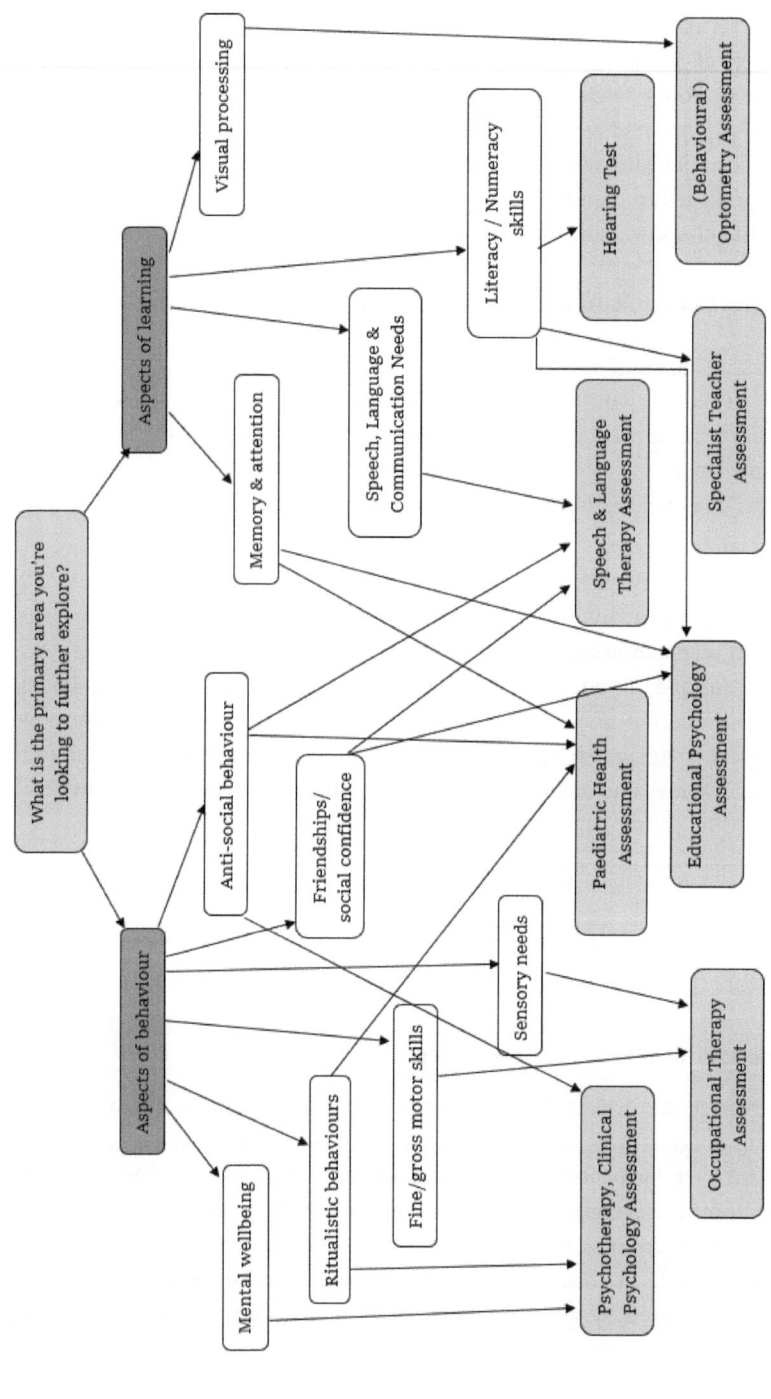

*Figure 10.4* A flow diagram of external specialists who may be able to help you depending upon the child's needs presenting

there are single gene disorders such as cystic fibrosis, conditions like autism and ADHD are likely to have a more complex origin. Instead, they should be considered multifactorial conditions, of which genetics is one of many influencing factors. Clinical geneticist, Dr Anne McCabe, explains "We often perform genetic testing to try and better understand children with developmental delays or learning problems and may find changes in individual genes or chromosomes which can help to explain this – there are many well-researched conditions which are often associated with behavioural and learning difficulties. However, when testing their parents, it is not uncommon to find that they share the same genetic alterations identified in their child but do not always experience the same issues".[6] She went on to say, "this suggests that whilst genetics clearly play an important role in the development of these disorders, they are certainly not the only influencing factor."

In our conversation together, we discussed the potential that mass genetic testing might uncover. It is feasible, for example, that if we tested everyone, we might find that lots of us have microdeletions and duplications in our DNA but which are not causing us significant issues. Dr Anne McCabe concluded, "there is still much to learn about the interplay between genetics and our environment in the development of learning difficulties". In other words, both genetic and psychotherapeutic research indicates that environment is critical to presentation. We have much more to understand when it comes to the influences interacting with individuals within their personal ecosystem, as we learnt in Chapter Seven.

Professor Robert Plomin, psychologist and geneticist at King's College London, calls these observable characteristics "extremes of quantitative dimensions"[7] and his work challenges us to consider how we might be able to implement treatment or intervention to improve the presentation of the dimension – dimensions like the ones we've been evaluating throughout this book.

While there is incredibly strong heritability in our genetic code, which explains why twins separated at birth who meet many years later tend to have followed similar life paths, "genes are not destiny" he argues. "You can change. But heritability means that

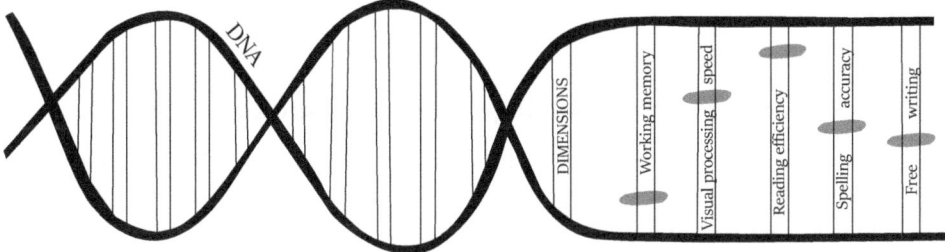

*Figure 10.5* A DNA mixing desk of psychological dimensions – Hannah's visual analogy to help you picture the screening scores and influences

| | |
|---|---|
| Some parents can find a label helps them to understand their child better. | Psychological research is beginning to indicate that diagnoses aren't always the most useful way to establish a personalised plan of support, as diagnoses aren't always reliably given - see the findings of the CALM Study at the University of Cambridge. |
| Likewise, some children and young people can find it helps them to form a more positive identity. | |
| A diagnosis can also make it easier to access additional funding and support - although this isn't actually legally necessary. | Genetic research has yet to find a "dyslexia", "autism" or "ADHD" specific gene, which means that in time we might begin to use other ways of categorising need, not labels of disability as we know them now. |
| There is a lot of support and advice from charitable bodies and local organisations who are designed to support children and young people with a diagnosis. | |
| Not having one might mean a child is not/less able to access additional support in non-educational settings, such as places of interest. | This screening process is broad and holistic. You might not get much more helpful information than that which you've already got from your own testing. (This is especially pertinent if a parent-carer is considering paying privately.) |

*Figure 10.6* Some reasons for and against undergoing diagnostic testing

some people are more vulnerable and find it more difficult to overcome".[8] For example, if you have quantitatively fewer phonological awareness genes, your sound desk slider might be naturally lower but with intervention (and sometimes *lots* of intervention), we are likely to be able to nudge it up a bit. Environment matters.

So, while it is still really important to consider advising further specialist assessment and advice if you need to, which may or may not lead to a diagnosis, it is possible that in the future, the diagnostic landscape will change dramatically. I think it's important to share that with you. For me, it also serves to further question the *real* reason for our focus on diagnoses, which, in education, more often seems to be about applying for further funding and accessing something additional or different from the standard options available. This probably tells us more about the system than it does the child . . .

## A word about using artificial intelligence strategies to support you. . .

With the rate of change in the field of AI, I expect that by the time this is published, we will have moved on a few notches yet again.

There is a real opportunity for us to gain exponentially by using AI to help us screen and support in our settings. There are companies exploring this right now. I will come back to the practical and ethical implications around using AI to diagnose in my "Final thoughts" but for now, let's consider how we might be able to use AI to help speed up our own internal screening policy and improve access to subsequent support.

Marking:

- Using AI to mark spelling and handwriting tests
- Using AI to mark paper-based tests you have used

Analysing and creating next steps:

- Using AI tools in your spreadsheets to help you crunch the data
- Using AI to create Schemes of Learning/Work and individual lesson plans to target needs identified through screening (Rockett AI and Twinkl are pioneering here)
- Using AI to deliver interventions (there are some good ones for precision teaching of maths facts, spelling and reading accuracy but be cautious of the pupil personal data you are handing over to access them)

Report writing:

- Likewise, whilst using AI to write reports might sound like near-perfection, saving hours and hours of time and reducing the likelihood of those pesky typos we all struggle with, it does need some caution about not putting personal pupil data into the AI programmes. However, there are undoubtedly massive benefits to explore. (Realfastreports and TeachMateAI are moving ahead quickly in this arena.)

**5. Feeding Back to Stakeholders**

## Summarising and sharing information with parents-carers

*Sharing outcomes*

I am a firm advocate for reporting back to parents-carers about the screening results. Firstly, I believe it helps parents-carers to feel more empowered at home by providing them with insights about their child or young person and strategies they can employ. Secondly, I think that in terms of someone's own data, they have a right to know important information about themselves – even if they're too little to understand it fully. They may wish to read it when they are older. Finally, I think it protects everyone: it proves you've taken your duty of care seriously, and it gives everyone an opportunity to ask questions and to make informed decisions in a pro-active way. Sharing outcomes, then, is critical.

o   On the website www.nochildismissed.org you will find a report proforma and a step-by-step guide for how you can write multiple reports using Mail Merge. This will help you to share outcomes more efficiently.

*Sharing advice and triaging level of need*

Advice does not have to be complicated – in fact, keeping it to simple and actionable advice makes it more likely that parents-carers can take on board your suggestions and fit them into a busy home environment.

Two important things I would mention in terms of managing parent-carer communications:

o   Time the release of reports so that they are near a parents-carers' evening which means you can summarise your findings into a much shorter face-to-face conversation rather than an in-school meeting if parents-carers want to talk to you about it. This is particularly helpful if you don't need a long meeting to discuss relatively minor issues.

o   If you do need to meet with a parent-carer, because needs are more complex, bear in mind the advice in Chapter Three about being open and honest about your level of experience in relation to any recommendations.

*Where to store/share it from*

If you've got a parent portal – somewhere where reports and communications can be stored digitally – we have found this to be a really useful way to share reports with parents-carers (it avoids paper, envelopes, stamps etc.) and it means that they have long-term access to your report. Paper tends to get misplaced and so it makes storage easier for Home, too. The requests for subsequent copies have dropped to zero!

## Summarising and sharing information with pupils

- *Sharing outcomes and advice*
- I'll be honest. This is still an area I am still exploring and I don't think there is a one-size-fits-all approach here. You will know your pupil, your family, your context and will have an idea about whether it is appropriate to share your screening findings directly and how you want to go about doing it, if so. I'm sure I will write more

about this in the future but for now I haven't perfected a system of feedback which I'm happy to share in a book.

What I would say is this however:

○ I think children know when they're struggling anyway so hiding it from them doesn't necessarily help. Research from Made By Dyslexia[9] shows that by the age of seven, children have a sense of their difficulties compared to peers. Acknowledging difficulties therefore actually enables you to be compassionate, empathetic and encouraging with your pupils in a way that can make them feel seen and heard.

○ I think our greatest weaknesses are also our greatest strengths – it just depends on the context. For example, in Chapter Seven we looked at "Shift" and how some children struggle to move on from something and become obsessive and hyper focused, which can be problematic. If you've ever written a book, you'll know that being obsessive and hyper focused (even if your children are clinging to your legs, yelling for their eleventh snack and you're typing with one hand whilst building a den with the other) is actually an enormous strength. It gets the job done! So I think it's important that we remember this when we're screening and identifying "weaknesses".

○ When we've had opportunities to talk through the results of a screening with a child or young person, we have been able to see a noticeable confidence shift in them. It can definitely be a powerful approach and is worth considering – perhaps as part of a mentoring session.

## Summarising and sharing information with staff

*Sharing outcomes*

Put together a list of all the possible outcomes from your screening in terms of the needs that can/do emerge. Going through the No Child is Missed Action Points in each chapter will help you to do this.

○ For example:

Receptive language needs

Colour vision deficiency

Focus and attention difficulties

*Sharing advice*

Now put a list (in brief) of all of the classroom advice you'd give in your setting associated with these needs. You're bound to have lots already but there's plenty in the No Child Misses Out Response Points if you need inspiration.

○ For example:

Giving thinking time for speech to be processed and a response considered

Labelling coloured pencils, pens and crayons.

Regular reminders and instructions available to check

*Where to store/share it from*

Look at your in-school information sharing processes. How can you share this information quickly and easily so relevant people can access it? (Especially supply/cover teachers)

○   For example, do you have a way to attach these simple outcomes and advice onto a child's profile which means you've got a longer-term plan for them which staff can access?

*Triaging level of need*

Decide on how significant the level of these needs are. Does this child have just one or two mild areas of need? Or are there more than this? Or more concerning in terms of the relative difficulty they present? If so, what might this suggest about the urgency of your next steps/advice/support?

*Access arrangements*

Deciding on the in-class access arrangements a teacher is responsible for will be a school-based decision. Access arrangements and what actually makes a difference is another research lacuna however. Dr Emily McGhee is a SENCO who explored this in her EdD thesis.[10] She found that there is a need for a more standardised approach across the UK, better resources for schools, and increased involvement of stakeholders in shaping policy. Her findings suggest that the current system requires significant reforms to ensure that all students who need access arrangements receive them equitably. Emily's findings highlight a global issue with equitable examination experiences. For example, in England pupils can get 25% extra time in their examinations. But in the USA, pupils receive 50% extra time. There doesn't seem to be any rhyme or reason for this. And, whilst different countries should rightly have their own processes, for me, it suggests we don't know enough about young people's needs and the impact of strategies for exam support to evaluate the value of time (which, given the importance of time in education overall, is surprising!) Much more work to do in this field, therefore, to evaluate which access arrangements make a difference and why!

**6. Developing a strategic approach**

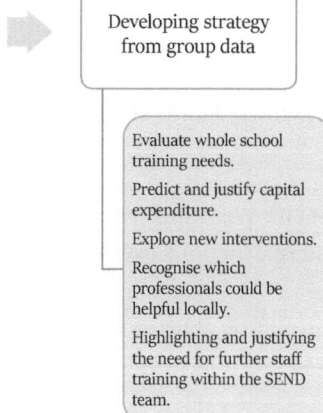

Developing strategy from group data

Evaluate whole school training needs.

Predict and justify capital expenditure.

Explore new interventions.

Recognise which professionals could be helpful locally.

Highlighting and justifying the need for further staff training within the SEND team.

This final section is only relevant if you've taken the plunge and screened a whole group of children. Having whole group data will allow you to think about your whole school needs: what the data tells you about this group, its support needs and even environmental factors which you could consider.

As a result you might better manage resources by:

- o  clear evidence-based decisions about where to target your CPD budget and time, focusing on teacher training to meet need. If you're seeing significantly lower working memory scores across the year group, you might want to invest in some executive function training for your next training day, for example.
- o  predicting when you're going to need to invest finance into a new intervention or resource, e.g. a large capital expenditure like a sensory room or a computer reader software system
- o  seeing which year groups need most support and with what, e.g. developing a new small group intervention
- o  connecting with external professionals who you can call upon for help in a particular area, building your SEND ecosystem of support, e.g. putting together a list of local professionals, groups and charitable endeavours who you can call upon and also recommend to parents-carers
- o  justifying the need for further staff training and qualifications in assessment within the SEND team, e.g. the CCET or a Level 7 qualification to assess
- o  justifying the need for developing staffing expertise in a particular area which you hadn't engaged with as much before, e.g. putting a Teaching Assistant onto a higher-level training qualification or course, e.g. Elklan

## Final thoughts: Should we use AI to diagnose?

Given the huge shortage of educational psychologists, community paediatricians and other specialists in the diagnostic field, there's a lot of hope that **artificial intelligence** will be able to help close some of those gaps. Whilst that might fill us with a stream of different emotions, from horror to hope, the idea that computers would be able to match and even supersede the human mind has been knocking around since at least 1950.[2] And by 1954, there was evidence to suggest that computers were actually *better* than humans when it came to the skill of prediction.[11] So, whilst apocalyptic fears of robots taking over the world are good for cinema ticket sales, our growing reality is that we seem to be the better for it: more productive, more useful, more included. Just look at how Stephen Hawking wrote his speeches and books with eye-gaze technology and just the twitch of his cheek, for example. And now, for those who are blind or have low-vision, there are even smart-canes which give audible navigation and way-finding prompts. With a simple command such as "Navigate to home", a digital stick can now guide you there with

---

2  With the Turing Test.

real time information.[12] Far from it being an existential crisis, the merger of mind and machine has enabled some of the most inspiring developments ever known. And this could easily include better diagnostics for us all.

---

**Artificial Intelligence (AI):** There are three types of AI: narrow (performing specific tasks, like Siri and Alexa); reactive machines (that react to stimuli, like a spam filter or a recommender system like Netflix uses) and limited memory AI (useful for making predictions, like chatbots and self-driving cars). Generative AI, like ChatGPT and other similar technologies, is a form of narrow AI, trained to recognise patterns in the data and draw conclusions from them.

**AI hallucination:** is an incorrect or misleading result generated through AI modelling.

**Co-morbidity:** the simultaneous presence of two or more diseases or medical conditions in a patient.

---

The challenge ahead, however, is the same theme we've been bumping into throughout this book: the sensitivity and specificity of the data. Can we provide the computer with *sufficient detail*[3] so it is sensitive enough and *of the right kind*[4] so it is specific enough? In getting to this diagnostic utopia, we have to navigate through at least three challenges to help us avoid the very real risks of AI **"hallucinations"** on the way.

The first challenge, and I'd say it's a pretty massive one, is that we simply don't have that kind of data to draw upon. We aren't yet clear enough ourselves what conditions such as dyslexia or autism are: we have multiple definitions which we haven't all agreed on as being "the one". Not only that, but many children and young people will present with characteristics of more than one diagnostic label at the same time, known as a **co-morbidity**. And whilst, "you can't please all of the people all of the time" is certainly true, when it comes to applying a diagnostic label on a child, which then signals a lifetime disability and a potential course of treatment, we're going to want to be quibbling over a few minor details, not major points of contest. Certainly, when we look at the data from the CALM project I mentioned a few pages back, we can see that diagnostic labels are inconsistently given by humans, which should cause us to take stock. When viewed at scale, similar cognitive profiles are often given different labels, depending on the opinion and qualification of the assessor.[13] In addition, not all diagnoses take biopsychosocial factors into consideration, which we now know can be highly influential. So, do we have data that is sensitive enough and specific

---

3   Not too much that it over-identifies, not too little that it under-identifies.
4   Enough clear examples of when it is and when it's not so it can learn the difference.

enough to feed to computers so that they can confidently and reliably diagnose conditions like autism or dyslexia right now? I'd argue no. We're a long way off (even if the test's webpage tells you otherwise). The data we have is simply too myopic and scattered. It's going to be a long time before computers can code for the autism that represents "millions of different stories".[14] But that's not to say it couldn't happen in the future.

The second challenge, which is a possible knight in shining armour to the first (depending on whether it turns out to be a frog or a prince in the costume), is the use of technology to *gather* that data in the first place. We could put children and young people through computer screening which harvests their data to help us build datasets to diagnose. We use basic screening technology in schools already so this is really only an extension and development of the data use. Surely it's an easy decision: it's cheap and it's quick, and the precedent has already been set. The problem really lies, not so much in the use of technology to gather data (although there are certainly challenges with that, including the inaccuracy of technologies like facial recognition), or to analyse patterns within it, but in the subsequent commercial use of that data. If companies like Palantir or Meta, and the Chinese government's Sesame Credit, hold vast datasets *now* about individuals which are used to influence, and in some cases, to limit and prevent access, then we must place the potential benefits of a quick and cheap diagnosis alongside some pretty enormous risks. Risks to children's future freedoms, both online and in the real world. Are we, as teachers, really knowledgeable enough or skilled enough in confidently interpreting and navigating those risks?

Far from being a fair data swap, even when we're filling in silly questionnaires online about whether we're more like a puppy or a penguin, or where we should go on our next holiday, we're not always aware of the consequences of what we're trading. Can you imagine the commercial value of children's cognitive data we're ploughing into businesses in the name of cost- and time-efficiency? And the subsequent power it then gives them? As Professor Hannah Fry, the mathematician who studies models of human behaviour, argues "It's rarely obvious what our data can do, or, when fed into a clever algorithm, just how valuable it can be. . . [and]. . . how cheaply we were bought".[15] So, whilst we certainly need more data, who will own what we're so readily handing over about our next adult generation? And how and where will it be stored? Did we – or they – *really* consent to it in full knowledge (rather than just blithely accepting fourteen pages of font size 6 terms and conditions)? How much is it worth and to whom? And, perhaps most importantly, how will it be used to make decisions not just about the diagnostic question in hand but other, as yet unknown, far more sinister ones too?[5]

---

5  Let's not forget that the research into working memory and attention was powered by Winston Churchill during World War Two in order to put the pilots with the best attention spans in the new RAF planes; and that Brigham Yerkes' Alpha and Beta test results were used to decide who would be in direct mortal combat and who would be calling the strategic shots from well behind enemy lines. This data has real world potential in all types of unforeseen contexts . . .

And herein lies the third problem. When we look back to mathematicians such as Sir Francis Galton and Karl Pearson, the values that they held and the algorithms they were building weren't ones which were targeted to help benefit humankind in the way that those of us who work in the field of education now try to. Theirs' was an altogether different and darker approach to evaluating and judging humans. If we think that computer screening and generative AI could help us to reduce systemic bias through more and better pattern spotting and predicting, we'd be very wrong. It might be called "generative" AI but the reality is, it's "regurgitative".[16]

AI technologies, when deployed without proper oversight, can not only perpetuate but exponentially increase systemic injustice in high stakes decision making such as the criminal justice system, healthcare and financial services.[17] There are huge ethical challenges which come from giving computers the power to make decisions without really understanding the algorithm that the neural network has taught itself. And, of course, if it's one which has been developed by a private company, that complex decision tree it has developed (rather disarmingly called "a random forest". . . aw, cute! I'd like to go there) is a commercially sensitive product. It is not in their financial interests to release the algorithm for it to be inspected on the grounds of transparency of decision-making. Simply put, we may never know whether we've been manipulated or discriminated against because we've unblinkingly trusted the secrets of a computer whose motives might be less than altruistic. Whether it's on age, gender, race or personality type, the chances are very high that we already have.

So, to build proper computer-based AI diagnostic tools to help us with the challenge of a shortage of specialist assessors in diagnosing children and young people, we need better data,[18] better transparency,[19] better contestability,[20] and a "human in the loop"[21] to help steer the ship. Well actually, we need more than one human, or even one type of human. We don't just need computer engineers, we need philosophers, ethicists, psychologists, teachers, doctors, therapists, we need people with lived experience to help shape the diagnostic tools. We need AI systems that are consciously designed by people who want to combat discrimination and promote equity, so that they in fact do.[22] And we need a more AI-literate society to better understand and expect higher ethical standards of these technologies to improve equity across those same old protected characteristics. Otherwise, AI has potentially unbridled permission to sabotage global efforts towards equality, diversity and inclusion; to undermine our universal human rights to be seen, heard and valued for who we really are; to diminish our basic human right to belong.

As Dr Joy Buolamwini says: "The rising frontier for civil rights will require algorithmic justice. AI should be for the people and by the people, not just the privileged few."[23]

# Chapter Summary

**Designing the screening protocol**

**What can we learn about this pupil?**

Follow recommended test protocol per age, as standard.

Make no assumptions.

Carry out any additional testing if needed. (Possibly at a different time.)

**Informing, guiding and respecting stakeholders**

Add a column to your spreadsheet to monitor opt-in or opt-out. Have evidence on record somewhere.

**Carry out the screening**

Gather group testing and biopsychosocial data.

Organise a room with dividers and arrange a timetable. (1 adult = 3x hour, + 1 adult to oversee)

Prepare yourself well practically - it goes fast.

Jot down little details you notice straightaway.

**Crunching the data**

Add in data to your spreadsheet.

Use conditional formatting and rules to help you.

There's an example on the website you can download and adapt.

**Supporting next steps**

**What support might make a difference to this pupil?**

Consider any relevant advice or strategies by linking known data to Response Points in the relevant chapter.

Note GDPR in any online interventions.

Does anyone need referring on to a specialist?

**Feeding back to stakeholders**

Publish a screening report for parents-carers. Use Mail Merge for batch reports. See website.

Time the reports to go out a few days before a parents evening.

Consider how you might be able to share outcomes with pupils.

Share key findings with staff. Give strategies for support, including access arrangements.

**Developing strategy from group data**

Evaluate whole school training needs.

Predict and justify capital expenditure.

Explore new interventions.

Recognise which professionals could be helpful locally.

Highlighting and justifying the need for further staff training within the SEND team.

# 11 We Are Extraordinary

Let's imagine, fed up with this education lark, you and I decide to rob a bank. A few weeks later, having discovered previously unknown talents for larceny, we find ourselves lounging on a tropical beach drinking mocktails and revelling in our spoils. With quite the tan, a new hair-do and having rediscovered the vigour of youth (no paperwork, no meetings, no stress), we *almost* look unrecognisable. And yet, sadly for us, after a few weeks of peace and paradise, Interpol track us down and take us in for questioning.

Now, of course, it's in both of our best interests to *stick to the story*. Back each other up. Admit nothing. Walk free.

But, in separate cells and with the offer of a lesser custodial sentence or even freedom if we give our interrogators damning information about the other, this kind of collusion now becomes a risk. What if I have been persuaded and you haven't? What if you get *all the blame* and I get to walk free? In separate cells, we cannot know what the other has chosen. This puts us into a really difficult dilemma: co-operate (trust) or defect . . . ? What are you going to choose?

|  | You Trust | You Defect |
|---|---|---|
| I Trust | Shared best outcome | Worst outcome for Me |
| I Defect | Worst outcome for You | Shared least worst outcome |

*Figure 11.1* The Prisoners' Dilemma[1] Theory

Now however (or so the Prisoners' Dilemma Theory goes), despite initial intentions, unless we have *very* high levels of trust in each other, it is actually better to cut our losses and to *defect* on our promises. Whilst we will both get some kind of penalty, it will be a shared, lesser penalty. We will have chosen a path that is not in our mutual best interests, but it's not in our individual worst interests either.

In the game we call Life, this same social dilemma plays out over and over again in different guises: will we work with and support each other within this particular context or not? In fact, we see it play out in spectacular style when it comes to children, particularly when resources are stretched, pitting settings or sectors against each other. Education versus health or social care. Schools versus **local authorities**, parents or the government. Who will acknowledge a need and fund an assessment or provision? The

DOI: 10.4324/9781032663968-14

best outcome for the child would be for the two sides to trust and support each other. The number of parents-carers having to fight for the needs of their child in court[2] and the high level of exclusions in some schools would suggest that defection is all too common.[3]

In securing better outcomes for children and young people, the critical challenge then should be to prioritise building trust and collaborative working between the adults around each child. This is undoubtedly in our shared best interest. If a lack of resources often prevents collaborative working, then the simple solution to growing trust must surely be better funding.

Simple solutions are, however, never *usually* that simple.

Let's return to the story of education.

> **Local authorities:** local government overseeing town or county services, which include education.
>
> **Individualism:** the political notion that a country should operate with minimal state intervention in people's lives, keeping taxes low and allowing people their personal freedoms. The result of this policy in practice often means keeping statutory support for those in poverty to a minimum to encourage them to become more economically productive and independent.
>
> **Handicapped:** this term is an historic term, dating from King Henry VIII, used to describe people with physical disabilities who were allowed to beg for money "cap in hand" if unable to work.
>
> **Warnock Report:** a report put to the British government in 1978 to recommend changes to education, including the introduction of the term special educational needs.
>
> **Paradigm shift:** a deep change in how something is collectively perceived or understood.

## Funding education for the masses

Back in 1870, when Sir Francis Galton was intent upon measuring the value of people, and when education first became compulsory for all children of primary age in Britain, the mandate from politicians was clear. Newly enfranchised working-class men should be educated in order to "use their vote wisely" through "the extension of sound and cheap elementary instruction to all classes of the people".[4] Fuelled with the Liberal values of **"Individualism"**, it's fair to say that the reluctance to use taxpayers' money to fund this massive social experiment was palpable. To ensure a return on investment (and that public funds should not be siphoned off by unscrupulous educators), in 1872 politicians set up a revised code of regulations. Along with the initial funding per capita schools would receive, there would be an additional amount for when pupils met the standards set by government. Pupils had to master the 3Rs – Reading, wRiting and aRithmetic.

Compared to today, the expected standards were pretty low, but it started education off on a particular footing; one which might feel rather familiar. Funding and expected outcomes were based upon the calculations of the Treasury and the economic needs of the country (not on the complex needs of children themselves). In fact, not all children were even able to access education: equality, diversity and inclusion wasn't a thing. It wasn't until a century later, in 1971, that "the **handicapped**" would be included in the education calculations. Before then, some children were simply not part of the equation.

Towards the end of the 1970s, radical educational recommendations were made with the publication of the **Warnock Report**, significantly impacting funding and provision; the kind of changes that academics refer to as "a **paradigm shift**". Not only did the term "special educational needs" emerge and become legal terminology from 1981 with the Education Act (which other English-speaking countries use in a similar way[1]) but the framing of "educational needs" instead of "handicaps" moved the dial considerably. Each child's difficulties were placed within a context and could be supported and improved by the practice of professionals in school, aided by local authority specialists. As such, "integration" and specialist training for all teachers, particularly those in mainstream, became a priority.

The Warnock Report encouraged educators to question their own practices and assumptions about children's potential, testing and stretching previous educational and caring boundaries. This new emphasis pushed the dial even further in 1988, when the Education Reform Act stated that children in government funded schools must experience a broad, balanced and differentiated curriculum, which included all children in specialist provision, too. The expectation set out by government was clear for all – albeit with additional and different approaches for those who needed it. In spite of all this promise and hope for children's education, people raised concerns about "the inadequacy of funding" which left "much to be achieved".[5] It wasn't all roses.

On the subject of valuing the needs of children and young people, the Warnock committee had tried, but failed, to remove a "deeply engrained" millstone around the neck of educational thinking: "that there are two types of children, the handicapped and the non-handicapped".[6] The language might have changed; the percentage of children who became eligible for additional support under this new framework may have grown; and the education budget and curriculum expectations may have increased as a result, but as for the millstone? The dichotomy of SEND/non-SEND still lives on today. Why would we calculate its percentage in annual government statistics if it didn't?

---

1   In England and Wales, it's "a learning difficulty or disability which calls for special educational* provision to be made for them" which is "a significantly greater difficulty in learning than the majority of others of the same age" or "which prevents or hinders him from making use of facilities of a kind generally provided for others of the same age" (SEND Code of Practice, 2014). In Scotland, "a child or young person has additional support needs . . . [where] the child or young person is . . . unable without the provision of additional support to benefit from school education provided" (Statutory Guidance to the Education (Additional Support for Learning) (Scotland) Act 2004 as amended). In the USA, the law states, "The term 'child with disability' means a child – with [and then lists specific categories which qualify] . . . who, by reason thereof, needs special education and related services" (Individuals with Disabilities Education Act, 2004). In Australia, they have a very detailed list of what it means to have a disability and provide clear instructions about providing "reasonable adjustments" to provide special provision (Disability Standards for Education, 2005) which result from the child being "unable (because of his or her disabilities) to receive a substantial part of the benefits ordinarily available to children enrolled there" (States Grant (Primary and Secondary Education Assistance) Act 2000).

This taxonomy of separating "those who can" from "those who can't without additional or different provision" leads us straight to the conclusion that those with SEND are an additional cost to society. And, depending on your political and economic views, one you might be very reluctant to pay for. To understand why, we need to get to grips with some twentieth-century economics. Bear with.

## Twentieth-century values

Back in the 1930s, deep in America's Great Depression, the economist Simon Kuznets was commissioned by the Senate to develop a way to measure economic growth. He was successful in this endeavour, developing the concept that we now commonly refer to as a country's **Gross Domestic Product (GDP)**. For the less acquainted, GDP measures the market value of goods and services produced through business. The more we produce, the better we're doing. And, as a result, the more likely we'll avoid mass unemployment and recession. His theory was highly successful and helped to get America out of its devastating depression, which is why, nearly a century later, you will still regularly hear politicians around the globe chiming for their country's economic growth; and news updates commenting on the percentage of growth in the economy this month. However, as economist Kate Raworth explains in her catchily titled book *Doughnut Economics*, that we can just keep growing our economy forevermore to avoid catastrophe is a cushioning thought but one that actually comes with huge, hidden costs to the environment and to certain groups in society. Kuznets, too, was well aware of the shortcomings of GDP. He knew that, whilst it might be a helpful measure of a country's wealth, it wasn't a measure of a country's wellbeing.

**Top Tip:** If you're looking for a book to read to understand economic theory better and would like to explore how we might change our economic habits for the twenty-first century, *Doughnut Economics* is a great book to read. My summary below is the richer for it.

GDP only measures the output from business: the goods and services produced from offices and factories. What it doesn't measure is the value of goods and services produced by the household and by society. It doesn't measure, for example, the economic value of a parent hugging their child or tending to their grazed knees after a fall. It doesn't measure the economic value of friendship and sacrifice, sharing food with the people around you, providing a listening ear and some sage wisdom if needed. It doesn't measure the economic value of being able to go for a walk on common land; to get out of breath climbing a hill, inhaling lungfuls of life-giving fresh air, and drawing inspiration from the view at the top. We might call these "the things that money can't buy" but, make no mistake: there is enormous economic value in all of these things. We just don't capture it in the narrow calculation we call GDP, rendering its value largely unquantified and invisible.

Why does this matter? And more importantly, why does this matter to SEND?

It matters tremendously. What we value economically, we support with time and resources. And how we get to use our time *really* matters. Time, after all, is freedom. Big GDP contributors, the bigger earners in society, have more *control* over how they use their time. Their financial flexibility means they can afford to work fewer hours if they choose to and to outsource those time-consuming life admin jobs that most people have to squeeze in around work. Instead, they get to do something that restores them – like go for a run or on a mini-break. Financial flexibility affords better foods, better holidays and better access to healthcare, rewarding the wealthy with longer lives and with better health and wellbeing into old age. Higher income therefore allows people to better manage their other vital personal resources which, in turn, leads to more wealth.

The reverse is also true. Lower earners, generally those who take on roles that contribute to the household or to society rather than GDP – nurturing or teaching children are good examples – have less control over how they use their time. Less investment from the State equates to smaller budgets and fewer resources. This results in more intense working days as more has to be crammed into less; lower salaries for the workers leading to less capacity to outsource life admin; and, less free time resulting in fewer opportunities to maintain a healthy diet and exercise habit to foster good health.[2] Just keeping all the plates spinning is enough and then it's time for bed. Same again tomorrow. Cumulatively, this pattern leads to less wealth and less health.

There are many shades of grey in between these two stereotypes of course, but because GDP does not capture the economic value held within the household and society, overall this omission has led to stark and deeply discriminatory trends in health and wealth. In terms of education specifically, what it takes (and costs) to nurture and support children from different starting points towards greater independence simply hasn't been accurately valued; the invoice has been left blank.

To big budget holders, this doesn't seem to matter. In fact, it's fully justifiable and not worth spending time working out – or so economists and politicians would have us believe – because of Kuznets' second highly seductive and staggeringly influential theory: Kuznets' Curve.

The theory of **Kuznets' Curve** shows that whilst inequality will initially rise when an economy grows its GDP, ultimately when it has increased its productivity sufficiently, it will improve the wellbeing of all and therefore reduce the pernicious aspects of inequality. Some will just be wealthier than others in an otherwise productive sea of wealth. In that sense then, inequality and stress should be expected and can be justified as simply an uncomfortable first part of the journey to a better life. Short-term pain, long-term gain.

---

2   May The Force be with you if you are a parent *and* a teacher – you're doubly screwed over when it comes to GDP. At least we only work 9–3 and have all those holidays, eh?

## Kuznets' Curve

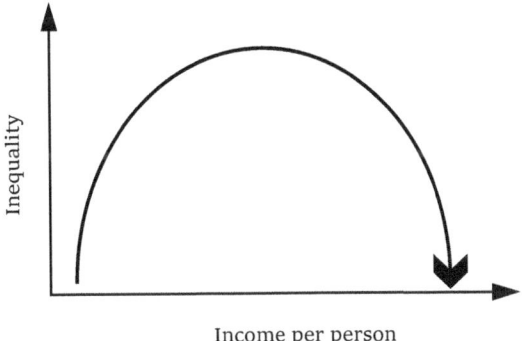

*Figure 11.2* Kuznets' Curve

**Gross Domestic Product (GDP):** measures the market value of goods and services produced through business.

**Kuznets' Curve:** shows that while inequality will initially rise, when an economy grows everyone will benefit thereby reducing inequality.

As Raworth points out, the problem with Kuznets' Curve is it was based on a unique and limited set of data and on assumptions that Kuznets privately disclosed he had "no evidence whatsoever".[7] When viewed over a longer time period and with more data, other economists have proved Kuznets' Curve wrong.[8] Inequality just leads to . . . you guessed it . . . *greater* inequality.[9]

Nevertheless, just like GDP, it has been – and *continues to be* – the backbone of much political and economic decision-making. "We have to tolerate the inequality as a way to achieve greater prosperity and opportunity for all" said Lord Griffiths of Goldman Sachs, to justify the huge bankers' bonuses the year after the 2007 economic crash.[10] Austerity policies from that same economic crash forced public sector cuts which directly ate into the reserves of the household and of society: community services, schools, youth centres, healthcare, public transport – all reducing or ceasing goods and services which help keep communities together and foster wellbeing. Instead, the deficits have had to be absorbed by the "invisible" economy, causing huge inequalities between the business "providers" and the household and society "nurturers", often with a huge gender pay gap to boot. The increase in number of children and families struggling and the growing inequalities more than a decade later is no coincidence.

It turns out that, far from the wealth we'd been promised, countries with greater societal inequalities have more teenage pregnancy, mental illness, drug use, obesity, prisoners, children not in education, fractured communities, lower life expectancy, more women out of work, and lower levels of trust. The same trust that allows communities to work together towards shared best outcomes. In 2009, research proved that "inequality does not make economies grow faster: if anything, it slows them down. And it does so by wasting the potential of much of the population."[11] Eating into the invisible economy means people (often parents, most often mothers, and acutely within that, black and ethnic minority mothers[12]) who could be working simply can't sustain the increased demands upon their time on such comparatively poor pay. Instead of bringing in revenue for their household and the local and national economies through working, this penalty plunges families into living on a time and resource breadline, resulting in high levels of stress, poorer levels of health and greater strain on family relationships.

Ignoring this makes no sense from an evolutionary biology point of view, either. The "cost to global health is immense",[13] says researcher Cat Bohannon. Every society needs mothers to be healthy to reproduce and nurture offspring, so to continue with policies and practices that reduce maternal health and wellbeing is "the biological equivalent of cutting your nose off to spite your face".[14] Calculating the value of the hidden economy *does, in fact, matter.* And it matters greatly to the prevalence of needs we see in children and young people today, and to schools' and parents' abilities to meet them. Just as we learned, all those chapters ago, the map of education continues to discriminate along the fault lines of gender, race and socioeconomic status.

## The cost of wasted potential

"Instead of prioritising metrics like GDP", the Nobel-Memorial prize-winning economist Amartya Sen wrote, "the aim should be to enlarge people's capabilities – such as to be healthy, empowered and creative – so that they can choose to be and do things in life that they value".[15] (Can I hear an Amen?!) But for that, we need to work together to reappraise, better understand, value and resource that which has been hidden and misunderstood for so long. Only then will we begin to learn about and release the potential encoded into society, rather than waste it.

For many used to twentieth-century economic mantras and those holding the reins of power, accepting a different interpretation of the potential and purpose encoded into society, in all its diversity, might fill them with horror. The idea of valuing and maximising the diverse strengths of humanity rather than simply championing the growth of the economy might feel deeply threatening to a very successful political and economic model. What if, in recognising the true cost of raising healthy, empowered children and young people, it actually puts the economy and our country at risk? Surely economic safety and conservatism should be prioritised over the need for equality, diversity and inclusion? The dawning reality, however, seems to be that valuing the power of diversity is actually our safety-valve.

When the world watched in horror at the terrorist attacks on the Twin Towers and the Pentagon in September 2001, there were some very difficult questions to answer. How could such a huge act of war have possibly been allowed to happen? It didn't take long for **CIA** agents to be accused of "sleeping on the job". But when the dust and rubble had been cleared from Ground Zero and in the months and years after 9/11, a new truth started to emerge. Warning signs were missed, yes; and critical actions weren't taken. But it wasn't as a result of poor work ethic – agents had been working extraordinarily hard in a dangerous and complex world. It was, in fact, because the CIA lacked diversity amongst their agents in the field and lacked diversity of perspective in their analysis, to fully appreciate the data that they had. This "collective blindness", as the British journalist Matthew Syed puts it,[16] built flawed information gathering and data analysis systems, which led them to misunderstand the holes in their systems and to drastically underestimate the level of threat. Far from keeping her safe, the lack of value for diversity within the CIA put America at significant risk.

I wonder, to what extent, this might be a metaphor for many other complex and dynamic problems we currently face? Though the thought of seismic re-evaluation of our economic values might seem frightening to some, or just completely alien to others, the risks that come from inertia don't look any easier to navigate:[17] food inequality, global warming, water contamination, gender inequality and violence against women and girls, obesity and chronic ill-health from ultra-processed foods and a stressful lifestyle, war, injustice and discrimination. We must then recognise that seeing the world through one single frame of reference and ignoring or diminishing the value of others doesn't make the problems go away – if anything, it fertilises them. The answer, from a global perspective at least, seems to be that for peace and prosperity and reduced risk of crisis, we must find ways to capitalise on the power of diversity, not quash it.

When we think about all that we've learnt over the last few chapters, we could say much of the same about education as the economy. After all, they are, in essence, an extension of each other. The first line of England's Department of Education priorities is to "drive economic growth through improving the skills pipeline, levelling up productivity and supporting people to work".[18] Valuing only pupil productivity through speed and accuracy of sensorimotor response in timed conditions and against age expectations, standardised into a bell curve, is a monoculture world view: it is a form of collective blindness that we have inherited. And yet, whilst the tide *is* slowly turning, we still have a strong undercurrent in education that fears seeing the world through any other lens. Whether it's "trauma-informed", valuing equality, diversity and inclusion, or assessing skill outside of an exam hall, voicing a different perspective can be perceived as pedalling lower standards for education, as if there is a "trade-off" between excellence and diversity. Culture within the CIA was similar before 9/11.

Agents had perceived no benefit to widening the frame of what excellence looked like to them[3] – until they zoomed in on what their aims and values truly were and realised their recruitment processes needed to change to meet them. Who they looked for and what they valued had to adapt if they really wanted to keep America safe. Our very own **GCHQ** actively look for cultural- and neurodiversity in their recruitment processes, too. If our "most intelligent" members of society are recognising the power of diversity to capitalise upon it, then in schools, surely we should be reflecting deeply on what our aims and values truly are and whether we need to change our processes to meet them, too. So, why aren't we?

---

3   White, male, middle-class, Christian, university-educated . . .

**Central Intelligence Agency (CIA):** America's intelligence system which captures and uses information to keep America safe.

**GCHQ:** the UK's intelligence, security and cyber agency whose mission is to help keep the country safe.

## Managing the economy of education

"The customer can have any colour. . ." Henry Ford is famously supposed to have said of his cars ". . . so long as it's black". And, we might accept, perhaps reluctantly or with resignation, that this is the cost of mass-production and the benefit of utilitarianism: "the greatest good for the greatest number". In choosing to design a "sound" and "cheap" education system which meets the expectations of the Treasury, it is entirely logical to focus on pupil productivity to feed the country's future GDP, while also keeping the cost of education as low as possible. It balances the demand of educating an efficient workforce of the future to help our economy grow, whilst also managing our capital resources effectively in prioritising GDP over the household and society. We want adults who can produce goods and services quickly and accurately to boost our economy so everyone gains. As a result, some will necessarily have to compromise on their preferred choice or way of working because anything else has lesser return on investment. After all, "you cannot please all the people all of the time" or, if you're Karl Pearson, some are just "better stock".

Flawed though utilitarianism may be as an approach to ethical decision making, given that its ideals necessitate denying the needs of some, "the greatest good for the greatest number" is an approach we tend to use readily. When there are no easy answers, supporting the needs of the majority first makes sense. The minority, whoever they are, will just have to make do in whatever way they can. Those with SEND are a prime example. For a decision or design to meet this threshold however, we have to *know* that the greatest number are indeed benefitting, and that those who are disadvantaged by it are very small in number. Otherwise it's just an **oligarchy** in all but name. The growing number of people calling for change in education – teachers, SENCOs, parents, social workers, local authorities, children and young people themselves – would suggest that this assumption needs careful review. If the priorities of education are to "improve skills", "level up" and "support people" then we need to know that we, as the enactors of this system in daily practice, are actually achieving that. Let's do a mini stocktake to see.

**Oligarchy:** a small group of people having control promoting their own interests above others.

**Education Health and Care Plan:** (England only) This is for children and young people aged up to 25 who need more support than is available through special educational needs support. It is a legal document which requires provision to be made by the educational setting and is reviewed annually by professionals and parents-carers on behalf of, and often with, the pupil.

## Stocktaking our education system

We could count the cost of court cases where parents have had to take their local authority to court on behalf of their children who have been struggling in school. The reputable British parent support and information website, *Special Needs Jungle*, has calculated that nearly half a billion pounds[4] from the public purse has been spent on tribunals in the last decade, to prevent additional costs going towards children's education. In the academic year 2022–2023, local authorities *lost* 98.3% of the tribunal cases they'd initially refused to fund.[19] Shocking though these wasted costs are, not to mention the personal life stories which come with them, they still represent a minority of children. Only 4.3% of children and young people have an **Education, Health and Care Plan** (EHCP)[20] and only a fraction of those will need to go down the route of tribunal. So we're still talking about "the few".

We could count the number of those opting out of school altogether. In a post by the Children's Commissioner in February 2024, the number of children of compulsory school age not in school was recorded at 120,000;[21] a massive increase of 25% on the year before. But even then, we're still only talking about 1.3% of children and young people in compulsory education in that same year.[22] It's far worse however, when we see that 22.3% of all pupils persistently avoided school in 2022–2023.[23] If we extend our frame of reference and look at these same metrics within the teaching workforce, we see an equally worrying picture. According to a government school workforce report, almost 10% of teachers left the state-funded sector in 2022–2023, with teacher vacancies increasing by 20%, having already more than doubled over the previous three years. And in the same year, 66.2% of teachers were absent due to ill-health, with an average of eight days off per teacher.[24] Recruitment and retention is now a major issue with high workload, insufficient pay compared to other degree-level professions, and the increasingly high level of needs of the children themselves; all of which are regularly cited as reasons to leave the workforce. Recruitment and retention for teaching assistants to help support children with additional needs is also similarly affected.

We could even cross-check teacher claims by counting the number of children and young people with identified special educational needs and disabilities in the same year – which, the data corroborates, is on the rise at 17.3%.[25] The percentage of those identified as SEND but without an EHCP jumped 5% in one year alone. "The few" are no longer a small minority, it seems. But this is where I think it all starts to get really rather murky. You see, having worked in this field for quite some time now – long enough to write a book about it – I've come to a very unsettling conclusion. When we talk about totalling the national number of children and young people with "special educational needs and disabilities" I don't think we really know what we're talking about.

Let me repeat that again, in case the weight of that statement didn't grab you the first time. When we talk about "special educational needs and disabilities" I don't think we really know which children we're talking about, or in fact, what those needs

---

4   And it's growing at an exponential rate, currently £1 billion a year.

actually are. The 2021 research by the Education Policy Institute,[26] showing that the school a child attends makes a far greater difference to their chances of being identified with SEND than other factors, is an example of the confusion that I'm talking about. It leads me to the conclusion that "SEND" is a misnomer and a distraction. It's a nebulous construct that doesn't really have any clear, applicable meaning.

And if we don't have any shared meaning for what on earth we're really talking about, then we can't be clear that our education system design does in fact meet the needs of the majority to maximise productivity. Worse still, the warning signs might be right there in front of us, big obvious signs, and yet we're collectively blind to them because we haven't been trained to look for them or we're focussing our attention on something else instead. Underestimating the data we have, and underappreciating the black holes that are in it, risks permeating our "skills pipeline". It might be leaking all manner of potential productivity for all we know, leading us towards a far shallower pool of future resource: an educational and an economic crisis. In fact, some would say we've already reached it.

## What do we mean when we talk about SEND?

We can, of course, cite a legal definition, like the one currently in force in England: "a child or young person with special educational needs is one for whom a learning disability or difficulty calls for special educational provision to be made for them", "which is a greater difficulty than the majority of others of the same age".[27] We can point out the children in our classes who appear to be struggling and say they need additional support. We can even name the children and the necessary provision for those with an EHCP. But, when it comes to actually measuring the number, using shared language and definitions, agreed criteria, and no ulterior prisoners' dilemma motives, I don't think we could yet truly define special educational needs and disabilities with any sensitivity or specificity, to be able to put a figure on prevalence.

It is another result of the hidden economy. Like a Russian doll, the strengths and needs of children and young people are a hidden economy within the hidden economy of education. And I think that this is because when we talk about SEND we're still clinging rather helplessly to an outdated definition and estimation from 1978. A year when the Ford Cortina was Britain's best-selling car, now available in many more colours than just black, with its four gears and stereo/cassette player, playing infamous hits like the Rivers of Babylon by Boney M; and where vol-au-vents and prawn cocktails graced the tables of dinner parties across the land.

Back in 1978, when the Warnock Report was first published, the number of children thought to need some kind of special educational provision was pitched at somewhere between 16–20%. "About one in six children at any one time, and up to one in five children at some time in their school career" the report states,[28] and about 2% of children will have a higher degree of complexity. These figures were shocking, especially compared to the 2% of handicapped children that had been previously calculated, and were based upon a wide range of **epidemiological studies** at the time.

But let's just pause for a moment. Let's stand back and really consider the context of these figures. For a start, in 1978, computers were only just beginning to introduce spellcheck and most people were very unlikely to have used one, let alone owned one. Nearly fifty years on, our world (just like our technology) is dramatically different to the one on which this research and report was written. Dyslexia was still the myth of the middle classes and children couldn't be diagnosed with well-known conditions that we have today, such as ADHD or autism.[5] Epidemiological studies have been updated since then and we are increasingly aware of not only a greater range of conditions, but also that previously known medical conditions, like asthma and diabetes, are growing rapidly in prevalence, too, with potential adverse effects on educational outcomes. But our national SEND data is still bobbing around the original estimation from back in the day. It doesn't make sense to me.

You see, for there to be an accurate figure of prevalence, there has to be sufficient expertise, resourcing, shared responsibility and trust between professionals and parents to agree that a child has a need in the first place. And for that to happen, we have to have enough professionals who have a clear sense of what the needs of children actually are to be able to draw a meaningful comparison, as well as the incentive to do so. And we don't. We have huge lacunas in our research on children and the impact of the nested structures around them. So, given that much of the economy of education is hidden and largely undervalued, the likelihood of an outcome we're all happy to agree on is pretty slim. There is still so much we don't see and know about this cloaked and undervalued world of education. No wonder we're calling it a crisis.

My professional hypothesis – my hunch, if you want to call it that – is that when we do eventually unveil this hidden world, we will see that there are not two types of children, instead we will just see enormous diversity and a whole host of risk and protective factors influencing it. Children and young people, all genetically predisposed to have purpose in their unique and individual ways, exposed to multifarious risk and protective factors – some biological, some psychological, some social – affecting their success in the classroom. The more risk factors present at any one time in a pupil (which will, of course, be different and dynamic, but cumulative), the greater the draw on someone's potential, changing the course of their lives, and even potentially the generations to follow.

---

**Epidemiology:** the study of the prevalence of diseases; their occurrence and distribution amongst different groups of people and why.

**Fractal:** an infinitely complex mathematical shape.

---

5  Whilst children displayed difficulties associated with these now well-known conditions, it was not until 1987 when a revised version of the *Diagnostic and Statistical Manual of Mental Disorders* (DSM) – III included them, that these diagnoses could officially be given to children and young people.

## We are extraordinary

"Unless you take into account the diversity of individuals," warns Matthew Syed, "you are likely to design systems, guidelines and much else that are defective or restricting or both."[29] My screening and teaching experience leads me to vigorously agree. We are *all* neuro-diverse. We are all wonderfully extraordinary in our own unique ways. When I drill down, like you will when you start screening at scale, I just see this diversity staring back at me on the page. No binary distinctions. Everyone is different. But of course we don't see this when we only test a few children and assume that everyone else is typical.

Perhaps I *am* just one of those 'raving loony women' after all . . .?

Or perhaps my relatively tiny data sets are indicative of the patterns you will find within your school walls too? Perhaps you too will find that your own school community is really rather diverse: full of human **fractals**, all a little bit different from each other, with their own unique profiles of strengths and needs, risks and protective factors? Perhaps you too will find that there's more pupils than you first thought who'd enormously benefit from an education system, and indeed a world, which is designed to see them for who they really are and the value they offer? No "SEND children", but *every* single child and young person with risk and protective factors in their lives. I wonder how that changes things for you? It shook me deeply. After all, I too have been immersed in this monoculture perspective for a long time, with all its assumptions and preconceptions.

The power we have with this mindset is enormous, however. Many of those risks, whether the result of nature, nurture or a bit of both, can be mitigated by protective factors in our environment. We can change how we structure, organise and deliver 'school'. We can invest in better maternal and paediatric health, support and economic opportunities. We can evaluate the wealth that comes from a father investing in their child. We can actively empower the children and young people themselves by providing better support and better self-awareness. But to do this, we need to acknowledge, understand and quantify the value encoded into the household and on society. We need to critically evaluate our economic and educational aims and values. We have to be adaptive and we have to be brave. After all, what are we *really* trying to achieve and are we effective in making it happen?

And, if what I've described does indeed turn out to be the case, then we've got some paradigm-shifting of our own to do, you and I. To finally quash the millstone in education that continues to believe that there are two types of children: ones who can drive shiny black Ford Cortinas and ones who can't. A twenty-first century education takes much more than just offering one-size-fits-all solution, which the car industry learnt nearly a century ago. It's time we did, too.

Admiration for a fast speed of visual processing, for example, must be tempered by the need to appreciate the comparatively slower but arguably equally beautiful and valuable nature of colour perception that some people have. The gains of a strong working memory and calculating complex numerical problems must be weighed and measured against the shared best outcomes we all benefit from when parents and carers are able to love and grow their children in a stress-free home – children in all their wonderful diversity – into adulthood. Understanding how we create a system which does this goes well beyond education alone, of course, but let's not get overwhelmed by the size of that. Let's start where we are, one step at a time, and commit to exploring what we can about the biopsychosocial factors which can influence someone to experience a happy and purposeful time in school. After all, as we learnt in Chapter One, crises are actually fertile ground.

## Final thoughts: the path to growth and freedom

Learning, changing and understanding ourselves is perhaps the most intense yearning we feel throughout our entire lives. It can empower some with confidence and bravery until their dying breath, and it can eat others alive every day in self-loathing. Gently helping someone to discover parts of themselves they didn't previously understand and to embrace themselves in all their technicolour is honestly the greatest privilege. In screening and feeding back, I believe we empower a child and their family to admire their diversity for what it is; to recognise their unique strengths and empower them with tools and strategies they can use to navigate any challenges. To not be afraid of their future but to write it.

As I sit here drinking my now lukewarm coffee, typing these final few paragraphs of the book, I feel my own growing sense of the peace that comes with acceptance. The closing of my own metaphorical life chapter as I finish writing this book. I, too, have learned, changed and understood myself a little bit better than when I first started. I have travelled a few steps further in my own ever-evolving journey in discovering pieces of who I am and where I've come from. Knowing yourself better is, indeed, the path to growth and freedom.

In reading this book, I hope that you have also met parts of yourself in these pages and understood yourself just a little better, too. Perhaps you have sensed the depth of the empowerment I'm talking about; the self-awareness that maximises potential? What an honour and a privilege you now have. A gift you can share with others in enabling them to feel the same. And, even if the responsibility of developing a screening process in your setting feels a little overwhelming on top of everything else you need to do, know that Nelson Mandela was right when he stated, "it always seems impossible until it's done". You can absolutely do this.

It was this very same quotation that kept me clinging on for dear life when we first started planning the National SENCO Workload Survey. I just kept repeating it to myself over and over again, when gathering the views of as many SENCOs as we could persuade to participate, seemed like an impossible task. And yet, as a national team of SENCOs, we rose to the challenge spectacularly. We combined our efforts and brought together data from a deeply hidden economy. Data that has been read and used by SENCOs in schools, as well as journalists, departmental ministers, civil servants, advocates and researchers. It is research that has left an indelible mark.

Not long ago, I read an article for my professional doctorate and it made me catch my breath. It said: "Teacher research is revolutionary; it upsets the educational hierarchy, much like feminism upsets the patriarchal hegemony."[30]

*Teacher* research is revolutionary.
Teacher research is *revolutionary.*

It changes things.
Our research changes things.

The fact that it's revolutionary is, I think, another mark of our hidden value. We perceive ourselves as professionals who bring curriculums or laws into fruition, not as researchers, as well, evaluating the impact of those very same curriculums or laws on our people. We are nurturers not fact checkers, verifying that national decisions do in fact provide "the greatest good to the greatest number". We are not usually funded with enough flexibility of resourcing to do anything more than carry out our daily responsibilities with the children in front of us. And yet, what another huge waste of potential, that is!

\*

As I've been crafting and editing this book in the small hours of the morning before school, it has slowly dawned upon me that there is another purpose concealed within these chapters. It was hidden even from me when I first started writing, which is ironic because it's been obvious since the moment I first introduced you to Jack. Let me remind you of what I wrote: "Jack helped me to see that regardless of what had gone before, I was the custodian of my classroom now. It was my own research insights that mattered to today's children, and that I could make a difference where I was."

And so, I will leave you with this additional opportunity: to consider yourself a researcher, too. A virtual colleague with me, gathering together our children's data, to better understand it so that decision-making isn't just perpetual "regurgitation" or good old prisoners' dilemma defection. Instead, let's take our findings to the rooms where it happens and invite ourselves to the table with our research. We are the ones who see it all and have access to the children and young people of today to be able to tell their story. We hold great potential to amplify it and to change things.

The truth is, if we want to improve a complex system we need to find the "leverage points" – "places . . . where a small shift in one thing can produce big changes in every-thing", says economist Donella Meadows.[31] "Get the beat of the system, even if it is an ailing economy, a dying forest, or a broken community", she says. "Watch and understand how it currently works and learn its history . . . Ask what's wrong [but] also ask: how did we get here, where are we headed, and what is still working well?"[32] Uncovering the hidden economy of education through screening, and through analysis of the data gathered will expose the holes in the current system. It means we stand a chance of finding those leverage points and capitalising upon them.

This kind of living requires a commitment from us to be brave and to see the world through a more intelligent lens – one which gathers diverse data and *adapts to what it perceives*. As a result, the world will undoubtedly look a bit different to the one we know and live in now. But that's evolution for you . . . I can see Darwin and Galton smiling and nodding their heads approvingly – even if the understanding we now have takes us further away from the solutions that Galton, in particular, foresaw.

Like them, we may never live to see the true legacy of these changes, some of which will be generational. But we will know that we will have taken our shared responsibility for humanity seriously, and we will have done the best we could with what we had, until we knew any better. As the Holocaust survivor, Viktor Frankl, is believed to have said: "Between stimulus and response there is a space. In that space is our power to choose our response. In our response lies our growth and freedom."[33]

To screen children in your setting is to play your part in this process. In so doing, you will know that you are dismantling the visible and invisible barriers children and young people, and their families, are facing. You will see it and you will feel it. In systematically screening everyone, you will have given a voice to those facing injustice when they couldn't speak, when they weren't even asked, or like philosopher Miranda Fricker identified and as generative AI technologies have taught us, when they *didn't even know.*

In becoming researchers together as well, however, perhaps we might stand a chance of finding those "leverage points" – those places in a complex system where making a small change in one thing can lead to a big change in everything. I'm intrigued to see whether we can achieve it. Aren't you?

www.nochildismissed.org

*End Note*

Perspective is a funny thing. Hopefully, having now read this book, you will see some of the problems which can come from upholding one truth and ideology above others. Through this same prism, you will also recognise that this interpretation of mine is my own, built from a lifetime of personal sensations and perceptions, biology and lived experiences. I have tried to share many other views, to celebrate the power of diversity, as these views have shaped mine; but if I have missed a point or left a gap in the message that needs filling, let's change that. Your view counts, too. Join in the conversation. As the great educator and philosopher, Paolo Freire, says: *"Liberation is a praxis: the action and reflection of men and women upon their world in order to transform it."*

# Acknowledgements

To the broad church of professionals, parents and pioneers, past and present, who have been a huge inspiration since my first day in teaching: thank you. One of the greatest joys of writing this book has surely been to collate and celebrate the swathes of your expertise from across the globe and across time. You've pursued theory and perfected practice that has made a huge difference to millions of children, young people, parents and professionals worldwide. I am in awe and it has been a privilege to have collaborated with you, including your work in mine.

To my little global village of family, friends and colleagues whom I am lucky enough to do life with: you are my absolute rock. To Rich, Simeon, Theo, Mum, Dad, Jess, Dan, Laurence, Amelie, Elowen, Joel, Gareth, Gilly, Jim, Yvonne, Kevin, Leslie, Garry, Molly, Stuart – thank you for listening to me go on about it and still looking interested; I am finished. I promise! To my Home crew who have championed and supported me over the past fifteen months: Jude, Roisin, Tanya, Kate, Fiona, Holly and the many who have asked me how it's going. It has lifted me, especially when it's been tough going. To my Away crew who have encouraged me now as professionals as well as childhood mates: Sophie, Joel, Becca, Helen – I love that our lifelong connection still lives on. Thank you for your support and professional expertise. To my SEND colleagues over time: Teresa, Kate, Claire, Kathy, Sally, Alison, Vanessa, Lou, Jo, Amy, Michelle, Lesley, Ruth, Carole, Rosie, Angie, Elspeth, Sophie, Debbie, Liz and Sherralyn – I have learnt so much from you all; it's been a privilege to work with every single one of you. To my SENCO ecosystem of local and national professionals and friends whom I've called upon for help with this massive writing endeavour: Katrina, Conor, Kelly, Sarah, Kiri, Tania, Anne, Ben and to my reviewers – thanks a bunch for your feedback and your guidance; I'm indebted to you. To Team HAHA: Helen, Anne and Adam – thank you for believing in the SENCO research project and for working to bring it to life; for all those late night online meetings – we were a great team. Perhaps we can do it all again some time? To all the educators who have poured into me their knowledge, energy and perspectives – thank you for passing it on; especially Jack Whitehead when he was at the University of Bath, and Stuart Read and Agnieszka Bates at Bath Spa University who are a great support with my crazy ambitions to change the world (go big or go home, right?!) and who continue to challenge me to be better . . . To Team Speechmark (Routledge) – Clare, thank you for letting me go wild with a laptop and "get it all out". Writing this has given me an opportunity to write the book I think I needed to read – and one which I hope will make a difference to SENCOs, SEND teams and school leadership everywhere. And to you, whoever you are, for reading this and for caring so deeply about children and young people, building opportunities for them to thrive. Let's keep making a difference together . . .

# Appendix 1

# Chapter and NCIM Summaries

| IQ and Cognitive Ability Tests | Phonological Processing | Visual Processing | Handwriting and Sensory Integration | Executive Function | Social, Emotional, Mental Health | Physical Health |
|---|---|---|---|---|---|---|
| Intelligence is the result of quick and accurate sensorimotor responses – how efficiently the nervous system processes sensory inputs. IQ tests use the "deviation IQ" method, with scores on a bell curve, showing standardised scores where results between 85–115 are average, <84 is below average and >115 is above average, based on someone's age. Individual scores of Verbal, Numerical and Non-Verbal abilities tell us more than one composite. Early and detailed cognitive testing helps identify opportunities to close gaps. | Phonological processing is crucial for learning speech, language, reading, and writing. Accurate perception of sounds builds vocabulary. Phonological awareness is the ability to distinguish and manipulate sounds. Reading development involves both phonological skills and sight word recognition. Spelling relies on phonological awareness and the ability to segment words into sounds. | Visual acuity tests by optometrists assess clarity but may miss functional reading issues. A reduced functional field of view affects reading fluency, comprehension, attention and social confidence. Chronic stress leads to visual perception problems, clumsiness, and learning difficulties. People have different experiences of colour. Many children with colour vision deficiency go undetected. Speed and accuracy of vision depends on experience and exposure. | Handwriting is a complex sensorimotor skill. Good posture and balance are essential. Proprioception helps regulate movement for efficient handwriting. Visual perception guides letter formation, spacing, and alignment. The ability to cross the body's midline is important. Motor planning is necessary for coordinating movements. Sensory integration combines input from multiple senses to perform coordinated actions. Children with sensory processing issues may experience hyper- or hyposensitivity, affecting their ability to regulate behaviour and complete tasks. | EF regulates thoughts and behaviours. Hot EF involves managing emotional, impulsive responses. Cool EF helps with logical decision-making, planning, and memory. Working memory allows children to hold and manipulate information, aiding comprehension, problem-solving, and task completion. The ability to control impulses and resist distractions is crucial for academic success and social interaction. Cognitive flexibility allows children to adapt to change and think creatively, while rigid thinking leads to challenges in social interactions and problem-solving. | Students with strong self-efficacy take more risks to overcome challenges, while low self-efficacy leads to disengagement. Trauma, including adverse childhood experiences (ACEs), has long-term effects on students' emotional, social, and academic development, affecting behaviour and learning in school. Students can mask their true identities to fit in, leading to internalised stress, anxiety, and a lack of belonging. School avoidance can be triggered by anxiety, sensory overwhelm, or social challenges. Prolonged internal stress can manifest in physical symptoms, such as exhaustion and withdrawal from school environments. | Biological, psychological, and social data can reveal patterns of underachievement. Chronic health conditions such as asthma, diabetes, and epilepsy are risk factors for underachievement. Poorly managed asthma can lead to issues with concentration and learning. The quality of food pupils consume directly impact upon blood sugar levels, cognitive function, and overall academic performance. External environmental factors such as pollution, pollen levels, and living conditions can exacerbate health issues. |
| **2.1 Cognitive Ability** | **4.1 Speech, Language and Communication** <br> **4.2 Phonological Awareness** <br> **4.3 Reading Comprehension** <br> **4.4 & 4.5 Spelling** | **5.1 Visual Stress** <br> **5.2 Colour Vision Deficiency** <br> **5.3 Rapid Automatic Naming Speed** <br> **5.4 Reading Efficiency** | **6.1. Handwriting Efficiency** <br> **6.2. Motor Planning (Praxis)** <br> **6.3. Sensory Integration** | **7.1 Social and Economic Risk Factors** <br> **7.2 Working Memory** <br> **7.3 Impulsivity/ Inhibition** <br> **7.4 Shift** | **8.1 Self-Efficacy for Learning and Pupil Wellbeing** <br> **8.2 SEMH - Trauma** <br> **8.3 SEMH – School Avoidance** | **9.1 Asthma and Oxygen Efficiency** <br> **9.2 Food and Blood Sugar** <br> **9.3 Impact of Autoimmune Conditions and Allergies** |

No Child is Missed

No Child Misses Out

This summary details screening advice from chapters 2, 4–9

# Appendix 2

# An Overview of the Age Group Screening Protocols – Core and Additional

**No Child is Missed: Core Screeing Protocol – Pre School to Age Five**

| Risk/protective Factors | Screening Focus | NCIM Action Points/ Data to gather |
| --- | --- | --- |
| **Sense of safety and capacity** | Basic health checks: hearing (4) and vision (5) | 5.2 Colour Vision Deficiency |
| | Relationship with food (8 & 9) | Appendix 9: EYFS & Primary Parent-Carer Conversation Form |
| | Bladder & bowel control | 7.1: Social &Economic Risk Factors |
| | Parenting supportt & Child Social & Economic Risk Factors | |
| | Social & Emotional Development (7) | |
| | Physical & sensory development:(6) | 6.2& 3: Praxis and Sensory Integration |
| **Ability to express themselves and be heard** | Attention and Listening | 4.1: Speech, language and Communication |
| | Receptive & Expressive Language | |
| | Social Communication | |
| | Speech Sounds | |
| | Play (4) | |
| **Ability to sustain attention and delay gratification** | Impulse control | Appendix 7: Observations in setting (EYFS & Early Primary) |
| | Remaining focused | |
| | Thinking ahead (7) | |
| **Developing independence** | | |

**No Child is Missed: Core Screening Protocol - Ages Five to Seven**

| Risk/Protective Factors | Screening Focus | NCIM Action Points/ Data to gather |
|---|---|---|
| **Sense of safety and capacity** | Basic health checks: hearing (4) and vision (5) Relationship with food (8 & 9) Bladder & bowel control (7) | Appendix 9: EYFS & Primary Parent-Carer Conversation Form |
| | Parenting support, Child Social & Economic Risk Factors Social & Emotional Development (7) | 7.1: Social & Economic Risk Factors |
| **Ability to understand & express themselves** | Phonological Awareness (4) | 4.2 Phonics Screening Test/ Non-Word test evaluating phonemic decoding 4.4 Spelling |
| | Reading Comprehension (4) | 4.3 Reading Comprehension |
| **Ability to correctly interpret visual information at speed** | Colour Processing (5) | 5.2 Colour Vision Deficiency |
| | Speed of sight-sound correspondence (5) | 5.3 Rapid Automatic Naming (RAN) Speed |
| **Pencil hold and early writing skills** | Handwriting grip and hand strength and visuo-motor skills (6) | 6.1-2: Early Handwriting & Praxis skills |
| **Ability to sustain attention and delay gratification** **Developing independence** | Updating (working memory) Focus and attention (7) | 7.2 Appendix 5 Executive Function (Core only; Additional if needed) |

**No Child is Missed: Core Screening Protocol - Ages Seven to Eighteen**

| Risk/Protective Factors | Screening Focus | NCIM Action Points/ Data to gather |
|---|---|---|
| **Sense of mental and physical health** | Basic health checks Safeguarding checks | Appendix 4: Starter Questions Known Health data (use Appendix 10 if needed) |
| **Sense of academic, emotional and social confidence** | Self-efficacy (8) Impulsivity & Shift (7) | 8.1: Self-efficacy questionnaire 7.4 Strengths & Difficulties questionnaire (Age 11+) |
| **Literacy skills: accuracy and speed of working** | Reading efficiency Reading comprehension (4) Spelling (4) Handwriting efficiency (6) | 5.4 Reading efficiency 4.3 Reading comprehension 4.4 Spelling accuracy 6.1 Handwriting efficiency |

| Risk/Protective Factors | Screening Focus | NCIM Action Points/ Data to gather |
|---|---|---|
| **Visual processing speed and colour accuracy** | Colour processing (5) Speed of sight-sound correspondence (5) | 5.2 Colour Vision Deficiency 5.3 Rapid Automatic Naming (RAN) Speed |
| **Ability to sustain attention and delay gratification** | Updating (working memory) Focus and attention (7) | 7.1: Social & Economic Risk Factors 7.2 Appendix 5 Executive Function (Core only; Additional if needed) |
| **Cognitive profile** | Cognitive Ability / Intelligence (2) | 2.1 Cognitive Ability |

**No Child is Missed: Additional Protocol - Complex Behaviours and Trauma/Mental Health**

| Risk/Protective Factors | Screening Focus (Chapter reference) | NCIM Action Points/ Data to gather |
|---|---|---|
| **Speech, Language and Communication Skills** | Attention and Listening Receptive & Expressive Language Social Communication Speech Sounds Play (4) | 4.1: Speech, Language and Communication |
| **Stress in the school day Quality of Life** | Sensory integration (6) Basic health checks Safeguarding checks Relationship with food Bladder and bowel control(8 & 9) | 6.3 Sensory Integration 8.2 Quality of Life, ACES Appendix 9 or 10: Age-appropriate Parent-Carer Conversation Form |
| **Typical behaviours observed in school** | Profile of common behaviours and challenges inside school (7) | 7.3 & 7.4 Impulsivity, Shift, Strengths & Difficulties Appendix 7 or 8: Age-appropriate observations in setting |
| **Influences and choices outside of school** | Profile of risk exposure outside of school (8) | 8.2 Consider local Youth Offending resources |

### No Child is Missed: Additional Protocol - School Avoidance

| Risk/ Protective Factors | Screening Focus (Chapter reference) | NCIM Action Points/ Data to gather |
|---|---|---|
| **Speech, Language and Communication Skills** | Attention and Listening Receptive & Expressive Language Social Communication Speech Sounds Play (4) | 4.1: Speech, Language and Communication |
| **Stress in the school day Quality of Life** | Sensory integration (6) Basic health checks Safeguarding checks Relationship with food Bladder and bowel control (8 & 9) | 6.3 Sensory Integration 8.2 Quality of Life, ACES Appendix 9 or 10: Age-appropriate Parent-Carer Conversation Form |
| **Barriers to attendance, including sense of belonging and identity** | Social., Emotional & Mental Health (8) | 8.3 School Avoidance and Perceived Stress |

### No Child is Missed: Additional Protocol - Learning Delays

| Risk/ Protective Factors | Screening Focus (Chapter reference) | NCIM Action Points/ Data to gather |
|---|---|---|
| **Speech, Language and Communication Skills** | Attention & Listening Receptive & Expressive Language Social Communication Speech Sounds Play (4) | 4.1: Speech, Language and Communication |
| **Handwriting & Spelling Difficulties** | Rhyme and Alliteration Shared sounds Dividing and blending syllables Segmenting phonemes Manipulating phonemes (4) | 4.2 Phonological Awareness 4.5 Spelling accuracy (additional) |
| | Handwriting & Praxis (6) | 6.1 & 6.2 Appendix 6: Handwriting & Praxis Checklist |
| **Stress in the school day** | Sensory integration (6) | 6.3 Sensory Integration 8.3 Perceived Stress |
| **Quality of Life** | Basic health checks Safeguarding checks Relationship with food Bladder and bowel control (8&9) | 8.2 Quality of Life, ACES Appendix 9 or 1o: Age-appropriate Parent-Carer Conversation Form |

This summary details advice from Chapter 10

# Appendix 3

# An Overview of the Screening Process

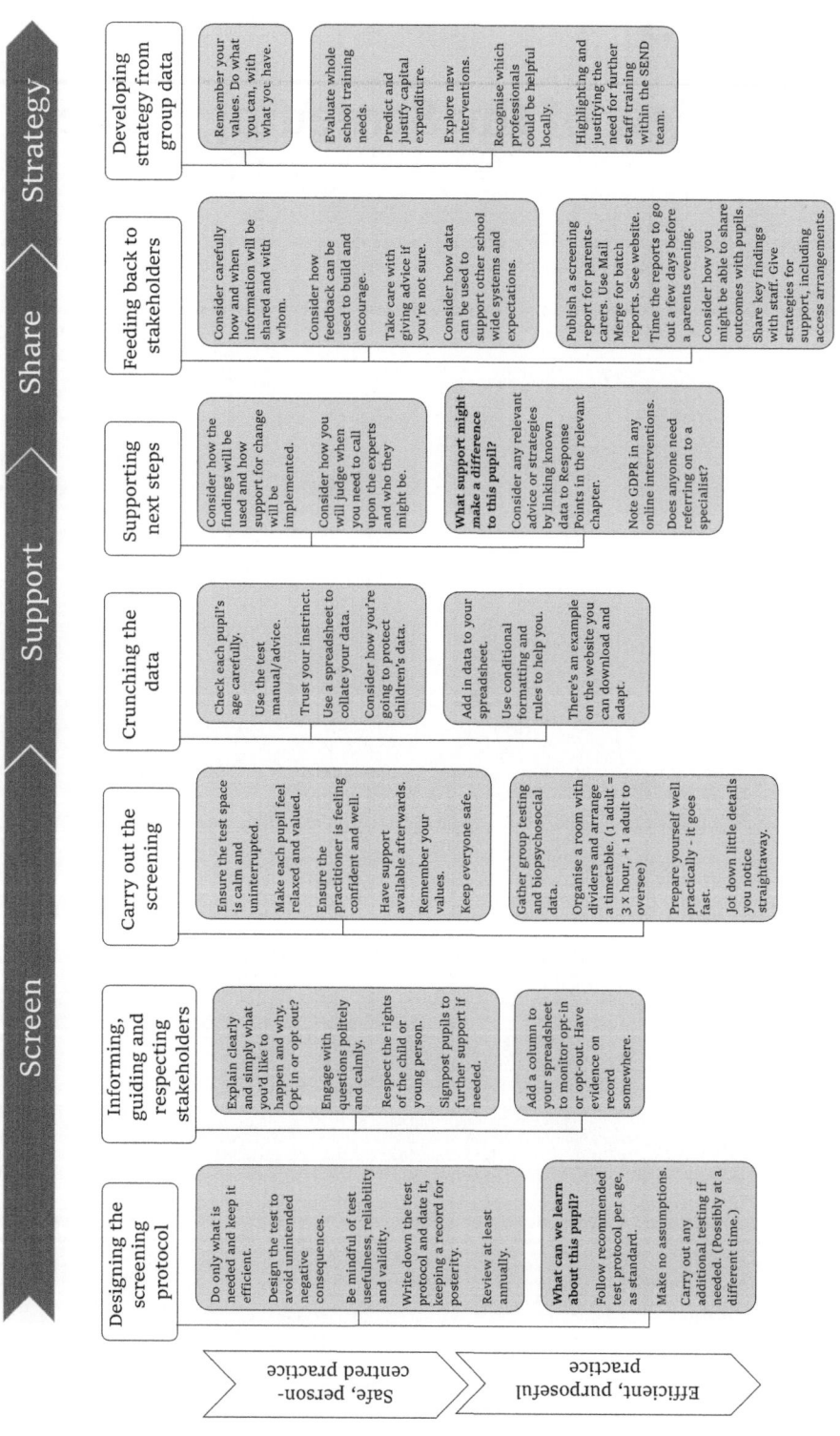

**Screen | Support | Share | Strategy**

**Screen**

**Designing the screening protocol**

- Do only what is needed and keep it efficient.
- Design the test to avoid unintended negative consequences.
- Be mindful of test usefulness, reliability and validity.
- Write down the test protocol and date it, keeping a record for posterity.
- Review at least annually.

**What can we learn about this pupil?**
- Follow recommended test protocol per age, as standard.
- Make no assumptions.
- Carry out any additional testing if needed. (Possibly at a different time.)

**Informing, guiding and respecting stakeholders**

- Explain clearly and simply what you'd like to happen and why. Opt in or opt out?
- Engage with questions politely and calmly.
- Respect the rights of the child or young person.
- Signpost pupils to further support if needed.

- Add a column to your spreadsheet to monitor opt-in or opt-out. Have evidence on record somewhere.

**Support**

**Carry out the screening**

- Ensure the test space is calm and uninterrupted.
- Make each pupil feel relaxed and valued.
- Ensure the practitioner is feeling confident and well.
- Have support available afterwards.
- Remember your values.
- Keep everyone safe.

- Gather group testing and biopsychosocial data.
- Organise a room with dividers and arrange a timetable. ( 1 adult = 3 x hour, + 1 adult to oversee)
- Prepare yourself well practically - it goes fast.
- Jot down little details you notice straightaway.

**Crunching the data**

- Check each pupil's age carefully.
- Use the test manual/advice.
- Trust your instinct.
- Use a spreadsheet to collate your data.
- Consider how you're going to protect children's data.

- Add in data to your spreadsheet.
- Use conditional formatting and rules to help you.
- There's an example on the website you can download and adapt.

**Share**

**Supporting next steps**

- Consider how the findings will be used and how support for change will be implemented.
- Consider how you will judge when you need to call upon the experts and who they might be.

**What support might make a difference to this pupil?**
- Consider any relevant advice or strategies by linking known data to Response Points in the relevant chapter.
- Note GDPR in any online interventions. Does anyone need referring on to a specialist?

**Feeding back to stakeholders**

- Consider carefully how and when information will be shared and with whom.
- Consider how feedback can be used to build and encourage.
- Take care with giving advice if you're not sure.
- Consider how data can be used to support other school wide systems and expectations.

- Publish a screening report for parents-carers. Use Mail Merge for batch reports. See website.
- Time the reports to go out a few days before a parents evening.
- Consider how you might be able to share outcomes with pupils.
- Share key findings with staff. Give strategies for support, including access arrangements.

**Strategy**

**Developing strategy from group data**

- Remember your values. Do what you can, with what you have.
- Evaluate whole school training needs.
- Predict and justify capital expenditure.
- Explore new interventions.
- Recognise which professionals could be helpful locally.
- Highlighting and justifying the need for further staff training within the SEND team.

This summary details advice from chapters 3 and 10

**Safe, person-centred practice**

**Efficient, purposeful practice**

# Appendix 4

# Example Starter Questions and Test Flow

These two questions ensure that you're measuring ability on top of any identified vision support needs. Asking about the opticians helps you to advise later on.

This section is critical. Never skimp on it. You will always want to know these four pieces of information.

This question targets assent and gives a baseline figure.

These health-related questions help you to build a sense of their overall health.

Sleep is critical in attention and focus. This measures insomnia. Recommend visiting GP if it takes 45m+. Asking about tech might help you advise on sleep hygiene.

An enjoyable question for them but one which can be very revealing for you.

Time the child reading. Carry out a brief miscue analysis to gain a sense of reading efficiency.

Measure accuracy of response. Include different types of questions e.g. factual recall, inference, vocabulary. Reflect on their response speed. Fast? Slow? Do they need questions repeated? Do they need to re-check the text to answer?

---

**Pupil Name:** _____  **Date of Birth:** _____

**Date of Assessment:** _____  **Assessor:** _____

How are you feeling right now?          1   2   3   4   5

1-2 Pupil Voice questions               1   2   3   4   5

Wearing glasses? Y / N       Last eye test within 2 years? Y / N

When is bed time? _____  How easy is sleep? 10-20 / 45 mins+

How many hours on tech after school?    1   2   3   4   5

What food do you enjoy? _____

How much water do you drink a day?  500ml   11   1.51   21

Are you on any regular medication? Y / N  If so, what? _____

If you could be an animal, what would you be and why? _____

**Reading Comprehension**

Giraffes are the tallest animals in the world, with long necks that help them reach leaves high in trees. They live in Africa, where they roam the savannas. A giraffe's tongue can be up to 18 inches long, helping them grab food. They also have unique spots that work like fingerprints, making each giraffe different.

1. Where do giraffes live?
2. What helps giraffes reach leaves high in trees?
3. Which word in the text means *wander*?
4. How might the length of a giraffe's tongue help it survive?
5. Why are giraffe spots special?
6. What purpose do you think a giraffe's unique spots serve in the wild?
7. How might a giraffe's height impact its interactions with other animals in its ecosystem?

Errors: _____
Time: _____

**Digits Forwards**

Continue through the test until the pupil fails to complete both trials of a pair. "Listen carefully as I say some numbers. When I finish, you say them." Administer both trials of each item.

Comment on retrieval speed: _____

---

A core test of executive function. What does their pattern of response indicate? Zoning in and out? Impulsivity? Anxiety or rushing? Are they especially fast or slow responders? What is their standardised score?

| Item | First Trial | ✓ ✗ | Second Trial | ✓ ✗ | Total |
|------|-------------|-----|--------------|-----|-------|
| A | See the Turner Ridsdale test for the numbers to say. | | See the Turner Ridsdale test for the numbers to say. | | |
| B | See the Turner Ridsdale test for the numbers to say. | | See the Turner Ridsdale test for the numbers to say. | | |
| C | See the Turner Ridsdale test for the numbers to say. | | See the Turner Ridsdale test for the numbers to say. | | |
| D | See the Turner Ridsdale test for the numbers to say. | | See the Turner Ridsdale test for the numbers to say. | | |
| E | See the Turner Ridsdale test for the numbers to say. | | See the Turner Ridsdale test for the numbers to say. | | |
| F | See the Turner Ridsdale test for the numbers to say. | | See the Turner Ridsdale test for the numbers to say. | | |
| G | See the Turner Ridsdale test for the numbers to say. | | See the Turner Ridsdale test for the numbers to say. | | |
| H | See the Turner Ridsdale test for the numbers to say. | | See the Turner Ridsdale test for the numbers to say. | | |
| | See the Turner Ridsdale test for the numbers to say. | | See the Turner Ridsdale test for the numbers to say. | Forwards: | |

**Digits Backwards**

"Repeat these numbers after me but this time I want you to say them backwards."

Give to practice trials of two digits first – any two numbers. If the child gets them wrong, correct them. If they repeat the digits forwards, remind them that they should be reversed.

Continue through the test until the pupil fails to complete both trials of a pair.

| Item | First Trial | ✓ ✗ | Second Trial | ✓ ✗ | Total |
|---|---|---|---|---|---|
| A | *See the Turner Ridsdale test for the numbers to say.* | | *See the Turner Ridsdale test for the numbers to say.* | | |
| B | *See the Turner Ridsdale test for the numbers to say.* | | *See the Turner Ridsdale test for the numbers to say.* | | |
| C | *See the Turner Ridsdale test for the numbers to say.* | | *See the Turner Ridsdale test for the numbers to say.* | | |
| D | *See the Turner Ridsdale test for the numbers to say.* | | *See the Turner Ridsdale test for the numbers to say.* | | |
| E | *See the Turner Ridsdale test for the numbers to say.* | | *See the Turner Ridsdale test for the numbers to say.* | | |
| F | *See the Turner Ridsdale test for the numbers to say.* | | *See the Turner Ridsdale test for the numbers to say.* | | |
| G | *See the Turner Ridsdale test for the numbers to say.* | | *See the Turner Ridsdale test for the numbers to say.* | | |
| | *See the Turner Ridsdale test for the numbers to say.* | | *See the Turner Ridsdale test for the numbers to say.* Backwards: | | |

Part two of the core test of executive function. If you still have questions about EF (or handwriting), you could also consider carrying out the additional Luria tests at this point.

## Rapid Automatic Naming Speed

Time: _____
Errors: _____

| 3 | 6 | 2 | 4 | 8 | 1 | 9 | 2 |
|---|---|---|---|---|---|---|---|
| 5 | 7 | 4 | 2 | 8 | 3 | 1 | 4 |
| 6 | 3 | 5 | 8 | 2 | 9 | 7 | 1 |
| 8 | 1 | 6 | 7 | 9 | 4 | 5 | 3 |

Time: _____
Errors: _____

| s | a | t | p | i | n | a | c |
|---|---|---|---|---|---|---|---|
| k | t | m | s | o | c | k | a |
| i | n | c | t | s | o | n | p |
| k | c | m | o | a | n | p | s |

## Reading Efficiency

Part two looking at vision. You will probably see similarities in RAN and Reading Efficiency. This test will help you identify whose fluency is below and needs targeted intervention with precision teaching (and/or phonics).

| | | | | |
|---|---|---|---|---|
| 1. Cat | 2. Dog | 3. Ball | 4. Hat | 5. Cup |
| 6. Tree | 7. Sun | 8. Book | 9. Fish | 10. Car |
| 11. Apple | 12. Chair | 13. Shoe | 14. House | 15. Water |
| 16. Bread | 17. Bird | 18. Table | 19. Milk | 20. Coat |
| 21. Bicycle | 22. Garden | 23. River | 24. Window | 25. Pillow |
| 26. School | 27. Pencil | 28. Jacket | 29. Island | 30. Mountain |
| 31. Helicopter | 32. Dictionary | 33. Calendar | 34. Medicine | 35. Architecture |
| 36. Telescope | 37. Container | 38. University | 39. Laboratory | 40. President |
| 41. Technology | 42. Atmosphere | 43. Hypothesis | 44. Pollution | 45. Ecosystem |
| 46. Phenomenon | 47. Psychology | 48. Revolution | 49. Astronomy | 50. Democracy |
| 51. Synchronization | 52. Neuroscience | 53. Cosmopolitan | 54. Biochemistry | 55. Catastrophic |
| 56. Nanotechnology | 57. Quantitative | 58. Photosynthesis | 59. Anthropology | 60. Metamorphosis |
| 61. Dichotomy | 62. Etymology | 63. Epistemology | 64. Hypothetical | 65. Constellation |
| 66. Cryptography | 67. Paradigm | 68. Discrepancy | 69. Algorithm | 70. Magnanimous |
| 71. Heterogeneous | 72. Irreconcilable | 73. Symbiosis | 74. Obfuscation | 75. Multilateralism |

This is really a gut-reaction judgement compared to peers, but it might indicate a further conversation is needed with home about eating habits, health or issues of safeguarding.

This is comparative data to before. It gives you a sense of the experience and an opportunity to reassure and support if it has gone down. If you notice lots feeling lower than when they started, review your procedures.

| | | | | |
|---|---|---|---|---|
| 76. Ephemeral | 77. Paradoxical | 78. Perpendicular | 79. Transcendental | 80. Circumlocution |
| 81. Disestablishment | 82. Pseudoscientific | 83. Quintessential | 84. Inconsequential | 85. Perfunctory |
| 86. Ambidextrous | 87. Conflagration | 88. Epistemological | 89. Metaphysical | 90. Indefatigable |
| 91. Substantiate | 92. Existentialism | 93. Incommunicable | 94. Defenestration | 95. Anthropocentric |
| 96. Oscillatory | 97. Synecdoche | 98. Compartmentalize | 99. Circumscription | 100. Thermodynamics |

Total correct: _____

Well done! Great job.
And how are you feeling now?

**Observation only:**     Height + / -     Weight + / -

1   2   3   4   5
**None**

Once you've collated and standardised this information and also your outsourced information gathering (handwriting, spelling, sense of self-efficacy, other data), you are ready to input the data into your spreadsheet. If you wish to do additional tests with a child or young person, it is easier to do them at a separate time to the Core tests, rather than interrupt flow and exhaust a pupil at the same time. Go to www.nochildismissed.org to download an example excel sheet and report to help you so you can mail merge the data quickly.

# Appendix 5

# Testing Executive Function

## 1. The Turner Ridsdale Digit Memory Test (Core)

Unfortunately, due to copyright reasons, we cannot publish the test directly here; however, if you search online you will readily find the test and worked examples. Links will also be available on www.nochildismissed.org

**Don't forget the top tips in administering this type of test!**

### Additional Top Tips from Hannah

- When a child is taking this test, you may notice a pattern emerging. We regularly see some children doing really well on one prompt and then getting the following one wrong. This seems to indicate difficulties maintaining attention and focus: zoning in and out. This is can be particularly relevant if a pupil is naturally well-mannered and calm in class: their frequent inattention is invisible.
- You can also see evidence of impulsivity in this test, too. Listen out for the pupils who interrupt you before you've got to the end of the string of numbers. This is their inhibition getting the better of them. I always make a note of it by writing an "i" in a circle (like the © sign but with an i) each time it happens.
- The speed at which pupils complete this task is also an indicator of their speed of working. Speed is not always an indicator of their level of accuracy, however. Some are fast and wrong, others can be slow and correct. I think the speed can sometimes be more indicative of their mental health and ability to cope with discomfort, than their memory competence.
- This test can occasionally provoke an emotional reaction in pupils. Although it seems quite a fun challenge to most, be mindful that for those with underlying anxiety or heightened stress responses, this task can be triggering. Noticing how a pupil is finding this test is important and using your professional instinct to judge whether to continue or to end the test early, perhaps

trying again another day, is something to keep in mind. Also, we've found it best to avoid putting it last in the screening battery. Finish on something less intense instead.

- Hopefully what the above has taught you is to notice the pupil as well as their responses. You can learn a huge amount from just watching and observing *how* they complete a task.

**Below is also an example of how you might format the test for your own use.**

Pupil Name:_____ Date of Birth: _____

Date of Assessment: _____ Name of Assessor: _____

### Digits Forwards

Continue through the test until the pupil fails to complete both trials of a pair.

"Listen carefully as I say some numbers. When I finish, you say them." Administer both trials of each item.

| Item | First Trial | ✓✗ | Second Trial | ✓✗ | Total |
|---|---|---|---|---|---|
| A | | | | | |
| B | | | | | |
| C | | | | | |
| D | | | | | |
| E | | | | | |
| F | | | | | |
| G | | | | | |
| H | | | | | |
| | | | | Forwards: | |

### Digits Backwards

"Repeat these numbers after me but this time I want you to say them backwards."

Give to practice trials of two digits first – any two numbers. If the child gets them wrong, correct them. If they repeat the digits forwards, remind them that they should be reversed.

Continue through the test until the pupil fails to complete both trials of a pair.

| Item | First Trial | ✓✗ | Second Trial | ✓✗ | Total |
|------|-------------|-----|--------------|-----|-------|
| A | | | | | |
| B | | | | | |
| C | | | | | |
| D | | | | | |
| E | | | | | |
| F | | | | | |
| G | | | | | |
| | | | | Backwards: | |

### Final Score

| Total Forwards & Backwards Scores | |
|-----------------------------------|---|
| Standardised Score Equivalent | |

Use the table of standardised scores to work out how strong your pupil's working memory is.

## 2. Luria's Three Step Motor Sequence Test (Additional)

### Instructions

- Ask the pupil to observe you carefully and follow your movements.
- Perform the following actions sequentially:

  1. **First Action**: Make a fist.
  2. **Second Action**: Place your palm flat on the table.
  3. **Third Action**: Use the side of your hand to "karate chop" the table.

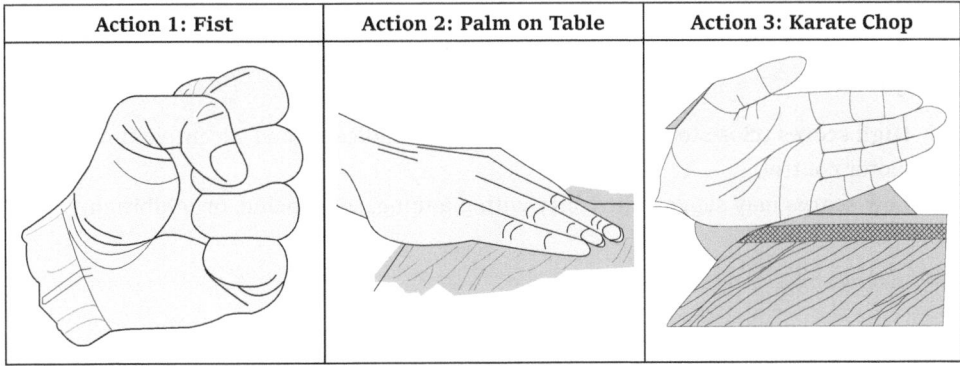

| Action 1: Fist | Action 2: Palm on Table | Action 3: Karate Chop |
|----------------|-------------------------|-----------------------|

- After demonstrating the sequence, instruct the pupil to repeat it. Pay attention to their ability to copy the sequence of moves that you performed, which must be in the same order that you showed them.

### Scoring

- **0 points:** The pupil is unable to follow the sequence after multiple attempts.
- **1 point:** The pupil makes some errors or performs the sequence with hesitation, but eventually gets it right.
- **2 points:** The pupil correctly performs the sequence without errors.

You can continue to do this, increasing the length of instructions as you go, just like the working memory test. Monitor how difficult a pupil finds this. Although there are no standardised score tables you can use (that I can find), you can use this indicatively to evaluate a child's confidence in completing the test. The more times they score 0 or 1, indicates that this isn't easy for them.

## 3. The Go/No-Go Test (Additional)

### Inhibition Task (Go/No-Go Task)

- Tell the pupil: "When I say 'Go,' tap the table once. When I say 'Stop,' do nothing."
- Then, alternate between saying "Go" and "Stop," and gradually speed up.
- Evaluate whether the pupil can inhibit their response appropriately when told to stop.

### Scoring for Inhibition Task

- **0 points:** The pupil fails to inhibit actions and taps inappropriately.
- **1 point:** The pupil makes a few errors but can correct themselves after feedback.
- **2 points:** The pupil successfully inhibits their responses as required.

### Interpretation

- **High scores** (close to 2 in each task) typically indicate good executive function and motor control.
- **Low scores** may suggest difficulty with planning, sequencing, or inhibition.

# Appendix 6

# Handwriting and Praxis Checklist

Pupil Name:_____ DOB:_____ Date:_____

**Writing Speed:**

Word Count:_____Words per Minute Score: _____**Slow/Average/Fast**

## Writing Accuracy and Clarity

Look at the following and tick the relevant observations. Total each section.

### *It's difficult to read:*

|  | **The shape of the letters** |
|---|---|
|  | Are they difficult to read? |
|  | Are letters left unclosed, e.g. a looks like a u, a g could be a y? |
|  | Are letters unfinished e.g. n looks like an r, a looks like an o? |
|  | Are ascenders or descenders too short? |
|  | Are the bodies of letters too large or inconsistently sized? |
|  | Are there mirror-reversals e.g. b/d, p/q? |
|  | Are letters unusually shaped? |
|  |  |
|  | **Letter placement** |
|  | Do the words change direction throughout the sentence or paragraph? |
|  | Do letters rise off the line or dip below it? |
|  | Do lead-in strokes come up at different angles? |
|  | Does the work look rushed e.g. thinking is too fast for the hand to cope? |
|  |  |
|  | **Spelling and Punctuation** |
|  | Are capital letters inappropriately used e.g. within words or sentences? |
|  | Is spelling unusual or inconsistent? |
|  | Is there difficulty in error-spotting and proof-reading work? |
|  |  |

| | Word placement |
|---|---|
| | Do words drift across the page away from the margin? |
| | Are words inconsistently placed e.g. bunched together/spaced too far apart? |
| | Do words rise up off the line? |
| | **Visual Perception Indicators Total:** **out of 17**<br>*If you notice several of these, further support for visual perception is needed* |

## *It's not 'enough' (quality/amount)*

| | Content |
|---|---|
| | Is the quality of written content less than their oral communication ability? |
| | Is their spelling inaccurate in relation to age expectations? |
| | Is their spelling broadly accurate but vocabulary used overly simplistic? |
| | Do they miss out words within sentences? |
| | Do their sentences flow from one to the next? |
| | Is the grammar passably accurate, e.g. do they use tenses correctly? |
| | Is their written structure disjointed? |
| | Is there a general structure, e.g. have they planned their response? |
| | **Phonological Processing & Executive Function Indicators Total:** **out of 7**<br>*If you notice several of these, further support for PP and EF is needed* |
| | |

www.nochildismissed.org

## *It doesn't flow*

| | The flow of the writing |
|---|---|
| | Is the writing joined up? |
| | Is there a lot of pressure on the nib when writing? |
| | Does the handwriting look intense? |
| | Is the writing too small or too large? |
| | **Vestibular and Proprioceptive Indicators Total:** **out of 4**<br>*If two or more, it might be worth observing the pupil writing. Likely support for fine and gross motor skills needed* |

## *Additional Observation of Handwriting*

| | Observations of the Writing Process |
|---|---|
| | Do they regularly fidget, wriggle or move about on their chair? |
| | Do they appear to have low motivation for writing? |
| | Do they appear to grip the pen or pencil tightly? |

| | |
|---|---|
| | Do they rest their head in their hands when writing? |
| | Do they lean right over so they are very close to the page? |
| | Do they seem to use excessive or insufficient force when holding pens/pencils? E.g. breaking or dropping them |
| | Do they struggle to copy accurately from the board? |
| | Do they hold the pen in an awkward grip? |
| | Do they complain of pain or discomfort from writing, or look uncomfortable? |
| | Are they left-handed? |
| | Do they struggle/forget to place the paper at an angle? (E.g. 11 to 5 o'clock if right-handed, or 7 to 1 o'clock if left-handed) |
| | Do they move the trunk of their body along the page, left to right, with the pen? |
| | Does the paper seem to move around when they write? |
| | Do they wrap their feet around the chair legs? |
| | Do they regularly rock on their chair? |
| | **Vestibular and Proprioceptive Indicators Total:** out of 14 <br> *If you notice several of these, further support for fine and gross motor skills is needed and it might be worth carrying out further Praxis screening* |

### *Further Praxis Checklist*

| | |
|---|---|
| | **Other observations** |
| | Do they appear clumsy, awkward, inefficient? |
| | Do they seem to take a long time to master an action or skill? |
| | Do they get easily frustrated in multi-step tasks and give up easily? |
| | Do they generally move, think and speak more slowly? |
| | Do they have difficulties or are they slow getting changed? |
| | Do they struggle to 'cross their midline'? For example, when they play sports, do you see their whole trunk change direction to be able to catch a ball, rather than being able to move arms and hands across the body to meet the ball? |
| | Do they prefer individual sports/activities rather than team sports/activities? |
| | Do they struggle to follow directions and initiate tasks? |
| | Do they struggle to keep their physical space organised e.g. is desk area cluttered, is equipment/coat/bag stored untidily? |
| | Do they tend to keep their routines narrow and rigid e.g. avoidant of new things? |
| | Do they struggle with self-care skills e.g. getting dressed or eating? |
| | **Praxis Indicators Total:** out of 11 <br> *If you notice several of these, then a refer to an occupational therapist for assessment* |

# Appendix 7

# No Child is Missed – Pre-School Observation

| Name: | Room/Group: | Observed by: | |
|-------|-------------|--------------|--|
| Activity: | Date: | Time: | |

| Observation | |
|-------------|--|
| **What do you notice?**<br><br>Jot down both what you see and what you *don't* see. Both can be important. | **Possible Actions** |
| **Environment and Context:**<br>• *behaviour of other children*<br>• *stimulating activity/activities*<br>• *engagement of adults in the room*<br>• *environment and notable room features* | Follow-up discussion with practitioner/s |
| **Phonological Processing:**<br>***Responses and awareness to sound:***<br>• *sound? hyper-/hypo-sensitivity*<br>• *reactions? what's going on around them, proportionate*<br>• *positioning? proximity to others*<br>• *voice? intonation, volume, pitch, matches body*<br><br>***With peers:***<br>• *engagement? joins in with others*<br>• *comfort? relaxed with others*<br>• *support needs? who is in their toolkit*<br>• *chats with others? age-appropriate, laughs*<br>• *initiates conversation? asks questions of others*<br><br>***With adult:***<br>• *comprehension? length and accuracy of response, can infer/guess*<br>• *oracy? uses appropriate vocabulary, sentence structure*<br>• *confidence? fluency, hesitations, volume, response time*<br>• *verbal responses? short, lengthy, coherent, grammatically correct*<br>• *instructions? follows instruction for adult-selected activity* | Hearing Test<br><br>More detailed 1:1 Speech and Language Screening<br><br>Referral to Speech & Language Therapist<br><br>More detailed assessment of English as an Additional Language |

| | |
|---|---|
| **If using assistive tools/tech:**<br><br>• visual aids (e.g. widget symbols)<br>• ear defenders/protection/hearing aids | |
| **Visual Processing:**<br><br>• light? frowning, blinking, distraction<br>• tracks objects and faces? looking at the adult, peers<br>• task accuracy and fluency? confidence<br>• depth perception? executes movements accurately<br>• behaviour reactions? proportionate, appropriate<br>• can correctly identify colours? stilted, error-prone?<br>• relaxed with others? interprets social situations calmly<br><br>**If using assistive tools/tech:**<br><br>• wearing glasses?<br>• image/text size? zoomed in/normal/zoomed out<br>• proximity of tech? close to eyes<br>• confidence? efficient/error-prone | Sight Test |
| **Posture and Movement:**<br><br>• muscle tone? flexibility, posture, physical strength<br>• balance? use of props to support standing or sitting, feet position<br>• body positioning when sitting? discomfort, changing position<br>• activity completion? fidgeting, foot tapping, knee movement, rocking, easily tired<br>• tension? static, tight<br>• speed of movements?<br>• self-dressing? can put shoes/coat on | Referral to Health Visitor/<br><br>Occupational Therapist |
| **Focus, Health and Wellbeing:**<br><br>• repeated movements/stimulation? chewing, stroking<br>• fidgeting? foot tapping, knee movement, rocking, squirms<br>• impulsive? easily distracted? zoning-out?<br>• communication with others? appropriate length/style/frequency<br>• responds in a timely manner to the adult, neutral/positive<br>• independence? how much prompting<br>• presentation? hygiene, clothing, weight, height<br>• eating? range of food choices, hand/eye/mouth co-ordination, balance, chewing, swallowing<br>• toileting? is wearing nappies, is aware of toileting need<br>• sleep? is relaxed, achieves sustained sleep easily<br>• comfortable with temperature changes/extremes?<br>• emotional response to disappointment age-appropriate in intensity/length/frequency? | Sensory Screening/ SDQ Age 2-4<br><br>Referral to Health Visitor/<br><br>Occupational Therapist/ Feeding Therapy/ Family Support |

| **Anything else?** | **Other Actions/Next Steps** |
|---|---|
| | |

# Appendix 8

# No Child is Missed – Pupil Observation and Work Review (Upper Primary and Secondary)

| Name: | Year Group: | Observed by: |
|---|---|---|
| Subject/Topic: | Date: | Time: |

| Observation | |
|---|---|
| **What do you notice?**<br><br>Jot down both what you see and what you *don't* see. Both can be important. | **Possible Actions** |
| **Environment and Lesson Context:**<br><br>• *behaviour of other pupils*<br>• *pace and challenge of lesson*<br>• *lesson design and resources*<br>• *environment and notable classroom features* | Follow-up discussion with practitioner/s |
| **Phonological Processing:**<br>*Responses and awareness to sound:*<br><br>• *sound? hyper-/hypo-sensitivity*<br>• *reactions? what's going on around them, proportionate*<br>• *positioning? proximity to others*<br>• *voice? intonation, volume, pitch, matches body*<br><br>**With peers:**<br><br>• *engagement? acknowledges others*<br>• *comfort? relaxed with others*<br>• *support needs? who is in their toolkit*<br>• *incidental conversation? age-appropriate, humour*<br>• *initiates conversation? asks questions of others*<br><br>**With teacher:**<br><br>• *comprehension? responses to teacher*<br>• *oracy? planned, executed clearly, tier 3 vocabulary?*<br>• *confidence? fluency, hesitations, volume, response time*<br>• *verbal responses? short, lengthy, coherent, grammatically correct* | Hearing Test<br><br>More detailed 1:1 Speech and Language Screening<br><br>More detailed Phonological Awareness / Spelling Assessment<br><br>More detailed assessment of English as an Additional Language |

| | |
|---|---|
| • *instructions? follows whole-class instruction*<br>• *appropriateness of communication with context?*<br>**If using assistive tools/tech:**<br>• *speech-to-text software use*<br>• *ear defenders/plugs* | Referral to Speech & Language Therapist |
| **Visual Processing:**<br>• *light? frowning, blinking, distraction*<br>• *tracking? looking at teacher, peers*<br>• *reactions? proportionate, appropriate*<br>• *reading fluency? stilted, error-prone?*<br>• *eye-contact? sustained, appropriate, tracking*<br>**If using assistive tools/tech:**<br>• *wearing glasses*<br>• *text size? normal, larger than average*<br>• *screen tint? coloured, light/dark screen*<br>• *proximity of tech? close to eyes*<br>• *confidence? efficient/error-prone*<br>• *text-to-speech software use* | Sight Test |
| **Posture and Movement:**<br>• *muscle tone? (slouching, head in hands)*<br>• *balance? (use of props to support, feet position)*<br>• *body positioning on chair? (discomfort, changing position)*<br>• *fidgeting? (foot tapping, knee movement, rocking)*<br>• *tension? (static, tight)* | Further Praxis screening<br><br><br>Referral to Occupational Therapist |
| **Focus, Health and Wellbeing:**<br>• *repeated movements/stimulation? chewing, stroking*<br>• *fidgeting? (foot tapping, knee movement, rocking)*<br>• *impulsive? easily distracted? zoning-out?*<br>• *communication with others? Appropriate*<br>• *responds in a timely manner to the teacher*<br>• *independence? how much prompting*<br>• *presentation? hygiene, uniform* | Further Sensory Screening & SDQ<br><br><br>Referral to<br><br>Occupational Therapist |

| | |
|---|---|
| **Executive Function, Engagement in Learning** <br><br> • *responding? work-rate, questions* <br> • *pace? consistent/interrupted* <br> • *exercise book/notes? ordered, completed* <br> • *equipment layout on desk? messy/contained* <br> • *location of bag/coat?* | Referral to Paediatrician <br><br><br> Mental Health / wider support |
| **Handwriting** <br><br> • *script? letter formation, positioning on page* <br> • *hand dominance? left/right?* <br> • *pen grip? normal/unusual, tight, body weight distribution* | Further evaluation of handwriting |
| **Use of Technology** <br><br> • *NWOW? keyboard, stylus, read aloud app* <br><br><br> | Touch typing testing <br><br><br> More training |
| **Anything else?** <br><br><br><br><br><br><br><br> | |

# Appendix 9

# No Child Misses Out

## EYFS and Primary Parent-Carer Conversation Form – *Working Together*

| Child's Name: | Room/Group: | | Date: |
|---|---|---|---|
| Parent-Carers: | Staff: | | |

**Conversation Record:**

A. Information sharing:

    1. The strengths and recent developments we've observed.
    2. Do you notice these at home? What other strengths and recent developments have you observed?

    3. The areas which seem to be tricky/more difficult that we've observed.
    4. Do you notice these at home? What else, if anything, seems tricky from your perspective?

(if not already covered/known)

    5. What are bed time and sleep like?
    6. What are mealtimes like? (food groups avoided/allergies/limited range/(in)digestion?)
    7. What are toileting habits like?
    8. How are any medical conditions being supported (by health services and at home)?

**B. Solution finding:**

  9. What are the actions we could take to support tricky areas/difficulties?
 10. Can we use any known strengths to support weaker areas?

**Actions for the setting:**

**Actions for Home:**

**Have we covered everything we wanted to today? If not, what else?**
**Additional family support needed?**

**Date & Time of next meeting:**

Copy of minutes for file and for home

# Appendix 10

# No Child Misses Out

## Upper Primary and Secondary Parent-Carer Conversation Form – *Working Together*

| Child's Name: | Class: | Date: |
|---|---|---|
| Parent-Carers: | Staff: | |

**Conversation Record:**

A. **Information sharing:**

1. The strengths we've observed.
2. Do you notice these at home? What other strengths and recent developments have you observed?

3. The areas which seem to be tricky/more difficult that we've observed.
4. Do you notice these at home? What else, if anything, seems tricky from your perspective?

5. Use of technology at home? (What, how long, internet safety?)
6. What are bed time and sleep like?
7. What are mealtimes like? (food groups avoided/allergies/limited range/(in) digestion?)
8. How are toileting, personal hygiene and dressing habits/skills?
9. How are any medical conditions being supported (by health services and at home)?

**B. Solution finding:**

    **10. What are the actions we could take to support tricky areas/difficulties?**
    **11. Can we use any known strengths to support weaker areas?**

**Actions for School:**

**Actions for Home:**

**Have we covered everything we wanted to today? If not, what else?**
**Additional family support needed?**

**Date & Time of next meeting:**

Copy of minutes for file and for home

# Notes

## Preface

1 Department for Education. (2015). *The SEND code of practice: 0 to 25 years*.
2 Hutchinson, J. (2021). *Identifying pupils with special educational needs and disabilities*. Education Policy Institute.
3 Curran, H., Moloney, H., Heavey, A., & Boddison, A. (2018). *It's about time: The impact of SENCO workload on the professional and the school*. Bath Spa University.
4 Schools in England face funding crisis as costs soar, study warns. (2022, August 2). *The Guardian*. https://www.theguardian.com/education/2022/aug/02/schools-in-england-face-funding-crisis-as-costs-soar-study-warns
5 Department for Education. (2019). *Research on the educational psychologist workforce* (Clare Lyonette, Gaby Atfield, Beate Baldauf, & David Owen, The Institute for Employment Research, University of Warwick). https://www.rcpch.ac.uk/resources/community-paediatric-workforce-short-report-2017

## Chapter 1

1 Gardner, H. (1983). *Frames of mind: The theory of multiple intelligences*. Basic Books.
2 Darwin, C. (1859). *On the origin of species by means of natural selection, or preservation of favoured races in the struggle for life*. John Murray.
3 *The Guardian*. (2019, October 3). Eugenics and Francis Galton. https://www.theguardian.com/commentisfree/2019/oct/03/eugenics-francis-galton-science-ideas (accessed July 14, 2023).
4 Pearson, K. (1901). *National life from the standpoint of science*. Adam & Charles Black (pp. 16–17).
5 Gould, S. J. (1981). *The mismeasure of man*. W.W. Norton & Company.
6 Burt, C. (1966). The genetic determination of differences in intelligence: A study of monozygotic twins reared together and apart. *British Journal of Psychology, 57*(1), 137–153.
7 Hearnshaw, L. S. (1979). *Cyril Burt, psychologist*. Hodder & Stoughton.
8 Whitehead, J. (2023). *Action research*. https://actionresearch.net/ (accessed July 14, 2023).
9 Gardner, H. (1983). *Frames of mind: The theory of multiple intelligences*. Basic Books.
10 Gould, S. J. (1981). *The mismeasure of man*. W.W. Norton & Company.
11 Goleman, D. (1996). *Emotional intelligence: Why it can matter more than IQ*. Bloomsbury.
12 Gladwell, M. (2008). *Outliers: The story of success*. Little, Brown and Company.
13 Flynn, J. R. (2009). *What is intelligence? Beyond the Flynn Effect* (Expanded edn). Cambridge University Press.
14 Kanner, L. (1949). Problems of nosology and psychodynamics of early infantile autism. *American Journal of Orthopsychiatry, 19*(3), 416–426.
15 Rimland, B. (1964). *Infantile autism: The syndrome and its implications for a neural theory of behavior*. Appleton-Century-Crofts.
16 Bettelheim, B. (1967). *The empty fortress: Infantile autism and the birth of the self*. Free Press of Glencoe.

17 Fisher, N. (2021). *Changing our minds: How children can take control of their own learning.* Robinson (p. 117).

18 Hippocrates. (1849). *Aphorisms.* In *The genuine works of Hippocrates* (The Sydenham Society).

19 National Audit Office. (2019). *Support for pupils with special educational needs and disabilities in England.*

20 Dobson, G. J. (2019). Understanding the SENCo workforce: Re-examination of selected studies through the lens of an accurate national dataset. *British Journal of Special Education.*

21 Dyslexia History. (n.d.). Brief history of dyslexia. https://dyslexiahistory.web.ox.ac.uk/brief-history-dyslexia (accessed July 20, 2023).

22 BBC Panorama. (2023, May 20). *Private ADHD clinics exposed* [Television broadcast].

23 Smith, S. (2020, February 28). Uncovering the origin of the EHCP "golden ticket" narrative. Special Needs Jungle. https://www.specialneedsjungle.com/uncovering-origin-ehcp-golden-ticket-narrative/ (accessed July 20, 2023)

24 Special Needs Jungle. (n.d.). https://www.specialneedsjungle.com (accessed July 20, 2023).

25 Pearson, K. (1914–1930). *The life, letters, and labours of Francis Galton* (3 vols.) "Men who leave their mark on the world are very often those who, being gifted and full of nervous power, are at the same time haunted and driven by a dominant idea, and are therefore within a measurable distance of insanity."

26 Cooke, L. (2022). *Bitch: What does it mean to be female?* Basic Books (p. 288).

27 *Quote attributed to Margaret Mead.* Planetary Citizen of the Year Award in 1978.

## Chapter 2

1 Hippocrates. (1849). *Aphorisms.* In *The genuine works of Hippocrates* (The Sydenham Society).

2 Robinson, K., & Robinson, K. (2022). *Imagine if . . .: Creating a future for us all.* Penguin Books.

3 Hippocrates. (1849). *Aphorisms.* In *The genuine works of Hippocrates* (The Sydenham Society).

4 Your EP might have differing views to me – see references below. Using IQ test data to support understanding a pupil's presentation for me, as a SENCO working with huge numbers of pupils in schools bearing responsibility for hundreds and hundreds of children's outcomes, is without doubt a very powerful source of information for schools which can be used *for good*. There is, I think, a distinction between the remit of an external professional to the school working uniquely for a few hours with a handful of pupils through pieces of commissioned work, and an internal professional working to identify and support needs at scale. Eminent psychologists, both in research and practice, explain their views about testing for cognitive ability in these papers so you can learn more here: Hussain, N. (2023). Special educational needs and disabilities: Where to focus finite amount of time and resources? *DECP Debate, 184,* 7–11; Fletcher, J. M., & Miciak, J. (2017). Comprehensive cognitive assessments are not necessary for the identification and treatment of learning disabilities. *Archives of Clinical Neuropsychology, 32*(1), 2–7; Schneider, W. J., & Kaufman, A. S. (2017). Let's not do away with comprehensive cognitive assessments just yet. *Archives of Clinical Neuropsychology, 32*(1), 8–20. Alongside this, Cathy Atkinson et al., explore the differences between EPs and other educational practitioners in this paper: Atkinson, C., Barrow, J., & Norris, S. (2022). Assessment practices of educational psychologists and other educational professionals. *Educational Psychology in Practice, 38*(4), 347–363.

5 Criado Perez, C. (2019). *Invisible women: Exposing data bias in a world designed for men.* Chatto & Windus.

6 There is more than a century of research into this – some of which, if you've read Chapter One, you'll know is very uncomfortable reading. That said, more recent research with arguably better ethical and conceptual awareness also shows an enormous genetic influence over our intelligence. You can read more here: Deary, I. J., Johnson, W., & Houlihan, L. M. (2009). Genetic foundations of human intelligence. *Human Genetics, 126,* 215–232; Plomin, R., DeFries, J. C., Knopik, V. S., & Neiderhiser, J. M. (2013). *Behavioral genetics* (6th edn). Worth Publishers.

7 Organisation for Economic Co-operation and Development (OECD). (2016). *PISA 2015 results (Volume II): Excellence and equity in education.* OECD Publishing.

8 This phrase is often attributed to Albert Einstein, but there is no clear evidence that he said or wrote it exactly in this form. It is believed to be a paraphrase of his ideas about simplicity in

scientific theories. A similar sentiment is found in his lecture "On the Method of Theoretical Physics" (1933), where he discusses the importance of simplifying concepts without oversim-plification. The exact wording seems to have evolved over time through reinterpretation.

9 I am grouping several concepts into one here: notably, IQ and the many facets which make up executive function. Reference about the stability of IQ can be read about in the references of note v and executive function, here: Friedman, N. P., Miyake, A., Young, S. E., DeFries, J. C., Corley, R. P., & Hewitt, J. K. (2008). Individual differences in executive functions are almost entirely genetic in origin. *Journal of Experimental Psychology: General, 137*(2), 201–225.

10 Maté, G., & Maté, D. (2022). *The myth of normal: Trauma, illness & healing in a toxic culture* (p. 61). Penguin: London.

11 Candace Lewis is quoted in Maté, G., & Maté, D. (2022). *The myth of normal: Trauma, illness & healing in a toxic culture* (p. 60). Penguin: London.

## Chapter 3

1 Schacter, D., Gilbert, D., Wegner, D., & Hood, B. (2020). *Psychology: Third European Edition.* Macmillan Higher Education.

2 This is known as the Diathesis-Stress model which theorises that a person may be genetically or contextually predisposed to a mental disorder that remains unexpressed until it is triggered by stress.

3 Duncan, S. [@autismfather] (2012, November 10). #Autism is one word attempting to describe millions of different stories [Tweet on X]. My thanks to Stuart for his permission to include this tweet.

4 Engel, G. L. (1977). The need for a new medical model: A challenge for biomedicine. *Science, 196*(4286), 129–136.

5 Chodkiewicz, A. R., & Boyle, C. (2017). Positive psychology school-based interventions: A reflection on current success and future directions, *Review of Education, 5*(1), 60–86.

6 Cromby, J., Harper, D., & Reavy, P. (2013). *Psychology, Mental Health and Distress.* Red Globe Press.

7 Health & Care Professions Council. (2023). *Practitioner psychologists: Standards of proficiency* (valid from September 2023). Health & Care Professions Council.

8 Edmondson, A. C. (2012). *Teaming: How organizations learn, innovate, and compete in the knowledge economy.* Jossey-Bass.

9 Coyle, D. (2018). *The Culture Code: The secrets of highly successful groups.* Random House Business Books (p. 13).

10 Gladwell, M. (2005). *Blink: The power of thinking without thinking.* Little, Brown and Company.

11 BBC News. (2023, July 19). https://www.bbc.co.uk/news/education-60197150

12 The Good Childhood Report 2022. The Children's Society.

13 NHS Digital. (2022). *Autism statistics: January to December 2022.* https://digital.nhs.uk/data-and-information/publications/statistical/autism-statistics/january-to-december-2022

14 Royal College of Paediatrics and Child Health. (2017). *Community paediatric workforce short report.* https://www.rcpch.ac.uk/resources/community-paediatric-workforce-short-report-2017

15 Department of Education. (2019). *Research on the Educational Psychologist Workforce* (C. Lyonette, G. Atfield, B. Baldauf, & D. Owen, eds). The Institute for Employment Research, University of Warwick.

16 Early Day Motion 239. (1990, December 13). Referring to the shortage of Educational Psychologists tabled by Gerry Steinberg MP.

17 Department for Education. (2023). *Educational psychology services: Workforce insights and school perspectives on impact Research report.* DfE.

## Chapter 4

1 Bonacina, S., Krizman, J., White-Schwoch, T., & Kraus, N. (2024). Clapping in time parallels literacy and calls upon overlapping neural mechanisms in early readers. *Annals of the New York Academy of Sciences, Special Issue: The Neurosciences and Music VI, Original Article.*

2 Poudel, S., Denicola-Prechtl, K., Nelson, J. A., Behboudi, M. H., Benitez-Barrera, C., Castro, S., & Maguire, M. J. (2024). Rethinking household size and children's language environment. *Developmental Psychology, 60*(1), 159–169.

3 Hart, B., & Risley, T. R. (2003). The early catastrophe: The 30 million word gap. *The American Educator, 27*, 4–9.

4 Sperry, D. E., Sperry, L. L., & Miller, P. J. (2019). Reexamining the verbal environments of children from different socioeconomic backgrounds. *Child Development, 90*(4), 1303–1318.

5 Department of Speech, Hearing and Phonetic Sciences. (n.d.). *Speech and phonetic sciences course: Week 7.* University College London. https://www.phon.ucl.ac.uk/courses/spsci/iss/week7.php (accessed April 10, 2024).

6 Department of Speech, Hearing and Phonetic Sciences. (n.d.). *Speech and phonetic sciences course: Week 7.* University College London. https://www.phon.ucl.ac.uk/courses/spsci/iss/week7.php (accessed April 10, 2024).

7 Horst, J. S., Parsons, K. L., & Bryan, N. M. (2011). Get the story straight: Contextual repetition promotes word learning from storybooks. *Frontiers in Psychology, 2*, 17; Damhuis, C., Segers, E., & Verhoeven, L. (2014). Stimulating breadth and depth of vocabulary via repeated storybook readings or tests. *School Effectiveness and School Improvement, 26*, 1–15.

8 Stein, B. E., Meredith, M. A., Huneycutt, W. S., & McDade, L. (1989). Behavioral indices of multisensory integration: Orientation to visual cues is affected by auditory stimuli. *Journal of Cognitive Neuroscience, 1*, 12–24.

9 Hjetland, H. N., Lervåg, A., Lyster, S.-A. H., Hagtvet, B. E., Hulme, C., & Melby-Lervåg, M. (2019). Pathways to reading comprehension: A longitudinal study from 4 to 9 years of age. *Journal of Educational Psychology, 111*(5), 751–763.

10 Ford-Connors, E., & Paratore, J. R. (2015). Vocabulary instruction in fifth grade and beyond: Sources of word learning and productive contexts for development. *Review of Educational Research, 85*(1), 50–91.

11 Bercow, J. (2018). *Bercow: Ten years on. An independent review of provision for children and young people with speech, language and communication needs in England.* London: ICAN.

12 McNamara, N. (2012). Speech and language therapy within a forensic support service. *Journal of Learning Disabilities and Offending Behaviour, 3*(2), 111–117.

13 Frith, U. (1985). Beneath the surface of developmental dyslexia. In K. E. Patterson, J. C. Marshall, & M. Coltheart (Eds), *Surface dyslexia: Neuropsychological and cognitive studies of phonological reading* (pp. 301–330). London: Lawrence Erlbaum.

14 Rose, J. (2006). *Independent review of the teaching of early reading: Final report.* Department for Education and Skills.

15 Rose, J. (2006). *Independent review of the teaching of early reading: Final report.* Department for Education and Skills.

16 American Dyslexia Association. (n.d.). *Phonics for teenagers and adults.* Dyslexics.org.uk. https://www.dyslexics.org.uk/phonics-for-teenagers-and-adults/ (accessed April 12, 2024).

17 Brunswick, N. (2009). *Dyslexia: A beginner's guide.* Oxford: Oneworld Publications.

18 Goddard Blythe, S. (2014). *The well balanced child: Movement and early learning.* Hawthorn Press.

19 Adams, R. (2017, October 3). School results improve when children take music lessons alongside maths, study finds. *The Guardian.*

20 Loui, P., Kroog, K., Zuk, J., Winner, E., & Schlaug, G. (2011). Relating pitch awareness to phonemic awareness in children: Implications for tone-deafness and dyslexia. *Frontiers in Psychology, 2*, 111.

21 Carroll, J.M., Breadmore, H.L. (2018). Not all phonological awareness deficits are created equal: Evidence from a comparison between children with Otitis Media and poor readers. *Developmental Science*, May; 21(3), e12588. doi: 10.1111/desc.12588. Epub 2017 Sep. 7. PMID: 28880490; PMCID: PMC5947145.

22 Education Endowment Foundation. (n.d.). *Oral language interventions.* https://educationendowmentfoundation.org.uk/education-evidence/teaching-learning-toolkit/oral-language-interventions (accessed April 04, 2024).

23 Brackett, M. (2019). *Permission to feel.* Quercus Publishing.

24 Daikoku, T., Yatomi, Y., Kamiya, K., & Osaka, N. (2024). Bodily maps of uncertainty and surprise in musical chord progression and the underlying emotional response. *iScience.*

25 There is plenty of current research on loneliness, including the appointment of a Minister for Loneliness in Britain since 2018, given its prominent factor in health and wellbeing. There is also recent research which indicates that loneliness in childhood can lead to significant mental health difficulties in adulthood. *Neuroscience News*. (2024, April 9). Childhood loneliness linked to adult psychosis risk. https://neurosciencenews.com/childhood-loneliness-psychosis-25891/ (accessed April 10, 2024).

26 UCL Institute of Education. (n.d.). Seeing the importance of breaktimes for children's development. University College London. https://www.ucl.ac.uk/ioe/ioe120/seeing-importance-breaktimes-childrens-development (accessed April 13, 2024).

27 Snow, C. E. (2002). *Reading for understanding: Toward a research and development program in reading comprehension*. RAND Corporation.

28 Duke, N. K., & Pearson, P. D. (2002). Effective practices for developing reading comprehension. *What Research Has to Say About Reading Instruction* (pp. 205–242). 3rd edn. International Reading Association.

29 Nagy, W. E., & Scott, J. A. (2000). Vocabulary processes. *Handbook of Reading Research*, 3, 269–284.

30 Vygotsky, L. S. (1978). *Mind in society: The development of higher psychological processes*. Cambridge, MA: Harvard University Press.

31 George Berkeley (1685–1753) was an Anglo-Irish philosopher who advanced the idea of "immaterialism" in his work: Berkeley, G. (1710). *A treatise concerning the principles of human knowledge*. Dublin: Aaron Rhames.

32 Fricker, M. (2007). *Epistemic injustice: Power and the ethics of knowing*. Oxford: Oxford University Press.

33 Macpherson, W. (1999). *The Macpherson report*. London: The Stationery Office.

34 Henderson, D.J. (1974). Incest, in *Comprehensive Textbook of Psychiatry*, eds A.M. Freeman and H.I. Kaplan, 2nd edn (1536). Baltimore: Williams & Wilkins.

35 Van der Kolk, B. (2014). *The body keeps the score: Mind, brain and body in the transformation of trauma*. Penguin Random House (p. 22).

36 U.S. Department of Health & Human Services, Administration for Children and Families, Administration on Children, Youth and Families, Children's Bureau. (2023). *Child maltreatment 2022*.

37 Rape Crisis England & Wales. (n.d.). Statistics on sexual violence. https://rapecrisis.org.uk/get-informed/statistics-sexual-violence/ and NSPCC. (n.d.). Child sexual abuse: Statistics briefing. https://learning.nspcc.org.uk/research-resources/statistics-briefings/child-sexual-abuse (Both accessed August 23, 2023).

## Chapter 5

1 Thorpe, S., Fize, D., & Marlot, C. (1996). Speed of processing in the human visual system. *Nature*, *381*(6582), 520–522.

2 Wolfe, J. M., & Cave, K. R. (2022). *Sensation and perception* (International Sixth Edition). Oxford University Press.

3 This is known as "transduction" and two interesting research pieces about this are: (breathing) *Neuroscience News*. (2023, April 6). The rhythm of breathing shapes memory formation. https://neurosciencenews.com/memory-breathing-23360/ (Accessed October 3, 2023) and (saccades) Wolfe, J. M., & Cave, K. R. (2022). *Sensation and perception* (International Sixth Edition). Oxford University Press.

4 Carrasco, M., Evert, D. L., Chang, I., & Katz, S. M. (2005). The eccentricity effect: Target eccentricity affects performance on conjunction searches. *Perception & Psychophysics*, *57*(8), 1241–1261; Wolfe, J. M., O'Neill, P., & Bennett, S. C. (1998). Why are there eccentricity effects in visual search? Visual and attentional hypotheses. *Perception & Psychophysics*, *60*(1), 140–156.

5 Bayle, D. J., Schoendorff, B., Henaff, M. A., & Krolak-Salmon, P. (2011). Emotional facial expression detection in the peripheral visual field. *PLoS One*, *6*(6), e21584.

6 Bennett, D. M., Gordon, G., & Dutton, G. N. (2009). The useful field of view test: Normative data in children of school age. *Optometry and Vision Science*, *86*(6), 717–721.

7 American Institute of Stress. (n.d.). How stress affects your vision. https://www.stress.org/news/how-stress-affects-your-vision/ (Accessed May 13, 2024).

8 van der Kolk, B. A. (2014). *The body keeps the score: Brain, mind, and body in the healing of trauma*. Viking.

9 Yoonessi, A., & Yoonessi, A. (2011). Functional assessment of magno, parvo, and koniocellular pathways: Current state and future clinical applications. *Journal of Ophthalmic & Vision Research*, *6*(2), 119–126.

10 American Institute of Stress. (n.d.). How stress affects your vision. https://www.stress.org/news/how-stress-affects-your-vision/ (Accessed May 13, 2024).

11 Zachi, E. C., Costa, T. L., Barboni, M. T. S., Costa, M. F., Bonci, D. M. O., & Ventura, D. F. (2017). Color vision losses in autism spectrum disorders. *Frontiers in Psychology*, *8*, Article 1127.

12 Iregren, A., Andersson, M., & Nylen, P. (2002). Color vision and occupational chemical exposures: The usefulness of the Lanthony desaturated panel D-15. *NeuroToxicology*, *23*(6), 695–702; and Mergler, D., Blain, L., Lemaire, J., & Lalande, F. (1988). Colour vision impairment and alcohol consumption: A dose effect relationship. *NeuroToxicology*, *9*(1), 81–90.

13 Treisman, A. (1998). Feature binding, attention and object perception. *Philosophical Transactions of the Royal Society B: Biological Sciences*, *353*, 1295–1306.

14 Wolfe, J. M., & Bowers, P. G. (2000). Naming-speed processes and developmental reading disabilities: An introduction to the special issue on the double-deficit hypothesis. *Journal of Learning Disabilities*, *33*(4), 322–324.

15 Irlen, H. (n.d.). *Founder Helen Irlen*. Irlen Institute. https://irlen.com/founder-helen-irlen/ (Accessed July 28, 2023).

16 Have a look in Operation Diversity Community SEN Support EHCP Statements Help and Support Facebook group for example conversations about colour filters.

17 Suttle, C., Lawrenson, J., & Conway, M. (2018). Efficacy of coloured overlays and lenses for treating reading difficulty: An overview of systematic reviews. *Clinical and Experimental Optometry*, *101*(4), 514–520.

18 Gilchrist, J., Holden, C., & Warren, J. (2018). *Specific learning difficulties (SpLDs) and visual difficulties: A guide for assessors and SpLD practitioners*. SASC.

19 Difolco, M. (2025). *Supporting colour blindness in education and beyond: A practical guide for teachers and families*. Routledge.

20 Stanovich, K. E. (1986). Matthew effects in reading: Some consequences of individual differences in the acquisition of literacy. *Reading Research Quarterly*, *22*(4), 360–407.

21 Clear, J. (n.d.). Marginal gains: This coach improved every tiny thing by 1 percent and here's what happened. James Clear. https://jamesclear.com/marginal-gains

## Chapter 6

1 Lackner, J., & DiZio, P. (2005). Vestibular, proprioceptive, and haptic contributions to spatial orientation. *Annual Review of Psychology*, *56*, 115–147.

2 Briem, G. S., & Sassoon, R. (2010). *Improve your handwriting* (p. xiv). Hodder Headline.

3 Ayers, A. J. (1979). *Sensory integration and the child*. Los Angeles: Western Psychological Services.

4 Ayers, A. J. (1979). *Sensory integration and the child*. Los Angeles: Western Psychological Services.

5 Ayers, A. J. (1979). *Sensory integration and the child*. Los Angeles: Western Psychological Services.

6 Camarata, S., Miller, L. J., & Wallace, M. T. (2020). Evaluating sensory integration/sensory processing treatment: Issues and analysis. *Frontiers in Integrative Neuroscience*, *14*, 556660.

7 Camarata, S., Miller, L. J., & Wallace, M. T. (2020). Evaluating sensory integration/sensory processing treatment: Issues and analysis. *Frontiers in Integrative Neuroscience*, *14*, 556660.

8 De Phillips, F. A., Berliner, W. M., & Cribbin, J. J. (1960). Meaning of learning and knowledge. In *Management of training programs* (p. 69). Homewood, IL: Richard D. Irwin.

9 Limpo, T., Alves, R. A., & Connelly, V. (2018). Testing the effectiveness of handwriting interventions: Introduction to the special issue. *Reading and Writing*, *31*, 1249–1253.

10 Percival, A. [@primarypercival] (2023, December 20). Strategies used at Stanley Road Primary School [Tweet on X]. (With thanks to Andrew for allowing me to quote them.)

11 McLeod, A. (2013). *Handwriting: Reception to Year Two*. Scholastic.

12 Percival, A. [@primarypercival] (2023, December 20). Strategies used at Stanley Road Primary School [Tweet on X]. (With thanks to Andrew.)

13 Briem, G. S., & Sassoon, R. (2010). *Improve your handwriting* (p. 54). Hodder Headline.

14 Van der Weel, F. R., & Van der Meer, A. L. H. (2024). Handwriting but not typewriting leads to widespread brain connectivity: A high-density EEG study with implications for the classroom. *Frontiers in Psychology, 14,* 1219945. https://doi.org/10.3389/fpsyg.2023.1219945

15 Duncan, H., & Purcell, C. (2017). Equity or advantage? The effect of receiving access arrangements in university exams on Humanities 201 students with Specific Learning Difficulties (SpLD). *Widening Participation and Lifelong Learning, 19*(2), 6–26.

16 Tyldum, M. (2014) *The Imitation Game.* The Weinstein Company (film).

17 Karpinski, R. I., Kinase Kolb, A. M., Tetreault, N. A., & Borowski, T. B. (2018). High intelligence: A risk factor for psychological and physiological overexcitabilities. *Intelligence, 66,* 8–23.

## Chapter 7

1 Schacter, D., Gilbert, D., Wegner, D., & Hood, B. (2020). *Psychology: Third European Edition.* Red Globe Press.

2 Schacter, D., Gilbert, D., Wegner, D., & Hood, B. (2020). *Psychology: Third European Edition.* Red Globe Press.

3 Schacter, D., Gilbert, D., Wegner, D., & Hood, B. (2020). *Psychology: Third European Edition.* Red Globe Press.

4 You might be wondering why maths in particular? These papers are worth having a look at if you're interested: Bull, R., & Lee, K. (2014). Executive functioning and mathematics achievement. *Child Development Perspectives, 8*(1), 36–41; Clements, D.H., Sarama, J., & Germeroth, C. (2016). Learning executive function and early mathematics: Directions of causal relations. *Early Childhood Research Quarterly, 36,* 79–90.

5 Zelazo, P., & Carlson, S. (2012). Hot and cool executive function in childhood and adolescence: Development and plasticity. *Child Development Perspectives, 6*(4), 354–360.

6 Johnson, M. H. (2011). Interactive specialization: A domain-general framework for human functional brain development? *Developmental Cognitive Neuroscience, 1*(1), 7–21; and, Allan, N. P., & Lonigan, C. J. (2011). Examining the dimensionality of effortful control in preschool children and its relation to academic and socioemotional indicators. *Developmental Psychology, 47*(4), 905–915.

7 Zelazo, P., & Carlson, S. (2012). Hot and cool executive function in childhood and adolescence: Development and plasticity. *Child Development Perspectives, 6*(4), 354–360.

8 Erikson, E. H. (1950). *Childhood and society.* W. W. Norton & Company.

9 Based on the summaries created by Cherry, K. (2023, July 26). Erik Erikson's stages of psychosocial development. *Verywell Mind.* https://www.verywellmind.com/erik-eriksons-stages-of-psychosocial-development-2795740 (Accessed September 28, 2024) and Sutton, J. (2020). Erik Erikson's stages of psychosocial development. *Positive Psychology.* https://positivepsychology.com/erikson-stages/ (Accessed September 28, 2024).

10 Lucassen, N., Kok, R., Bakermans-Kranenburg, M.J., IJzendoorn, M., Jaddoe, V., Hofman, B., Verhulst, F., Berg, M., & Tiemeier, H. (2015). Executive functions in early childhood: The role of maternal and paternal parenting practices. *British Journal of Developmental Psychology, 33*(4), 489–505.

11 Trivers, R. L. (1974). Parent–offspring conflict. *American Zoologist, 14*(1), 249–264.

12 Cooke, L. (2022). *Bitch: What does it mean to be female?* (p. 135) Basic Books.

13 Altmann, J. (1980). *Baboon mothers and infants.* Harvard University Press.

14 Cooke, L. (2022). *Bitch: What does it mean to be female?* (p. 137) Basic Books.

15 Barrett, L., Dunbar, R., & Lycett, J. (2002). *Human evolutionary psychology.* Palgrave.

16 O'Sullivan, K. (2024). *Poor* (p. 147). Penguin Books.

17 Fay-Stammbach, T., Hawes, D.J., & Meredith, P. (2014). Parenting influences on executive function in early childhood: A review. *Child Development Perspectives, 8*(4), 258–264.

18 Cited from Bennett, T. (2020). *Running the room: The teachers' guide to behaviour.* John Catt.

19 Pierson, R. (2013, May). *Every kid needs a champion* [Video]. TED Conferences. https://www.ted.com/talks/rita_pierson_every_kid_needs_a_champion/transcript

20 Gill, K. (2017). *Making the difference: Breaking the link between school exclusion and social exclusion*. IPPR.

21 Harris, J. R. (1999). *The nurture assumption: Why children turn out the way they do*. Free Press.

22 Silk, J. B., Beehner, J. C., Bergman, T. J., Crockford, C., Engh, A. L., Moscovice, L. R., Wittig, R. M., Seyfarth, R. M., & Cheney, D. L. (2009). The benefits of social capital: Close social bonds among female baboons enhance offspring survival. *Proceedings of the Royal Society B: Biological Sciences, 276*(1670), 3099–3104.

23 Bathelt, J., Holmes, J., & Astle, D. (2018). Data-driven subtyping of executive function-related behavioural problems in children. *Journal of the American Academy of Child and Adolescent Psychiatry, 57*(4), 252–262.

24 Darley, J. M., & Batson, C. D. (1973). From Jerusalem to Jericho: A study of situational and dispositional variables in helping behavior. *Journal of Personality and Social Psychology, 27*(1), 100–108.

25 Tangney, J. P., & Dearing, R. L. (2002). *Shame and guilt*. Guilford Press.

26 Becker, S. P., Sidol, C. A., Van Dyk, T. R., Epstein, J. N., & Beebe, D. W. (2017). Predicting ADHD symptoms in adolescence from childhood sleep problems. *Journal of Attention Disorders, 21*(10), 872–882; Gruber, R., Xi, T., Frenette, S., Robert, M., Vannasinh, P., & Carrier, J. (2009). Sleep disturbances in prepubertal children: The effects of early school start time and sleep restriction on attention and performance. *Sleep Medicine, 10*(4), 473–480; Weiss, M. D., Wasdell, M. B., Bomben, M. M., Rea, K. J., & Freeman, R. D. (2006). Sleep hygiene and melatonin treatment for children and adolescents with ADHD and initial insomnia. *Journal of the American Academy of Child & Adolescent Psychiatry, 45*(5), 512–519; Owens, J. A., Maxim, R., Nobile, C., McGuinn, M., & Msall, M. (2000). Parental and self-report of sleep in children with attention-deficit/hyperactivity disorder. *Archives of Pediatrics & Adolescent Medicine, 154*(6), 549–555; Chorney, D. B., Detweiler, M. F., Morris, T. L., & Kuhn, B. R. (2008). The interplay of sleep disturbance, anxiety, and depression in children. *Journal of Pediatric Psychology, 33*(4), 339–348.

27 Advice by @the.holistic.psychologist. (2023, October 27). How to (actually) regulate your emotions: A step-by-step guide. [Instagram post].

28 Education Endowment Foundation. (n.d.). *Improving behaviour in schools: Guidance report*. https://educationendowmentfoundation.org.uk/education-evidence/guidance-reports/behaviour (Accessed May 22, 2024).

29 Rogers, C. R. (1956). *Client-centered therapy* (3rd edn). Boston: Houghton-Mifflin.

30 Rogers, C. R. (1986). Client-centered approach to therapy. In I. L. Kutash & Wolf, A. (eds), *Psychotherapist's casebook: Theory and technique in practice* (pp. 197–208). Jossey-Bass.

31 A paraphrased version from Wallace, D. F. (2005, May 21). This is water: Some thoughts, delivered on a significant occasion, about living a compassionate life [Commencement speech]. Kenyon College.

32 Bronfenbrenner, U. (1979). *The ecology of human development: Experiments by nature and design* (p. 3). Harvard University Press.

33 Bronfenbrenner, U. (1979). *The ecology of human development: Experiments by nature and design*. Harvard University Press.

## Chapter 8

1 Curran, H., Moloney, H., Heavey, A., & Boddison, A. (2018). *It's about time: The impact of SENCO workload on the professional and the school*. Bath Spa University, Bath.

2 Curran, H., Moloney, H., Heavey, A., & Boddison, A. (2018). *It's about time: The impact of SENCO workload on the professional and the school* (p. 24). Bath Spa University, Bath.

3 Curran, H., Moloney, H., Heavey, A., & Boddison, A. (2018). *It's about time: The impact of SENCO workload on the professional and the school* (p. 19). Bath Spa University, Bath.

4 Children's Commissioner. (2022). *Back into school: New insights into school absence – evidence from three multi academy trusts*. https://assets.childrenscommissioner.gov.uk/wpuploads/2022/07/cc-new-insights-into-school-absence.pdf (Accessed January 2, 2024).

5 Curran, H., Moloney, H., Heavey, A., & Boddison, A. (2018). *It's about time: The impact of SENCO workload on the professional and the school* (p. 21). Bath Spa University, Bath.

6 Bandura, A. (1977). Self-efficacy: Toward a unifying theory of behavioral change. *Psychological Review, 84*, 191–215.

7 Zakariya, Y. F., Nilsen, H. K., Goodchild, S., & Bjørkestøl, K. (2020). Self-efficacy and approaches to learning mathematics among engineering students: Empirical evidence for potential causal relations. *International Journal of Mathematical Education in Science and Technology, 53*(4), 827–841.

8 Rosenthal, R., & Jacobson, L. (1968). *Pygmalion in the classroom: Teacher expectation and pupils' intellectual development*. Holt, Rinehart & Winston.

9 Hendrick, C., & Macpherson, R. (2017). *What does this look like in the classroom?: Bridging the gap between research and practice* (p. 216). Hodder Education.

10 Felitti, V. J., Anda, R. F., Nordenberg, D., Williamson, D. F., Spitz, A. M., Edwards, V., Koss, M. P., & Marks, J. S. (1998). Relationship of childhood abuse and household dysfunction to many of the leading causes of death in adults: The Adverse Childhood Experiences (ACE) Study. *American Journal of Preventive Medicine, 14*(4), 245–258.

11 Bellis, M. A., Lowey, H., Leckenby, N., Hughes, K., & Harrison, D. (2013). Adverse childhood experiences: Retrospective study to determine their impact on adult health behaviours and health outcomes in a UK population. *Journal of Public Health, 36*(1), 81–91; Bellis, M. A., Hughes, K., Leckenby, N., Perkins, C., & Lowey, H. (2014). National household survey of adverse childhood experiences and their relationship with resilience to health-harming behaviors in England. *BMC Medicine, 12*(1), 72.

12 Brown, D. W., Anda, R. F., Tiemeier, H., Felitti, V. J., Edwards, V. J., Croft, J. B., & Giles, W. H. (2009). Adverse childhood experiences and the risk of premature mortality. *American Journal of Preventive Medicine, 37*(5), 389–396.

13 Jung, C. (1963). *Memories, dreams, reflections*. Crown Publishing Group/Random House. (Original work published 1961).

14 Finch, C., & Loehlin, J. (1998). Environmental influences that may precede fertilization: A first examination of the prezygotic hypothesis from maternal age influences on twins. *Behavioral Genetics, 28*(2), 101–108.

15 Wolynn, M. (2022). *It didn't start with you: How inherited family trauma shapes who we are and how to end the cycle* (p. 29). Penguin: London.

16 Cairns, K. (2024, July 9). Collective trauma, disorganised attachment [Blog post]. Retrieved from https://kca.training/blog/collective-trauma-disorganised-attachment

17 Brown, B. (2021). *Atlas of the heart* (pp. 162–163). Random House.

18 Browne, K., Blundell, J., & Law, P. (2016). *Sociology for AQA: Volume 2, 2nd year A-Level* (3rd edn) (p. 384). Polity Press.

19 Sebastian, C., Viding, E., Williams, K. D., & Blakemore, S.-J. (2010). Social brain development and the affective consequences of ostracism in adolescence. *Brain and Cognition, 72*(1), 134–145.

20 Holt-Lunstad, J., Smith, T. B., Baker, M., Harris, T., & Stephenson, D. (2015). Loneliness and social isolation as risk factors for mortality: A meta-analytic review. *Perspectives on Psychological Science, 10*(2), 227–237.

21 Maté, G., & Maté, D. (2022). *The myth of normal: Trauma, illness & healing in a toxic culture* (p. 313). Penguin: London.

22 Maté, G., & Maté, D. (2022). *The myth of normal: Trauma, illness & healing in a toxic culture* (p. 312). Penguin: London.

23 Meyer, I. H. (2003). Prejudice, social stress, and mental health in lesbian, gay, and bisexual populations: Conceptual issues and research evidence. *Psychological Bulletin, 129*(5), 674–697.

24 Miller, D., Rees, J., & Pearson, A. (2021). "Masking is life": Experiences of masking in autistic and nonautistic adults. *Autism in Adulthood, 3*(4), 330–338.

25 Belcher, H. (2022). *Taking off the mask*. Jessica Kingsley Publishers.

26 Perry, B. D., & Winfrey, O. (2021). *What happened to you?: Conversations on trauma, resilience, and healing*. Macmillan.

27 Cassidy, S., Bradley, L., Shaw, R., & Baron-Cohen, S. (2018). Risk markers for suicidality in autistic adults. *Molecular Autism, 9*(42), 1–14.; Williams, A. J., Arcelus, J., Townsend, E., & Michail, M. (2019). Examining risk factors for self-harm and suicide in LGBTQ+ young people: A systematic review protocol. *BMJ Open, 9*(11), e031541.

28 Meyer, I. H. (2003). Prejudice, social stress, and mental health in lesbian, gay, and bisexual populations: Conceptual issues and research evidence. *Psychological Bulletin, 129*(5), 674–697.

29 Heyne, D., Rollings, S., King, N. J., & Tonge, B. J. (2002). *School refusal* (1st ed.). Wiley-Blackwell.

30 Thambirajah, M. S., Grandison, K. J., & De-Hayes, L. (2008). *Understanding school refusal: A handbook for professionals in education, health and social care.* Jessica Kingsley Publishers.

31 Flakierska-Praquin, N., Lindström, M., & Gillberg, C. (1997). School phobia with separation anxiety disorder: A comparative 20- to 29-year follow-up study of 35 school refusers. *Comprehensive Psychiatry, 38*(1), 17–22.

32 Maté, G., & Maté, D. (2022). *The myth of normal: Trauma, illness & healing in a toxic culture* (p. 26). Penguin: London.

33 Epel, E. S., Blackburn, E. H., Lin, J., Dhabhar, F. S., Adler, N. E., Morrow, J. D., & Cawthon, R. M. (2004). Accelerated telomere shortening in response to life stress. *Proceedings of the National Academy of Sciences, 101*(49), 17312–17315.

34 Maté, G., & Maté, D. (2022). *The myth of normal: Trauma, illness & healing in a toxic culture* (p. 48). Penguin: London.

35 Bladon, S. [@75ThunderRoad] (2024, June 21). Reframing attendance – A thread [Tweet on X]. (With thanks to Steve for allowing me to quote him).

# Chapter 9

1 National Health Service (NHS). (2024, January 4). *Asthma.* https://www.nhs.uk/conditions/asthma/

2 World Health Organization (WHO). (1948). *Constitution.* World Health Organization.

3 Union of the Physically Impaired Against Segregation (UPIAS). (1976). *Fundamental principles of disability.* UPIAS.

4 Union of the Physically Impaired Against Segregation (UPIAS). (1976). *Fundamental principles of disability.* UPIAS.

5 Shakespeare, T. (2006). *Disability rights and wrongs.* Routledge.

6 Van den Ven, L., Post, M., de Witte, L., & van den Heuvel, W. (2005). It takes two to tango: The integration of people with disabilities into society. *Disability and Society, 20*(3), 311–329.

7 World Health Organization (WHO). (1984). *Health promotion: A discussion document on the concept and principles: Summary report of the Working Group on Concept and Principles of Health Promotion, Copenhagen, 9–13 July 1984.* Regional Office for Europe. World Health Organization.

8 Davies, W. (2015). *The happiness industry: How the government and big business sold us well-being.* Verso.

9 National Institute for Health and Care Excellence (NICE). (2024, January 2). Managing long-term conditions in children. https://www.nice.org.uk/about/what-we-do/into-practice/measuring-the-use-of-nice-guidance/impact-of-our-guidance/niceimpact-children-and-young-peoples-healthcare/ch2-managing-long-term-conditions-in-children

10 Department for Education. (2024, January 2). Schools, pupils and their characteristics: January 2018. https://www.gov.uk/government/statistics/schools-pupils-and-their-characteristics-january-2018

11 Royal College of Paediatrics and Child Health (RCPCH). (2024, January 2). State of child health: At a glance. https://stateofchildhealth.rcpch.ac.uk/evidence/at-a-glance/#page-section-8

12 I reference here the case of Awaab Ishak who died aged two from living in a mould infested home run by Rochdale Borough Housing, in Rochdale UK in December 2020.

13 Campaign for Better Transport. (2023, June). Better transport for better health: Campaign briefing. https://bettertransport.org.uk/wp-content/uploads/2023/06/2023-06-better-transport-for-better-health-campaign-briefing.pdf

14 Centre for Longitudinal Studies. (2010). *Millennium cohort study, briefing 9: Parent and child health.* Centre for Longitudinal Studies, Institute of Education, University of London. Based on *Children of the 21st century (Volume 2): The first five years* (K. Hansen, H. Joshi, & S. Dex, Eds). The Policy Press.

15 General Medical Council (GMC). (2020). *Decision making and consent.* (into effect from November 9, 2020).

16 University College London. (2024, March). Analysis: Child health crisis in the UK – Here's what needs to change. UCL News. https://www.ucl.ac.uk/news/2024/mar/analysis-child-health-crisis-uk-heres-what-needs-change (Accessed October 7, 2024).

17 Royal College of Paediatrics and Child Health (RCPCH). (2024, January 2). State of child health: At a glance. https://stateofchildhealth.rcpch.ac.uk/evidence/at-a-glance/#page-section-8

18 I refer here to the case of Molly Russell, as an example, of the impact of social media on teenage mental health. BBC News. (2022, September 21). Molly Russell inquest: Online life was "the bleakest of worlds". BBC News. https://www.bbc.co.uk/news/uk-england-london-62981964

19 Bordoloi, M., Durkin, I., & Aggarwal, A. (2024). Effects of pornography on youth: A review. *Missouri Medicine*, 121(3), 195–197.

20 Royal College of Paediatrics and Child Health. (2017). *The inaugural State of Child Health report 2017*. Royal College of Paediatrics and Child Health.

21 National Health Service (NHS). (2024, January 4). Asthma. https://www.nhs.uk/conditions/asthma/

22 Toyran, M., et al. (2020). Asthma control affects school absence, achievement and quality of school life: A multicenter study. *Allergologia et Immunopathologia (Madr)*, 48(6), 545–552.

23 Cortese, S., Sun, S., Zhang, J., Sharma, E., Chang, Z., Kuja-Halkola, R., . . . & Faraone, S. V. (2018). Association between attention deficit hyperactivity disorder and asthma: A systematic review and meta-analysis and a Swedish population-based study. *The Lancet Psychiatry*, 5(9), 717–726.

24 Neuroscience News. (2023, April 6). The rhythm of breathing shapes memory formation. https://neurosciencenews.com/memory-breathing-23360/ (Accessed October 3, 2023).

25 Ritz, T., et al. (2014). Controlling asthma by training of capnometry-assisted hypoventilation (CATCH) verses slow breathing: A randomized controlled trial. *Chest*, 146(5), 1237–1247.

26 Swami, R., Ballentine, R., & Hymes, A. (1998). *Science of breath: A practical guide* (p. 45). Himalayan Institute Press.

27 Weyand, A. C., Chaitoff, A., Freed, G. L., Sholzberg, M., Choi, S. W., McGann, P. T. (2023, June 27). Prevalence of iron deficiency and iron-deficiency anemia in US females aged 12–21 years, 2003–2020. *JAMA*, 329(24), 2191–2193. doi: 10.1001/jama.2023.8020. PMID: 37367984; PMCID: PMC10300696.

28 Barr, E., et al. (2007). Risk of cardiovascular and all-cause mortality in individuals with diabetes mellitus, impaired fasting glucose, and impaired glucose tolerance. *Circulation*, 116(2), 151–157.

29 French, R., Kneale, D., Warner, J. T., Robinson, H., Rafferty, J., Sayers, A., Taylor, P., Gregory, J. W., & Dayan, C. M. (2022). Educational attainment and childhood-onset type 1 diabetes. *Diabetes Care*, 45(12), 2852–2861.

30 Jamie's School Dinners was a documentary series in 2005 which raised the profile of the nutritional value of school dinners, leading to a national campaign "Feed Me Better" aimed at improving school dinners throughout Britain.

31 Leavy, K. M., Cisneros, G. J., & LeBlanc, E. M. (2016). Malocclusion and its relationship to speech sound production: Redefining the effect of malocclusal traits on sound production. *American Journal of Orthodontics and Dentofacial Orthopedics*, 150(1), 116–123.

32 Bouvard, V., Loomis, D., Guyton, K. Z., Grosse, Y., El Ghissassi, F., Benbrahim-Tallaa, L., . . . & Straif, K. (2015). Carcinogenicity of consumption of red and processed meat. *The Lancet Oncology*, 16(16), 1599–1600.

33 N. Raven Morris, personal communication, February 12, 2024.

34 Goday, P. S., Huh, S. Y., Silverman, A., Lukens, C. T., Dodrill, P., Cohen, S. S., & Phalen, J. A. (2019). Pediatric feeding disorder: Consensus definition and conceptual framework. *Journal of Pediatric Gastroenterology and Nutrition*, 68(1), 124–129.

35 American Psychiatric Association. (2013). *Diagnostic and statistical manual of mental disorders: DSM-5* (5th edn). American Psychiatric Association. – to find the definition for ARFID.

36 Goday, P.S., Huh, S.Y., Silverman, A., Lukens, C.T., Dodrill, P., Cohen, S.S., Delaney, A.L., Feuling, M.B., Noel, R.J., Gisel, E., Kenzer, A., Kessler, D.B., de Camargo, O.K., Browne, J., Phalen, J.A. (2019). Pediatric feeding disorder: Consensus definition and conceptual framework. *Journal of Pediatric Gastroenterelogy and Nutrition*, 68(1), 124–129.

37 Epilepsy Society. (2024, January 7). How epilepsy can affect learning and university experience. https://epilepsysociety.org.uk/living-epilepsy/university-and-epilepsy/how-epilepsy-can-affect-learning-and-university-experience

38 Lystad, R. P., McMaugh, A., Herkes, G., Badgery-Parker, T., Cameron, C. M., & Mitchell, R. J. (2022). The impact of childhood epilepsy on academic performance: A population-based matched cohort study. *Seizure: European Journal of Epilepsy, 99*, 91–98.

39 Marcotte, D. (2015). Allergy test: Seasonal allergens and performance in school. *Journal of Health Economics, 40*, 132–140.

40 Walker, S., Khan-Wasti, S., Fletcher, M., Cullinan, P., Harris, J., & Sheikh, A. (2007). Seasonal allergic rhinitis is associated with a detrimental effect on examination performance in United Kingdom teenagers: A case-control study. *Journal of Allergy and Clinical Immunology, 120*(2), 381–387.

41 Marcotte, D. (2015). Allergy test: Seasonal allergens and performance in school. *Journal of Health Economics, 40*, 132–140.

42 Requia, W. J., Kill, E., & Amini, H. (2021). Proximity of schools to roads and students' academic performance: A cross-sectional study in the Federal District, Brazil. *Environmental Research, 202*, 111770.

43 BBC News. (2024, January 28). Ella Adoo-Kissi-Debrah: Air pollution a factor in girl's death, inquest finds. https://www.bbc.co.uk/news/uk-england-london-55330945

44 Branum, A. M., & Lukacs, S. L. (2008). Food allergy among U.S. children: Trends in prevalence and hospitalizations. NCHS Data Brief, No. 10. National Center for Health Statistics; and Gupta, R. S., Springston, E. E., Warrier, M. R., Smith, B., Kumar, R., Pongracic, J., & Holl, J. L. (2013). The prevalence, severity, and distribution of childhood food allergy in the United States. *JAMA Pediatrics, 167*(11), 1026–1031.

45 Asthma + Lung UK. (n.d.). Toxic air: Playgrounds and schools [Webpage]. Asthma + Lung UK. https://www.asthmaandlung.org.uk/toxic-air-playgrounds-qr

46 These suggestions are taken from the findings of the INSCHOOL research: Spencer, B. K. C., Hugh-Jones, S., Cottrell, D., & Pini, S. (2023). The INSCHOOL project. Young people with long-term physical health conditions: An in-depth qualitative study of their needs at school. *Journal of Adolescence*, 1–13.

47 Dr B. Sinclair, personal communication, June 22, 2024. Dr Sinclair works at Dr Finlay's practice www.drfinlays.co.uk My thanks to Dr Sinclair for his time and contribution to this chapter.

48 Criado-Perez, C. (2019). *Invisible women: Exposing data bias in a world designed for men* (p. 196). Chatto & Windus.

49 Independent Review of Gender Identity Services for Children and Young People. (2024). *The Cass Review: Final report*. NHS England.

50 As evidenced throughout the book and summarised in this quotation by Professor David Crews, cited in Cooke, L. (2022). *Bitch: What does it mean to be female?* (p. 276). Basic Books.

51 West-Eberhard, M. J. (2003). *Developmental plasticity and evolution*. Oxford University Press.

## Chapter 10

1 *The Guardian*. (2024, April 9). Senior Labour figures call for "life-transforming" Sure Start policy. https://www.theguardian.com/education/2024/apr/09/senior-labour-figures-call-for-life-transforming-sure-start-policy (Accessed April 24, 2024).

2 Erikson, E. H. (1950). *Childhood and society*. W. W. Norton & Company.

3 Erikson, E. H. (1950). *Childhood and society*. W. W. Norton & Company.

4 Holmes, J., Guy, J., Kievit, R. A., Bryant, A., Mareva, S., CALM Team, & Gathercole, S. E. (2021). Cognitive dimensions of learning in children with problems in attention, learning, and memory. *Journal of Educational Psychology, 113*(7), 1454–1480.

5 Jay, T., & Betenson, J. (2017). Mathematics at your fingertips: Testing a finger training intervention to improve quantitative skills. *Frontiers in Education, 2*, Article 22.

6 Dr. A. McCabe, personal communication, September 5, 2024.

7 Plomin, R. (2019). *Blueprint: How DNA makes us who we are* (p. 62). Penguin Books.

8 Plomin, R. (2019). *Blueprint: How DNA makes us who we are* (p. 92). Penguin Books.

9 Made by Dyslexia. (n.d.). Kids. *Made By Dyslexia*. https://www.madebydyslexia.org/kids/ (Accessed April 24, 2024).

10 McGhee, E. E. (2020). *Access arrangements for secondary students: Experiences and views of educational professionals, students and their parents/guardians* (Doctoral thesis, UCL). UCL Discovery.

11 Meehl, P. E. (1954). *Clinical versus statistical prediction: A theoretical analysis and a review of the evidence.* University of Minnesota Press.

12 WeWALK. (n.d.). *Homepage.* WeWALK. Retrieved August 29, 2024, from https://wewalk.io/en/ See also Hear See Mobility. (n.d.). *Homepage.* Hear See Mobility. https://www.hearseemobility.org (Accessed August 25, 2023).

13 Holmes, J., Gathercole, S. E., Place, M., Dunning, D. L., Hilton, K. A., & Elliott, J. G. (2020). Dimensional approaches to understanding the cognitive and neural underpinnings of specific learning difficulties. *Journal of Child Psychology and Psychiatry, 61*(10), 1087–1096; Holmes, J., Bathelt, J., & Astle, D. E. (2018). Look beyond the label. *Times Education Supplement,* (5324), 30–35.

14 Duncan, S. [@autismfather] (2012, November 10). #Autism is one word attempting to describe millions of different stories [Tweet on X].

15 Fry, H. (2018). *Hello world: How to be human in the age of the machine* (p. 25). W.W. Norton & Company.

16 Buolamwini, J. (2024, May 8). Unmasking AI: My mission to protect what is human in a world of machines [Audio podcast episode]. In Brené Brown (Host), *Dare to Lead Podcast.* Parcast. https://brenebrown.com/podcast/unmasking-ai-my-mission-to-protect-what-is-human-in-a-world-of-machines/#notes

17 Watkins, S. C. (2021, December). *Artificial intelligence and the future of racial justice* [Video]. TEDxMIT. https://www.youtube.com/watch?v=ic-RKkahD1o

18 Holmes, J., Gathercole, S. E., Place, M., Dunning, D. L., Hilton, K. A., & Elliott, J. G. (2020). Dimensional approaches to understanding the cognitive and neural underpinnings of specific learning difficulties. *Journal of Child Psychology and Psychiatry, 61*(10), 1087–1096.

19 Walmsley, J. (2021). Artificial intelligence and the value of transparency. *AI & Society.*

20 Walmsley, J. (2023). "Computer says no": Artificial intelligence, gender bias, and epistemic injustice. In M. L. Edwards & S. O. Palermos (Eds), *Feminist philosophy and emerging technologies* (pp. 249–263). Routledge.

21 Nyholm, S. (2018). Attributing agency to automated systems: Reflections on human-robot collaborations and responsibility-loci. *Science and Engineering Ethics, 24*(4), 1201–1210.

22 Watkins, S. C. (2021, December). *Artificial intelligence and the future of racial justice* [Video]. TEDxMIT. https://www.youtube.com/watch?v=ic-RKkahD1o

23 Buolamwini, J. (n.d.). *Unmasking AI.* https://www.unmasking.ai/ (Accessed August 29, 2024).

## Chapter 11

1 The Prisoner's Dilemma is a theory based on game theory developed by American mathematician Albert W. Tucker and has been extensively written about by others since.

2 Keer, M. (2023, December 15). Councils, stop wasting public funds: SEND appeals fail almost all the time. *Special Needs Jungle.* https://www.specialneedsjungle.com/send-tribunal-2023-councils-stop-wasting-public-funds-send-appeals-fail-almost-all-time/ (Accessed 18.08.2024)

3 BBC News. (2024, July 27). Why school exclusions are at record levels. https://www.bbc.co.uk/news/articles/cgerplykjy9o

4 Newcastle Report. (1861). *The state of popular education in England* (Vol. I, p. 7). London: HM Stationery Office.

5 Haviland, J. (Ed.). (1988). *Take care, Mr. Baker.* London: Fourth Estate.

6 Department of Education and Science. (1978). *Special educational needs (The Warnock Report)* (p. 36). London: HMSO.

7 Kuznets, S. (1954, August 15). Letter to Selma Goldsmith, US Office of Business Economics. *Papers of Simon Kuznets, Harvard University Archives, HUGFP88.10 Misc. Correspondence, Box 4.* http://asociologist.com/2013/03/21/on-the-origins-of-the-kuznets-curve/

8 Krueger, A. (2002, April 4). Economic scene: when it comes to income inequality, more than just free market forces are at work. *New York Times.*

 9  Piketty, T. (2014). *Capital in the twenty-first century.* Cambridge, MA: Harvard University Press.

10  Quinn, J., & Hall, J. (2009, October 21). Goldman Sachs vice-chairman says "learn to tolerate inequality" *Daily Telegraph.*

11  Wilkinson, R., & Pickett, K. (2009). *The Spirit Level.* London: Penguin.

12  Ville, L. (2024). *Double trouble: The ethnicity gender pay gap.* London: The Fawcett Society.

13  Bohannon, C. (2024). *Eve: How the female body drove 200 million years of human evolution* (UK edn, p. 417). Penguin Books.

14  Bohannon, C. (2024). *Eve: How the female body drove 200 million years of human evolution* (UK edn, p. 417). Penguin Books.

15  Sen, A. (1999). *Development as Freedom* (p. 285). New York: Alfred A. Knopf.

16  Syed, M. (2020). *Rebel ideas: The power of diverse thinking.* John Murray.

17  Both of these perspectives are well evidenced in: Stewart, R., & Campbell, A. (Hosts). (2023, June 12). Kate Raworth: Doughnut economics and thriving in balance [Audio podcast episode]. In *The Rest is Politics.* Goalhanger Podcasts. https://podcasts.apple.com/gb/podcast/kate-raworth-doughnut-economics-and-thriving-in-balance/id1665265193?i=1000616561557

18  UK Department for Education. (n.d.). *About us: Our priorities.* GOV.UK. Retrieved September 7, 2024, from https://www.gov.uk/government/organisations/department-for-education/about#our-priorities

19  Keer, M. (2023, December 15). Councils, stop wasting public funds: SEND appeals fail almost all the time. *Special Needs Jungle.* https://www.specialneedsjungle.com/send-tribunal-2023-councils-stop-wasting-public-funds-send-appeals-fail-almost-all-time/ (Accessed August 18, 2024).

20  Department for Education. (2023). *Special educational needs in England: 2022–23.* https://explore-education-statistics.service.gov.uk/find-statistics/special-educational-needs-in-england/2022-23 (Accessed August 19, 2024).

21  Children's Commissioner for England. (2024). Shocking new statistics show a huge increase in the number of children completely missing education. *Children's Commissioner for England.* https://www.childrenscommissioner.gov.uk/blog/shocking-new-statistics-show-a-huge-increase-in-the-number-of-children-completely-missing-education/ (Accessed August 18, 2024).

22  This figure was calculated by working out the number of children not in school in the previous reference, and comparing this to the number in education in the same year, from government figures at the following reference: Department for Education. (2024). *School pupils and their characteristics: 2023–24.* https://explore-education-statistics.service.gov.uk/find-statistics/school-pupils-and-their-characteristics/2023-24 (Accessed August 18, 2024).

23  Department for Education. (2023). *Pupil attendance in schools: 2023, week 29.* https://explore-education-statistics.service.gov.uk/find-statistics/pupil-attendance-in-schools/2023-week-29 (Accessed August 19, 2024).

24  Department for Education. (2024). *School workforce in England.* https://explore-education-statistics.service.gov.uk/find-statistics/school-workforce-in-england (Accessed August 19, 2024).

25  Department for Education. (2023). *Special educational needs in England: 2022–23.* https://explore-education-statistics.service.gov.uk/find-statistics/special-educational-needs-in-england/2022-23 (Accessed August 19, 2024).

26  Hutchinson, J. (2021). *Identifying pupils with special educational needs and disabilities.* London: Education Policy Institute.

27  The current law is: Department for Education, & Department of Health. (2015). *The special educational needs and disability code of practice: 0 to 25 years.* UK Government. This updates the definition originally legalised in the Education Act 1981. (1981). *Elizabeth II. Chapter 60.* London: Her Majesty's Stationery Office (HMSO).

28  Department of Education and Science. (1978). *Special educational needs (The Warnock Report)* (para 3.17). London: HMSO.

29  Syed, M. (2020). *Rebel ideas: The power of diverse thinking.* (p. 227). John Murray.

30  Christianakis, M. (2008). Teacher research as a feminist act. *Teacher Education Quarterly, 35*(4), 99–115 (p. 99).

31 https://donellameadows.org/archives/leverage-points-places-to-intervene-in-a-system/ (Accessed August 19, 2024).

32 Meadows, D. (1999). *Leverage points: Places to intervene in a system* (p. 1). Hartland, VT: Sustainability Institute.

33 This quotation is often attributed to Viktor E. Frankl, the Austrian neurologist, psychiatrist, and Holocaust survivor. However, it is not a direct quote from any of his writings.

# Index